External Events and Crises That Impact Firms and Other Entities

Heather C. Webb
Higher Colleges of Technology, Dubai, UAE

Hussain Al Numairy
Higher Colleges of Technology, Dubai, UAE

A volume in the Advances in Human Resources Management and Organizational Development (AHRMOD) Book Series

IGI Global
PUBLISHER of TIMELY KNOWLEDGE

Published in the United States of America by
IGI Global
Business Science Reference (an imprint of IGI Global)
701 E. Chocolate Avenue
Hershey PA, USA 17033
Tel: 717-533-8845
Fax: 717-533-8661
E-mail: cust@igi-global.com
Web site: http://www.igi-global.com

Library of Congress Cataloging-in-Publication Data

Names: Webb, Heather C., 1979- editor. | Al Numairy, Hussain A., 1986- editor.
Title: External events and crises that impact firms and other entities / Heather Webb and Hussain Al Numairy, editor.
Description: Hershey, PA : Business Science Reference, [2022] | Includes bibliographical references and index. | Summary: "This book will identify strategies of small and medium-sized enterprises or other entities that have recovered from the effects of the pandemic and detailing how they define recovered for preparation for future crises and other external impacts"-- Provided by publisher.
Identifiers: LCCN 2021037617 (print) | LCCN 2021037618 (ebook) | ISBN 9781799883463 (hardcover) | ISBN 9781799883470 (paperback) | ISBN 9781799883487 (ebook)
Subjects: LCSH: Business cycles. | Financial crises. | Small business--Management.
Classification: LCC HB3716 .E98 2022 (print) | LCC HB3716 (ebook) | DDC 338.5/42--dc23
LC record available at https://lccn.loc.gov/2021037617
LC ebook record available at https://lccn.loc.gov/2021037618

This book is published in the IGI Global book series Advances in Human Resources Management and Organizational Development (AHRMOD) (ISSN: 2327-3372; eISSN: 2327-3380)

British Cataloguing in Publication Data
A Cataloguing in Publication record for this book is available from the British Library.

For electronic access to this publication, please contact: eresources@igi-global.com.

Advances in Human Resources Management and Organizational Development (AHRMOD) Book Series

ISSN:2327-3372
EISSN:2327-3380

Editor-in-Chief: Patricia Ordóñez de Pablos, Universidad de Oviedo, Spain

MISSION

A solid foundation is essential to the development and success of any organization and can be accomplished through the effective and careful management of an organization's human capital. Research in human resources management and organizational development is necessary in providing business leaders with the tools and methodologies which will assist in the development and maintenance of their organizational structure.

The **Advances in Human Resources Management and Organizational Development (AHRMOD) Book Series** aims to publish the latest research on all aspects of human resources as well as the latest methodologies, tools, and theories regarding organizational development and sustainability. The **AHRMOD Book Series** intends to provide business professionals, managers, researchers, and students with the necessary resources to effectively develop and implement organizational strategies.

COVERAGE

- Human Relations Movement
- Employment and Labor Laws
- Process Improvement
- Executive Education
- Outsourcing HR
- Training and Development
- Human Resources Development
- Work-Life Balance
- Job Enrichment
- Executive Compensation

IGI Global is currently accepting manuscripts for publication within this series. To submit a proposal for a volume in this series, please contact our Acquisition Editors at Acquisitions@igi-global.com or visit: http://www.igi-global.com/publish/.

The Advances in Human Resources Management and Organizational Development (AHRMOD) Book Series (ISSN 2327-3372) is published by IGI Global, 701 E. Chocolate Avenue, Hershey, PA 17033-1240, USA, www.igi-global.com. This series is composed of titles available for purchase individually; each title is edited to be contextually exclusive from any other title within the series. For pricing and ordering information please visit http://www.igi-global.com/book-series/advances-human-resources-management-organizational/73670. Postmaster: Send all address changes to above address.

Titles in this Series

For a list of additional titles in this series, please visit:
http://www.igi-global.com/book-series/advances-human-resources-management-organizational/73670

Ergonomics and Business Policies for the Promotion of Well-Being in the Workplace
Mildrend Montoya-Reyes (Autonomous University of Baja California, Mexico) Ismael Mendoza-Muñoz (Autonomous University of Baja California, Mexico) Gabriela Jacobo-Galicia (Autonomous University of Baja California, Mexico) and Samantha E. Cruz-Sotelo (Autonomous University of Baja California, Mexico)
Business Science Reference • © 2022 • 303pp • H/C (ISBN: 9781799873969) • US $195.00

Gender Perspectives on Industry 4.0 and the Impact of Technology on Mainstreaming Female Employment
Shashi Bala (V. V. Giri National Labour Institute, India) and Puja Singhal (Sashakt, India)
Business Science Reference • © 2022 • 305pp • H/C (ISBN: 9781799885948) • US $215.00

Handbook of Research on Key Dimensions of Occupational Safety and Health Protection Management
Snežana Živković (Faculty of Occupational Safety, University of Niš, Serbia) Bojan Krstić (Faculty of Economics, University of Niš, Serbia) and Tamara Rađenović (Faculty of Occupational Safety, University of Niš, Serbia)
Business Science Reference • © 2022 • 512pp • H/C (ISBN: 9781799881896) • US $295.00

Analyzing Telework, Trustworthiness, and Performance Using Leader-Member Exchange COVID-19 Perspective
Michael A. Brown Sr. (Right Fit Communications LLC, USA)
Business Science Reference • © 2022 • 263pp • H/C (ISBN: 9781799889502) • US $215.00

Future Advancements for CSR and the Sustainable Development Goals in a Post-COVID-19 World
Andrea Pérez (University of Cantabria, Spain)
Business Science Reference • © 2022 • 355pp • H/C (ISBN: 9781799880653) • US $225.00

For an entire list of titles in this series, please visit:
http://www.igi-global.com/book-series/advances-human-resources-management-organizational/73670

IGI Global
PUBLISHER of TIMELY KNOWLEDGE

701 East Chocolate Avenue, Hershey, PA 17033, USA
Tel: 717-533-8845 x100 • Fax: 717-533-8661
E-Mail: cust@igi-global.com • www.igi-global.com

Table of Contents

Detailed Table of Contents

It was reported that almost 3,800 companies closed during the height of the COVID-19 pandemic in Singapore. Sometime between April 2020 to August 2020, the pandemic became the litmus test that shattered the fragile small and medium-sized businesses (SMEs) into dissolution. This chapter discusses the impact of the pandemic on Singaporean SMEs and the challenges ahead post recovery. It also discusses possible strategies for SMEs as well as possible governmental strategies.

The purpose of the study is to explore the role of service quality in reviving the United Arab Emirates hospitality sector post COVID-19 pandemic. Various factors contribute to the success of the hospitality industry in UAE; some of them are strategic location, leisure facilities, and business-friendly policies. Nevertheless, the COVID-19 pandemic has impacted the hospitality industry all over the world. Therefore, it is necessary to find ways to revive the hospitality sector during and post pandemic. Thus, the findings of this research give insight into customer preference and expectations as well as the need to invest and implement technology to deliver exceptional service. Therefore, it emphasizes that organizations operating in the hospitality sector should understand the customer needs, develop appropriate strategies, and invest in technology. Specifically, this research stresses that service quality dimensions improve customer satisfaction, enhances customer loyalty, and regain trust with consumers.

Pandemics generally affect businesses due to their nature. Business owners have little to no knowledge of when crises such as pandemics will occur or how severe they will be. Each pandemic is different in nature as its spreadability is different; therefore, the outcome of no two pandemics can be the same. This chapter discusses the historical impact previous pandemics had on businesses. Then it presents information about the COVID-19 pandemic and how the United Arab Emirates (UAE) government and businesses dealt with this particular pandemic. More specifically, the authors focus on Dubai's banking sector response.

This chapter makes an effort to highlight the challenges faced and strategies adopted by businesses in India. An effort has been made to describe the economic condition of the economy before the onset of the COVID pandemic and the resulting outcome of the havoc so created by the pandemic and resulting lockdowns. An analysis has been done to clarify how large corporations and small businesses faced the combined blunt of poor economy and COVID. Case story-based approach has been adopted to highlight responses of few large corporations and how they turned the pandemic into an economic opportunity to churn out super normal profits. The chapter also highlights how the number of billionaires in India has increased during this time. Struggles of small businesses are also highlighted, and how they struggled for survival and sustenance and changes they have made in the way they function or carry out day-to-day business operations have also been discussed. A very small proportion of businesses did stand up for the welfare of the public and made an effort to facilitate their workforce.

Preface

Historically, academics and practitioners have developed various management methodologies and technologies to help business managers deal with challenges in their environments, yet many businesses fail. Thus, these challenges need to be researched more closely in order to overcome business failure. Many of these challenges are external events in which firms need to adapt and react. Getting the right adaptation and reaction to these external events will depend on whether a firm succeeds or fails altogether. Companies may fail due to their inability to properly respond to a crisis, whether it be a business or organizational crisis. A business or organizational crisis is defined as a low-probability, high-impact event that threatens the organization's viability, and thus, companies need crisis management strategies (Pearson and Clair, 1998).

A crisis of high consequences implies that a business cannot afford to ignore the threats as the impact can be financially enormous (Singh, 1994). An organization's successes can be derailed in a short period by a crisis. Therefore, crisis management is an important task. A crisis of low frequency indicates that the next crisis an organization faces is unlikely to be similar to any of its previous crises. Therefore, it becomes difficult for an organization to learn from history. Sometimes, though, organizations are reluctant to share their experiences with others, which can compromise the opportunity to learn from others and acquire knowledge. However, learning is crucial in order for businesses and other organizations to improve their chances of surviving future crises.

Whilst crises do not occur frequently, their impact can be devastating as organizations are still vulnerable to manufactured and natural crises. Thus, businesses can suffer the loss of profit and the ultimate demise of their business. It becomes increasingly complex, at times, to prevent crises such as these. It then becomes difficult to develop practical means to mitigate their undesirable effects once they occur.

A crisis is not a new phenomenon. The reaction to dealing with crises is just as complex and dramatic. From terrorism, environmental, scientific, financial, political, pandemic to natural disasters, crises can occur at any moment, and if not managed efficiently and effectively, the ramifications can be devastating. The study of crisis management is still a relatively young field. Thus, there has been no agreed-upon theoretical construct for crisis management (Zdziarski et al., 2007; Pearson and Clair, 1998; Auerbach and Kilmann, 1977; Hermann, 1972). For instance, globally, businesses and industries of all sizes have experienced the effects of COVID-19, an external pandemic. The recovery process requires SMEs to rearrange and reestablish their missions, goals, and business infrastructure. This is an overwhelming challenge of recovering.

The disruptive nature of crisis events can significantly interfere with the normal operations of any organization and government (Seymour and Moore, 2000). Crises are generally perceived negatively. However, optimistically, organizations can improve their standing, business model, or strategy. As such cases, they move into the e-commerce arena. Although, individual businesses that are stronger and more financially stable can adapt to a new norm following a crisis (Harrell, 2008). In comparison, other companies have barriers such as infrastructure problems, lack of access to capital, or vulnerability to cash flow interruption, which impedes recovery (Runyan, 2006).

With this book, we wanted to identify strategies of SMEs or other entities such as education or non-profit organizations that have recovered and how they define recovered for preparation for future crises and other external impacts. Harrell (2008) explains the term recovery when the business is profitable within a new economic environment, the company remains viable to meet its mission, and the business is self-sufficient for at least one-year post-event. We realize that the response to the Covid-19 pandemic is still ongoing, but reviewing organizations' strategic responses now could potentially help others that are still struggling.

ORGANIZATION OF THE BOOK

The book was organized into nine chapters. A brief description of each of the chapters follows:

Chapter 1 presents information on the FinTech industry. The FinTech industry has been growing rapidly and significantly, becoming the go-to service provider for some of the most important financial services, such as lending and payments. Since 2020, the onset of COVID-19 has substantially impacted the industry, both positively and negatively. This chapter discusses the recent performance of the FinTech industry based on a large-scale survey across the globe. The chapter then focuses on analysing the 'new normal' in banking, after the pandemic era, based on the findings of the global survey, with an explicit focus on the FinTech sector, followed by further implications on the pandemic's impact in the traditional banking sector. The paper concludes by providing an overview of the emerging opportunities that appear in the FinTech sector.

Chapter 2 discusses policy impact on employees. Given the intimacy of food preparation and service, the close proximity of diners and staff, the general inability to eat comfortably while masked, the warm emotional atmospherics of restaurants, and the limits to restaurant ventilation, the current SARS-CoV-2 / COVID-19 pandemic has meant shutdowns of restaurants across the United States early in the pandemic and then partial reopenings later with public health constraints. Some restaurants applied for the Small Business Administration (SBA)'s Paycheck Protection Program's funds in March 2020 to cover 2.5 months maximum of costs. Huge swaths of the restaurant industry have closed permanently, and many others are slated to close in the near future. Based on content analysis, this work explores the plight of restaurant workers in academic research and mass media literature and applies abductive reasoning to propose an approach for a policy mix that may better inform the present challenges with social justice considerations.

Chapter 3 focuses on a family-run business. A sub-class of small and medium(-sized) enterprises (SMEs) are family-run groceries and restaurants, both businesses hard hit by the SARS-CoV-2 / COVID-19 pandemic, given the high-contact person-to-person nature of both. In one American Midwestern town, there are two stores that carry Asian foodstuffs. These are B2C and B2B businesses with a limited client base and tight profit margins. Theirs are pressured businesses given the racialized cultural atmosphere around COVID-19 in the U.S. Both businesses take different and limited strategies to survive in this COVID-19 era. This work uses qualitative research techniques: primary mixed methods research (in a light auto-ethnography) and publicly available data sources to conduct an in-depth content analysis to examine the two family-run stores. Some ideas are advanced about ways to support such hyperlocal stores.

Chapter 4 reviews supply chain strategies in India and their impact on businesses. Due to COVID-19, the supply chains have got disrupted in many ways. This chapter aims to identify the strategies that can help the Micro, Small and Medium Enterprises (MSMEs) develop a resilient supply chain strategy that can handle any kind of disruption. Five strategies are determined from the literature review. A questionnaire is being developed for survey-based research in the MSMEs of India. For data analysis, exploratory factor analysis and structural equation modeling are used. An empirical investigation is carried out to present our research framework in this research. The proposed hypotheses were accepted, and the developed model satisfied all the parameters.

Chapter 5 presents the impact of the Covid-19 Pandemic on SMEs in Singapore and the challenges ahead post-recovery. It also discusses possible strategies for both SMEs and the government. It was reported that almost 3,800 companies closed down during the height of the Covid-19 Pandemic in Singapore. Sometime between April 2020 to August 2020, the pandemic became the litmus test that shattered the fragile Small and medium-sized businesses (SMEs) into dissolution.

Chapter 6 looks at the impact on service quality. The chapter explores the role of service quality in reviving the United Arab Emirates' hospitality sector post-COVID-19 pandemic. Various factors contribute to the success of the hospitality industry in UAE; some of them are strategic location, leisure facilities, and business-friendly policies. Nevertheless, the COVID-19 Pandemic has impacted the hospitality industry worldwide. Therefore, it is necessary to find ways to revive the hospitality sector during and post-pandemic periods. Thus, the findings of this research give insight into customer preference and expectations as well as the need to invest and implement technology to deliver exceptional service. Therefore, it emphasizes that organizations operating in the hospitality sector should understand the customer needs, develop appropriate strategies, and invest in technology. Specifically, this research stresses that service quality dimensions improve customer satisfaction, enhance customer loyalty, and regain consumer trust.

Chapter 7 discusses the historical impact previous pandemics had on businesses. Then it presents information about Covid-19 Pandemic and how the United Arab Emirates (UAE) and businesses dealt with this particular pandemic. As consumption for goods and services reduced, a pattern of demand and supply shocks was identified. More specifically, we focus on Dubai's banking sector response as the banks' management strategies will influence the economy's recovery.

Chapter 8 highlights the challenges faced and strategies adopted by businesses in India. This chapter looks at the pre-Covid and post-Covid economic conditions. An analysis has been done to clarify how large corporations and small businesses faced the combined blunt of poor economy and COVID. A case story-based approach has been adopted to highlight the responses of a few large corporations and how they turned the pandemic into an economic opportunity to churn out supernormal profits. The chapter also highlights how the number of billionaires in India has increased during this time. Struggles for small business survival are also highlighted, and sustenance and changes in how they function or carry out day-to-day business operations are discussed. A very small proportion of businesses did stand up for the public's welfare and made an effort to facilitate their workforce.

Chapter 9 discusses the condition of employees, migrant workers, and middle classes in India during COVID-19. The chapter specifically looks at how each of them faced the pandemic and how their conditions deteriorated drastically. The chapter highlights how labour laws changed, how training and development programs were shelved, and how millions of employees ended up losing jobs during the pandemic. The impact of job loss and its trickledown effects changed how the Indian Middle class was living and forced them to take up a war of their own. The changed socio-economic scenario forced several Micro, Small and Medium enterprises to close their shop. SMEs rose to the challenge and either changed the line of business or adopted innovative business practices to survive and sustain. The changing socio-economic environment became more complex and volatile as few large corporations, pharmaceutical companies, health care providers, and hospitals in India started considering the pandemic as an opportunity to make supernormal profits. Indian Middle Class rose to the challenge and proved their Never Say Die Attitude!

Heather C. Webb
Higher Colleges of Technology, Dubai, UAE

Hussain Al-Numairy
Higher Colleges of Technology, Dubai, UAE

REFERENCES

Auerbach, S., & Kilmann, P. (1977). Crisis intervention: A review of outcome research. *Psychological Bulletin*, *84*(6), 1189–1217. doi:10.1037/0033-2909.84.6.1189 PMID:928575

Harrell, A. J. (2008). Factors that influence the recovery of small family-owned residential-care facilities for senior citizens in New Orleans, Louisiana after Hurricane Katrina. *Academy of Strategic Management Journal*, *7*, 49–53.

Hermann, C. F. (1972). *International Crises: Insights from Behaviour Research*. The Free Press.

Pearson, C., & Clair, J. (1998). Reframing Crisis Management. *Academy of Management Review*, *23*(1), 59–76. doi:10.2307/259099

Runyan, R. (2006). Small Business in the Face of Crisis: Identifying Barriers to Recovery from a Natural Disaster1. *Journal of Contingencies and Crisis Management*, *14*(1), 12–26. doi:10.1111/j.1468-5973.2006.00477.x

Seymour, M., & Moore, S. (2000). *Effective crisis management: Worldwide principles and practice*. Cassell.

Singh, J. (1994). Organizational Niches and the Dynamics of Organizational Mortality. *American Journal of Sociology*, *100*(2), 346–380. doi:10.1086/230540

Zdziarski, E., Dunkel, N., & Rollo, J. (2007). *Campus crisis management*. Jossey-Bass.

Chapter 1
Global Fintech Market:
Recent Performance and the Effect of COVID-19 - Investigating the Impact of the Pandemic in the Financial Technology Sector

Konstantinos Tsanis
Hult International Business School, Nigeria

Vasilios Stouraitis
https://orcid.org/0000-0001-5825-2604
Glasgow Caledonian University, UK

ABSTRACT

The FinTech industry has been growing rapidly and significantly, becoming the go-to service provider for some of the most important financial services, such as lending and payments. Since 2020, the onset of COVID-19 has substantially impacted the industry, both positively and negatively. This chapter discusses the recent performance of the FinTech industry based on a large-scale survey across the globe. The chapter then focuses on analysing the 'new normal' in banking, after the pandemic era, based on the findings of the global survey, with explicit focus on the FinTech sector, followed by further implications on the impact that the pandemic had in the traditional banking sector. The chapter concludes by providing an overview of the emerging opportunities that appear in the FinTech sector.

DOI: 10.4018/978-1-7998-8346-3.ch001

1. INTRODUCTION

The FinTech industry has been growing rapidly and significantly, becoming the go-to service provider for some of the most important financial services, such as lending and payments. Since 2020, the onset of COVID-19 has substantially impacted the industry, both positively and negatively. This paper aims to discuss the recent performance of the FinTech industry – across different verticals and regions – to speak to the different ways in which COVID-19 is shaping the current FinTech market and impacting its future. The unexpected disruption caused by COVID-19 has prompted many to reflect on the extent of company preparedness and risk-evaluation processes (Jaques, 2010), as well as crisis management more broadly (see Deloitte, 2020; Dobrowolski, 2020; Fasth, *et al.*, 2021). Thus, the paper will also explore the actions taken by FinTechs in light of the COVID-19 pandemic.

The paper is structured as follows. First, it will provide a detailed overview of the survey data, focusing on the distribution of survey respondents (Section 2.1), the recent market performance of FinTechs (Section 2.2), the initiatives of the FinTech market in light of COVID-19 (Section 2.3), and offering a summary of the findings (2.4). The paper then focuses on analysing the 'new normal' in banking, after the pandemic era, based on the findings of the global survey. It focuses explicitly on the impact on the FinTech sector, followed by further implications on the impact that the pandemic had in the traditional banking sector. The paper concludes by providing an overview of the emerging opportunities that appear in the FinTech sector.

2. SURVEY DATA: THE GLOBAL COVID-19 FINTECH MARKET RAPID ASSESSMENT REPORT

In order to better understand and assess the impact that Covid had in the global FinTech markets, the World Bank Group, along with the World Economic Forum and Cambridge Center for Alternative Finance conducted a large scale survey[5]. The findings of the survey are presented in the following section.

2.1 Distribution of Survey Respondents[67]

In this research project, titled ''Global Covid 19 FinTech market rapid assessment study'' we had the participation of 1035 FinTechs. Graph 1 represents the distribution among primary FinTech verticals. As expected, Digital Lending is a primary activity, with 21% of surveyed FinTechs focusing on it. Digital Payments is the second most popular vertical with 18% of FinTechs involved. Capital management was another field with large representation, with 14% and 8% of FinTechs engaged in a Digital Capital Raising and Wealthtech verticals, respectively.

Surprisingly, only 1% of surveyed FinTechs work on Digital Savings, a percentage which is much lower than that of areas, such as ETP (9%), Insurtech (7%), RegTech (6%), Digital Banking (6%), Alternative Credit & Data Analytics (3%), Digital Identity (3%), and Digital Asset Exchange (3%).

Figure 1. Survey Sample Distribution Among Primary FinTech Verticals

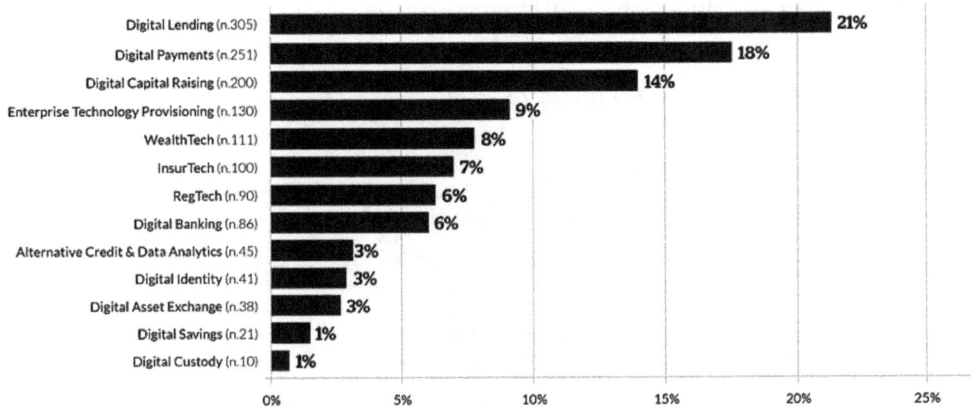

Figure 2. Geographical Distribution of Survey Respondents

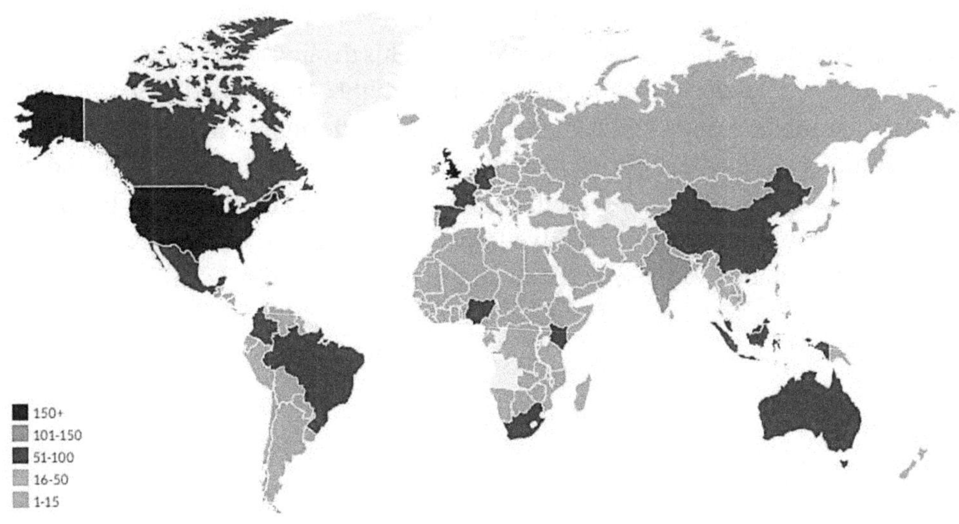

Figure 2 displays the geographical distribution of survey respondents. Most surveyed FinTechs are based in the US followed by India. Representation is high across western Europe, LATAM, Asia, Canada, and Australia as well. Fewer FinTechs are based in Eastern Europe, CIS, and Africa.

2.2 FinTech Market's Recent Performance

The next element of this research focused on assessing the impact that Covid 19 could have in the different fintech verticals. Figure 3 showcases the uneven distribution of the growth performance across different verticals.

Figure 3. The Global FinTech Market Growth Across Verticals

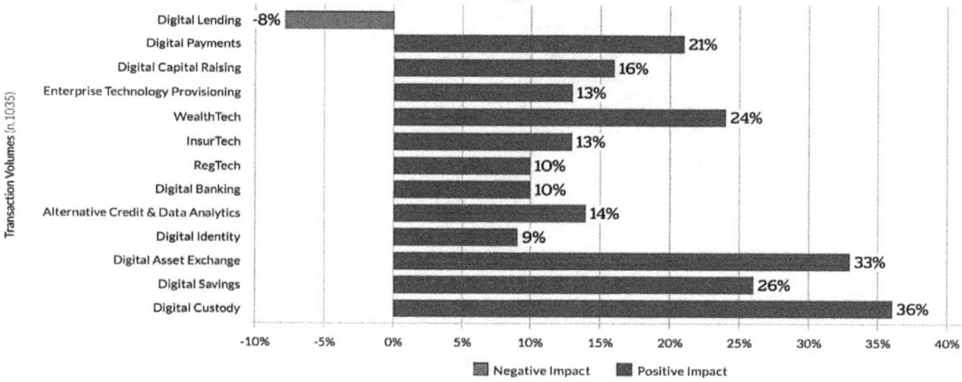

Despite being the dominant competence for FinTechs, Fintech focusing on Digital Lending saw a decline in its transaction volume. This decline is partially attributable to the tendency of lenders to become risk-averse in light of the COVID-19 pandemic. Contrary, wealthTech and Digital Payments recorded the highest transaction volume growth among popular categories, mainly due to customers handling their money online during the pandemic. Although Digital Custody and Digital Asset Exchange verticals display an impressive positive impact, this might be overestimated due to the low representation of these verticals in the survey.

Figure 4. The Global FinTech Market Growth Across Markets

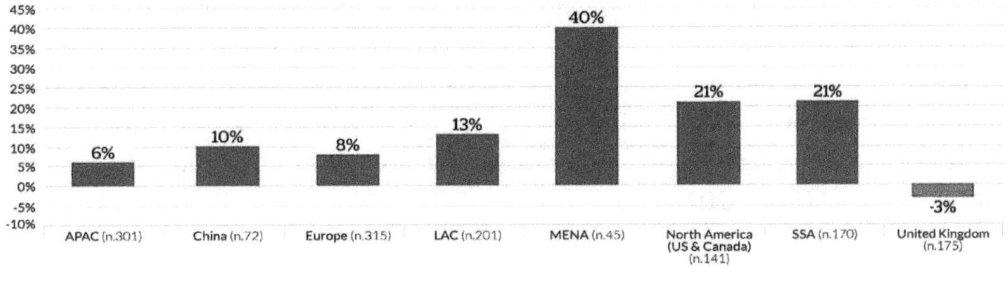

Another way to capture the impact of Covid-19 in the FinTech sector is by analyzing the transaction volumes of the products being offered. Figure 4 presents transaction growth volumes across different regions. As evident, the growth is uneven both geographically and vertically. FinTechs based in MENA reported highest transaction growth volume, amounting to 40%. North America and SSA also had an impressive performance throughout H1 2020. Results displayed by FinTechs based in APAC, China, Europe, and LAC are moderate, whereas United Kingdom had a negative impact – which might be due to the combination of the COVID-19 pandemic and Brexit.

Figure 5. The Global FinTech Market Performance between Emerging Markets and Developing Economies and Advanced Economies

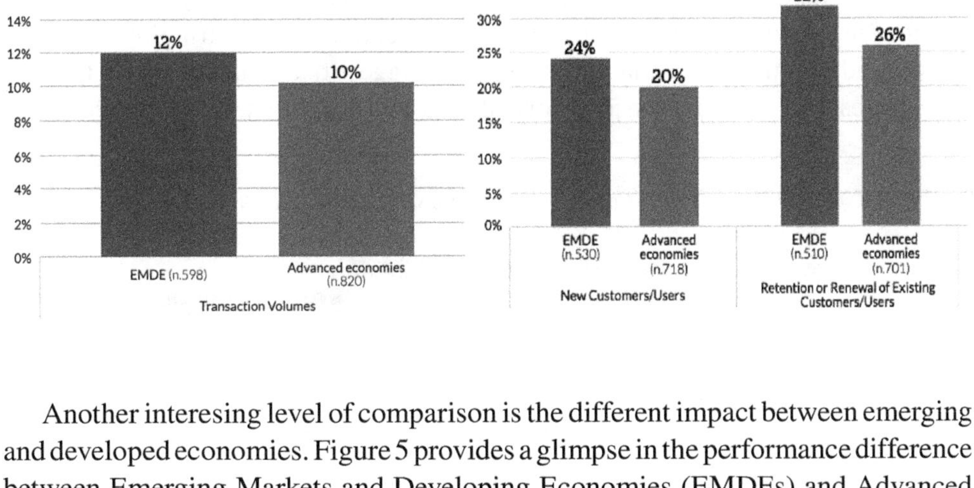

Another interesing level of comparison is the different impact between emerging and developed economies. Figure 5 provides a glimpse in the performance difference between Emerging Markets and Developing Economies (EMDEs) and Advanced Economies (AEs). According to the data collected, FinTechs in EMDEs outperformed their peers in all surveyed indicators, recording higher transaction volume growth, as well as better customer acquisition and retention rates. These results are connected to the fact FinTech players are now beginning to capture the previously-untapped market in EMDEs.

Another very interesting level of comparison is the impact of the lockdown itself in the markets in which FinTechs operate. Specifically, the ''stringency'' of lockdowns sems to have been a factor quoted widely as a factor affecting markets during covid-19 (Lara, 2020).

Figure 6. Impact of Lockdown Stringency on the Performance of FinTechs

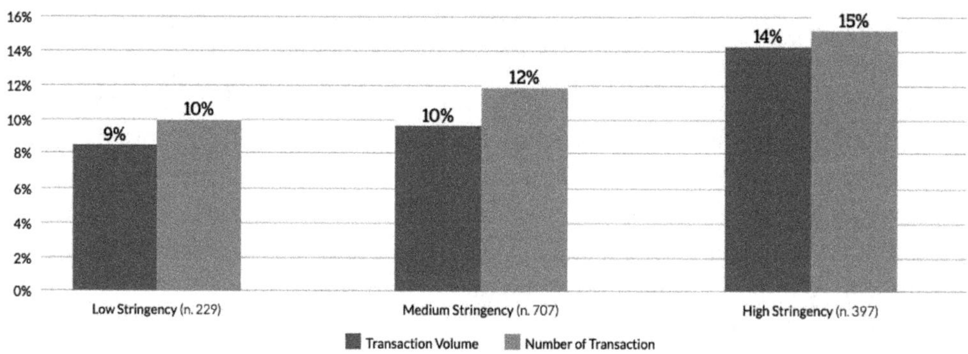

Figure 6 provides an overview the impact of different COVID-19 lockdown strategies on the performance of FinTechs. FinTechs based in countries with higher stringencies report higher transaction growth rates. This is mainly related to the increased use of online or digital as the best option for transactions in highly restricted areas. In addition, this correlation might also suggest that countries with highest stringencies were able to go back to normality faster than ones with less restrictions.

Figure 7. COVID-19's Impact on Financial Position of FinTechs

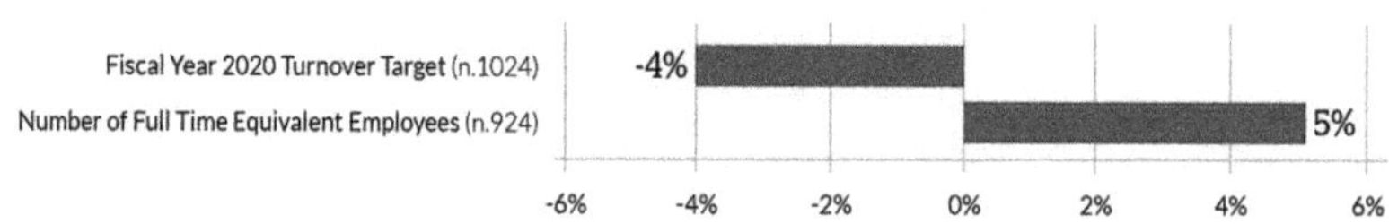

Figure 8. COVID-19's Impact on Financial Position of FinTechs

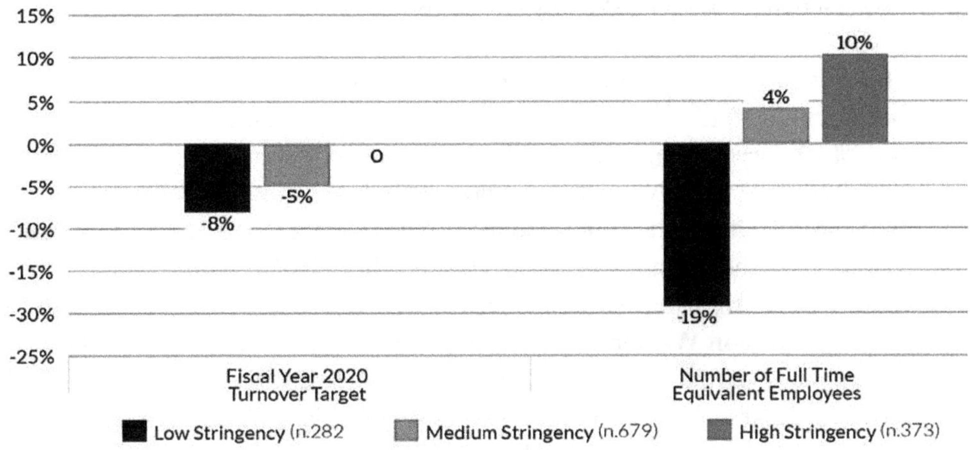

Figures 7 and 8 display a negative impact of COVID-19 on turnover targets. FinTechs operating in low/medium stringency markets didnt meet their targets by 8% and 5% on average. Despite financial hardship, most companies grew in terms of new employees, with FinTechs in high stringency markets reporting a 10% average staff growth.

2.3 Initiatives of the FinTech Market Due to COVID-19

The previous sections highlighted clearly the impact that Covid-19 had in the performance of FinTechs, and the importance of Covid measures implementation on the performance of FinTechs. As a resust, Fintechs in different markets responded to Covid-19 in different ways, which is topic of discussion of the following section.

Figure 9. Adjustments made by FinTechs in light of COVID-19

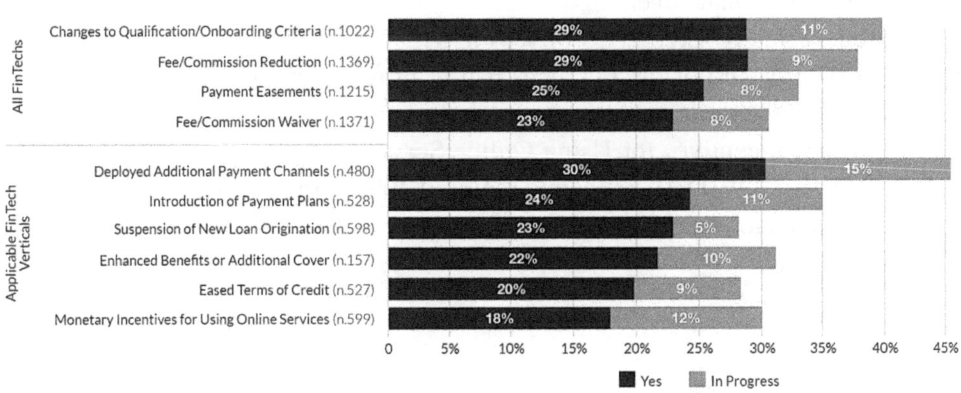

Graph 9 outlines the actions taken by FinTechs to adjust to the COVID-19 reality. Figure 9 presents the actions taken by all FinTechs:

- **Changes to qualification / onboarding criteria** – In light of ongoing lockdown regulations, digital onboarding became pressing issues, with as far as 40% of surveyed FinTechs having to implement adjustments. Out of this 40%, 29% have already finished the process, whereas 11% are still in progress
- **Fee/Commission reduction** – FinTechs had to adapt to worsening economic conditions of their customers, with 29% reporting a fee/commission reduction, while 9% are still working on this provision.
- **Fee/Commission Waiver** – Considering the worsening economic conditions, 31% of surveyed FinTechs abolished commissions and fees altogether.
- **Payment Easements** – With the changes in lifestyle, payment systems had to go through major adjustments. As much as 25% of surveyed FinTechs have already eased their solutions, while for 8% of the companies, this is still a work-in-progress.

The actions taken by all FinTech verticals survey are as follows:

- **Deployed Additional Payment Channels** – As already mentioned, offering more accessibility became of paramount importance. Hence, 45% of surveyed FinTechs report working on adding alternate payment channels.
- **Introduction of Payment Plans** – Paymnet plans became important measure for offering more transparency, and while 24% of the companies have already done that, 11% are still in the implementation phase.
- Suspension of New Loan Origination: With worsening economy, FinTechs had to tighten their fiscal policies, with 28% suspending new loan origination during COVID-19.
- Enhanced Benefits or Additional Cover: In order to reinforce customer-employee loyalty, 32% of surveyed FinTechs have enhanced benefits and offered additional cover.
- Eased Terms of Credit: To offset the negative economic impact caused by COVID-19, 29% of the FinTechs had to provide greater accessibility to the capital for their clients.
- Monetary Incentives for Using Online Services: Adjusting to the conditions during the COVID-19 pandemic required 30% of the FinTechs to incentivize their clients to use online services.

Figure 10. New Products, Services, and Features launched by FinTechs

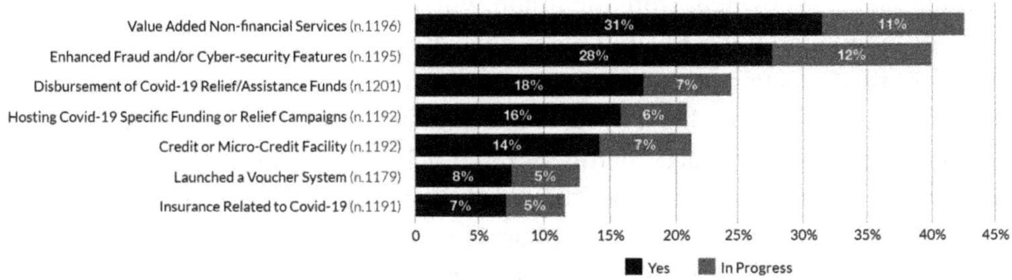

Figure 10 showcases new products, services, and features launched by surveyed FinTechs. Since financial institutions are increasingly involved with non-financial services, 42% of surveyed FinTechs have launched – or are in the process of launching – at least one non-financial service. With business moving in the digital realm, improving cyber-security is now one of the major challenges facing FinTechs, with 40% of respondents working on features to do address this issue.

Dealing with the negative impacts of Covid has been a major challenge for most FinTechs, with the majority launching products with the objective of offsetting negative impacts. Amongst the most popular products are:

- Direct solutions:
  - Disbursement of COVID-19 Relief / Assistance Funds (25%)
  - Hosting COVID-19 Specific Funding or Relief Campaigns (22%)
  - Insurance Related to COVID-19 (11%)
- Indirect solutions:
  - Credit or Micro-Credit Facility (21%)
  - Launched a Voucher System (13%)

Figure 11. FinTechs Willingness to Work with Governments on COVID-19 Relief Measures

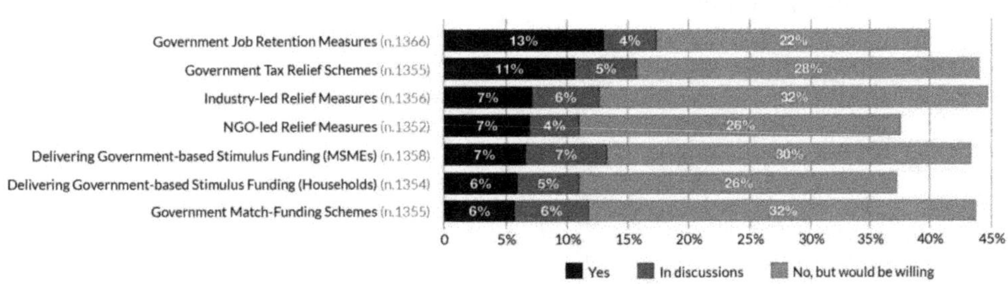

Figure 11 shows FinTechs willingness to work with Governments on COVID-19 relief measures. As evident from the graph, FinTechs are keen on getting involved across different directions. Overall, more than 40% of surveyed FinTechs declared readiness to participate in relevant relief measures, with particular interest in Industry-led relief measures. Around 45% of surveyed companyes reported to be either willing to participate or already participating in relief activities. Nevertheless, it is worth noting that FinTechs remain underutilized. In the majority of verticals, although FinTechs have demonstrated ready to participate, they are yet to be involved are not actively involved. The highest participation falls within job retention measures, where 13% of surveyed FinTechs are already actively involved.

Figure 12. Regulatory Support Needed by FinTechs

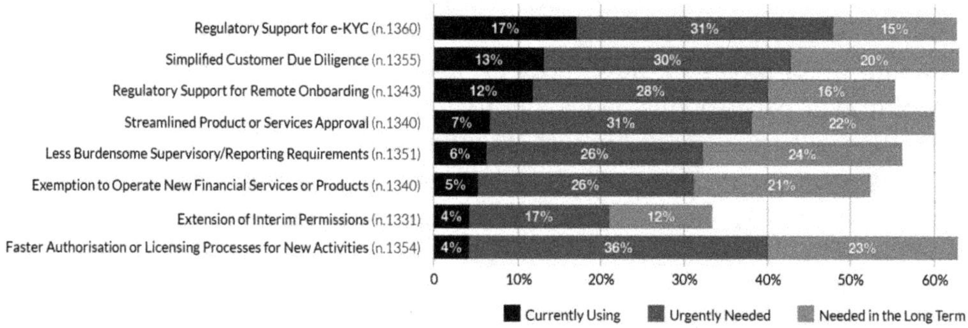

Figure 12 indicates that regulatory support for FinTechs is lagging in most cases. There is fierce competition within the FinTech industry, and companies are resorting to rapid development in order to edge out competitors. However, in some cases, regulatory support is lagging. Indeed, over 55% of the surveyed FinTechs identify the need for some form of support in all the areas shown in the graph above, apart from the extension of interim permission. Importantly, most of the FinTechs reported e-KYC, CDD and Onboarding as the areas representing the most pressing need for regulatory support.

Figure 13. Participation in Regulatory Innovation Initiatives

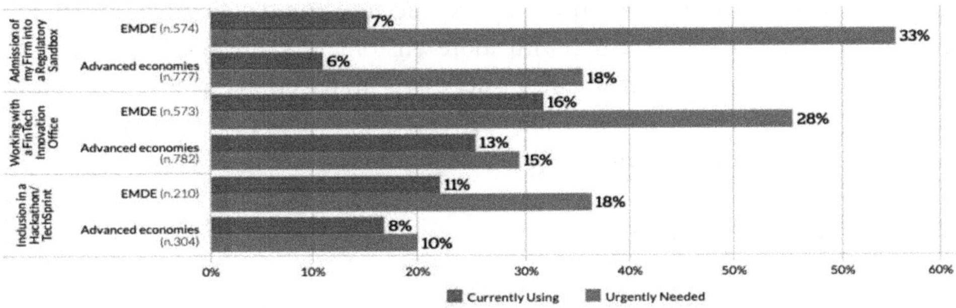

Figure 13 shows that FinTechs based in EMDEs require more support than their peers operating in AEs. Apparently, regulators in EMDEs are less agile and their frameworks are outdated in comparison with regulators in AEs. Once again, it is worth mentioning that less initiatives are currently used than what is needed. Currently, only 7% of the surveyed FinTechs located in EMDEs are admitted into the regulatory sandbox, with 33% in the need of urgent admission. The difference is less striking for AEs with 6% and 18%, respectively. FinTech innovation offices are more inclusive in AEs, with 13% of FinTechs currently using them and only 15% having an urgent need compared with 16% and 28%, respectively in EMDEs. Lastly, inclusion in Hackathons is the least pressing issue, with 18% of the FinTechs in EMDEs and 10% of those in AEs having the need of urgent inclusion.

Figure 14. Operational Challenges faced by FinTechs

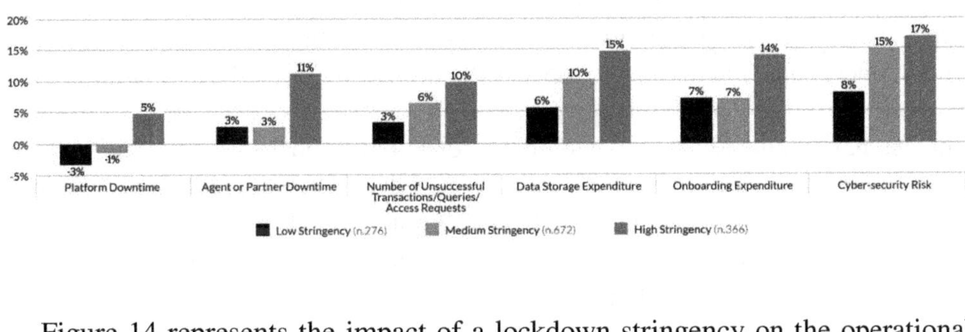

Figure 14 represents the impact of a lockdown stringency on the operational processes of FinTechs. All surveyed FinTechs reported a growth in operational problems, compared to H1 2019. FinTechs working in a markets with more restrictions during the COVID-19 pandemic had to change their processes drastically and at a rapid pace. Consequently, this posed more operational challenges. Overall, FinTechs with higher lockdown stringency reported a substantially higher number of operational issues than companies in other markets. The most impacted area was growing cyber-security risk, followed by expenditures on developing onboarding services and data storage. Lastly, with more customers using digital services to perform transactions, the number of unsuccessful transactions queries also grew. Surprisingly, platform downtime is the only category where FinTechs operating in low/medium stringency reported improvement.

2.4 Summary of Findings

The survey suggests that COVID-19 had a varied impact on the FinTech industry. Across some verticals, COVID-19 had a positive impact, yet, there have been negative implications as well. Indeed, lockdowns and customers' inability to use physical services spurred rapid digitization and improvements in digital services and features. A closer look at a survey's results provides insights into the key features that FinTechs have been developing throughout the pandemic. For instance, over 45% of surveyed FinTechs have already deployed or are in the process of delivering additional payment channels. Moreover, there are visible improvements in cybersecurity, and the fact that 42% of the surveyed respondents are working on developing non-financial value-added services suggests that the focus of financial institution is expanding towards creating eco-systems rather than delivering standalone platforms.

The competitive environment in which FinTechs operate, coupled with a shrinking economy is forcing most of the surveyed companies to review their fee/commission strategies – in most cases, organizations report reductions and waivers. For instance, 35% of surveyed organizations are working on the introduction of payment plans, which suggests that customers will get better products at a more affordable price.

Nevertheless, the COVID-19 pandemic has had negative impacts on the FinTech industry as well. Indeed, the growing demand of the digital services has created several operational challenges. Amongst them, growth in platform downtime has been one of the most visible problems during the pandemic. Most of the surveyed Fintechs have indicated that expenditures for client onboarding and data storage are growing exponentially, which, in light of a decline in revenue from services might become a serious financial challenge. As mentioned earlier, with businesses moving to the digital realm, cybersecurity risks have increased exponentially. For example, the survey shows that, across FinTechs operating in markets with strong lockdown stringency, cybersecurity risks grew by 17%, and the situation is similar for markets with medium to low lockdown stringencies.

COVID-19 undoubtedly had a negative impact on FinTechs financial position. Surveyed FinTechs reported that they were unable to meet their fiscal year turnover goals by 4% on average. Interestingly, there is a correlation between lockdown stringency and the reaching of turnover goals. In fact, FinTechs operating in low stringency markets were unable to meet their goals by 8% on average, whereas in high stringency markets, most FinTechs managed to meet their goals.

The most part of surveyed FinTechs demonstrated willing to participate in COVID-19 relief measures. In order to ensure their inclusion, collaboration with regulatory entities is of paramount importance. However, survey results suggest that, in some cases, regulators are unable to adapt to market changes, suggesting that FinTechs are not getting enough support. For example – 32% of FinTechs have an urgent need for support with e-KYC, 30% need simplifications in customer due diligence, and 28% require assistance with digital onboarding.

When it comes to fostering innovation, challenges to companies' inclusion become evident . This problem is especially pressing for FinTechs operating in EMDEs, where 33% of surveyed companies report that they need urgent admision into regulatory sandboxes and only 7% already have an access. 28% declare an urgent need to work with innovation offices. Here only 16% already have an opportunity to do so. FinTechs operating in AEs have on average higher inclusion rates. However, the number of FinTechs that are not yet fully integrated remains high. For example, when it comes to admision into regulatory sandboxes, 18% do not have access to them, 15% have the ability to work with innovation offices, while 10% are included in hackathons and techsprints .

3. THE 'NEW NORMAL' IN FINTECH AND BANKING

3.1 The Impact of COVID-19 on the FinTech Industry

The FinTech sector is witnessing tremendous amount of volatility in both its structure and work, which have been significantly amplified by the COVID-19 pandemic. Most FinTech companies have displayed flexibility, managing to shift entirely to online technology. Due to the pandemic, a lot of companies focusing on product and process innovation have become more customer centric and have built the capacity to handle large disruptions.

It is estimated that the spread of COVID-19 and the consequent lockdown measures have led to between a 24% and 32% increase in the relative rate of daily downloads of finance mobile applications. In absolute terms, this equates to an average daily increase of roughly 5.2 to 6.3 million application downloads and an aggregate increase of about 316 million application downloads since the outbreak of the pandemic. Most regions across the world exhibit notable increases in terms of absolute, relative, and per capita increase. Preliminary analysis of country-level characteristics suggests that market size and demographics – rather than level of economic development and ex-ante adoption rates – drive differential trends (Remolina, 2020).

In addition, emerging market economies have been increasingly committing resources to support FinTech innovation, mainly through infrastructure development and relaxed market regulations – many also have been creating start-up hubs, accelerators, incubators, and public-private partnership (PPP) programs to foster the development of the FinTech industry (Varma et al., 2021).

During the COVID-19 pandemic, moving payments to digital channels has been one of the hottest topics of debate. Since cash is seen as one of the potential carriers of the coronavirus, cash-based transactions have been declining throughout the pandemic and further reduction is expected. In this context, digital payments have witnessed a massive increase in the rate of adoption.

The lending vertical has been impacted as well. Most FinTech lenders developed their companies on the premise that consumers income levels are rising and the economy is shrinking, which, combined with the tightening of lending policies, had a negative impact on a market size. COVID-19 has also caused a potentially long-lasting effect on the micro, small, and medium sized enterprise (MSME) lending sector due to the sudden interruption in supply chain and subdued demand, which have left MSME's in urgent need to generate cash flow.

Even though FinTechs focused on lending have been struggling throughout the pandemic, the economy is expected to recover rapidly once the lockdowns are lifted. More specifically, Peer-to-Peer (P2P) lending gained traction during the pandemic, during which the FinTech P2P lending has become the most viable alternative credit option available to borrowers. These findings are significant and likely to be of interest to borrowers, investors, practitioners, academics, and policymakers because they highlight the usefulness of P2P lending platforms and their potential to increase or replace lending provided by traditional or conventional banking institutions (IFC, 2021).

The Wealthtech segment – which comprises various sub segments such as digital discount brokers, robo-advisors, mutual fund advisors, personal finance management apps, micro investing platforms, and foreign investing apps – have reported an upsurge in number of new accounts opened and volume of transactions, resulting in entry of new investors in capital markets.

The Insurtech sector, however, reports controversial results. On the one hand, the outbreak of the pandemic meant an increase in insurance premium among the non-life insurance segment. Yet, the increase in demand for insurance products remains volatile. On the other hand, since the travel industry was severely hit by the pandemic, the demand for travel and vehicle insurance decreased significantly, offsetting the increase in demand for health insurance policies. Digitization drastically helped insurers – especially life and health – to create and distribute simplified, digital-native solutions in a cost-effective manner.

The impact of COVID-19 on Neobanks has been varied. Although these companies are facing challenges to attract deposits, their flexible model allows to keep discretionary costs reduced and keeping ongoing programs on hold, effectively maintaining a capital-light model. The biggest opportunity for Neobanks lies in providing value added services, Credit and Saving Accounts (CASA) accounting, and expense management. Due to their innovative business models and digital payments channels, Neobanks have seen a surge in adoption globally due to swift transition to work from home model resulting in the growth of digital financial services.

The Emerging Tech segment, which comprises software like SaaS, B2C, and FinTechs offering digital onboarding, chatbots, customer relation management, API platforms and productivity tools has stayed active even during the pandemic. The vertical growth is expected to continue in the post-pandemic era. With a greater number of online options, FinTech enablers could offer cloud-based solutions which are guaranteed to experience higher demand. AI is also expected to be one of the most in-demand technologies for products and services like conversation solutions for call center chatbots, fraud detection, as wll as workflow automation. Digital identity provides (DaaS) are also expected to be in-demand as increasing regulatory support is likely to translate in more KYC process being digitalized.

Technologies such as machine learning algorithms can put FinTechs – from P2P lending platforms, such as Funding Circle to digital banks that provide lending to small and medium enterprises (SMEs), such as OakNorth and Iwoca – at an advantage as they are called to assess the credit worthiness of businesses and distribute loans rapidly by automating due diligence processes (Deloitte, 2020).

In addition, FinTechs may be able to serve customers that are usually excluded by the traditional banks, for instance, due to lack of collaterals. Bigger and older financial institutions operating with legacy technologies and models can potentially struggle to work at this pace and be more reluctant to offer lending to businesses using alternative data for their credit assessment. Considering that most SMEs have limited liquidity, time here is of the essence. Being digitally native, FinTechs will also be better equipped for remote working, and will potentially be more prepared to respond to such calls and to service businesses remotely (Khakan et al., 2021).

FinTechs have adopted a mix-and-match of broad coping strategies to survive and sustain their businesses amid the 'new normal'. First, FinTechs have increased digital interaction with customers across all customer touchpoints from onboarding to providing customer support. In the absence of physical interaction, FinTechs have been using online and social media channels like WhatsApp and Facebook. Second, customers have increasingly adopted digital platforms, including financial services platforms. This has been consistent across different customer segments from low-to high-income customers. Such platforms have opened up new opportunities for FinTechs to expand their customer reach digitally with low customer acquisition costs. At the same time, digital platforms have widened the offerings of FinTechs to encompass compatible services, such as bookkeeping with lending on their platforms. These value-adding activities have helped increase the 'customer stickiness' on their platforms. Third, the pandemic helped some FinTechs gain perspective on eliminating operational redundancies through several steps. These include reducing staff, cross-skilling teams, automating processes, and re-strategizing their businesses to ensure survival over growth. In addition, credit FinTechs have begun partnering with payment gateways and developing APIs for loan repayment collections. These measures would reassure investors, gain investment, and increase runways.

Lastly, FinTech appears to be closing gender gaps, but special attention needs to be paid to ensure that women are not left behind during the pandemic. Stakeholders noted that several barriers to digital financial inclusion – such as access to resources (mobile phone, internet), cultural or social norms, and digital and financial literacy – may be higher for women (Sridhar & Gamser, 2020).

3.2 Post-COVID-19's Opportunities for FinTechs

As already discussed, the economic shifts caused by the pandemic have placed tremendous stress on FinTechs. However, most FinTechs leveraged their flexibility to not only adapt to the 'new normal', but also to create competitive advantages through innovative approaches, products, and services. It is widely believed that adjustments made during the pandemic will provide new opportunities in the post-pandemic era. FinTechs tend to have some unique advantages that are allowing many to both create new ways of providing value in the current environment and to position themselves to thrive in the long-term. Among them, FinTechs are unburdened by complex legacy systems, which allows them to build platforms using a cloud-native approach that, with the widespread adoption of cloud systems, will allow them to integrate with one-another, as well as to build links with other financial institutions. Multiple alternatives shift power to the customer, whereas most FinTechs are laser-focused on a seamless and delightful digital customer experience allowing them to create best-in-class products.

For most FinTechs access to funding was exceedingly difficult during pandemic, and this was especially heightened for early-stage companies. This forced most FinTechs to reexamine their mission and business models not only during the pandemic but also looking forward. FinTechs were the first to react to the fact that social distancing was accelerating customers' use of online – especially mobile – channels to view and manage their finances. Consequently, many FinTechs switched to a mobile-first approach. Additionally, being customer-centric, FinTechs often excel in digital onboarding, data visualization, and in providing convenient customer journeys for transactions. These capabilities proved to be the right recipe for surviving and will likely become even more relevant as a greater number of customers and businesses switch to the digital realm. Deloitte's research identified key areas in which FinTechs' business model can be used to create new opportunities in a post-pandemic world:

- **Expanding partnership strategies** – Growth in open banking and banking-as-a-service regulations and initiatives will play an important role.
- **Advancing financial inclusion programs** – The economic disruption of the pandemic highlights the importance of serving people who are currently outside the financial system.
- **Accelerating economic relief efforts** – FinTechs in digital payment's verticals may be well positioned to provide rapid disbursement of government relief funds.
- **Empowering gig workers** – This is a growing segment whose unpredictable revenue patterns create unique financial, insurance, and tax requirements, which FinTechs are best positioned to serve.
- **Harnessing the Internet of Things** – More and more contactless payment-enabled devices create the need for flexible API integration services.

The pandemic has highlighted the important role of FinTechs in advancing the digitization of the whole financial services ecosystem, especially in providing services such as financial management, banking services, lending, accounting, e-payments, and insurance, to name a few. Beyond financial services, the SMEs can also gain through the provision of non-financial services as well. Providing SMEs with the digital tools they need means providing them with the opportunity to advance their business, and for many of them, the chance to survive during the pandemic (Jaques, 2010).

It should be noted that before COVID-19, less than 15% of SMEs in emerging economies had access to the resources they needed to grow and create wealth, with the unmet financing need of SMEs in developing countries estimated at $5.2 trillion every year. During the pandemic, access to financing from traditional banks has dried up even more, contributing to slow economic growth. In response, SMEs have turned to FinTech as one way to meet their financing needs. The term originally referred to the back-end systems of established financial institutions, but it is clear that it now includes a myriad of sectors that seek to improve the delivery and use of online financial services.

It is important to note that the potential of FinTech potential has attracted investor attention. In 2019, investment in FinTech companies amounted to $135.7 billion, with a total 2,693 deals around the globe. During the pandemic, many of these digital lending platforms moved quickly to respond to the surge of loan applications triggered by business shutdowns and layoffs. As mentioned earlier, because FinTechs use cutting edge technology to assess the creditworthiness of borrowers through alternative data and electronic platforms to process requests, their services have been more accessible and faster to small and medium-sized enterprises (Paolo et al., 2020).

Recently, an increasing number of FinTech lenders for SMEs are offering a new model of lending that is faster, easier, more cost-effective, as well as more transparent. For the first time, SMEs can share what data they have in exchange for access to credit to help them grow. By using advanced analytics platforms and artificial intelligence to assess transactional and alternative data (at times as simple as a bank statement that shows an SME's cash flow), FinTech lenders are gaining a much deeper understanding of SMEs. They can establish SMEs' creditworthiness, evaluate their risk more easily, and issue loans in as little as 24 hours. Today, these new, innovative, data-and artificial intelligence-led solutions are better positioned to serve SMEs' financing needs, lead them out of the imminent financial crisis, and unlock their potential (Paolo et al., 2020).

More specifically, many FinTechs are innovating to create new products that address the rapidly evolving economic environment:

- In the UK, Trade Ledger, Wiserfunding, Nimbla, and NorthRow have formed a business-lending taskforce to provide a turnkey origination and underwriting platform that allows banks, alternative lenders, and private debt lenders to digitally deploy funds to businesses during the COVID-19 outbreak.
- Israeli FinTech company Innovesta launched its COVID-19 Resilience Innodex (CRI). Using a proprietary artificial intelligence technology, the CRI assigns risk scores based on a business' ability to withstand the effects of the pandemic.
- British company Iwoca – an online lender – announced OpenLending, a platform that allows FinTechs and banks to extend iwoca's lending capabilities to more than two million UK businesses.
- Finally, a number of US-based FinTech companies – those that provide financial services as well as those that enable financial services – are helping to facilitate the financial relief provided under the CARES Act:
    - nCino has a developed a new solution to optimize the PPP loan process.
    - ODX, a subsidiary of OnDeck, has developed a solution that is specially configured to the CARES Act.
    - Lendio is enabling small businesses to apply for loans.
    - Unqork developed a small business digital lending platform (Johnathan and Mishra, 2020).

It is also important that governments make actions to allow faster and more effective digital transformation in the banking industry. The following are several considerations specific to governments.

- **Promote better payment services through FinTech during and after the COVID-19 crisis** – FinTech can allow users to transfer money to any bank account, pay for bills and services to merchants and businesses in any part of the country and across borders. Financial technology can also provide a framework to incorporate and leverage technological opportunities to promote access and use of transaction accounts. When such framework is in place, individuals employed in urban areas can pay bills, and can easily send money to their loved ones in rural areas to help them cope with the economic consequence of the COVID-19 crisis.
- **Increase trust and cybersecurity in FinTech** – Governments should encourage FinTech businesses should emphasize greater transparency in their business operations, alongside security.
- **Regulators should be proactive and assume FinTech will breach user privacy and plan to mitigate damage by protecting users** – This can be assumed because of the fact that FinTech are essential teams of young people, trying to offer products, without having received compliance training. The fact that FinTech are unregulated creates even more risks on the potential, and the WireCard scandal is a prominent example in this category.
- **Prioritize digital financial services for remittances** – Many families and individuals around the world rely on payments sent from migrant workers abroad using international digital payment systems. As such, these international firms are targeting the needs of the unbanked across the world and using mobile devices to send remittances is becoming an efficient instrument in the push toward financial inclusion.
- **Do all it takes to get money to people as fast as possible** – Getting money to people quickly during the COVID-19 crisis is important. Governments should make cash transfers to their citizens if they have the capacity to do so. Priority should be given to unconditional cash transfers to poor individuals and households, and such transfers should be sent early and often.
- **Reassure individuals and households that their money and financial transactions are safe** – Governments should reassure members of the population that their money and financial transactions are safe. The government should also reassure the people that there will be uninterrupted access to financial services during the crisis, and even during lockdowns.[10]

3.3 The Early Impact of COVID-19 on Financial Institutions (FIs)

Seven months from the outbreak of the COVID-19 pandemic – as most countries had begun easing the lockdown restrictions – the vast majority of FIs were reporting lower loan collection and disbursement levels; government moratoria and voluntary deferrals affected over half of FI portfolios. Despite the widespread restructuring of portfolios, FIs started to register significant increases in non-performing assets. Furthermore, COVID-19 has affected the operations, strategic direction, funding, portfolios and asset quality.

Even though the COVID-19 has slowed down or stopped the operation of many industries, it did not have the same effect in the data-driven finance world. Indeed, traditional FIs and FinTechs are trying to leverage on data-driven solutions to respond to the challenges associated with the pandemic. For instance, as mentioned earlier, data-driven financial companies are participating to the lending programs for small businesses launched by several governments, whereas in previous crisis only traditional institutions with traditional credit risk models participated to these programmes (Deloitte, 2020).

In terms of operations, the impact of the pandemic on operations as of October-November 2020 was consistent across all regions. Roughly one in five respondents reported operating at pre-crisis levels, and the majority of these FIs were in upper middle-income countries. In addition, the impact of the pandemic on new loan disbursements was larger for the riskier MSMEs and retail segments. At the time of the survey, IFC clients reported that loan disbursements decelerated due to the crisis, on average at about 80% of pre-crisis levels. FIs in South Asia recorded the lowest disbursement levels as of October-November 2020. Microfinance Institutions (MFIs) and nonbank financial institutions (NBFIs) were disbursing just over three quarters of pre-crisis loan volumes.

Focusing on strategic direction, digital transformation gained priority for more than half of IFC clients. While digital transformation was already a corporate priority for nearly all IFC clients, 62% of respondents stated that investments in digital channels such as mobile and internet banking have become an increased or urgent priority as a result of the COVID-19 crisis. In addition, diversification of funding sources is now a strategic priority for the majority of IFC clients. In particular, the development of retail deposits increased in importance for one in three respondents. Lastly, mixed impacts on lending priorities are consistent with high levels of uncertainty and reduced lending activities. Retail and MSME lending decreased or ceased to be a priority for 27% and 18% of respondents, respectively. However, 21% of FIs stated a new importance for retail lending and 25% reported a higher priority for lending to MSMEs.

Portfolio-wise, outstanding loan portfolios remained at pre-crisis levels with over 50% of portfolios interested by moratoria and deferrals. Government moratoria on loan repayments – in addition to voluntary deferral and restructuring efforts – affected over half of client portfolios on average. In terms of asset quality, portfolios had begun to show signs of deterioration at the time of the survey, despite the masking effect of government moratoria and deferrals. Indeed, approximately 96% of institutions reported that their portfolios were negatively affected by the crisis (Deloitte, 2020). Over 60% of lenders have tightened their credit criteria, with over half discontinuing new lending entirely; only 37% reported that they continue lending to both existing and new customers (Fasth et al., 2021).

The pandemic has challenged traditional banking models and products, changed the competitive landscape, and served as a catalyst for digitization. Now, banks will need to get to know their customers again. More specifically, they first need to gain a better understanding of the shifts occurring in customers' preferences. Second, banks should rethink how to conduct business and transition from physical to digital customer relationship management. Third, banks are being pushed to explore process innovation to facilitate business sustainability and reduce costs. This signifies designing new customer offerings supported by new tools/ partnerships, proper planning for post-crisis operating models, and managing people 'in the cloud' (Sridhar & Gamser, 2020).

4. CONCLUSION

In conclusion, the impact of COVID-19 has significantly evolved the financial services industry – from the big banks accelerating their digital transformation to increasing number of and products from the FinTech players. Focusing on the FinTech industry, payments and wealth management have benefited the most while lending experienced a downturn. By geography, the FinTech industry has been growing much faster in emerging markets than in more developed markets. Indeed, lockdowns and customer's inability to use physical services spurred rapid digitization and improvements in digital services and features.

In addition to the recent performances, COVID-19 has also changed the initiatives and operations of many FinTech players. The most part of surveyed FinTechs declare willingness to participate in COVID-19 relief measures, signalling that collaboration with regulatory entities is of paramount importance.

Looking forward, FinTechs and banks – and the financial services industry as a whole – need to consider key necessary changes in their business model to operate in the 'new normal'.

*Dr. Konstantinos Tsanis is a Digital Transformation and FinTech expert in the World Bank Group, and a Lecturer in Innovation and Strategy, at the University of Hult Business School

**Dr. Vasilios Stouraitis is a lecturer in International Business and Management at Glasgow Caledonian University in the UK and visiting lecturer in several institutions abroad including Italy and Panama. Specializing in small and medium-sized enterprises and with a background in International Business and Economics, he holds a PhD from Henley Business School/University of Reading, an Msc in Development studies from University College London and an MBA and Bsc from the University of Kent. He has worked on development issues (agribusiness and governance) for the United Nations (Food and Agriculture Organization and the International Fund for Agricultural Development) and European Commission (DG Enterprise and Industry) and is also a published author in international business strategy and entrepreneurship. Regarding academic work, he has taught in several institutions (Edinburgh Business School at Athens, The American University of Rome, Link Campus Rome, Swiss School of Management Rome) and supervised several BA/BSc and MA/MSc theses on International Business topics and Food Economics.

REFERENCES

Carrasco C. (2021). *Digital Marketplaces, and how to survive COVID-19.* Smefinanceforum.org

CCAF, World Bank, & World Economic Forum. (2020). *The Global COVID-19 FinTech Market Rapid Assessment Report*. University of Cambridge, World Bank Group, and the World Economic Forum.

Deloitte. (2020). *Addressing the impact of COVID-19: Crisis management and resilience planning*. Author.

Deloitte. (2020). *Beyond COVID-19: New opportunities for fintech companies.* Deloitte Center for Financial Services.

Dobrowolski, Z. (2020). After COVID-19: Reorientation of crisis management in crisis. *Entrepreneurship and Sustainability Issues*, *8*(2), 1–12.

Fasth, J., Elliot, V., & Styhre, A. (2021). Crisis management as practice in small- and medium-sized enterprises during the first period of COVID-19. *Journal of Contingencies and Crisis Management*, 1–10.

Fu & Mishra. (2020). *The Global Impact of COVID-19 on Fintech Adoption*. Swiss Finance Institute Research Paper Series 20-38, Swiss Finance Institute.

Giordani & Rullani. (2020). *The Digital Revolution and COVID-19*. Working Papers 6, Department of Management, Università Ca' Foscari Venezia.

IFC. (2020). *The early impact of Covid-19 on financial institutions. In Insights from a survey of IFC financial institution clients*. IFC.

IFC. (2021). *The Effects of COVID-19 and the Need for Bank Restructuring*. IFC.

Jaques, T. (2010). Reshaping crisis management: The challenge for organizational design. *Organization Development Journal*, *28*(1), 9–17.

Lara. (2020). *Need financing because of the pandemic? SMEs turn to fintech companies*. IFC.

Lyons, A., Kass-Hanna, J., & Polato e Fava, A. (2021). Fintech Development and Savings, Borrowing and Remittances: A Comparative Study of Emerging Economies. *Borrowing and Remittances: A Comparative Study of Emerging Economies*.

Najaf, Subramaniam, & Atayah. (2021). Understanding the implications of FinTech Peer-to-Peer (P2P) lending during the COVID-19 pandemic. *Journal of Sustainable Finance & Investment*, 1-16.

Ozili, P. K. (2020). *Financial inclusion and Fintech during COVID-19 crisis: Policy solutions*. Academic Press.

Remolina, N. (2020). Towards a data-driven financial system: the impact of COVID-19. *SMU Centre for AI & Data Governance Research Paper*, *8*, 1-24.

Sahay, R., Eriksson von Allmen, U., Lahreche, A., Khera, P., Ogawa, S., Bazarbash, M., & Beaton, K. (2020). *The Promise of Fintech, Financial Inclusion in the Post COVID-19 Era. Departmental Paper No. 20/09*. IMF.

Sridhar & Gamser. (2020). *Member Survey Results on the Impact of COVID-19*. UKRI.

Varma, J., & Saxena, S. (2021). *Impact of COVID-19 on FinTechs*. Academic Press.

Zachariadis, M., Ozcan, P., & Dinçkol, D. (2020). The Covid-19 impact on fintech: now is the time to boost investment. *LSE Business Review*, 1-3.

Chapter 2
"Where the Next Meal Is Coming From": Policy Mix to Support Restaurant Workers in the U.S. During the COVID-19 Pandemic

Shalin Hai-Jew
https://orcid.org/0000-0002-8863-0175
Kansas State University, USA

ABSTRACT

Given the intimacy of food preparation and service, the close proximity of diners and staff, the general inability to eat comfortably while masked, the warm emotional atmospherics of restaurants, and the limits to restaurant ventilation, the current SARS-CoV-2/COVID-19 pandemic has meant shutdowns of restaurants across the United States early in the pandemic and then partial re-openings later with public health constraints. Some restaurants applied for the Small Business Administration (SBA)'s Paycheck Protection Program's funds in March 2020 to cover 2.5 months maximum of costs. Huge swaths of the restaurant industry have closed permanently, and many others are slated to close in the near future. Based on a content analysis, this work explores the plight of restaurant workers in the academic research and mass media literature and applies abductive reasoning to propose an approach for a policy mix that may better inform the present challenges with social justice considerations.

DOI: 10.4018/978-1-7998-8346-3.ch002

INTRODUCTION

For a disease-causing virus to have pandemic potential for humanity, it has to cause disease and death in people, and it has to be spread so quickly and easily and in silent (asymptomatic) ways that it can stealthily move in a population, even when the population is somewhat aware of its presence. If it has too fast of a death rate, people will succumb before they can pass it on to others. If the death rate is "too high," people may go to ground *en masse*, and the transmission may end. But what about a virus that affects different parts of a population very differently, so much so that people can deny that the virus causes a fatal disease that can stop a person's heart within days or weeks…even when treated with the best of modern science? In many ways, SARS-CoV-2 (severe acute respiratory syndrome coronavirus 2) which can develop into COVID-19 (corona virus disease 2019) fits the bill based on empirical health outcomes data. The world at this moment is in its grip. The numbers are devastating.

In mid-December 2020, about a year from when humanity became aware of this pathogen, there are currently 75,148,314 active coronavirus cases and 52,715,399 recovered. There have been 1,665,481 deaths worldwide, and in the U.S., on Dec. 17, 2020, 316,906 deaths [and projections of half a million dead by the end of February 2021 (IHME COVID-19 Forecasting Team, Oct. 23, 2020)] by a team that has proved its predictive mettle at virtually every phase of this pandemic. At this time, humanity finally has some therapeutics that may be somewhat effectual, and they have some novel mRNA vaccines coming online with high efficacy (94 – 95%) against infection and some protectiveness against serious COVID-19 even if infected. Diagnostics has become more available but was never sufficient to use for actual contact tracing and suppression of viral spread; rather, American communities had to make do without actual sufficient awareness of viral hotspots. Many carried the infection asymptomatically and spread the infection to others. For the past many months, however, humanity did not have a truly credible defense except social distancing, face-masking (against the passing of bio-aerosols), hand hygiene, and some other protective measures reminiscent of those practiced in the 1918 influenza (Spanish flu) pandemic that resulted in some 50 million deaths around the world (Scerri & Grech, Nov. 12, 2020) with hope that present-day collaborations could lower the numbers of deaths (Webel, & Freeman, June 5, 2020). At this moment, the U.S. is in its third wave; others suggest that the U.S. never really left the first wave and has never been able to bring down the base load of infection in society. Coming into the Fall 2020 and Winter 2021, there are fears that people returning indoors given the colder weather will mean a large jump in infections, and the numbers seem to be bearing that out. Family gatherings around the winter holidays—Thanksgiving;

Hanukkah, Christmas, Kwanzaa; the New Year's celebration, and such—are also expected to seed more outbreaks.

Researchers have been teasing out various evolving social patterns of viral spread in different locales, based on available data. One study found that "younger persons, having first acquired their infections through increasing social contact with their peers, then transmitted their infections to older, less socially mobile individuals. Without such cross-infection, an isolated epidemic among older people in Florida would be unsustainable" (Harris, 2020, p. 1019). This particular study used available mobility data and restaurant reservation data, among others.

Government Partial Shutdowns and Partial Reopenings to "Flatten the Curve"

Government shutdowns of non-essential businesses and restrictions on citizen mobility to "flatten the curve" of infections have affected different sectors disproportionately. This is especially so as the pandemic has dragged on for approximately a year now. U.S. citizens, even a few months into the shutdowns, were projected to have average income losses at $5,293 and average wealth losses at $33,482 (Coibion, Gorodnichenko, & Weber, May 2020); certainly, the losses have worsened given the continuing waves of infections and resulting partial or total shutdowns across the country. Another work examined the effects of COVID-19 on households in a region in California. They write: "Assuming a shelter-in-place period of three months, the poverty rate would temporarily increase from 17.1% to 25.9% in the Bay Area in the absence of social protection, and the lowest income earners would suffer the most in relative terms" (Martin, Markhvida, Hallegatte, &Walsh, 2020, p. 453).

A team has aggregated private sector data to capture insights on "consumer spending, employment rates, incomes, business revenues, job postings, and other key indicators" in real time in an automated data pipeline and made available for free on a platform to enable more informed policymaking and decision-making by "policymakers, non-profits, and the public" (Chetty, Friedman, Hendren, Stepner, & Opportunity Insights Team, May 7, 2020, pp. 0 and 13). The data are reported "by county and by industry and, where feasible, by initial (pre-crisis) income level and business size (Chetty, Friedman, Hendren, Stepner, & Opportunity Insights Team, May 7, 2020, p. 0). The co-researchers suggest that his data may enable "rapid diagnosis of the root causes of economic crises" (Chetty, Friedman, Hendren, Stepner, & Opportunity Insights Team, May 7, 2020, p. 0), without the typical time lag given episodic reportage.

The team made observations from micro-economics data that explores the effects of policymaking. They discovered that "high-income individuals reduced spending sharply in mid-March 2020, particularly in areas with high rates of COVID-19 infection and in sectors that require in-person interaction. This reduction in spending greatly reduced the revenues of small businesses in affluent ZIP codes...State-ordered reopenings of economies had small impacts on spending and employment. Stimulus payments to low-income households increased consumer spending sharply, but little of this increased spending flowed to businesses most affected by the COVID-19 shock, dampening its impacts on employment...These results suggest that traditional macroeconomic tools—stimulating aggregate demand or providing liquidity to businesses—have diminished capacity to restore employment when consumer spending is constrained by health concerns" (Chetty, Friedman, Hendren, Stepner, & The Opportunity Insights Team, June 2020, p. 0).

Other researchers suggest, too, that "most of the short-run increase in own-state unemployment was not directly due to the state-level NPIs that we consider. State-level restaurant and bar limitations, non-essential business closures, stay-at-home orders, large-gatherings bans, school closures, and emergency declarations collectively account for 12.4% of the increase in UI claims from March 14 – 28, 2020. Using high-frequency proxy data, we find that the different policies have heterogeneous effects. Restaurant and bar limitations and non-essential business closures account for 6.0% and 6.4% of the 10.2 million UI claims filed during this period. On the other hand, large-gatherings bans, school closures, and emergency declarations did not significantly impact UI claims. Stay-at-home orders had significant effects when considered in isolation, but their effect disappears after controlling for non-essential business closures. These results point to a large role played by direct pandemic effects, local policies, and spillovers" (Kong & Prinz, 2020, p. 9). "NPIs" refer to non-pharmaceutical interventions, at the state level. "UI"s refer to "unemployment insurance" or "jobless claims."

Indeed, other studies of government policies in relation to cellular phone records data of consumer visits to various businesses during the pandemic concur: "Traffic started dropping before the legal orders were in place; was highly influenced by the number of COVID deaths reported in the county; and showed a clear shift by consumers away from busier, more crowded stores toward smaller, less busy stores in the same industry. States that repealed their shutdown orders saw symmetric, modest recoveries in consumer visits, further supporting the small estimated effect of policy. Although the shutdown orders had little aggregate impact, they did have a significant effect in reallocating consumer visits away from 'nonessential' to 'essential' businesses and from restaurants and bars toward groceries and other food sellers" (Goolsbee & Syverson, 2021, p. 1). Some parts of the population have been going to localized food supply chains even as they are "less cost efficient than the mainstream food system and offer less variety" (Hobbs, April 21, 2020, p. 7).

Still, while people did adhere to some shelter-in-place orders, it was never sufficiently air-tight. According to mobility data in 16 U.S. cities during lockdown, researchers found some proportion of visits to some points of interest (POI) remained stable in the social distancing period "while some POIs had an increased proportion of visits" such as Grocery Stores (Li, Bessell, Xiao, Fan, Gao, & Mostafavi, June 25, 2020, p. 1). Highly impacted locales included "Restaurants and Other Eating Places, Museums, Historical Sites, and Similar Institutions, Lessors of Real Estate, Elementary and Secondary Schools…Support Activities for Air Transportation…. and Religious Organizations (Li, Bessell, Xiao, Fan, Gao, & Mostafavi, June 25, 2020, p. 11). Lockdowns in the U.S. were always partial and never achieved the level of strictness that the public health officials requested, with many adhering to former lifestyles. Then, as summer turned to fall and fall to winter, people started engaging in riskier behaviors given what health professionals have termed "COVID fatigue." Government leaders were trying to reduce risks but also maintain some human activities (Karimi, May 15, 2020).

The government policies in the U.S. and abroad have almost always been contested, except for in countries where they have had prior experiences with air-transmissible pathogens. Protestors have been fighting stay-at-home orders, and anti-vaxxers have been militating against vaccinations (Smith, May 16, 2020). In the U.S., legislatures have challenges governor power to emplace stay-at-home orders. Various lawsuits have been filed by various arms of democratic government against each other in order to maintain "freedom" from "government overreach." For example, when restaurants and shopping malls were greenlighted to re-open albeit with public health restrictions in California, pastors filed suit because they felt slighted (Kim, May 21, 2020). Reopening itself was not necessarily a solution. When casinos reopened with required masks (even when smoking and drinking), social distancing, closed buffets, and fewer games (Hassan, May 19, 2020), some press coverage suggested that perhaps the new experience was not as entertaining as before. A prior high-service high-contact industry has changed fundamentally. In this sector, there has been a lot of anti-government sentiment, with violations of public health orders to try to protect livelihoods (Alsharaf, Nov. 27, 2020).

Globally, the social experiments have ranged from countries with little government restriction like Sweden (Leatherby & McCann, May 15, 2020) and Brazil and others. The most successful countries have been New Zealand, Australia, Taiwan, South Korea, China, and others. Some have opted to shut down virtually all businesses and pay workers to remain at home, with the idea that they will reopen when it is safe, on the other side of a mass vaccine rollout. It is much harder to set up a lockdown unless the government puts up the funds to enable the staying at home.

Several studies have found high variance between states in terms of both respective policies and policy impacts. Based on high-frequency data, one research team found that business closure policies were "associated with a 20 – 30% reduction of non-salaried workers in the food/drink and leisure/entertainment sectors during

March-April of 2020," significantly affecting small businesses (Huang, Makridis, Baker, Medeiros, & Guo, 2020, p. 1).

One study explored the effect of COVID-19 information (whether positive or negative) on the stocks of various market sectors in the U.S. The co-authors observe: "Results indicate that industries most impacted by negative aggregate demand shocks, such as petroleum and natural gas, restaurants, hotels and lodgings exhibited the largest increases in risk, whereas industries such as food production, beer and liquor with steady or increased demand exhibited smaller changes." (Baek, Mohanty, & Glambosky, 2020, p. 2).

Many small- and medium-sized enterprises (SMEs) or Micro, Small & Medium Enterprises (MSME), defined roughly as those with 100 or fewer employees, did not have the funds to weather the initial weeks-long shutdowns. They did not have "key person" insurance in case their leadership got ill. They often do not have backup if key staff are out. Then, as reopenings occurred to revive the economy and to protect jobs, insufficient guidance was provided by leadership about how the general population could try to stay safer against a highly infectious microbial pathogen. While the U.S. Centers for Disease Control and Prevention (CDC) offered clear guidance for various contexts ("Community, work, and school…" Nov. 13, 2020; Valencia & Kelly, May 19, 2020; Pinsker, May 7, 2020), this advisement was not adhered to by many. The CDC's "stricter road map to reopening" was offered but unsupported by the Trump administration (Holmes & Valencia, May 13, 2020). Various respectable journalistic publications shared information and advisement about how to proceed out of lockdown (Wafai, May 22, 2020). Many of these were fairly conservative and safety-focused. Based on rising numbers of infections, however, it does not seem like adherence was a priority for many.

One journalistic work observed: "All states except one, Connecticut, have loosened stay-at-home restrictions. In some states, people can get tattoos, go shopping inside malls and eat inside restaurants again" (Yan & Maxouris, May 18, 2020). [A virus is composed of genetic material (DNA or RNA), wrapped in a protein shell (or capsid). It is not considered alive in a classic sense. It cannot survive on its own outside of a host. It lives and multiplies in the cells of a host. It cannot travel on its own without being carried in a human or animal host. A pathogenic virus is one that causes disease.]

One hard-hit sector has been the restaurant industry of the hospitality sector. Restaurants are seen as entertainment (Kok, Jonkers, Gelissen, Meertens, Schaalma, & de Zwart, 2010). There was some $50 billion in revenue losses in April 2020 alone as compared to April 2019 (Grindy, 2020, as cited in Raj, Sundararajan, & You, June 12, 2020, p. 2) for the restaurant industry. A study of independent restaurant operator perspectives in South Carolina suggest that approximately 65% of the respondents would not be able to keep their restaurants open "if the pandemic restrictions remained in place until 2021" (Brizek, Frash, McLeod, & Patience, 2021, p. 1). With 32 million jobs in the U.S. related to "retail, leisure, and hospitality," one recent survey study found that "70 percent of smaller restaurants expect to be permanently closed if the COVID-19 crisis lasts four months or more" (Glaeser, May 1, 2020). The restaurants that have shut down include historically important restaurant sites nationally and locally (Anderson, Aug. 10, 2020). A number of restaurant chains have filed for bankruptcy, including Sizzler, California Pizza Kitchen, and Souplantation and Sweet Tomatoes (Valinsky, Dec. 12, 2020). By the end of May, there was the prediction of a fifth of restaurants closing due to the coronavirus pandemic (Pasquini, May 28, 2020). By late July, there were reports that there have been 26,160 restaurant closures and nearly 16,000 of those permanent ones; "60% of the restaurants that temporarily closed due to the pandemic have since shuttered for good" (McCarthy, July 24, 2020). The pandemic sped up the cycle of "creative destruction" in the small- and medium-sized enterprise (SME) business spaces. Restaurants "have lost more revenue and jobs than any other industry" based on U.S. Census Bureau data (McCarthy, July 24, 2020).

The reopening of (surviving) restaurants, even socially distanced, was set back with the research finding that indoor dining was a leading cause of COVID-19 superspreading, in a Stanford University study (Fantozzi, Nov. 13, 2020). Lowering the occupancy of a restaurant to 20% (to de-densify and lower human contacts) can reduce infections by "more than 80%" (Leskovec, as cited in Fantozzi, Nov. 13, 2020). The finding that outdoor spaces are safer than indoor ones given the improved airflow and direct sunlight (Pinsker, May 7, 2020) has informed some restaurant practices. In one locale, "bars and restaurants must close any inside services by midnight, and clear their premises by 12:30 a.m. They also must screen employees prior to each shift, and gathering sizes will still be limited to 50 people" (Brunner, July 17, 2020). The pattern of having COVID-19 flareups and then restaurant reclosings is a common one (Gibson, June 17, 2020). As cases climb, state governments have closed indoor operations for certain businesses, "including restaurants, bars, movie theaters and museums" to try to lower the burden on local hospitals (Higgins-Dunn, July 13, 2020).

Research approach. The severity of the restaurant shutdowns meant that rats themselves became more "aggressive" in searching for food and increasing "reports of rat cannibalism and infanticide in New York" (Kornfield, May 23, 2020). This work explores the plight of those who work in the restaurant industry. Based on a review of the literature and the application of abductive logic, in a content analysis, this work explores some potential practical supports from government but also from citizenry. This work focuses on some middle ground between absolute free-market hands-off approaches vs. full government support (minimum basic income for workers, sector supports, and others), while considering some aspects of social justice.

REVIEW OF THE LITERATURE

For all the lead-up research and academic writing and policy planning around a potential pandemic, SARS-CoV-2 / COVID-19 took the world by surprise. This has been so for the U.S. as well. In the U.S., a state of emergency was declared in January 2020, and by March, a number of states had put into place various shutdown, stay-in-place, and other self-quarantining policies. These shuttered many non-essential business but kept some essential ones open. Many workplaces closed or turned to remote work. Schools went to cyber-learning. In those early days, scientists were trying to understand how dangerous SARS-CoV-2 was, how COVID-19 manifested in various individuals and sub-populations, and way infections were transmitted and whether children could become infected and transfer it. Part of the challenge in early days was that the PRC where the zoonotic virus broke out managed to squelch their outbreak, so their information was only partial and often inferential. (They did not see much in the way of child infections. There were many gaps in the research literature.) One critical question in early days was: Are masks necessary, and do they work? What should masks be made of? How should they be worn? And when?

SARS-CoV-2 is thought to have spilled over from a host animal (some are thinking bats) into an intermediate species and then into people (Burki, Sept. 2020) and started transferred in airborne ways from person-to-person shortly thereafter. This was discovered in December 2019 in Wuhan, Hubei Province, in the People's Republic of China, which released information about this outbreak and the genetic sequence in early January 2020. SARS-CoV-2 is also thought to live in respiratory droplets for a number of days and can be transmitted that way. Virus that lands on surfaces and remain viable for a time may also be touched and transferred by a person to his / her mucosal tissues (eyes, nose, mouth) and spread from there into the lungs, where it can multiply and wreak havoc. The biological nature of SARS-CoV-2, with its contagious transmissibility through the air person-to-person (and to and from other non-human animals) and respiratory droplets, and the unpredictable severity of disease manifestation in COVID-19 (coronavirus disease 2019) affecting all body organs and leading to death for some, has meant that people have to change how they interact in fundamental ways, to protect the vulnerable.

Micro- to Macro Interventions

At the individual lived level, the current approach involves the following endeavors:

- Wear protective facemasks (N95, KN95, or three-tiered surgical masks, or multi-layered cloth masks…in the order of most protective to least protective) in all contexts where one is in proximity to others

- Practice good hand hygiene and overall sanitation
- Practice social distancing from others (at least six feet from others at all times)
- Avoid indoor congregate settings
- Avoid crowds of people
- Use contactless or no-contact ways of engaging others when engaging in commerce (purchasing services and products)

In theory, what should happen at the macro levels to face off with a pathogenic microbe is that there should be a low-cost diagnostic tool put into place to make infection clusters visible, so that infected (and exposed) people may be quarantined for the requisite 14 days until the infection passes, so the reproduction number (R_0) can be kept below 1, meaning that the infection spread slows and eventually stops. To contain the viral outbreak, government has to have eyes on the situation (through contact tracing, or track and trace), and they have to be able to suppress the viral spread. If the virus has spread too far into the community and is spreading invisibly, then the focus shifts from suppression to some sort of management or containment, to lower the amount of community spread—so as to protect life, so as to prevent the health system from becoming over-burdened.

Various Government Policies

Based on available state resources, the capabilities of government leaders, the advice of professionals (epidemiologists, medical doctors, public health workers, hospital administrators, and others), governments around the world applied different strategies and tactics to try to handle this pandemic. Some went along with ostensibly trying to "herd immunity" through natural infections, with the attendant outsized numbers of human deaths (and suffering). Others worked to suppress the spread of virus, at the cost of the gross domestic product (GDP) and many livelihoods. At every turn, the respective governments had supporters and detractors. Others went with some middle ground, like having an initial shutdown, reopening slowly (if not carefully), and then putting in place temporary pauses and shutdowns to keep the infections from over-whelming the health systems…until science-based solutions (therapeutics, vaccines) could be found. Given the power of what a research team calls "fearonomics" of COVID-19, future vaccines are being valued by some based on the freeing up of the economy that will follow mass population biosafety from inoculations (Ma, Kim, Cohen, & Neumann, 2020, p. 1405).

The U.S. Chamber of Commerce maintains a regularly updated dashboard on "COVID-19 Government Policies" that capture particular actions, the dates of those actions, various government aid and stimulus programs, reopening methods, and others ("Global Dashboard on COVID-19 Government Policies," n.d.). Theoretically, the policies can be measured against a country's population's infection rates and morbidity rates and mortality rates, but there is high variance in terms of access to diagnostic testing. Many suffer through an infection without medical care or testing. And many die without the diagnostic testing that would verify what they died of. Epidemiologists will be working through the actual infections, morbidity, and mortality, likely for years to come, once some semblance of control has been attained over this pandemic.

The shutdowns did suppress economic activity, and in many locations, it resulted in a so-called "induced recession." While many blamed government for the loss of their customers, various mobility data show that people started limiting their movements and potential contacts with others long before the government put restrictions into place, in the interests of preventing themselves from getting infected. This was even more pronounced with more data about the various negative health impacts of SARS-CoV-2, across a range of peoples and demographics. The collection of micro-economic data also identified this pause on citizen activities:

We illustrate the value of the tracker by analyzing the impacts of recent policy decisions in the COVID-19 crisis, focusing in particular on state shutdowns and re-openings. Perhaps surprisingly, we find these policies have little or no impact on economic activity. The decline in economic activity—consumer spending, the number of small business open, and employment—occurred in most cases before states 'shut down,' consistent with other recent work examining data on hours of work and movement patterns (Bartik et al. 2020, Villas-Boas et al. 2020). Moreover, we show that recent policies ending these shut-downs in certain states such as Georgia and South Carolina have not been associated with significant increases in economic activity. These findings suggest that the primary barrier to economic activity is the threat of COVID-19 itself as opposed to legislated economic shutdowns. (Chetty, Friedman, Hendren, Stepner, & Opportunity Insights Team, May 7, 2020, p. 2)

An early estimate of the potential cost of COVID-19 on the real U.S. GDP for 2020 is projected to be a decline of "5 percent for each month of partial economic shutdown" or $2.14 trillion (10%) in the first two months of shutdown alone (Makridis & Hartley, Apr. 6, 2020, p. 1). The current economy is both a factor of government policies and people's functional fears of infection and follow-on outcomes. It is unclear what pandemic-induced rolling openings, closings, re-openings, and re-closings (Hai-Jew, 2021) will mean for the economy. Researchers are also tracking and recording state-level policies given the devolution of such mandates to the respective states from the federal government for a more decentralized response (Chart: Each State's COVID-19 Reopening and Reclosing Plans and Mask Requirements, Dec. 14, 2020).

Certainly, this pandemic has had variant effects all the way up and down the hospitality value chain, with the restaurant industry one of the most negatively affected sectors. Some see the entire "tourism and hospitality industry" as under threat of non-survival with the pandemic (Kaushal & Srivastava, 2021, p. 1). Travel bans around the world affected "over 90% of the world population and wide-spread restrictions on public gatherings and community mobility, tourism largely ceased in March 2020 (Gössling, Scott, & Hall, 2021, p. 1). The "cancelled events, closed accommodations, and shut down attractions" affected "catering…laundry services… restaurants" (Gössling, Scott, & Hall, 2021, p. 2).

In the United States, consultancies such as McKinsey and Company (2020c) have reported that jobs in the accommodation and food services sector account for over 20% of all vulnerable positions, i.e., jobs that are subject to furlough, layoffs, or being unable to work as a result of social distancing. (Gössling, Scott, & Hall, 2021, p. 9)

These include to 13.4 million jobs that could be affected in the restaurant industry, 3.6 million in food preparation and serving, 2.6 million restaurant servers and 1.3 million restaurant cooks (Gössling, Scott, & Hall, 2021, p. 9). Job losses have numerous implications on human well-being because these threat housing loss and increased risks of SARS-CoV-2 infection (because of living in hotels / motels on vouchers, indoor congregate homeless shelters, and on the streets). There are potential health effects, from lack of health coverage and medical attention and poor diets. And there are the strains of job loss leading to even more acute mental health challenges (Khan, Mamun, Griffiths, & Ullah, 2020). Already, many who work in this market sector are low-paid and often low-skilled workers, who are already vulnerable. In the space, employees will have to upskill and be able to practice biosafety hygiene and sanitation (Kaushal & Srivastava, 2021, p. 1), to keep their jobs.

Among restaurant workers, their work status (working, furloughed, laid off) had implications on their stress levels and their turning to drug and alcohol use. One study found that "working employees experienced higher levels of psychological distress, drug and alcohol use than furloughed employees," and they found out that "psychological distress increased drug and alcohol use, as well as career turnover intentions" (Bufquin, Park, Back, de Souza Meira, & Hight, 2021, p. 1). All of the restaurant workers surveyed "indicated a desire to seek future employment in alternate industries during the pandemic" (Bufquin, Park, Back, de Souza Meira, & Hight, 2021, p. 1), which might presage a mass exodus from the industry. In this stressful period, home drinking has risen as a form of stress relief leading to serious health issues like liver damage (Da, Im, & Schiano, 2020).

Job insecurity has negative effects on the sense of work engagement of deluxe hotel employees, particularly those of Generation Y vs. Generation X (Jung, Jung, &

Yoon, 2021, p. 1) and raise the likelihood of individuals leaving the field, leading to employee turnover. Younger workers are more likely than older ones to experience the negative perceptions of job insecurity. Many employees in the hospitality are foreign-born workers. There were some 28.4 million foreign-born workers stateside in 2019 or 17.4% of the U.S.'s total workforce according to the Bureau of Labor Statistics (2020a, as cited in Sönmez, Apostolopoulos, Lemke, & Hsieh, 2020, p. 1). The occupations as "immigrant hotel and foodservice workers" involve high-stress, and risks to physical and emotional health, even as the wages are low and the work socially undesirable. COVID-19 adds to that risk, with "worker-to-worker disease transmission in the workplace poses a serious threat to labor capacity" (Sönmez, Apostolopoulos, Lemke, & Hsieh, 2020, p. 4). Some who work in this space are engaging in "undeclared work" which is "particularly prevalent in the hospitality, retail and personal services sectors" (Williams & Kayaoglu, 2020, p. 1). For some, the work is casual and part-time, a way to augment other income streams.

Restaurants (Indoor and Outdoor Spaces) in a Pandemic

Customer perceptions of the risks of infection by SARS-CoV-2 requires restaurants to align with "consumers' self-protection behaviour" and to enhance their localization strategies, practices and performance" to better connect with the various consumer bases (Foroudi, Tabaghdehi, & Marvi, 2021, p. 1). Consumer beliefs lead to their behavioral intentions and future desires, including whether or not they will patronize restaurants. The researchers observe: "Transparent information plays a vital role in consumers' behaviour, whereas the limitation and restrictions guidelines are more adaptable for people if they understand clearly the information provided by the authority" (Foroudi, Tabaghdehi, & Marvi, 2021, p. 9). Clear information from government helps citizens better manage risks, they suggest.

By the numbers, the restaurant industry in the U.S. "reached an all-time high of approximately 800 billion U.S. dollars in 2017" (Lock, Dec. 11, 2020). There are estimated to be 660,000 restaurants in the U.S., with 13.49 million employees (Lock, Dec. 11, 2020) although numbers have changed drastically in the pandemic. Where full-service restaurants have declined "by almost 50 percent," quick-service restaurants were able to adapt by building out their digital-facing services and delivery services (Lock, Dec. 11, 2020) and curbside pickups.

In the earliest shutdowns, restaurants were not deemed to be essential businesses. They were closed down in the initial response to the federal emergency. Thereafter, there have been partial reopenings with various public health guidelines and reclosings. The shutdowns of restaurants have led to some demand slumps, with "food at home" (FAH) practices vs. "food away from home" (FAFH) (Hailu, Apr. 18, 2020). FAH practices (retail) involve food from "grocery stores; warehouse clubs and supercenters; other stores and foodservice; mail order and home delivery; other food stores; convenience stores; mass merchandisers; direct selling by farmers, manufacturers, and wholesalers; and home production and donations" (according to USDA and Economic Research Service data from 2020, as cited in Hailu, Apr. 18, 2020, p. 166). FAFH (foodservices) include "limited-service restaurants; full-service restaurants; schools and colleges; food furnished and donated; retail stores and vending; hotels and motels; recreational places; and other FAFH sales, not elsewhere classified" (according to USDA and Economic Research Service data from 2020, as cited in Hailu, Apr. 18, 2020, p. 166). These were listed in the general descending order by percent of the category by purchases. Said another way, food is highly fungible and able to be acquired in any number of venues and channels, when available.

There were ensuing slumps in supply, too: "Non-essential industries such as Entertainment, Restaurants and Hotels, experience both a demand reduction (due to consumers seeking to avoid infection) and a supply reduction (as many workers are unable to perform their activities at home) (del Rio-Chanona, Mealy, Pichler, Lafond, & Farmer, 2020, p. 14).

Over time, it was learned that people singing in a closed space could spread the virus even if people themselves were not directly physically close to the infected individual (Hamner, et al., May 15, 2020). In indoor congregate settings, air may be moved in a way that picks up shed virus and distributes it within the space, enabling those physically distant from an infected person to become infected. On the one hand, recycling air quickly is thought to remove concentrations of virus from the human space; on the other hand, the movement itself can enable transfer. Aerosolized SARS-CoV-2 remains in the air for several hours (Azuma, et al., 2020, p. 1) or longer. The questions about how to make indoor spaces safer from aerosolized virus particles depend on a body of research, some of which has not yet been conducted. Various technologies have been brought to bear, such as various filters for the air handling units; ultraviolet (UV) light and / or chemicals applied to air to kill microbes, including pathogens, in recycled air; high heat applications for particular time periods to kill pathogenic microbes; and others. Ideally, in closed spaces, air should not be recirculated; fresh ventilation is preferred. The virus has been found to persist on surfaces for "at least 3 days depending on the conditions" (Azuma, et al., 2020, p. 1). On a cruise ship, researchers found coronavirus RNA on Princess Cruise surfaces "up to 17 days after passengers disembarked" (Feuer, Mar. 28, 2020). For fomite (materials that can carry and enable the transfer of infections) transfers, regular cleaning of surfaces inactivates the virus. In sunlight, the virus in the air is disabled in 7 – 14 minutes (Mandal, May 26, 2020; Ratnesar-Shumate, et al., May 20, 2020). How long SARS-CoV-2 remains in the air and remains viable as an inoculum depends on the air temperature and relative humidity (Azuma, et al., 2020,

p. 2). Fluid mechanics has been applied to the study of SARS-CoV-2 transmission dynamics in indoor spaces. Researchers observed that "indoor transmission of the virus far outstrips outdoor transmission, possibly due to longer exposure time and the decreased turbulence levels (and therefore dispersion) found indoors" (Bhagat, Wykes, Dalziel, & Linden, 2020, p. 903 F1-1). Various methods of displacement ventilation are explored.

Other studies suggest that various variables may interact for the creation of safer indoor spaces. One study suggests that "increasing social distance (e.g., halving occupancy density) can significantly reduce the infection rate (20 – 40%) during the first 30 min even under current ventilation practices" (Sun & Zhai, 2020, p. 1). These researchers also suggest that "minimum ventilation or fresh air requirement should vary with distancing condition, exposure time, and effectiveness of air distribution systems" (Sun & Zhai, 2020, p. 1). Certainly, in-world conditions vary from lab ones, and there are dynamic factors at play (people, and others) as well as uncontrollable factors (weather). Sobering, too, has been the fact that many who have become infected cannot name where they think they might have gotten infected; many profess that they followed all the guidelines to the best of their abilities and still became infected. In some cases where people identify where they think they became ill—working in healthcare, shopping at a big box store, engaging in a COVID-19 party (because the individual did not believe the virus was real)—most were pursuing essential activities of work or shopping.

The virus survives differently on various non-porous and porous surfaces. Environmental conditions also affect the viability of the virus on surfaces: "These findings suggest that a potential for fomite transmission may persist for hours to days in indoor environments and that the survivability of fomites is affected by temperature and relative humidity, as well as by the presence of protein found in human sputum" (Azuma, et al., 2020, p. 4). A number of outbreaks—in a call center in S. Korea, the choir practice in Washington State, a meat processing plant in Germany—"suggest that in a confined, crowded, and poorly ventilated environment where conversations, loud vocalizations, and heavy breathing take place, SARS-CoV-2 can spread through the air at a distance of 2 m or more and may result in a large number of secondary infections" (Azuma, et al., 2020, p. 7). Follow-on research suggests a variety of interventions. This research has also been applied to how to ensure ventilation in a car with multiple riders, by opening all windows (Mathai, Das, Bailey, & Breuer, Dec. 4, 2020).

An important (and mass-salient) study suggested that air conditioning in a restaurant spread SARS-CoV-2 between people who were in the same interior space but not in close proximity physically (Lu, et al., July 2020). This same event is described in another work:

On January 24, 2020, a COVID-19 outbreak occurred in a restaurant in Guangzhou, China, infecting ten people in three families. The minimum length of time during which the index-infected person was present with the secondary infected person was 46 min, and the possibility of contact infection was considered to be low based on in-store camera recordings. Fifty percent (five of ten) of those at the same table as the infected person were found to be infected within the next 7 days. At the adjacent leeward table, 75% (three of four) were infected. Two of the seven people at the windward table were infected. Other diners who were located away from the airflow around the infected tables, as well as the staff, were not infected. Lu et al. concluded that the airflow from the air-conditioners promoted droplet infection and recommended that distances between people are maintained and ventilation improved. (Azuma, et al., 2020, p. 6)

Later research suggests that indoor congregate settings such as restaurants and religious establishments are locales for superspreader and other infections (Chang, Pierson, Koh, Gerardin, Redbird, Grusky, & Leskovec, Nov. 10, 2020). These findings extended the hesitancy of going to restaurants even as states lifted restrictions (albeit with the guidance that restaurants have limited capacity to de-densify the spaces and to offer services outdoor for *al fresco* dining where possible).

In restaurants, patrons cannot eat while masked. They tend to socialize, talk, laugh, cough, and engage. If restaurant patrons are infected, with or without symptoms, they may spread the SARS-CoV-2 infection. In other words, there is not a safe way to turn a restaurant into a Level 4 Biosecurity Lab, even if a restaurant has social distancing decals on the floor, staff wearing cloth masks, and all sorts of signage about their hygienic practices (all common self-depictions of many restaurants on social media). The uses of testing at the point-of-service is also a porous practice as may be seen in the "cruise to nowhere," which ended when a prior-tested passenger came down with COVID-19 during the cruise (Chappell, Dec. 9, 2020). The virus is so widespread that every location is a "hot zone," even a cruise ship with state-of-the-art sanitation, testing of all before boarding, and other measures to "bubble" or "pod" (group-isolate those deemed free of active SARS-CoV-2 infection) those on the cruise. Even without the risks to health and life, going to restaurants with signage, masked staff, hand sanitizer stations all around, floor decals for social distancing, and other aspects take away from the atmospherics and ambiance of typical restaurants, with background chatter, lighting, people, and music. For many, a "lockdown palate" may have changed their food preferences.

Restaurants may be part of a draw to mass-scale events, such as the Sturgis Motorcycle Rally, which turned out to be a COVID-19 superspreader event. This event involved half a million motorcycle enthusiasts, who were shown on mass media socializing unmasked in many cases, indoors and outdoors. This annual event drew people from all over the U.S. and ran from Aug. 7 – 16, 2020. Infected people attended and infected others, with repercussions around the country as people returned to their respective home states. Researchers write about their findings based on a dose response difference-in-differences model:

...counties that contributed the highest inflows of Sturgis attendees saw COVID-19 cases rise by 6.4 to 12.5% following the Sturgis event relative to counties without any detected attendees. Descriptive evidence suggests some evidence of variation in local COVID-19 spread depending on the stringency of local contagion mitigation policies. We conclude that the Sturgis Motorcycle Rally generated substantial public health costs, which may range from $3.8 and $8.7 billion using the statistical value of a median COVID-19 case estimated by Kniesner and Sullivan (2020)...Our findings underscore that local COVID-19-related policy decisions over events that generate large local economic benefits, but diffuse external health costs (such as the decision by South Dakota policy officials to hold the Sturgis event) may not be socially optimal. (Dave, McNichols, & Sabia, 2020, p. 4)

The actions of local decision-makers to benefit their local economies can entail a cost in lives and suffering...and mass public health encumbrances.

Well-intentioned efforts may have unintended consequences. The U.K.'s "eat-out-to-help-out" effort was studied for its effects. Clearly, the intention was to have citizen enhance the potential survival of restaurants hurt by the initial lockdowns. This "large-scale government subsidy aimed at encouraging people to eat out in restaurants in the wake of the first 2020 COVID19 wave in the United Kingdom" resulted in "a notable increase in new COVID19 infection clusters within a week" (Fetzer, Oct. 2020, p. 1). Closer analysis of the data suggests "the program is accountable for between 8 to 17 percent of all new infection clusters during that time period" (Fetzer, Oct. 2020, p. 1).

Similar dynamics happened with various state reopenings in the U.S. Some misread reopening as suggesting that "it was safer to eat out" and led to a rise in COVID-19 infections with state openings (Glaeser, Jin, Leyden, & Luca, Aug. 2020). This suggests that the general public has a responsibility to interpret the context, find trusted and reliable sources of information, and respond accordingly. Their own health is a personal responsibility, not a responsibility of the state per se, in a liberal democracy.

Researchers draw on the challenges with meat-packing plants early in the pandemic when many workers in that sector were getting infected and dying. There were reports of a lack of personal protective equipment. The food production lines had people working shoulder-to-shoulder without any protections against airborne viral pathogen spread between workstations. The thinking is that those on the front lines should have a voice in the decision-making of the companies for which they work since they have expertise and since their well-being depends on proper decision-making. The co-authors pose important questions:

Who has the power to identify 'the COVID-19 problem,' and for whom? Who has the ability to define solutions and nudge pandemic trends? To say when it is 'safe enough' to return to factories and begin gathering in restaurants? Deciding those questions is not neutral—they are frequently embedded in life-worlds where entrenched hierarchies of knowledge and malignant power inequalities prevail. (Iles & de Wit, 2020, p. 1)

Beyond meat-processing plants: "Similar conflicts in expert politics are now rippling across the fast food, restaurant, fruit-packing, and farm sectors. Unions and worker movements insist that they, too, must have a say in defining the problem, finding solutions, and stopping production if necessary. They are claiming sovereignty over their knowledge. More responsible companies are listening and devising work procedures to protect their employees. Such conflicts have literal life and death consequences, not only for people in the US but in regions from Europe to Latin America" (Iles & de Wit, 2020, p. 2).

This is not to say that experts always know best. One research study of the restaurant industry in the Netherlands explored whether entrepreneur resilience and innovation could make a difference in terms of generating revenue in a time of a pandemic. This work involved interviews of some members of small and medium enterprises (SMEs) (Dijk, 2020, p. 1) in the restaurant sector. Here, "entrepreneur resilience" as "the capacity of the entrepreneur to bounce back from adversities by creating new opportunities (Dijk, 2020, p. 2); this characteristic is often positively correlated with innovation (p. 2). In the interviews, the listed innovations include the following: "1.5 meter tables, rally tour, bike tour with mealbox, take-out via a new platform, Mother's Day mealbox, Barbecue platter, foodtruck, cocktail service, webshop for online orders" and others (Dijk, 2020, p. 4). The small qualitative study found that there is "no direct impact of entrepreneur resilience on the utilization of innovation in dealing with adversities like the COVID-19 pandemic, because the urgency of creating revenue in the 'contain phase of this pandemic forces entrepreneurs to become innovative and causes entrepreneur resilience to becomes (sic) secondary" (Dijk, 2020, p. 0). This is about what works in the crisis environment, in the real, in the high-risk and low-cash environment, to achieve sales. Given the scope of the pandemic, those entrepreneurs that were more resilient were not found to be more successful in dealing with the pandemic. Nor was there much evidence in this small study that more innovativeness led to better dealing with the consequences of COVID-19. And the third hypothesis was also rejected; this read: "Entrepreneurs that are more resilient, are utilizing innovation more in dealing with the COVID-19 pandemic crisis" (Dijk, 2020, p. 5), perhaps suggesting that many external factors are too overwhelming for individual actions to be able to affect. To make sense of some of these findings, the author observes that the restaurateurs may have health conditions that inform their vulnerability to SARS-CoV-2. And some innovations may be expensive in a time when financial resources are low (Dijk, 2020, p. 6) and so are less likely to be pursued fully or even partially. In many cases, people are over-matched by the scope of the challenges from the virus and the follow-on implications.

A study of six hospitality firms in Austria looked at various forms of "business model innovation" and a changing of the value proposition of these entities in a time of COVID-19. The researchers interviewed managers to understand how they strove to create new revenue streams and increase liquidity for their firms through various adaptive innovations. Here, the business model is "the firms' unique configuration of its value proposition (i.e., what does the firm offer to whom?), value creation (i.e., how is this value proposition created?) and value capture (i.e., how does the firm generate profits from this?) approach (Clauss, 207; Clauss et al., 2019, as cited in Breier, Kallmuenzer, Clauss, Gast, Kraus, & Tiberius, 2021, p. 1). The challenge is to find what business configuration works temporarily for the present moment but also what previously unexploited opportunities should be pursued into the future and become more permanent. This research involves a small number of restaurants and bars and a hotel in the Austrian context, with closed borders on all sides but an opening up by May: "The staff had to wear masks or face visors. Also, guests had to wear a mask when entering a facility. Guests were allowed to sit at the table with a maximum of four people and a minimum distance between the tables was imposed. The closing time was legally set at 23:00" (or 11 p.m.)" (Breier, Kallmuenzer, Clauss, Gast, Kraus, & Tiberius, 2021, p. 4). The within-case analyses found that the various firms mostly considered BMI but found furloughs as their most important measures. In many cases, rent was sales-related; in others, the managers owned the buildings from which they conducted business. Only one of the firms resorted to dismissals of staff, while the others went with temporary furloughs (Breier, Kallmuenzer, Clauss, Gast, Kraus, & Tiberius, 2021, p. 5). Some of the firms report BMI, with some "financial support, psychological support, marketing channel, idea generator, furlough, and decrease of VAT on non alcoholic drinks" as some types, along with uptake of government support, and other adjustments (Breier, Kallmuenzer, Clauss, Gast, Kraus, & Tiberius, 2021, p. 6). This work shows that different contexts enable different affordances, and custom solutions may have to be originated for each firm. The researchers observe that a crisis may be a trigger for "general BMI" but is not sufficient alone as such; a number of "influencing factors" affects the decision of whether to pursue BMI or not (Breier, Kallmuenzer, Clauss,

Gast, Kraus, & Tiberius, 2021, p. 8). Another note: many firms seem to respond much more to policy than science-based understandings of the pathogen and its transmission modalities. And finally, some of the main challenges for firms seem to come from the high cost of human labor, forcing employee furloughs to survive. Another work examines business model changes across a range of industries in the time of COVID-19, based on various features of the industries given the new emerging rules of competition (Seetharaman, 2020).

Some self-recreation efforts of firms involve both public (government) and private (corporate) sectors cooperating to engage the present pandemic moment and to plan for a future rebound (Loi, Lei, & Lourenço, 2020). One move to protect the hospitality industry was to cut labor costs and operating costs ("in particular marketing expenses"), for firm survival (Loi, Lei, & Lourenço, 2020, p. 4). To be ready for the rebound, the basic infrastructure of the physical locations were maintained, and the "software" of people were retrained for bio-safety as a new business norm (Loi, Lei, & Lourenço, 2020, p. 5). One work provides ways to retrain hospitality workers for "deep compliance with COVID-19 safety measures" through psychological processes (Hu, Yan, Casey, & Wu, 2021, p. 1), with a "safety first" approach (p. 6). Indeed, the new normal is about a "socially distant servicescape" (Taylor, 2020, p. 1), with various applied efforts—partitioning and uses of mannequins to enable social distancing in the COVID-19 era—and testing for customer preferences.

The various entities in the food industry space have had to adapt. Luxury food service has engaged in "social bricolage entrepreneurial thinking" (Batat, 2020, p. 1) to remain relevant and to position for the post-COVID-19 marketplace. Some strategic efforts have been to engage in philanthropy to support the larger community and to support "medical and frontline workers" and contribute to "community-based sponsorships, donations and support for both vulnerable populations and health professionals" (Batat, 2020, p. 5). Such efforts are covered heavily by the press. In luxury dining, chefs have important personalities, and they drive a brand. Their meals are their artistic self-expressions "on a plate," their self-identities; these are expressed across a range of perceptions: sight, smell, taste, touch, and hearing, because food is so multi-dimensional and sustaining. On mass media, chefs are stars of their own broadcast shows and describe how their cooking and menu plans and dishes are extensions of their own food histories, stories, lived experiences, personalities, palates, locales, and other features. Their respective intermingled personal and professional brands are imbued with emotion and passion and sentiment. Then, too, celebrity chefs of luxury brands demonstrate being "socially responsible" by supporting their employees and work on "new taste combinations" for haute gastronomy (Batat, 2020, p. 8). Part of the luxury dining experience involves taking photos with the head chef, in many cases. One eatery in Belgium moved operations into a "spacious village church" to enable social distancing (Casert, Oct. 25, 2020).

On the other end of the spectrum is street food, which is an important part of a country's cuisine, its food culture, and its lifestyle. "Street food" is created by cooks who set up shop on roadsides, on boats, and other pop-up locales. Some "2.5 billion people around the world consume street food every day" (Ranka, June 2020, p. 2). In a time of COVID-19, the outdoors dining enables a heightened sense of biosafety given the movement of air. Such vendors need to practice social distancing between staff (and each other) and enforce distance between the diners (Ranka, June 2020, p. 1). Still, those who would run such businesses need to practice proper hygiene and sanitation and avoid cross-contamination of food (Ranka, June 2020, p. 4). Street food is "an important source of affordable and ready to eat food available to common people" and a possible opportunity for employment for those in the food sector (Ranka, June 2020, p. 1).

Some researchers have studied particular customer segments to understand preference. For example, Chinese tourists are found to prefer "separated dining when traveling with a tour group" after the 2003 SARS epidemic (Zhang, et al., 2005, as cited in Wen, Kozak, Yang, & Liu, 2020, p. 7). In a time of a pandemic, when SARS-CoV-2 and COVID-19 are top-of-mind, survey respondents prefer private dining facilities and private dining tables (Kim & Lee, 2020, p. 67), so as to avoid others. This is so even if the privacy of the room may not necessarily provide any bio-safety given air handling across rooms in a building. This work suggests other possible solutions to create a sense of bio-safety by offering single plated food instead of shared food; doing away with shared utensils; not offering buffet or hot pot services (with shared communal food). They propose that food may be pre-packed and sanitized for tourists (Wen, Kozak, Yang, & Liu, 2020, p. 7). They suggest de-densifying seats on vehicles by not booking all of them. They point to differing tourist locations that allow for more social distancing, such as in outdoors spaces.

Lessons Across Borders

In China, with the pandemic outbreak, many restaurants found themselves under pressure:

The catering industry, for example, which greatly drives China's consumption, was pressured from both sides—drop in operating revenue and high-fixed cost. The restaurant industry suffered an 80% drop in revenue in the first quarter of 2020, due to a ban on crowd gathering, leading to the shutdown of many restaurants. Meanwhile, the high cost of rent and employee wages made the situation in the catering industry even worse. In order to cope with the operational risks caused by COVID-19 and ensure that firms can smoothly survive the pandemic, managers tend to increase firms' cash holding level in the short term through bank loans or equity financing to ease the cash flow pressures. However, the financing capacity of the firms is different, so it is debatable whether the companies can raise the cash in time. (Qin, Huang, Shen, & Fu, 2020, pp. 2243-2244)

Their pursuit of short-term credit is informed in part by "goodwill" defined as "the potential economic value that can bring excess profits to the business operation in the future, or the capitalized value that the expected profitability of a business exceeds the normal profitability of identifiable assets, such as the average rate of return on investment" (Godfrey & Koh, 2001, as cited in Qin, Huang, Shen, & Fu, 2020, p. 2246). The "goodwill" (overpayment for a particular business) provides a sense of potential for the business operation and may be a factor by banks and others providing loans for the potential of the firm. Firms then not only strive to heighten cash holdings (against present and future contingencies) in the face of systemic risks but also work to control costs.

In the food service space for Canada, the pandemic has effected demand-side shocks as including "consumer panic buying…the sudden change in consumption patterns away from the food service sector to meals prepared and consumed at home" (Hobbs, April 21, 2020, p. 1). Some restaurants have lost large amounts of goods to spoilage, such as $15,000 in beer in kegs, which cannot keep (Kesslen, Oct. 30, 2020). Supply-side disruptions include "labor shortages, disruptions to transportation networks, and 'thickening' of the Canada-U.S. border with respect to the movement of goods" (Hobbs, April 21, 2020, p. 1).

The pre-COVID conditions of U.S. restaurant firms enable some to be more resilient to stock declines in the pandemic; these factors include the following: "larger size, more leverage, more cash flows, less ROA (return on assets), and more internationalization" (Song, Yeon, & Lee, 2021, p. 1). Other variables, like "dividend, franchising, international ownership, and managerial ownership" did not seem to have any significant moderating effect on the relationship between COVID-19 and stock returns. Those firms not built for resilience against such catastrophic threats have to deal with what resources they have.

Financial fragility is a common state for many restaurant firms.

The median firm with expenses over $10,000 per month has only enough cash on hand to last for two weeks. Three-quarters of respondents state that they only have enough cash on hand to cover two months of expenses or less. Parsa et al. (2005) also note the fragility of small restaurants. Firms with more cash on hand are relatively more optimistic that they will remain open at the end of the year. (Bartik, Bertrand, Cullen, Glaeser, Luca, & Stanton, April 2020, p. 3)

With the long-livedness of the pandemic (even though this will have been comparatively short in terms of global pandemics), there has already been damage to the economy and its various businesses (Bartik, Bertrand, Cullen, Glaeser, Luca, & Stanton, April 2020, p. 15).

In the U.S., some aspects of cultural practices have enabled creative adaptivity that include outside moves. Certainly, restaurants have had a long history of creativity to survive. Some dinner restaurants are built around "murder mysteries," so there is live storytelling while diners eat. There are pop-up restaurants that appear transiently in various venues, in expensive cities with sky-high rents. (The author was in one such presentational experience, with some 8 servers for the family, and a bill of over $1500 prior to the tip. There were a number of mini dishes with unique flavors and accompanying stories.) There are creative brands, with celebrity individuals and salient stories, for different restaurant personalities. Some trim menu options to save money (Knowles, Ettenson, Lynch, & Dollens, 2020, p. 4). In the pandemic economy, one restaurant turned into a "bottle shop" for "small producers and wineries"; this enabled the restaurant owner to use the extant restaurant space and create value (Willens, Shaffrey, & Hajela, Dec. 11, 2020). Some restaurants in a smaller town served customers on outdoor dining platforms, set up by the city to help restaurants survive (Simmons, Oct. 13, 2020) and to draw foot traffic to the downtown shopping district. Many of these show outside-the-box types of thinking.

For some restaurants in the U.S., online food-ordering and delivery platforms have come to the rescue by providing another income stream (Raj, Sundararajan, & You, June 12, 2020). One study found that "small restaurants experience significant increases in total activity, orders per day, and orders per hour following the closure of the dine-in channel" by using food ordering and delivery platforms (Raj, Sundararajan, & You, June 12, 2020, p. 1), in the shift from brick and mortar. This capability is also a part of grocery shopping, with the popularization of an "online grocery delivery sector" (Hobbs, April 21, 2020, p. 1). Car culture has also had a salutary effect, with people doing take-out from drive-throughs and curbside pickups. In some locales, people have engaged in a concerted effort to order takeout "hoping to help them survive this crisis" (Tufekc, May 12, 2020). Some go beyond mere patronizing restaurants. Some supporters are leaving large tips for staff (to the tune of thousands of dollars) (Elassar, Dec. 20, 2020). There are press reports of wait staff being stiffed by patrons in this time (Meyer, Oct. 23, 2020). Other research suggests that the pandemic has exacerbated sexual harassment of waitstaff (Saxena, Dec. 1, 2020).

The digital aspects of life have also been harnessed, with heightened uses of online food shopping (Chang & Meyerhoefer, 2020). Electronic word-of-mouth (e-WOM) is as important as ever. While social media have included social influencers who review various restaurant foods and experiences, there are also risks in media attention, such as reputational harms in media depictions of restaurants implicated in COVID-19 infections, including misinformation (Brennen, Simon, & Nielsen, Oct. 10, 2020).

Even as the U.S. government made available CARES Act PPP loans to businesses, some 13% of respondents said that they would not be taking out such loans because of the "application hassle, distrust that the federal government will forgive the loans, or worry about complicated eligibility rules"; in this study, those surveyed said that they would not likely be able to stay in business past the four month mark (Bartik, Bertrand, Cullen, Glaeser, Luca, & Stanton, July 28, 2020, p. 17666). The maximum amount of the loan would be for 2.5 months of expenses. Based on extrapolations, researchers suggest that the volume of loans taken would be "approximately $410 billion" (Bartik, Bertrand, Cullen, Glaeser, Luca, & Stanton, July 28, 2020, p. 17666). At present, there are debates on how much insurers have to potentially cover work stoppages at restaurants based on business interruptions based on infectious disease (Richter & Wilson, 2020, p. 191).

A Restaurant Future Imagined

The longer the pandemic lasts, the more people may be fundamentally changing their mental concepts of food and their food behaviors, given "the near-complete loss of the food service distribution channel" (Chenarides, Manfredo, & Richards, 2020, p. 1). There have been reports of "wasted food, failing suppliers, and food shortages" (Chenarides, Manfredo, & Richards, 2020, p. 1), reminding all of the need to improve food chain resilience into the future. The is a need for a broader managerial imagination" (Chenarides, Manfredo, & Richards, 2020, p. 8). One research team has made a brutal observation that COVID-19 is not so much about government support needs but that the pandemic is exposing "firms that likely should not have existed in the first place" (Chenarides, Manfredo, & Richards, 2020, p. 8).

In a time when there is less demand and little traffic at restaurants, ironically, there are increased demands from the airborne lethal pathogen contributes to rising labor costs in the restaurant industry (Luna, Sept, 16, 2020).

The tourism industry is remaking itself in a bid to attract customers in the post-COVID-19 era to particular target audiences and their preferences (Wen, Kozak, Yang, & Liu, 2020). Various people are rethinking how people may interact in the future and how the "new normal" might look. The hospitality industry has to figure out "will make customers return" (Gursoy & Chi, 2020, p. 527), given the wide reluctance of large swaths of the general public to engage in tourist travel and dining in.

There are challenges, too, with trying to reformulate the distribution of food, to address the reality of "food deserts" that "contain more fast food restaurants than grocery stores" and which have citizens with higher risks of obesity and breathing disorders that put them at higher risks of negative outcomes from COVID-19 (Singu, Acharya, Challagundla, & Byareddy, 2020, p. 6). The question is how to remake the future to not dispossess some citizens.

Given the importance of health, there has been exploratory research in terms of how much more people are willing to pay in order to have "increased safety precautions" (Gursoy & Chi, 2020, p. 528), such as point-of-service test, track and trace capabilities, short of everyone having achieved herd immunity through vaccinations.

For the firms that survive the pandemic, they would do well to "explore effective quality signaling cues that influence customers' perceived uncertainty risks, which ultimately affect restaurant performance after restrictions are eased" (Kim, Kim, & Wang, 2021, p. 2) since strong branding is seen to lead to higher sales (p. 6). Consumers may be lured with discounts (Kim, Kim, & Wang, 2021, p. 5). Those "destination-dining" establishments with ties to tourism tend to be vulnerable to "stay-at-home orders and excessive restrictions," which suggests the need for differentiated efforts for different restaurant types (Kim, Kim, & Wang, 2021, p. 9). Ultimately, there is a need for customer participation "for building a safety culture and sanitation guidelines" (Kim, Kim, & Wang, 2021, p. 9).

A research team, in studying press releases from various restaurant enterprises, identified "corporate social responsibility" (CSR) moves through three phases of the crisis, termed "incubation, acceleration, and climax" (Ou, Wong, & Huang, 2021, p. 1), or the beginning of the outbreak, its intensification, and the peak (indicated as early May in the research article but without apparent awareness that the peak of the crisis was still many months away). This work suggests that food service conglomerates do well to focus on CSR for their shareholders. Core animating values for an organization may support a stronger sense of corporate identity within and help bridge to consumers externally.

For U.S. restaurants, based on a meta-analysis, firm size moderates the effects of corporate social responsibility (CSR) endeavors on outcomes such as corporate financial performance (CFP), or the bottom line. The larger size of firms was not found to moderate the effective of negative CSR on CFP but only positive (Youn, Hua, & Lee, 2015, p. 127).

For small firms in the hospitality space, a common strategy involves "actioning alternative measures to create much-needed revenue streams, and preparing for a new post-COVID-19 operational regime" (Alonso, et al., 2020, p. 1). A more passive (but perhaps effective) approach involved "biding time in anticipation of a changing business and legal environment" (Alonso, et al., 2020, p. 1)

More Artificial Intelligence (AI) and Robotics

Hospitality is a high-touch, high-interpersonal, and service-oriented space. However, in a context where humans themselves can be the carriers of a pathogen that can infect, harm, and even result in the deaths of others, various technologies have been brought into play to reduce the contact, internationally:

Robotics, artificial intelligence, and human-robot interactions have gained an increased presence to help manage the spread of COVID-19 in hospitals, airports, transportation systems, recreation and scenic areas, hotels, restaurants, and communities in general. Humanoid robots, autonomous vehicles, drones, and other intelligent robots are used in many different ways to reduce human contact and the potential spread of the SARS-CoV-2 virus, including delivering materials, disinfecting and sterilizing public spaces, detecting or measuring body temperature, providing safety or security, and comforting and entertaining patients. While controversial in the past due to concerns over job losses and data privacy, the adoption of robotics and artificial intelligence in travel and tourism will likely continue after the COVID-19 pandemic becomes less serious. (Zeng, Chen, & Lew, 2020, p. 1)

Robot "dogs" patrol parks in Singapore to warn people not to get to close to each other ("Coronavirus: Robot dog…" May 11, 2020). Robot dogs take vital signs of people hospitalized with COVID-19 (Peters, Sept. 3, 2020).

Technologies are not necessarily seen in a positive light in this space. While some have suggested that digital technologies may enhance work in the restaurant space, such as turning to food delivery apps, other research suggests that the uses of digital tools in hospitality management may lead to a sense of "self-control depletion" and "disengagement from work" (Chadee, Ren, & Tang, 2021, p. 1); a counter-weight to such downsides may be social "relational energy" between people members of "a wider network of work colleagues" (p. 3). The working from home (WFH) with digital technologies is seen in this work as somewhat "debilitating" (Chadee, Ren, & Tang, 2021, p. 7) and in need of management attention.

The Imagined Future of Chefs by Chefs

Chefs who took part in a survey mused on how they foresaw changes to their professions, with the researchers observing optimistic and pessimistic senses of the future. More and different food safety regulations will be put into place, with COVID-19 certifications for kitchen staff to ensure proper handling of food for biosafety. Some respondents imagine robots in the kitchen almost as augmentation to people, who will not be replaced. Others suggest a massive economic contraction in the space. Some chefs will leave their professions (Bucak & Yiğit, 2021, p. 4). Some suggest that open buffets may be a practice of the past (Bucak & Yiğit, 2021, p. 5), given the risks of having people share access to public trays.

With the sector under threat, elite chefs have been lobbying the U.S. president for more aid and support (Gillison, May 22, 2020), to no effect then. As of mid-December 2020, with the U.S. Congress considering another aid package, the "restaurant" portion of the bill was not being championed.

Food Safety Re-Imagined

In a cautionary work, one research team asserts that "food can, if not directly, be a carrier of the virus. Particular attention should be paid to this indirect pathway when considering the potential for the spread of an epidemic and the development of prevention principles" (Duda-Chodak, Lukasiewicz, Zieć, Florkiewicz, & Filipiak-Florkiewicz, 2020, p. 145). This concern has been a part of the public discussion with members of the broad public asking if it is safe to order takeout food or how to decontaminate food packaging delivered by restaurants in contactless ways. The researchers write: "To date, the detailed SARS-CoV-2 infection pathways are still unclear, but studies indicate the possibility of virus entry not only through the respiratory system but also the digestive tract. This is due to the fact that the SARS-CoV-2 entry receptor, ACE2, shows significant expression in lung AT2 cells, upper and layered epithelial cells, and epithelial enterocytes from the ileum and colon." (Duda-Chodak, Lukasiewicz, Zieć, Florkiewicz, & Filipiak-Florkiewicz, 2020, p. 152) This work makes the point that food safety may mean newer ways of ensuring non-contamination. Others suggest a need for vigilance of the potential contamination of food with SARS-CoV-2 given the role of people in the whole process even though "the possibility of COVID-19 transmission through the food sector is considered negligible" (Rizou, Galanakis, Aldawoud, & Galanakis, 2020, p. 297).

A Light Summary of the Mass Media Coverage

Where academic research has been focused on public health and economics and the restaurant sector, public mass media coverage has been focused on personal health, survival, household incomes, homelessness, food insecurity, and limited government aid. There are evocative stories of over-run hospitals. There are memorials to the many dead. There are stories of "long haulers" who have experienced devastating and continuing health effects, from brain fog to amputations to weakened hearts, and others. A roughcut summary of these articles may be seen in Figure 1. (The articleset was too large to run in the autocoding for automated topic modeling or theme and sub-theme extraction. The journalistic articles were all read by the author, and some of the works are cited in this chapter.)

Figure 1. Word Cloud from "Restaurant and COVID-19" Journalistic Set

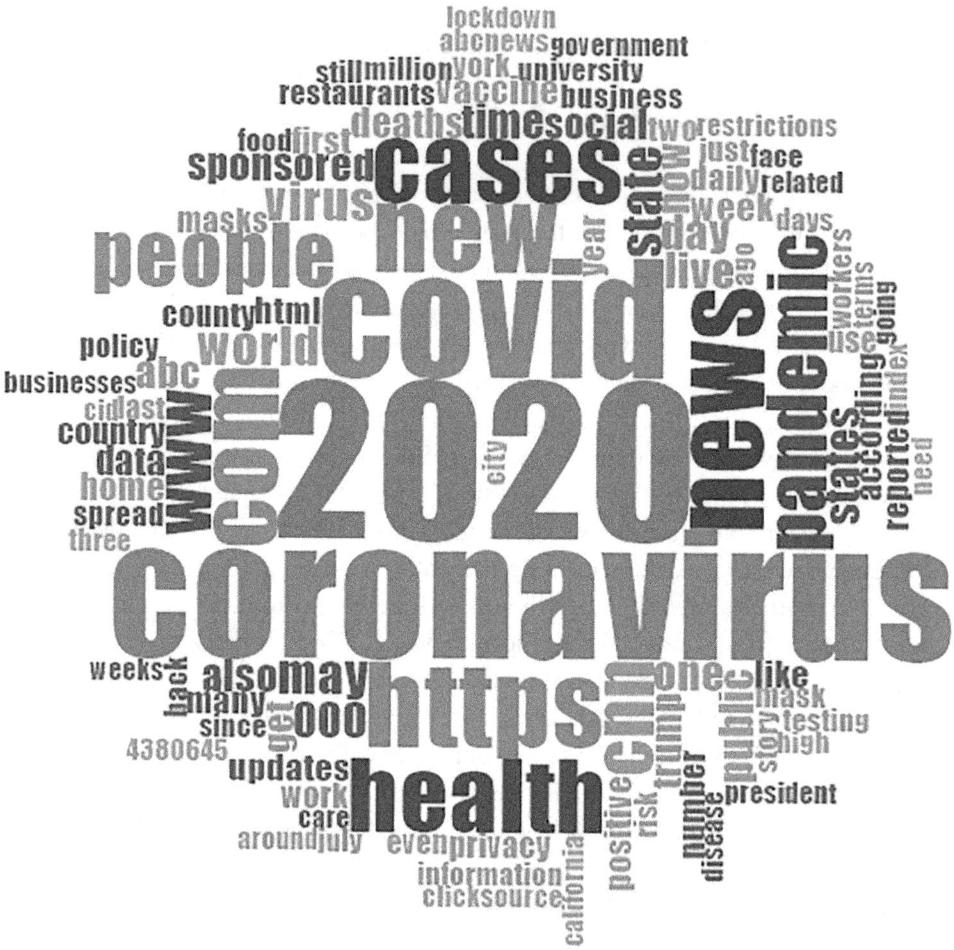

A word tree was extracted from the articleset. This word tree has hundreds of branches and runs some 30 inches in height as a visual. The size of this word tree shows the forefronted concerns of "restaurant"(s) in the context of the pandemic in terms of academic research and news coverage (with much more of the latter than the former). An excerpt of this word tree follows (Figure 2).

Figure 2. Word Tree around "Restaurant" in "Restaurant and COVID-19" Journalistic Set

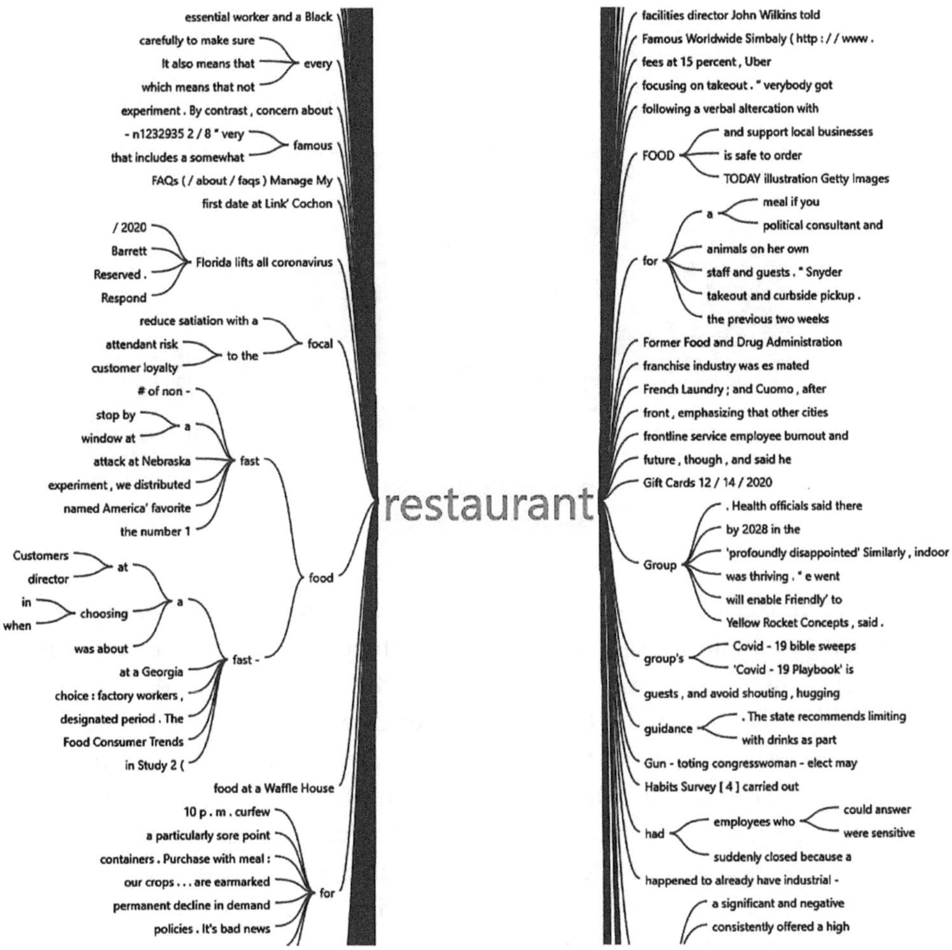

A computational sentiment analysis of this articleset shows that much of the writing runs "moderately negative" and "very negative." The mass media coverage finds little "very positive" (Figure 3).

Figure 3. Autocoded Sentiment Analysis of "Restaurant and COVID-19" Journalistic Set

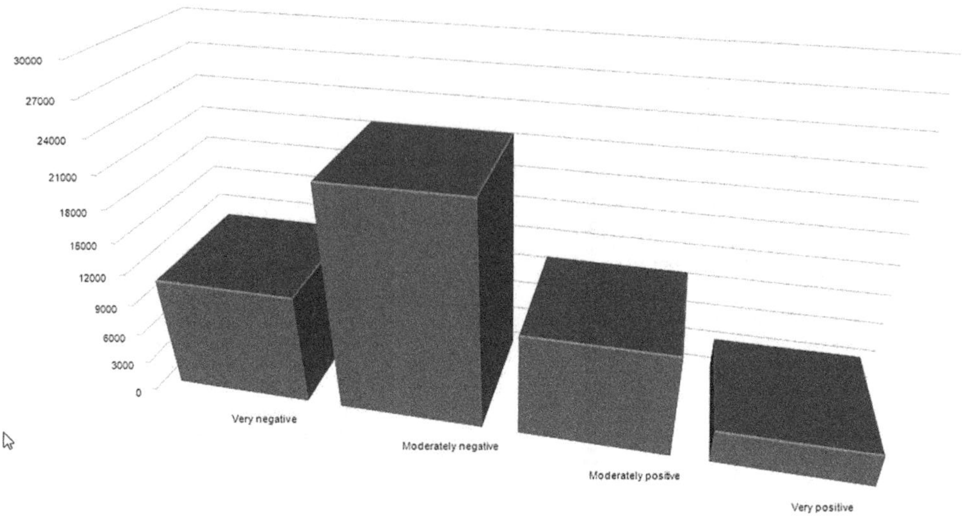

What the thinker Umberto Eco (1991) observed in the American preference for themed restaurants and various simulacrum and "total fakes" in their entertainment environments, like an everyday Disneyland. Indeed, restaurants do design full experiences for their clientele, from the moment they smell the foods and drinks and see the signs and hear the music. There are physical centerpieces in themed restaurants. One chain has dinosaurs and fake flora and fauna for a "jungle" experience. A chain marketing towards children's birthdays has video games and ball pits and indoor climbers. A major fast food chain has a clown as its primary mascot. An up-scale restaurant features plenty of wall art and sculptures. Another has a main interior water feature in the waiting area and art throughout. The staff are trained to communicate over-friendliness and a sense of occasion around the food. There may be actual preparation of the food at the table, such as through hibachi-grill action or hot pot cooking. There may be live entertainment: singing, live music, mysteries and dinner theatre, comic performances, dance performances, and others, to draw traffic, set the mood, and justify higher prices. To keep the visits "fresh," there are changing menus of chef's specials with time-sensitive available vegetables, seafood, and other ingredients.

In the Social Imagery From "COVID and Restaurants" Imageset

Social imagery may be informative of dynamics in the pandemic (Hai-Jew, Apr. 2020). The available social imagery (766 from Google Images from the seeded query "COVID 19 restaurants" and downloaded on Dec. 14, 2020) show a data-centered response from humanity. One seminal one featured on the CDC site shows a data visualization of places with the highest risks of infection in a state of societal reopening ("COVID-19 Science Update released: November 24, 2020 Edition 66," Nov. 24, 2020; Chang, Pierson, Koh, Gerardin, Redbird, Grusky, & Leskovec, Nov. 10, 2020). In descending order of highest risk to lowest, the list reads: full-service restaurants, fitness centers, cafes & snack bars, hotels & motels, limited-service restaurants, religious organizations, offices of physicians, grocery stores, used merchandise stores, pet stores, sporting goods stores, other general stores, hobby & toy stores, hardware stores, automotive parts stores, department stores, gas stations, pharmacies & drug stores, convenience stores, and new car dealers. The name of the visual is "The numbers of additional infections (per 100k), compared to not reopening (per POI)" where "POI" refers to a point of interest and the data are modeled off of 10 metro areas. A different data source showing a set of pie charts suggests that there is high variances in the places where people become infected in various states. There are other data visualizations, in reference to predicted infections and deaths; estimated costs of losses for restaurants under various conditions (shutdown, partial reopening, and others), choropleth maps with intensities of viral spread mapped. The data visualizations are of various common types: area charts, bubble charts, scatter graphs, bar graphs, filled maps, data tables, pie charts, and social network analysis graphs. The data are from global, national, state, and county-level reports.

There are diagrams: floorplans of restaurants and classrooms with overlays of air flow patterns and depictions; simulations of viral transmission between people through various airborne transmission and fomite transfer surfaces; explanations of various contagious disease spread models. There are visuals of planning out needs for ICU beds at hospitals, based on a 72-hour bed demand model, for when to trigger various surge capacities. One digital visual shows chefs behind transparent barriers and spaces for diners at the counter with the stools socially distanced.

There are photographs: experiments of airborne viral spread from breathing, talking, coughing, sneezing, and others, with and without facial masking of various types; photos of restaurants being shuttered by staff; photos of diners eating across from each other and interacting through transparent plexiglass and plastic barriers; COVID patients in ICU beds; dining tables set up in a city scape on a roof space; signs of closed spaces due to COVID, signs of proper behaviors in restaurants, posters of how to wear face masks properly; screengrabs from television news broadcasts, of government announcements, of press conferences, and of weather reports, among others; digital COVID-19 dashboards; an empty restaurant with a series of seating booths; masked people standing in line in a socially distanced way; diners in tented "pods" or "bubbles" on the sidewalk; slideshow slides with various rules and guidance; a masked person at a counter of a government office being served by a masked clerk;

a drive-through testing site; a row of masked individuals shoulder to shoulder on an airplane; empty tables and chairs in an outdoor dining space; a masked waiter holding a "sanitized" (labeled as such) menu in a plastic cover while an unmasked man in a baseball cap looks at his plate of a sandwich and fries; a screengrab of a Twitter message decrying the messaging around SARS-CoV-2 as exaggerated, and others. There are photos of various testing lines for SARS-CoV-2, along with healthcare workers with gloves, face masks, face shields, PPE gowns, and other protections. Some visuals are of the first pages of academic papers. Some photos show famous tourist destinations (like the Space Needle in Seattle). One photo shows a jogger running past an outdoor shopping mall area decked in Christmas decorations. One photo shows a single rider in a face mask on a subway train car. These images are evocative of a particular slice-in-time. These complement published works.

Restaurants Upstream and Downstream

The plight of the restaurant industries around the world has also led to greater observations of their embeddedness in human societies, both upstream and downstream. The pandemic has highlighted threats to "food and nutrition security" (Love, et al., 2020, p. 2). Upstream, the seafood sector had to readjust to restaurant shutdowns. In the "immobile" moment of COVID-19, the seafood industry was highly impacted based on its being "organized around continuous flow of product through global value chains" (Campling & Havice, 2018, as cited in Havice, Marschke, & Vandergeest, June 8, 2020, p. 1). Researchers found that some "supply chains, market segments, companies, small-scale actors and civil society" are more resilient than others (Love, et al., 2020, p. 2), in the face of such a shock. Many had to find alternate markets. Those providing "high-value marine fish species sold at restaurants" have been more impacted than "lower value farmed carp sold at retail outlets" (Love, et al., 2020, p. 4). It has been harder for firms engaged in "live-fresh supply chains" (delivering to restaurants) (Love, et al., 2020, p. 2). Beef cattle markets and producers have had to adapt to the lessened demand with the shutdowns of restaurants and food service (Martinez, Maples, & Benavidez, 2020, p. 1). The broiler industry has also had to adjust based on "detrimental impacts to chicken demand due to restaurant closures" and downward pressures on prices along with the rest of the livestock sector (Maples, Thompson, Anderson, & Anderson, 2020, p. 1).

Some worry about how the pandemic may affect future meat consumption given the spotlight on food safety issues from coverage of SARS-CoV-2. The general public has become more aware of "illnesses linked to animals," with resulting short-term reductions in meat intake. Perhaps present consumption may be part of "a shift away from overconsumption of meat, leading to potential health and environmental benefits in the longer term" (Attwood & Hajat, 2020, p. 3116).

Others see some silver linings. The foundational changes to people's ways of acquiring and consuming food globally is a global phenomenon. One study looked at changes to food consumption in a country in the Middle East. The pandemic has changed the way "consumers are eating, shopping, and interacting with food. Indeed, the survey results suggested (i) a shift toward healthier diets; (ii) an increase in the consumption of domestic products due to food safety concerns; (iii) a change in the modality of acquiring food (with a surge in online grocery shopping); (iv) an increase in culinary capabilities; and (v) the absence of panic buying and food stockpiling in Qatar" (Hassen, El Bilali, & Allahyari, Aug. 27, 2020, p. 1)

There may be pandemic impacts on fruit and vegetable markets. Some researchers suggest that consumers' may continue to engage in more online food-purchasing habits; the fruit and vegetable markets may experience "heightened constraints on immigrant labor markets, and tighter concentration in fresh produce distribution and perhaps retailing" in Canada (Richards & Rickard, April 13, 2020, p. 189). One work used as an example a firm in the fresh-produce sector that needs to be able to switch between "food service and retail distribution" to survive, for basic adaptivity (Chenarides, Manfredo, & Richards, 2020, p. 8).

A Long Overhang

Tens of trillions in wealth has been lost in this pandemic, along with dissipation of people's ambitions and dreams (Sheng, Nov. 5, 2020). Many who had been employed prior have dropped out of the job market and are no longer seeking work; they are now in the population of the long-term unemployed. The U.S. has not even started counting the costs of the mass stimulus funding to shore up industries and American jobs and general citizen well-being. The pandemic stands to have potential "long-run effects on health, labor, and human capital" given the direct effects of SARS-CoV-2 with its "geographic research, its relatively high ease of transmission, its comparatively low lethality, and its many emerging sequelae" and given the "large downturn, which in its own right has the capacity to permanently scar trajectories of health and income, even for those who do not fall ill themselves" (Arthi & Parman, 2020, p. 1). If past is prologue, the study of past pandemics and past depressions and recessions may inform what may work for humanity to come back from this precipice and to mitigate potential long-term scarring effects on peoples, livelihoods, public health, economies, and lived experiences (including subjective painful loss of work-based identities). The prior work shows something of the non-linearities of health issues that reverberate through generations…and economic effects that inform public health as well. The longer a pandemic lasts, the more devastation that occurs over time (Martin, Markhvida, Hallegatte, &Walsh, 2020), which explains the push for faster mass vaccinations to try to attain some level of pre-pandemic normalcy.

A more concerning issue is "if pandemics become the new normal, then tens of millions of urban service jobs will disappear" (Glaeser, May 1, 2020). This researcher suggests that billions of dollars need to be invested in "anti-pandemic health care infrastructure" to avoid a "labor market Armageddon" (Glaeser, May 1, 2020).

More specifically, the COVID-19 crisis has the U.S. restaurant industry predicting "a total of more than a USD 80 billion loss in sales in March and April 2020 alone, and the loss will be three times more by the end of 2020" (National Restaurant Association, 2020, as cited in Im, Kim, & Miao, 2021, p. 1). This continuing event is a "threat to employees, customers, the general public, and the fundamental survival of the company itself" (Im, Kim, & Miao, 2021, p. 1). Where some market sectors may really be building up pent-up demand, such as for durable goods like cars and appliances, people dissipate their hunger by foods purchased elsewhere. While there may be pent-up appetite for the thrill of dining out, people will be meeting their food needs likely once it is somewhat safer to do so, without having to worry that a meal out is a "last meal." There is no cuisine "to die for."

The U.S. population will spend many years examining the mistakes made. But early lessons are emerging. Government that uses multivocal approaches about public health will dilute the message, and biosafety will be much harder to achieve. If simple actions like face-masking are politicized, large swaths of the population will be led astray. People can be misled about what is actually credibly protective vs. what is merely theatrical and "pretend" biosafety. This deficit of trust is not only in the U.S., but other leaders who pushed their populations to continue working without bio-safety protections have incurred mass mistrust (Pedroso, Reverdosa, & Darlington, July 2, 2020). An important takeaway lesson really is that people have to be responsible for their own well-being and health, and no "nanny" government is going to step in to ensure their well-being (much less that they have housing, food, medical care, or other necessities for survival).

"WHERE THE NEXT MEAL IS COMING FROM": POLICY MIX TO SUPPORT RESTAURANT WORKERS IN THE U.S. DURING THE COVID-19 PANDEMIC

Restaurants do not exist in a vacuum. They are an integral part of a complex economy. A simplified conceptualization of upstream and downstream industries to restaurants may be seen in Figure 4. The light shaded areas show the upstream and downstream aspects, and the unshaded area shows some of the role-based functions related to restaurants.

Figure 4. Conceptualizing the Upstream and Downstream of (Generic) Restaurants

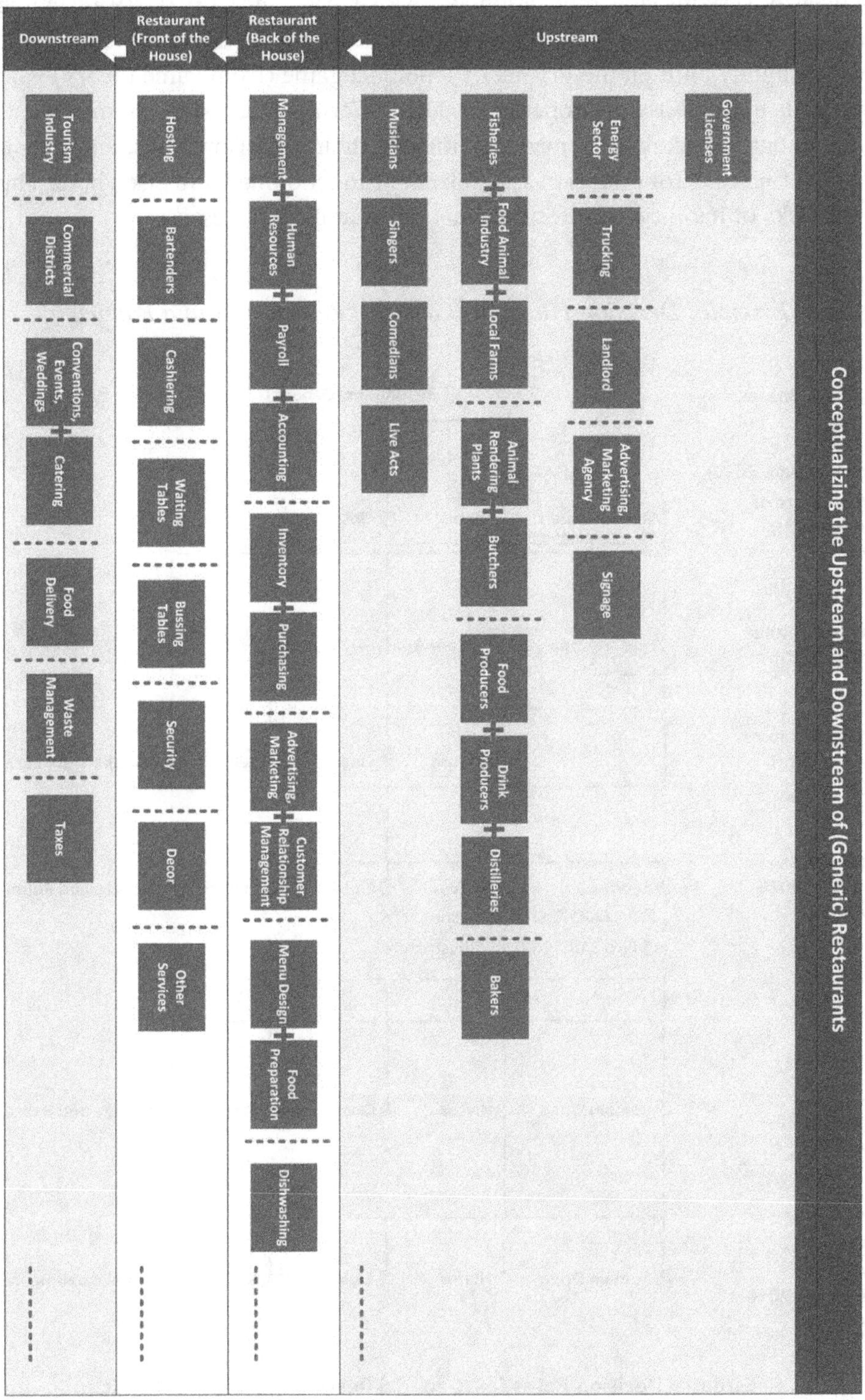

When restaurants close down, there are upstream and downstream repercussions.

Given the system-wide implications of SARS-CoV-2 and COVID-19, restaurants face critical decisions. A simplified decision flow may be seen in Figure 5. This flow was lightly built on the Prisoner's Dilemma game (from game theory) where individuals may choose to cooperate or defect. Certainly, a restaurant may want to continue, but the decision is made for them if their cash flow ends, and they are unable to find cash (or credit) to stay solvent or functioning from elsewhere. There are the risks of liability for infections that occur at the businesses.

Figure 5. Essential Decision Paths for (Generic) Restaurants in a Pandemic

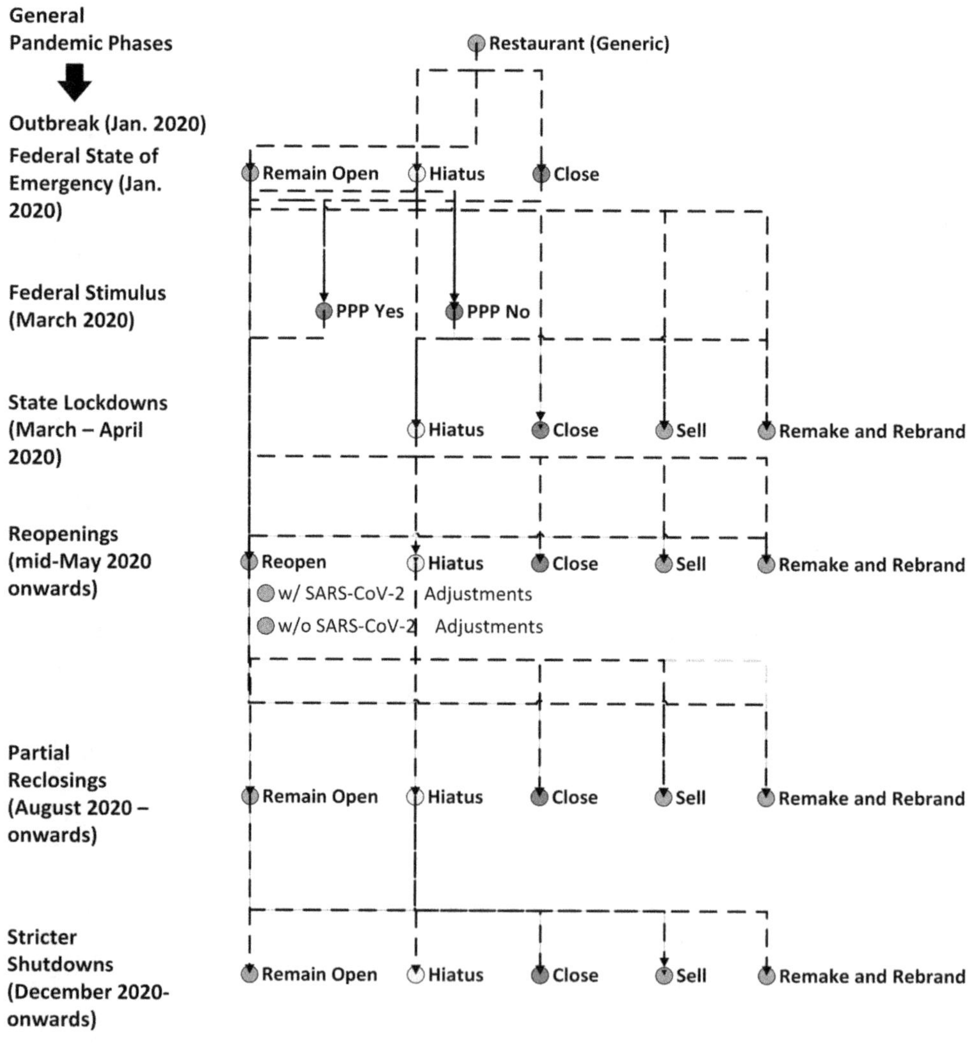

Essential Decision Paths for (Generic) Restaurants in a Pandemic

DISCUSSION

On the extreme of hands-off government, the extremes of the SARS-CoV-2 / COVID-19 pandemic would play out with winners and losers, and no tax payer dollars going to shore up failing businesses. The restaurant sector is part of entertainment, and it is not so critical that it has to be protected. The "utils" it provides may be subjective and idiosyncratic, based on people's palates and preferred dining-out experiences. It may be possible to argue a macro-level value, too, in terms of the promotion of spaces for accidental meetings and "bumps." One can maybe suggest that such restaurants are important places for disparate people (with different areas of expertise) to meet and socialize to enable "regional advantage" (Saxenian, 1996, 1994) by the seeding of innovations across various fields, to borrow a concept and to contort an argument. The opportunities to socialize and to make chance meetings in a restaurant may be valuable. This argument may be a bit of a stretch.

The creative destruction argument is that the market will decide whether or not firms survive, and interventions will merely corrupt the market mechanisms. The moneys and human endeavors may be better served if applied to other endeavors, other industries. On the other extreme would be full all-in investment with protections of all business and peoples until the long-running storm has passed. Human life, human health, and human well-being can be partially preserved from COVID-19, but shutdowns introduce other externalities that can be harmful to people: a lack of effective education for children, socially isolated people and families, and other harms. In between these two extremes of policy, these purposefully simplified contrasts, is the possible. Social justice considerations are also at play, especially given the "k-shaped" economic recovery underway (with a portion of the population getting richer and a majority getting poorer) and wide disparities between the sub-populations who are suffering most from this pandemic.

This work is not a prescriptive one given the many complexities of priorities for a nation of 320 million people, with complex responsibilities globally and at home. This work merely offers a light summary of research in this space and proposes some considerations of the various important factors at play, foremost, people.

Some Americans have a romantic notion about being the owners of their own businesses and the scheduler of their own hours. For this dream, they will sink life savings into a business; they will work without wages. They will put in very long work hours. They will expend beyond logical reason.

A former colleague of this author gave up his career and sunk his and his spouse's life savings into building out a rental for his new restaurant, which opened to great fanfare in the local community and brought out hundreds of celebrants. A year and a half later, without his having earned a cent of wages, the business went under, with full losses of all invested funds. The owner of the rental gained in terms of the interior build-out, for which he did not have to pay anything. The financial proposition was always going to be a tough one, with so many downward pressures on food prices, given their wide availability. The "business plan" that was proposed was more of a fairytale than anything actual, with no hard look at actual numbers. Though multiple people reached out to him and let him know about his risks…and the fact that he should extract some months of free rental for his build-out of the building owner's building, he brushed off the suggestions. His colleagues tried to support his effort by holding meetings in his space and ordering food out. He had made himself available for interviews in which he claimed to use high-quality meats from abroad. In these stories, he hyped his own career prior to becoming a restaurant owner. He waxed eloquent about his original special sauces for various hamburgers. Ultimately, even if parts of the general public believed his stories, there were not enough people to help the restaurant maintain. Essentially, with the month-on-month losses, he was essentially paying people to eat at his restaurant; he was subsidizing their meals. For others to survive this pressured moment, they have to be able to maintain life, hold off on rent payments due, protect brand reputation, and maintain morale—so as to have the drive to restart when the "all clear" is given (projected for mid-way into 2021 or later).

Small businesses have always been high-risk propositions in the U.S., given their high failure rate, with a third failing in the first two years (20% in the first year), and only half making it at least five years, according to the U.S. Bureau of Labor Statistics numbers. The end of a business may result in loss of investment and effort, but people can come back from that. People can find new jobs. People can learn new skills. People can reinvent themselves. And even better, government can help in such cases.

To summarize via a back-of-the-napkin SWOT analysis (Strengths, Weaknesses, Opportunities, Threats), restaurants during a pandemic with an airborne pathogen may look something like Table 1.

Table 1. A Back-of-the-Napkin SWOT Analysis of Restaurants in the COVID-19 Pandemic

Strengths	Weaknesses
• Brands • Loyal customers • Preferences for particular food tastes and dining experiences • Ability to set up businesses through rentals (lower cost) • Ability to sell foods through drive-through windows and curbside pickups • Sympathetic mass media coverage in broadcast media (stories of restaurant owners, stories of diners with high tips, and others)	• High-risk indoor eating spaces • Ties to super-spreader events in the news • Transient staff
Opportunities	**Threats**
• Ability to walk away from the industry and pursue other work for proprietors (and staff) • Ability to access PPP funds if eligible • Ability to receive government support for citizens • Ability to take tax write-offs for business expenditures • Ability to remake the physical space of the restaurant • Ability to plan for a re-opening once populations and societies are bio-safer • Ability to create trainings for safer food handling (including considering airborne transmissible pathogens in food)	• Changes in tastes over time • Changes in social dining habits over time • Fungible nature of food (with needs met in various locales) • Customer-favorite staff moving on • Physical risks to the staff and owners

The SWOT analysis shows a difficult hand that those in the restaurant and broader hospitality industry have been dealt. At this moment, there is little change in their predicament, more than a year in from the first case of SARS-CoV-2 stateside.

FUTURE RESEARCH DIRECTIONS

To build on this work, researchers may explore various policy mixes from around the world and examine the implications of those decisions and resourcing to better understand how government should function in such times…and what tradeoffs can be made to keep industries afloat while protecting human lives. In the future, some decisions made in the present era will be seen as brilliant, and others as wholly callous and destructive.

There may be studies of particular restaurant types within the SME / MSME category, the various applied survival strategies and tactics, and this research may provide a longer-term perspective optimally after the pandemic has ended and the proverbial dust has settled. Perhaps the restaurant owners may be debriefed in more depth post-pandemic for lessons learned.

There are further implications on research itself, which is now seen to be possible to be "near real-time" and "unfolding". Tens of thousands of research articles were published in 2020 and continued unabated into 2021. Some researchers published direct and hands-on lab research. Some works involved primary data. However, in addition, many researchers had to use the available information that they could collect remotely (online surveys, emails, and phone calls), indirectly (through passive collection of social media postings, and other means), and through journalistic publications that offer a first draft of history (with the attendant provisionality of the collected information).

CONCLUSION

On the streets, there are vast empty storefronts where restaurants once existed. For some, the signage and other signs of their prior existence have been removed. For others, there are zombie storefronts of former restaurants, with the owners enervated and no effort to do more than post signs that the restaurants are permanently closed. On social media, various websites for restaurants have disappeared. For others, they have not been updated and are the digital equivalent of zombie restaurants. Social ratings sites for restaurants (and tourist sites) indicate user notifications that the restaurants have closed for good. It is as if the owners themselves could not be bothered. Theirs has been a fast fade.

This current state is not a surprise. Most of the smaller restaurants, based on a number of surveys, would not pass a stress test by having some cash-on-hand for times of hardship. In most cases, too, hardships are conceptualized as maybe a month or two affair and generally limited. Most are not conceptualizing a challenge that affects the world...and will stretch past a year and maybe even into two. The full stoppage of so much of human endeavor breaks momentum in serious ways, and some harms will be permanent. In a way, the creating of restaurants with not extensive capital (depending on the restaurant type) and a "low cost of entry" may be on purpose, with a built-in brittleness that enables easy-in easy-out.

Public health officials estimate that by early 2021, a third of Americans (some 100 million) will have already been infected by SARS-CoV-2 and therefore potentially have some light immunity (Gottlieb, Dec. 7, 2020, as cited in "Dr. Scott Gottlieb...," Dec. 7, 2020); it is projected that the country will start seeing the downward side of the exponential infection decline by early January 2021. With mass-scale inoculations of the vaccines from Pfizer and Moderna (and others potentially coming online soon), many are anticipating that humanity still start gaining a handle on this pandemic soon.

The mutating SARS-CoV-2 / COVID-19 pandemic is an unprecedented mass casualty event, with far-reaching traumas for people around the world. At present, while many have become infected, with some recovered, some dead, a majority of the world's populations are still susceptible to infection and all potential outcomes if infected. Parts of the world's populations are under quarantine. Borders are mostly closed still, except between a few trusted zones or mass-scale bubbles where there is very low viral spread. If its virulence were higher, it would seem that humanity would have suffered even worse losses of human life—because of very inept responses in many parts of the world…and a lack of other options than to work through a pandemic for survival in many developing countries. Shockingly, in so many places, masking itself does not seem to be an option due to resource constraints and / or leadership and / or cultural practices. As a so-called 100-year-event, hopefully, something this devastating will not happen again for a long time (or ever). Optimally, the scientific advances in this year, 2020, may be protective for survivors and those of the future. However, given the microbial world and human engagements in the world and incursions into wildlife areas, the risks are ever-present. The devastations have not only been to people's lives and their senses of safety, but various industries have borne outsized destructive effects from this moment.

The U.S. Congress came to agreement on a $900 billion coronavirus relief package on December 20, 2020, and they have attached that to the $1.4 trillion omnibus spending bill (for the fiscal year beginning Oct. 1, 2020) (Shutt & Lerman, Dec. 20, 2020). The $120 billion RESTAURANTS Act [Real Economic Support That Acknowledges Unique Restaurant Assistance Needed To Survive (RESTAURANTS) Act] (Crowley, Oct. 2, 2020) did not make the cut, so small and medium-sized restaurants are on their own.

On the other side of this pandemic, perhaps some franchises will survive. Perhaps some of the larger corporations. It is hard to imagine hole-in-the-wall restaurants with questionable hygiene making it. It is hard to imagine strip malls filling up with small restaurants very quickly. The promised "snap back" that many politicians have touted, in an effort to be optimistic, is now not projected to occur with any speed, if at all.

The restaurant industry is a high profile one, with positive effects on various industries and on lived lives. Restaurants represent social gathering places where people connect, collaborate, socialize, share ideas, and innovate. Their full return will be much celebrated because it will mean that humanity has prevailed over an insidious lethal zoonotic virus, at least for the next while. And still, those that re-emerge or emerge post-pandemic will find a landscape of higher food and fuel prices and a lesser dollar, with inflation rising (in part from the wash of stimulus cash and other inputs into the U.S. economy).

Addendum: This work was written in early 2021. At this present moment, it is mid-summer, months later. Some 66.7% of Americans have received at least one dose of a vaccine against SARS-CoV-2 / COVID-19. There are three approved vaccines under the U.S. Food and Drug Administration's "emergency use authorization" (EUA). These are by Pfizer/BioNTech (two shots), Moderna (two shots), and Johnson & Johnson (one shot), for those 16 and older. There are reports of some rare blood clotting events in response to some of the vaccines, particularly by AstraZenica. There are reports of break-through infections but little in the way of serious illness or deaths, for those vaccinated with the approved vaccines. There are mutations arising from different regions of the world, some with much greater infection capabilities (and resulting higher R_0 scores). The "delta variant" (B.1.617.2) and "delta plus variant" (B.1.617.2.1) are the main mutations of concern at present even as others are identified and assessed. "Age de-escalation" trials are ongoing about the safety of various dosages for children and vaccine efficacy, among other factors. The United States waits full approval of the vaccines by the U.S. Food & Drug Administration. There is exploration of the need for boosters, particularly for those who first received their vaccines early in 2021.

Some restaurants have reopened, many with both in-restaurant dining as well as drive-through pickups. There are outdoor venues for *al fresco* dining. Many former-restaurant storefronts are still empty. There are many "help wanted" signs out and many jobs that restaurant owners are having trouble filling. Insufficient wages are an issue.

Masking policies have mostly been rolled back, even in places with high rates of low vaccinations, even in places with rising rates of infections. Those staff working in restaurants only sometimes mask up. Sometimes, the masking is a seen as a sign of politeness and social respect for customers; in other cases, it is taken as a political signal (non-conservative), and interpreted as an offense by some. The social implications of the pandemic have not diminished even a year and a half in. And counting. The country is now in the Fourth Wave of the COVID-19 pandemic.

REFERENCES

Alonso, A. D., Kok, S. K., Bressan, A., O'Shea, M., Sakellarios, N., Koresis, A., Solis, M.A.B., & Santoni, L. J. (2020). COVID-19, aftermath, impacts, and hospitality firms: An international perspective. *International Journal of Hospitality Management, 91*, 1 – 11.

Alsharif, M. (2020, Nov. 27). *A Toronto restaurant owner was arrested after allegedly continuing to violate public health orders.* CNN.

Anderson, C. (2020, Aug. 10). *Many landmark restaurants, bars won't reopen after virus.* ABC News.

Arthi, V., & Parman, J. (2020). Disease, downturns, and wellbeing: Economic history and the long-run impacts of COVID-19. *Explorations in Economic History, 101381*, 1–20. PMID:33162564

Attwood, S., & Hajat, C. (2020, August 12). How will the COVID-19 pandemic shape the future of meat consumption? *Public Health Nutrition, 23*(17), 3116–3120. doi:10.1017/S136898002000316X PMID:32782062

Azuma, K., Yanagi, U., Kagi, N., Kim, H., Ogata, M., & Hayashi, M. (2020). Environmental factors involved in SARS-CoV-2 transmission: Effect and role of indoor environmental quality in the strategy for COVID-19 infection control. *Environmental Health and Preventive Medicine, 25*(1), 1–16. doi:10.118612199-020-00904-2 PMID:33143660

Baek, S., Mohanty, S. K., & Glambosky, M. (2020). COVID-19 and stock market volatility: An industry level analysis. *Finance Research Letters, 37*(101748), 1–10. doi:10.1016/j.frl.2020.101748 PMID:32895607

Bartik, A. W., Bertrand, M., Cullen, Z., Glaeser, E. L., Luca, M., & Stanton, C. (2020, July 28). The impact of COVID-19 on small business outcomes and expectations. *Proceedings of the National Academy of Sciences of the United States of America, 117*(3), 17656–17666. doi:10.1073/pnas.2006991117 PMID:32651281

Bartik, A. W., Bertrand, M., Cullen, Z. B., Glaeser, E. L., Luca, M., & Stanton, C. T. (2020, Apr.) *How are small businesses adjusting to COVID-19? Early evidence from a survey.* Working Paper 26989. National Bureau of Economic Research. NBER Working Paper Series.

Batat, W. (2020). How Michelin-starred chefs are being transformed into social bricoleurs? An online qualitative study of luxury foodservice during the pandemic crisis. *Journal of Service Management, 32*(1), 1–13. doi:10.1108/JOSM-05-2020-0142

Bhagat, R. K., Wykes, M. D., Dalziel, S. B., & Linden, P. F. (2020). Effects of ventilation on the indoor spread of COVID-19. *Journal of Fluid Mechanics, 903.*

Breier, M., Kallmuenzer, A., Clauss, T., Gast, J., Kraus, S., & Tiberius, V. (n.d.). The role of business model innovation in the hospitality industry during the COVID-19 crisis. *International Journal of Hospitality Management, 92*, 1 - 12.

Brennen, J. S., Simon, F. M., & Nielsen, R. K. (2020). Beyond (Mis) Representation: Visuals in COVID-19 Misinformation. *The International Journal of Press/Politics*, 1–26.

Brizek, M. G., Frash, R. E., McLeod, B., & Patience, M. M. (2020). Independent restaurant operator perspectives in the wake of the COVID-19 pandemic (R3). *International Journal of Hospitality Management*, 102766. PMID:33230361

Brunner, M. (2020, July 17). *Riley Co. extends restrictions on bars, restaurants.* WIBW.

Bucak, T., & Yiğit, S. (2021). The future of the chef occupation and the food and beverage sector after the COVID-19 outbreak: Opinions of Turkish chefs. *International Journal of Hospitality Management, 92*(102682), 1–8. doi:10.1016/j.ijhm.2020.102682 PMID:33071426

Bufquin, D., Park, J. Y., Back, R. M., de Souza Meira, J. V., & Hight, S. K. (2021, February). Employee work status, mental health, substance use, and career turnover intentions: An examination of restaurant employees during COVID-19. *International Journal of Hospitality Management, 93*(102764), 1–9. doi:10.1016/j.ijhm.2020.102764

Burki, T. (2020, Sept.). The origin of SARS-CoV-2. *The Lancet.* Retrieved Dec. 17, 2020, from https://www.thelancet.com/journals/laninf/article/PIIS1473-3099(20)30641-1/fulltext

Casert, R. (2020, Oct. 25). *Virus is pummeling Europe's eateries—and winter is coming*. ABC News.

Chadee, D., Ren, S., & Tang, G. (2021). Is digital technology the magic bullet for performing work at home? Lessons learned for post COVID-19 recovery in hospitality management. *International Journal of Hospitality Management, 92*(102718), 1–8. doi:10.1016/j.ijhm.2020.102718 PMID:33071425

Chang, H.-H., & Meyerhoefer, C.D. (2020). COVID-19 and the demand for online food shopping services: Empirical evidence from Taiwan. *American Journal of Agricultural Economics,* 1 – 18.

Chang, S., Pierson, E., Koh, P. W., Gerardin, J., Redbird, B., Grusky, D., & Leskovec, J. (2020, November 10). Mobility network models of COVID-19 explain inequities and inform reopening. *Nature*. PMID:33171481

Chappell, B. (2020, Dec. 9). *The coronavirus crisis: 'Cruise to Nowhere' returns to Singapore early after positive coronavirus test.* NPR.

Chart: Each State's COVID-19 Reopening and Reclosing Plans and Mask Requirements. (2020, Dec. 14). *National Academic for State Health Policy*. Retrieved Dec. 15, 2020, from https://www.nashp.org/governors-prioritize-health-for-all/

Chenarides, L., Manfredo, M., & Richards, T.J. (2020). COVID-19 and food supply chains. *Applied Economic Perspectives and Policy*, 1 – 10.

Chetty, R., Friedman, J. N., Hendren, N., & Stepner, M. (2020). Real-time economics: A new platform to track the impacts of COVID-19 on people, businesses, and communities using private sector data. *NBER Working Paper, 27431*, 1 – 26.

Chetty, R., Friedman, J. N., Hendren, N., Stepner, M., & the The Opportunity Insights Team. (2020, June). *How did COVID-19 and stabilization policies affect spending and employment? A new real-time economic tracker based on private sector data*. National Bureau of Economic Research. NBER Working Paper Series. Working Paper 27431.

Coibion, O., Gorodnichenko, Y., & Weber, M. (2020, May). *The cost of the Covid-19 crisis: Lockdowns, macroeconomic expectations, and consumer spending*. National Bureau of Economic Research. NBER Working Paper 27141.

Community, work, and school: Information for where you live, work, learn, and play. (2020, Nov. 13). *U.S. Centers for Disease Control and Prevention*. Retrieved Dec. 14, 2020, from https://www.cdc.gov/coronavirus/2019-ncov/community/index.html

Coronavirus: Robot dog enforces social distancing in Singapore park. (2020, May 11). BBC News.

COVID-19 science update released: Nov. 24, 2020 Edition 66. (2020, Nov. 24). *U.S. Centers for Disease Control and Prevention (CDC)*. Retrieved Dec. 20, 2020, from https://www.cdc.gov/library/covid19/112420_covidupdate.html

Crowley, C. (2020, Oct. 2). What is the RESTAURANTS Act—and can it really save the hospitality industry? *Grub Street*.

Da, B. L., Im, G. Y., & Schiano, T. D. (2020). COVID-19 hangover: A rising tide of alcohol use disorder and alcohol-associated liver disease. *Hepatology (Baltimore, Md.)*, *72*(3), 1102–1108.

Dave, D., McNichols, D., & Sabia, J. J. (2020). The contagion externality of a superspreading event: The Sturgis Motorcycle Rally and COVID-19. *Southern Economic Journal*, 1–39.

del Rio-Chanona, R. M., Mealy, P., Pichler, A., Lafond, F., & Farmer, D. (2020). *Supply and demand shocks in the COVID-19 pandemic: An industry and occupation perspective*. arXiv preprint arXiv:2004.06759.

Dijk, M. N. (2020). *How entrepreneur resilience impacts the utilization of innovation in dealing with adversities like the COVID-19 pandemic in the restaurant industry in the Netherlands* (Bachelor's thesis). University of Twente.

Duda-Chodak, A., Lukasiewicz, M., Zięć, G., Florkiewicz, A., & Filipiak-Florkiewicz, A. (2020). Covid-19 pandemic and food: Present knowledge, risks, consumers fears and safety. *Trends in Food Science & Technology*, *105*, 145–160.

Eco, U. (1991). *Travels in Hyperreality*. Harcourt Brace & Company.

Elassar, A. (2020, Dec. 20). *A customer at an Ohio restaurant left a $5,600 tip to split among the entire staff for Christmas*. CNN.

Fantozzi, J. (2020, Nov. 13). *Indoor dining major cause of COVID-19 'superspreader' events, Stanford-led study suggests*. Nation's Restaurant News (NRN).

Fetzer, T. (2020). Subsidizing the spread of COVID19: Evidence from the UK's Eat-Out-to-Help-Out scheme (No. 1310). University of Warwick, Department of Economics.

Feuer, W. (2020, Mar. 28). *CDC says coronavirus RNA found in Princess Cruise ship cabins up to 17 days after passengers left*. CNBC.

Foroudi, P., Tabaghdehi, A. H., & Marvi, R. (2021). The gloom of the COVID-19 shock in the hospitality industry: A study of consumer risk perception and adaptive belief in the dark cloud of a pandemic. *International Journal of Hospitality Management*, *92*(102717), 1–10.

Gibson, K. (2020, June 17). *After reopening, restaurants again shutting their doors as coronavirus flares*. MoneyWatch. CBS News.

Gillison, S. (2020, May 22). *Thought Experiment: Samantha Gillison: Is the coronavirus the end for fancy restaurants—and the start of a new dining era*. NBC News.

Glaeser, E. (2020, May 1). Looking beyond the urban jobs Armageddon. In How life in our cities will look after the coronavirus pandemic. Foreign Policy.

Glaeser, E. L., Jin, G. Z., Leyden, B. T., & Luca, M. (2020, Aug.). *Learning from deregulation: The asymmetric impact of lockdown and reopening on risky behavior during COVID-19*. National Bureau of Economic Research. NBER Working Paper 27650.

Global Dashboard on COVID-19 Government Policies. (n.d.). *U.S. Chamber of Commerce*. Retrieved Dec. 17, 2020, from https://www.uschamber.com/international-affairs-division/covid-dashboard

Goolsbee, A., & Syverson, C. (2021). Fear, lockdown, and diversion: Comparing drivers of pandemic economic decline 2020. *Journal of Public Economics*, *193*(104311), 1–8.

Gössling, S., Scott, D., & Hall, C. M. (2021). Pandemics, tourism and global change: A rapid assessment of COVID-19. *Journal of Sustainable Tourism*, *29*(1), 1–20.

Gottlieb, S. (2020, Dec. 7). *Dr. Scott Gottlieb on future of COVID-19, vaccine, and Pfizer*. USA Today. Retrieved Dec. 20, 2020, from https://youtu.be/PxJO8MrlGcg

Gursoy, D., & Chi, C. G. (2020). Effects of COVID-19 pandemic on hospitality industry: Review of the current situations and a research agenda. *Journal of Hospitality Marketing & Management*, *29*(5), 527–529.

Hai-Jew, S. (2020, Apr.). Emergent COVID-19 and SARS-CoV-2 in social imagery and social video: Initial three months of viral dispersion. In *Social World Sensing via Social Image Analysis from Social Media*. New Prairie Press. Retrieved Oct. 23, 2020, from https://kstatelibraries.pressbooks.pub/socialworldsensing/chapter/covid19-1/

Hai-Jew, S. (2021). Societal shutdown and reopening and reclosing in the U.S. as expressed in social imagery narratives: COVID-19 pandemic seven/eight months. In Z. Fields' (Ed.), *Handbook of Research on Using Global Collective Intelligence and Creativity to Solve Wicked Problems*. IGI Global.

Hailu, G. (2020, Apr. 18). Economic thoughts on COVID-19 for Canadian food processors. *Canadian Journal of Agricultural Economics/Revue canadienne d'agroeconomie*, 163 – 169.

Hamner, L., Dubbel, P., Capron, I., Ross, A., Jordan, A., Lee, J., Lynn, J., Ball, A., Narwal, S., Russell, S., Patric, D., & Leibrand, H. (2020, May 15). *High SARS-CoV-2 attack rate following exposure at a choir practice – Skagit County, Washington, March 2020*. Morbidity and Mortality Weekly Report (MMWR). U.S. Centers for Disease Control and Prevention. Retrieved Dec. 17, 2020, from https://www.cdc.gov/mmwr/volumes/69/wr/mm6919e6.htm

Harris, J. E. (2020). Data from the COVID-19 epidemic in Florida suggest that younger cohorts have been transmitting their infections to less socially mobile older adults. *Review of Economics of the Household*, 1019–1037.

Hassan, A. (2020, May 19). *Masks required, fewer games, buffet closed: Idaho casino offers glimpse of gambling's future.* NBC News.

Hassen, T.B., El Bilali, H., & S Allahyari, M. (2020). Impact of COVID-19 on Food Behavior and Consumption in Qatar. *Sustainability, 12*(17), 1 - 18.

Havice, E., Marschke, M., & Vandergeest, P. (2020, June 8). Industrial seafood systems in the immobilizing COVID-19 moment. *Agriculture and Human Values*, 1–2.

Higgins-Dunn, N. (2020, July 13). *California to close indoor restaurants, movie theaters and bars statewide as coronavirus cases rise.* CNBC.

Hobbs, J. E. (2020, April 21). Food supply chains during the COVID-19 pandemic. *Canadian Journal of Agricultural Economics*, 1–18.

Holmes, K., & Valencia, N. (2020, May 13). *CDC guidelines shelved by Trump administration spell out far stricter road map to reopening*. CNN.

Hu, X., Yan, H., Casey, T., & Wu, C. H. (2020). Creating a safe haven during the crisis: How organizations can achieve deep compliance with COVID-19 safety measures in the hospitality industry. *International Journal of Hospitality Management*, *92*, 102662.

Huang, A., Makridis, C., Baker, M., Medeiros, M., & Guo, Z. (2020). Understanding the impact of COVID-19 intervention policies on the hospitality labor market. *International Journal of Hospitality Management, 91*, 1 – 9.

IHME COVID-19 Forecasting Team. (2020, October 23). Modeling COVID-19 scenarios for the United States. *Nature*.

Iles, A., & de Wit, M. M. (2020). Who gets to define 'the COVID-19 problem'? Expert politics in a pandemic. *Agriculture and Human Values*, 1–2.

Im, J., Kim, H., & Miao, L. (2021). CEO letters: Hospitality corporate narratives during the COVID-19 pandemic. *International Journal of Hospitality Management*, *92*, 1–9.

Jung, H. S., Jung, Y. S., & Yoon, H. H. (2021). COVID-19: The effects of job insecurity on the job engagement and turnover intent of deluxe hotel employees and the moderating role of generational characteristics. *International Journal of Hospitality Management*, *92*(102703), 1–9.

Karimi, F. (2020, May 15). *The focus is shifting from trying to eliminate coronavirus to reducing the risks, a doctor says.* CNN.

Kaushal, V., & Srivastava, S. (2021). Hospitality and tourism industry amid COVID-19 pandemic: Perspectives on challenges and learnings from India. *International Journal of Hospitality Management, 92*(102707), 1–9.

Kesslen, B. (2020, Oct. 30). *'I'm going to church more': Restaurant owners wonder whether they'll survive winter.* NBC News.

Khan, K. S., Mamun, M. A., Griffiths, M. D., & Ullah, I. (2020). The mental health impact of the COVID-19 pandemic across different cohorts. *International Journal of Mental Health and Addiction*, 1–7.

Kim, A. (2020, May 21). *More than 1,200 pastors say they'll defy California's state order and resume in-person services.* CNN.

Kim, J., Kim, J., & Wang, Y. (2021). Uncertainty risks and strategic reaction of restaurant firms amid COVID-19: Evidence from China. *International Journal of Hospitality Management, 92*(102752), 1–10.

Kim, J., & Lee, J. C. (2020). Effects of COVID-19 on preferences for private dining facilities in restaurants. *Journal of Hospitality and Tourism Management, 45*, 67–70.

Knowles, J., Ettenson, R., Lynch, P., & Dollens, J. (2020). Growth opportunities for brands during the COVID-19 crisis. *MIT Sloan Management Review*, 1–6.

Kok, G., Jonkers, R., Gelissen, R., Meertens, R., Schaalma, H., & de Zwart, O. (2010). Behavioural intentions in response to an influenza pandemic. *BMC Public Health, 10*(174), 1–19.

Kong, E., & Prinz, D. (2020). Disentangling policy effects using proxy data: Which shutdown policies affected unemployment during the COVID-19 pandemic? *Journal of Public Economics, 189*(104257), 1–39.

Kornfield, M. (2020, May 23). Rats are getting aggressive hunting for food amid restaurant closures, CDC warns. *The Washington Post.*

Leatherby, L., & McCann, A. (2020, May 15). Sweden stayed open. A deadly month shows the risks. *The New York Times.*

Li, Q., Bessell, L., Xiao, X., Fan, C., Gao, X., & Mostafavi, A. (2020, June 25). *Disparate patterns of movements and visits to points of interests located in urban hotspots across U.S. metropolitan cities during COVID-19.* arXiv.

Lock, S. (2020, Dec. 11). *Restaurant industry in the U.S. – statistics & facts.* Statista.

Loi, K. I., Lei, W. S., & Lourenço, F. (2020). Understanding the reactions of government and gaming concessionaires on COVID-19 through the neo-institutional theory–The case of Macao. *International Journal of Hospitality Management, 102755,* 1 - 11.

Love, D., Allison, E., Asche, F., Belton, B., Cottrell, R., Froelich, H., Gephart, J.A., Hicks, C.C., Little, D.C., Nussbaumer, E.M., Pinto da Silva, P., Poulain, F., Rubio, A., Stoll, J.S., Tlusty, M.F., Thorne-Lyman, A.L., Troell, M., & Zhang, W. (2020). *Emerging COVID-19 impacts, responses, and lessons for building resilience in the seafood system.* Academic Press.

Lu, J., Gu, J., Li, K., Xu, C., Su, W., Lai, Z., Zhou, D., Yu, C., Xu, B., & Yang, Z. (2020, July). COVID-19 outbreak associated with air conditioning in restaurant, Guangzhou, China, 2020. Research Letter. *Emerging Infectious Diseases*, *26*(7).

Luna, N. (2020, Sept. 16). Compensation: Pandemic forces restaurant industry to rethink wages, tip credit. *Nation's Restaurant News*, 1 – 8.

Ma, S., Kim, D. D., Cohen, J. T., & Neumann, P. J. (2020). Measuring "fearonomic effects" in valuing therapies: An application to COVID-19 in China. *Value in Health*, *23*(11), 1405–1408.

Makridis, C.A., & Hartley, J.S. (2020, Apr. 6). *The cost of COVID-19: A rough estimate of the 2020 US GDP impact.* Policy Brief, Mercatus Center, George Mason University.

Mandal, A. (2020, May 26). Simulated sunlight kills SARS CoV-2 on surfaces in 7 to 14 minutes. *News Medical-Life Sciences.*

Maples, J.G., Thompson, J.M., Anderson, J.D., & Anderson, D.P. (2020). Estimating COVID019 impacts on the broiler industry. *Applied Economic Perspectives and Policy,* 1 – 14.

Martin, A., Markhvida, M., Hallegatte, S., & Walsh, B. (2020). Socio-economic impacts of COVID-19 on household consumption and poverty. *Economics of Disasters and Climate Change*, *4*, 453–479.

Martinez, C.C., Maples, J.G., & Benavidez, J. (2020). Beef cattle markets and COVID-19. *Applied Economic Perspectives and Policy*, 1 – 11.

Mathai, V., Das, A., Bailey, J. A., & Breuer, K. (2020, December 4). Airflows inside passenger cars and implications for airborne disease transmission. *Science Advances.*

McCarthy, K. (2020, July 24). *Nearly 16,000 restaurants have closed permanently due to the pandemic, Yelp data shows.* ABC News.

Meyer, Z. (2020, Oct. 23). The ugly truth about tipping waitstaff during COVID-19. *Fast Company.*

Ou, J., Wong, I. A., & Huang, G. I. (2021). The coevolutionary process of restaurant CSR in the time of mega disruption. *International Journal of Hospitality Management*, *92*(102684), 1–10.

Pasquini, M. (2020, May 28). TGI Fridays CEO says 20% of U.S. restaurants could close for good due to coronavirus crisis. *People Magazine.*

Pedroso, R., Reverdosa, M., & Darlington, S. (2020, July 2). *"Sending the population to the slaughterhouse": Restaurants and bars open in Rio, as experts warn worst is yet to come.* CNN.

Peters, A. (2020, Sept. 3). If you're in the hospital with COVID-19, this robot dog might come take your vital signs. *Fast Company.*

Pinsker, J. (2020, May 7). A guide to staying safe as states reopen. *Atlantic (Boston, Mass.).*

Qin, X., Huang, G., Shen, H., & Fu, M. (2020). COVID-19 pandemic and firm-level cash holding—Moderating effect of goodwill and goodwill impairment. *Emerging Markets Finance & Trade*, *56*(10), 2243–2258.

Raj, M., Sundararajan, A., & You, C. (2020). *COVID-19 and digital resilience: Evidence from Uber Eats.* arXiv preprint arXiv:2006.07204.

Ranka, S. (2020, June). How corona virus could affect the culture of eating, special reference to street food: The New Normal. *IOSR Journal of Business and Management*, *22*(6), 1–7.

Ratnesar-Shumate, S., Williams, G., Green, B., Krause, M., Holland, B., Wood, S., Bohannon, J., Boydston, J., Freeburger, D., Hooper, I., Beck, K., Yeager, J., Altamura, L. A., Biryukov, J., Yolitz, J., Schuit, M., Wahl, V., Hevey, M., & Dabisch, P. (2020, May 20). Simulated Sunlight Rapidly Inactivates SARS-CoV-2 on Surfaces. *The Journal of Infectious Diseases.* doi:10.1093/infdis/jiaa274

Richards, T.J., & Rickard, B. (2020, Apr. 13). COVID-19 impact on fruit and vegetable markets. *Canadian Journal of Agricultural Economics/Revue canadienne d'agroeconomie*, 189 - 194.

Richter, A., & Wilson, T. C. (2020). Covid-19: Implications for insurer risk management and the insurability of pandemic risk. *The Geneva Risk and Insurance Review*, *45*, 171–199.

Rizou, M., Galanakis, I. M., Aldawoud, T. M., & Galanakis, C. M. (2020). Safety of foods, food supply chain and environment within the COVID-19 pandemic. *Trends in Food Science & Technology*, *102*, 293–299.

Saxena, J. (2020, Dec. 1). Survey finds that pandemic has exacerbated sexual harassment of tipped workers. *Eater.*

Saxenian, A. (1996). Regional Advantage: Culture and Competition in Silicon Valley and Route 128. Harvard University Press.

Scerri, M., & Grech, V. (2020, Nov. 12). *To wear or not to wear? Adherence to face mask use during the COVID-19 and Spanish influenza pandemics.* US National Library of Medicine National Institutes of Health.

Seetharaman, P. (2020). Business models shifts: Impact of Covid-19. *International Journal of Information Management*, *54*(102173), 1–4.

Sheng, E. (2020, Nov. 5). *The $68 trillion transfer of wealth in America is evaporating amid crisis.* CNBC.

Shutt, J., & Lerman, D. (2020, Dec. 20). Deal reached on $900B coronavirus relief package; votes likely Monday. *Roll Call.*

Simmons, D. (2020, Oct. 13). *City of Manhattan installing outdoor dining platforms in front of seven downtown restaurants.* KMAN 1350 AM.

Singu, S., Acharya, A., Challagundla, K., & Byrareddy, S. N. (2020). Impact of social determinants of health on the emerging COVID-19 pandemic in the United States. *Frontiers in Public Health*, *8*, 1–18.

Smith, T.C. (2020, May 16). *Tara C. Smith Coronavirus vaccine and quarantine protesters in America form an unholy COVID-19 alliance. Thought experiment.* NBC News.

Song, H. J., Yeon, J., & Lee, S. (2021). Impact of the COVID-19 pandemic: Evidence from the U.S. restaurant industry. *International Journal of Hospitality Management*, *92*(102702), 1–7.

Sönmez, S., Apostolopoulos, Y., & Lemke, M.K. (2020). Understanding the effects of COVID-19 on the health and safety of immigrant hospitality workers in the United States. *Tourism Management Perspectives*, *35*(100717), 1–7.

Sun, C., & Zhai, Z. (2020). The efficacy of social distance and ventilation effectiveness in preventing COVID-19 transmission. *Sustainable Cities and Society, 62*, 1 - 10.

Taylor, S. (2020). The socially distant servicescape: An investigation of consumer preference's during the re-opening phase. *International Journal of Hospitality Management, 91*(102692), 1–9.

Tufekc, Z. (2020, May 12). How Hong Kong Did It: With the government flailing, the city's citizens decided to organize their own coronavirus response. *Atlantic (Boston, Mass.).*

Valencia, N., & Kelly, C. (2020, May 19). *CDC releases detailed guidance on reopening that had previously been shelved by White House.* CNN.

Valinsky, J. (2020, Dec. 12). *The 30 retailers and restaurant chains that filed for bankruptcy in 2020.* CNN.

Wafai, Y. (2020, May 22). Reopening phases in Washington state: When you can get a haircut, go to the gym, or eat at restaurants as coronavirus lockdowns are lifted. *The Seattle Times.*

Webel, M., & Freeman, M. C. (2020, June 5). *Compare the flu pandemic of 1918 and COVID-19 with caution.* University of Pittsburgh Medical School. https://inside.upmc.com/compare-the-flu-pandemic-of-1918-and-covid-19-with-caution/

Wen, J., Kozak, M., Yang, S., & Liu, F. (2020). COVID-19 potential effects on Chinese citizens' lifestyle and travel. *Tourism Review*, 1–19.

Willens, K., Shaffrey, T., & Hajela, D. (2020, Dec. 11). *New York City bars, restaurants pursue adaptation to survive.* ABC News.

Williams, C., & Kayaoglu, A. (2020). COVID-19 and undeclared work: Impacts and policy responses in Europe. *Service Industries Journal*, 1–32.

Yan, H., & Maxouris, C. (2020, May 18.) *Reopening the US: States relax rules, but some could return to stay-at-home orders if coronavirus cases surge.* CNN.

Youn, H., Hua, N., & Lee, S. (2015). Does size matter? Corporate social responsibility and firm performance in the restaurant industry. *International Journal of Hospitality Management, 51*, 127–134.

Zeng, Z., Chen, P.-J., & Lew, A. A. (2020). From high-touch to high-tech: COVID-19 drives robotics adoption. *Tourism Geographies*, 1–11.

ADDITIONAL READING

Hai-Jew, S. (2020, Apr.) Emergent COVID-19 and SARS-CoV-2 in social imagery and social video: Initial three months of viral dispersion. In *Social World Sensing via Social Image Analysis from Social Media.* New Prairie Press. Retrieved Oct. 23, 2020, from https://kstatelibraries.pressbooks.pub/socialworldsensing/chapter/covid19-1/

Hai-Jew, S. (2020, Apr. 15). *Social World Sensing via Social Image Analysis from Social Media.* New Prairie Press. Retrieved Aug. 21, 2020, from https://kstatelibraries.pressbooks.pub/socialworldsensing/

Hai-Jew, S. (2021). Incisive Real-Time Biosafety Decision-making under Societal Reopening: An Ego-Level Decision-Tree Understructure for A Serious Game (in the COVID-19 Pandemic Era). In Simulation and Game-Based Learning in Emergency and Disaster Management. IGI Global.

Hai-Jew, S. (2021). Observed Mass-Scale Call-Response Dynamics between Public Health Officials and American Public in Surging COVID-19 Pandemic Summer 2020: Content Analysis from Journalistic Articleset and Three-Phased Social Imagesets. In Practical Peer-to-Peer Teaching and Learning on the Social Web. IGI Global.

Hai-Jew, S. (2021). Societal shutdown and reopening and reclosing in the U.S. as expressed in social imagery narratives: COVID-19 pandemic seven/eight months. In Z. Fields (Ed.), *Handbook of Research on Using Global Collective Intelligence and Creativity to Solve Wicked Problems.* IGI Global.

Hai-Jew, S. (2021). Visual gists of home quarantines and self-quarantines from COVID-19 through social imagery: Four months into the SARS-CoV-2 disease outbreak. In Z. Fields (Ed.), *Handbook of Research on Using Global Collective Intelligence and Creativity to Solve Wicked Problems.* IGI Global.

Hai-Jew, S. (2021). Visual stories of COVID-19 social-physical distancing from tagged social imagery. In Z. Fields (Ed.), *Handbook of Research on Using Global Collective Intelligence and Creativity to Solve Wicked Problems.* IGI Global.

KEY TERMS AND DEFINITIONS

COVID-19: Corona virus disease 2019.

SARS-CoV-2: Severe acute respiratory syndrome coronavirus 2.

Undeclared Economy: Lawful work that is done under-the-table without reportage to the government; formerly, the underground economy; not the "black market" or "shadow economy," which refer to illegal dealing in illegal materials and forbidden work.

Chapter 3
A Tale of Two Hyperlocal Family-Run Stores:
Targeted Sector Supports for SMEs in the COVID-19 Pandemic Era

Shalin Hai-Jew
https://orcid.org/0000-0002-8863-0175
Kansas State University, USA

ABSTRACT

A sub-class of small and medium(-sized) enterprises (SMEs) are family-run groceries and restaurants, both businesses hard hit by the SARS-CoV-2/COVID-19 pandemic, given the high-contact person-to-person nature of both. In one American Midwestern town, there are two stores that carry Asian foodstuffs. These are B2C and B2B businesses with a limited client base and tight profit margins. Theirs are pressured businesses given the racialized cultural atmosphere around COVID-19 in the US. Both businesses took different and limited strategies to survive in this COVID-19 era. This work uses qualitative research techniques—primary mixed methods research (in a light auto-ethnography) and publicly available data sources—to conduct an in-depth content analysis to examine the two family-run stores. Some ideas are advanced about ways to support such hyperlocal stores.

INTRODUCTION

In the current SARS-CoV-2 / COVID-19 pandemic moment, almost a year to the day when the novel coronavirus was discovered in Wuhan, Hubei Province, in the

DOI: 10.4018/978-1-7998-8346-3.ch003

People's Republic of China, much of the world is again on lockdown, to try to "flatten the curve" against the virus' spread, to buy time for mass immunizations of people across the world. At this moment, the Pfizer vaccine immunizations have begun in the United Kingdom. If there is a glimmer of hope for the protection of human life, the effects are expected by the middle of 2021. Meanwhile, the pandemic has caused many businesses to shutter for good. Some of the most vulnerable businesses are small and medium-sized enterprises (SMEs), defined in different ways, but usually in reference to businesses and organizations with fewer than 100 staff. A particular sub-class of small and medium-sized enterprises are family-run stores, often carrying goods targeted to particular sub-populations. These are some of the most vulnerable businesses as the pandemic continues and as government supports of various types start to fade and the mass public remains in a low-mobility mode.

This work involves the observational and *in vivo* exploration of two competing stores in an American Midwestern town (as a light auto-ethnography based on 15 years of observations and lived experiences in the target town). These are both family owned stores that sell mostly Asian foodstuffs: noodles, rice, vegetables, fish, chicken, teas, coffees, canned goods, various bottled sauces, frozen dimsum, baked items, candies, and other goods. If the American grocery store is about "cultural meaning" and identity (Lorr, Jan. 29, 2021), these stores may be communicating messages of inclusion and sub-group support. These respective stores took different strategies and tactics to survive. Via these real-world cases, some ideas are extracted for ways that similar SMEs may be better protected as the world comes out of the pandemic's death-grip. This work was also supported by a deep review of the literature and related content analysis. The methods used are qualitative data analytics ones in combination.

REVIEW OF THE LITERATURE

This novel coronavirus pathogen was first identified in Wuhan, People's Republic of China, in December 2019. The first formal identified case in the U.S. was initially thought to be in February 2020, but more recent serologic testing of donated blood suggests that it may have already been stateside in December 2019 (Basavaraju, et al., Nov. 30, 2020). The morbidity and mortality effects of SARS-CoV-2 and its high infectivity (identified on all continents except Antarctica by February 2020), and its highly variant effects on the human body (with highly disparate effects on different sub-groups), have made this pandemic from the novel coronavirus one of the most serious threats that collective humanity has faced in 100 years. The pandemic is said to affect every aspect of people's lives.

At the moment of this work, the world has had 67.5 million known cases of infection by SARS-CoV-2, with 43.2 million recovered, and 1.54 million deaths. This is based on the COVID-19 Dashboard, maintained by the Center for Systems Science and Engineering (CSSE) at Johns Hopkins University & Medicine's Coronavirus Resource Center ("COVID-19 Dashboard," Dec. 7, 2020). In the U.S., at this dangerous moment, there have been 15.3 million cases and 290,323 deaths and 8.9 million recovered, according to the Worldometer count ("United States," Dec. 7, 2020, 23:23 GMT). These numbers are thought to be low, and an actual more accurate accounting will take place once SARS-CoV-2 / COVID-19 both have been contained (if that is possible). At the present moment, the epidemiological modelers have been exonerated, even as the terrible numbers manifest. Public health officials, with their consistent focus on the capabilities of the pathogenic virus and the actions of human populations, have stayed on message. By contrast, political leaders have been less consistent, and they have been much less committed to the health of the general public.

A Partial Bio-Defense Against SARS-CoV-2

In the current moment, humanity's only semi-credible defense at the micro and meso scales (individual and group levels) has been the following, with mindfulness in every context:

- wearing masks (ideally N95s, tested KN95s, or surgical masks, or multi-layered cloth ones, in that order of preference) in public places,
- donning face shields or goggles (or eyeglasses) in addition to protect the eyes,
- avoiding indoor congregate settings where others are present,
- social distancing from others,
- using proper hand hygiene by washing regularly,
- avoiding touching the eyes, nose, or mouth with the hands, and
- other practical good sense measures.

These disease countermeasures and defenses, even applied assiduously, are only partial. There are reports of fomite transfers of the virus. The environmental conditions can be a factor, such as air handling. In the ring of defenses for humanity, for those who do become infected, there are some limited therapeutics available to only a small minority of peoples in the world.

As free agents, people have chosen a range of lifestyles. At one extreme are those pretending everything is normal and that humanity is not in a pandemic. These go around maskless; they ignore social distancing; they socialize in indoor congregate settings. At the other extreme, there are shut-ins who try to live life in a contactless way. They sanitize everything that enters the home. They minimize exposure to others. Indeed, many did not need government advisement to start to socially distance for self-protection.

Temporary Government Shutdowns

In terms of macro-scale, global entities like the WHO and national-level governments have instituted border closings to institute a level of control over populations. They have instituted various lockdowns of domestic populations to try to slow the spread of transmission. The stay-at-home or shelter-in-place orders are emplaced to control for population mobility, de-densify indoor spaces, lower the demand on hospital care and especially intensive care unit (ICU) enrollments, to regain some measure of control. Some governments instituted the orders but avoided any enforcement. Others levied small fines for infractions. At the other end of the continuum, governments brought out national troops to enforce hard stay-at-home orders, and they even delivered food to shut-ins to maintain the strictness of the lockdowns. For the first time in human history, drones (in China) and robot dogs (in Singapore) were brought into play to enforce lockdowns.

Some governments were willing to take the hits to the economy and have massive lockdowns to save human lives. Others started out going for "herd immunity" through natural infection at a large loss of human life and no actual herd immunity achieved. And others tried a middle way: these countries saw full lockdowns as untenable for the economy and human well-being. They tried to keep essential businesses partially open even during lockdowns. Every approach has tradeoffs, and there are no costless options. In this pandemic moment (a year in), all countries are sobering about their own capabilities and national values and leadership capabilities.

The difficult balance for government is that the lockdowns do slow consumer activity and take away from the bottom lines of businesses. While these measures were credited with saving tens of millions of lives (Beaubien, June 9, 2020), these shutdowns led to the slowing and stoppage of much consumer behavior. Clusters of "essential workers" were infected due to poor mitigations in work places, like meat processing plants and factories and grocery stores. There are interruptions in various supply chains. As the virus spread in waves, the restarting and re-stopping wreaked more havoc, as governments tried to balance human health, school, economics, law enforcement, justice, and other public sector work. The government actions were also not without pushback, given citizen concerns about government intrusion into people's private lives and the potential eroding of citizens' rights. The rise of "severe moral communities," sub-populations triggered by fears into self-righteous and extremist ideas, has created an authorizing environment for swaths of the population not to follow basic health guidance in a pandemic.

"Severe Moral Communities" and Decision-Making Noise

While ICT has enabled some mitigations of pandemic disruptions, it has also enabled the rise and maintenance of what researchers call "severe moral communities," leading to "increasingly polarized, radicalized, and even extremist viewpoints" (Parra, Gupta, & Mikalef, 2021, p. 1) and poor decision-making behaviors in a time of a pandemic. Social media platforms offer the customization of contents, leading to "filter bubbles" and "echo chambers" that curtail a person's worldview. The confluence of ICT capabilities and the moment of pressures can lead to distortions in thinking. The co-authors write:

In sum, fear of threats brings about negatively-biased credulity. And threats concerning disease exposure elicits disgust, enhance in-group attraction, as well as the endorsement of binding moral foundations (i.e., in-group loyalty, authority/respect, and purity/sanctity). All of which may lead autopoietic social systems to adopt CPIs ("collectively prevalent interpretants") and CPCs ("collectively prevalent choices/capabilities"), amalgamated by fear and disgust, based on ethnocentrism and increased in-group attraction. (Parra, Gupta, & Mikalef, 2021, p. 7; parenthetical definition of terms quoted by author)

A sense of "disgust and anger" are described as "emotions of condemnation" and inform "the severity of moral judgments" (Parra, Gupta, & Mikalef, 2021, p. 8). People in such states are more open to being radicalized and turned extreme. Such a reaction may trigger various social schemas of others and exacerbate xenophobic out-group prejudices and induce negative reactions. In the present moment, such dynamics are leading to "severe moral communities choosing (NOT) to wear masks," with mask-wearing seen as "an offensive political statement, lacking virtue and even national pride" (Parra, Gupta, & Mikalef, 2021, p. 11). The same social-psychological dynamics may lead to people holding mass gatherings and congregating in closed indoor settings with others in unmasked ways (Parra, Gupta, & Mikalef, 2021, p. 13). Such polarized reactions to biosafety during a pandemic have clearly led to unnecessary infections, disease, and death.

Another research team has pointed to the importance of accurate knowledge of health risks and a cost-benefit calculus in which the person believes his or her actions outweigh the obstacles in order to create behavior change (based on the Health Belief Model). How a government communicates about the health threat affects how people respond. The co-researchers write:

In this study, perceived barriers were mainly the thought barriers about (the) current situation and they lacked the importance of disease prevention, felt there was much of media hype and secret organizations influenced political decisions which were the barriers in adopting preventive measures. Sudden influx of knowledge through different media (infodemic) made confusion among the public regarding behavioural changes. (Jose, Narendran, Bindu, Beevi, L, & Benny, 2020, p. 4)

People need to feel competent to follow through on particular behaviors and to take action, even in the face of "the perceived inconvenience, expense, danger (e.g., side effects of a medical procedure) and discomfort (e.g., pain, emotional upset" (Jose, Narendran, Bindu, Beevi, L, & Benny, 2020, p. 4).

Various studies have found varying abidance by government mandates, in the absence of full enforcement (which requires more resources than most nation-states have, with the PRC as the exception). In Australia, household travel and activities were found to result in border closings and the closing of non-essential venues to limit human contacts. Citizens limited their own mobility in order to protect themselves against the highly contagious and potentially fatal virus. From an average of 23.9 trips per week, by the end of March 2020, it was down to 11, "a reduction of over 50%"; younger households made more trips than middle and older aged ones, and "middle aged households in turn made significantly more than older households" (Beck & Hensher, 2020, p. 78). The population seemed to have responded well to public health messaging about the pandemic: "Over half of respondents (58%) are now extremely concerned about levels of hygiene on public transport, up from just 5% prior to COVID-19"; this finding was invariant across demographic groups (Beck & Hensher, 2020, p. 79). This study found a drop in virtually all forms of household trips by mode from pre-COVID to the COVID period studied: private car, taxi / ride-hailing, train, bus, ferry, and walking / bicycling (Beck & Hensher, 2020, p. 82) and citizens feeling "most comfortable" in private cars, then walking and bicycling and "least comfortable" in terms of bus riding, train / light rail, and taxi / ride-hail (p. 83). The researchers observed an overall shift to more essential types of mobility and less on recreational. Interestingly, the average day of stock of selected items varied: 11 days of food, 24 days of toilet paper, 20 days of tissues, 21 days of non-prescription medicine, and 15 days of sanitary products (Beck & Hensher, 2020, p. 88). Travel was influenced by work habits, with many working from home; others that became unemployed also traveled less.

Another study of mobility during a phase of the pandemic found, too, that "trip purposes, mode choice, distance traveled, and frequency of trips for the primary travel were significantly different before and during the pandemic" with a majority of trips made for shopping during the pandemic and a shift from public transport to private and to non-motorized modes (like bicycling and walking), although these were not at significant levels (Abdullah, Dias, Muley, & Shahin, 2020, pp. 1 and 12). Predictors of travel mode choice included "gender, car ownership, employment status, travel distance, the primary purpose of traveling, and pandemic-related underlying factors during COVID-19" (Abdullah, Dias, Muley, & Shahin, 2020, p. 1). Based on an online survey and outreach through a range of social media platforms, this research team also found that people traveled shorter distances during the pandemic for various purposes, including work, study, and shopping; people's frequency of trips also dropped (Abdullah, Dias, Muley, & Shahin, 2020, p. 4).

Just how much people in a community care for each other may be seen in responsiveness to government mandates. Those with high norms of reciprocity and trust and thus, stronger social bonds, and social capital, may be seen in the willingness to "bowl alone" or to be physically apart so as to break the chains of possible transmission. One empirical study of the February 17 – May 10, 2020 period found that several factors suppressed people's mobility in various countries: government adoption of shelter-in-place orders (SIPOs), rainy weather, and rising numbers of SARS-CoV-2 infections. This work identifies the outsized risks for those people with pre-existing medical conditions "and low levels of community level social capital," which put them at especial risk of severe COVID-19 health outcomes (Borgonovi & Andrieu, 2020, p. 1). This work enables a mapping of where major risks may reside based on the absence or presence of social capital and status. Those in high social capital counties "reduced mobility to non-essential activities compared to individuals in low social capital counties" (Borgonovi & Andrieu, 2020, p. 7).

Rethinking Social Contracts and Resets for the World

This forced global pause, a rare wholly discontinuous moment, is seen as a moment to reflect and make changes; it is an opportunity.

- How should the world recover from COVID-19, especially considering the needs of developing or emerging countries: joblessness, transportation, and sustainability?
- How can populations be lifted out of poverty (Momaya, 2020, p. 2)?
- How can people actualize "restarting supply chains to fill voids and restoring health (not only physiological, but also psychological…)? (Momaya, 2020, p. 1)
- How can food wastage be minimized? (Momaya, 2020, p. 4)

Given the current patchwork lockdowns around the world, what will the state of globalization be? Globalization is defined as "increased interconnectedness and interdependence of peoples and countries" often involving "the opening of international borders to increasingly fast flows of goods, services, finance, people and ideas, and the changes in institutions and policies at national and international levels that facilitate or promote such flows" (Jackson, 2020, p. 1). Globalization affects various dimensions of human cooperation: "economic, political, and social" (Jackson, 2020, p. 1), and certainly, health. In the pandemic era, the "collapse and re-engineering of vital structures (e.g., closure of educational establishments, businesses, with central banks adopting swift measures to support institutions, etc.)" (Jackson, 2020, p. 2) may result in new ways of functioning into the future. Even with the various setbacks from the pandemic, people should affirm the continuing importance of United Nations' 17 Sustainable Development Goals (Jackson, 2020, pp. 8-9). To address identified market failures, there need to be creative innovations and collaborations and insightful policies and practices (Jackson, 2020). The emerging countries cannot be forgotten in the reset after COVID-19.

Socio-economic Fallout

A global challenge of the magnitude of SARS-CoV-2 has resulted in "huge uncertainty" as indicated by various economic indicators hitting highs (Altig, et al., 2020, p. 1). Based on various indices, there has been "a 35% rise for the model-based measure of US economic uncertainty (relative to January 2020)" and "a 20-fold rise in forecaster disagreement about UK growth" (Altig, et al., 2020, p. 1). The projected economic volatility rises and falls with the infection patterns in world populations, and the unpredictability makes it harder to plan, invest, and act. Industrial production is projected to fall 12 – 19% (Altig, et al., 2020, p. 1). The world has experienced supply chain interruptions of personal protective equipment or PPE (Rowan & Laffey, 2020) and many other consumer goods besides. COVID-19 infection rates have a strong effect on financial markets and digital finance (Agosto & Giudici, 2020). Credit risks have heightened. Much rides on the suppression of the pathogen.

The U.S. has experienced similar headwinds. In the U.S., there have been high rises in unemployment:

To appreciate the tremendous speed with which the COVID-19 economic crisis unfolded and the magnitude of the shock, consider some observations for the United States. New claims for unemployment benefits in the early part of 2020 ranged from 200,000 – 280,000 per week. Relative to covered employment, these figures correspond to the slowest pace of new claims in the history of the series back to 1971. Over the ensuing twelve weeks 40 million Americans filed new claims, an astonishing surge without precedent in US history. As measured in the Current Population Survey, unemployment rose from 3.5% in February 2020—its lowest rate in over 60 years—to 14.7% in April, the highest rate in 80 years. US GDP fell 11.2% from 2019Q4 to 2020Q2, the largest drop since the Great Depression. A similar story of sharply contracting output emerged in the UK, with GDP falling a record 20.4% in April – June after a fall of 2.2% in January – March. In sum, the speed and scale of the COVID-19 contraction dwarfs that of any previous US or UK episode in the modern era. (Altig, et al., 2020, p. 2)

Citizens have experienced harsh socio-economic impacts, too. They have lost businesses. They have lost livelihoods. They have experienced food insecurity and hunger. They have experienced societal breakdowns in social order. In February 2020, the U.S. fell into recession (Smialek, June 8, 2020).

Hits to the "High-Contact" Hospitality Industry

Hospitality includes "lodging, food and drink service, event planning, theme parks, and transportation" and high-contact services in "hotels, restaurants, and bars" ("Hospitality industry," Dec. 3, 2020). This sector accounts for "20% of the U.S. GDP" and employs "30% of the U.S. labor force" according to the International Trade Administration, in 2018, as cited in Huang, Makridis, Baker, Medeiros, & Guo, 2020, p. 2). The pandemic-induced shutdowns and various government policies resulted in massive and precipitous job losses in the hospitality labor market: "a 20 – 30% reduction of non-salaried workers in the food/drink and leisure/entertainment sectors during March – April of 2020" (Huang, Makridis, Baker, Medeiros, & Guo, 2020, p. 1).

The U.S. eschewed a federal response to the pandemic, leaving states to fend for themselves for PPE, test kits, and other resources. States conduct their own disease surveillance. They output their own policies for shutdowns and other mitigations. This country has a "fragmented, arbitrary, and broken COVID-19 response" (Hotez, 2020, p. 398). Given the federated and patchwork state-by-state response to the pandemic in the U.S. (instead of a coordinated federal response), researchers have found "considerable differences…in the impact of policies on the labor market by state" based on high frequency data. Rises

in COVID-19 infections affect the labor market negatively because consumers will not venture out when there are high viral loads in the population. Various businesses have put in place heightened sanitation measures. They've set up plexiglass shields to separate customers from staff and also set up social distancing decals on floors (Huang, Makridis, Baker, Medeiros, & Guo, 2020, p. 7). These actions do not seem to have earned the confidence of potential consumers to contact-heavy industries.

Experts predict some 44 – 57 million U.S. jobs to be directly impacted by the pandemic and "roles in food services and accommodation are predicted to be most drastically affected" (McKinsey and Company, 2020, as cited in Huang, Makridis, Baker, Medeiros, & Guo, 2020, p. 2).

One particular hard-hit business category has been restaurants, which have been the target of various shutdowns because of the high-contact close-human proximity required for in-person dining. While outdoor dining and takeout have typically been allowed to continue, the restrictions on in-person dining with de-densification rules (e.g. restaurants can only open with 20 – 50% capacity) and phases of full shutdowns have taken a toll. One study explored U.S. restaurant firms' stock returns in the pandemic phase vs. pre-pandemic, with focuses on firm-level dimensions: "financial conditions, corporate strategies, and ownership structure" (Song, Yeon, & Lee, 2021, p. 1). They found that "restaurant firms with past characteristics of larger size, more leverage, more cash flows, less ROA (return on assets), and more internationalization" tend to be more resilient to stock declines (Song, Yeon, & Lee, 2021, p. 1); surprisingly, managerial ownership" did not show any significant moderating effect on the relationship between COVID-19 and stock returns" (p. 1). Leverage has been found to have mixed implications. There are some indications that there is "a negative moderating role of leverage, in that more leverage of a firm under external shock signals a potential increase in business risks" but also a positive moderating effect of leverage that "restaurant firms with more leverage are more resilient in the face of stock reactions to COVID-19 shock" (Song, Yeon, & Lee, 2021, p. 6), which the co-authors suggest might seem less of a concern given the magnitude of the shock affecting the whole sector.

Government policies to fight the pandemic directly affect consumer behaviors, such as panic buying. One study found that the lockdown policy (LDP) and Timed Intervention Policy (TIP) of "phased lockdowns and social distancing measures at different times based on the virus-status within the community" have both intended and unintended effects (Prentice, Chen, & Stantic, 2020, p. 1). Lockdowns tend to occur in escalatory phases:

The first stage of lockdown normally takes place at the epicenter – the place of the outbreak of the virus. The second stage is closure of institutions such as universities, schools, and places where there may be large gatherings. The third stage is home quarantine with limited mobility and access only to essential activities. The final stage is large-scale lockdown with complete restrictions on mobility. (Prentice, Chen, & Stantic, 2020, p. 1)

It is difficult to get the timing right, especially in the absence of perfect awareness and complete information, and often in the face of resistance from the general population. This study examined to see if there was a link between government COVID-19 measures and panic buying based on social data from the microblogging site, Twitter. Initial shutdowns did indeed trigger the mass purchasing of essential items, given fears of shortages from disruptions to the supply chain. In terms of panic buying: "Items that were most popular were toilet paper, staples (e.g. rice, pasta), flu related medicine, long-life products, canned and frozen food, and consumer electronics. There was a 35% increase in retail food spending, a 60% jump in the pharmacy and toiletry spend, and a 22% rise in electronic purchases" (Prentice, Chen, & Stantic, 2020, p. 5). One social media post shows a man stands by the side of the road with a sign: "Will work for toilet paper" (Prentice, Chen, & Stantic, 2020, p. 7). There were also ties between releases of stimulus packages to the public and panic shopping. On social media, initial sentiment towards panic buying was negative but turned positive over time, possibly due to increased efficiencies in various stores getting needed items on the shelves. (Prentice, Chen, & Stantic, 2020, p. 10)

Another study also explored panic buying in this pandemic. Such consumer behavior was common across the board in March "but with significant variation in the timing and severity of panic between countries" (Keane & Neal, 2020, p. 1). Based on Google search data, these researchers conducted "a daily index of consumer panic (buying) for 54 countries from January 1st to April 30th 2020" and found that both domestic and world virus transmissions affected consumer panic buying behaviors. Government policy and internal (within-country) movement restrictions led to "substantial short run panic" that lasted a week to 10 days and then faded. These co-researchers found that early restrictions to citizen movement engendered more panic than later ones. Stimulus announcements had impacts also on panic buying but at a lesser level. Finally, "travel restrictions" were not found to generate consumer panic (Keane & Neal, 2020, p. 2).

On a Section of Main Street

In the U.S., small businesses have a high failure rate. A fifth (20%) fail in the first year. By the fifth year, 50% of new businesses have failed. This is so across various industries, from manufacturing to construction to hospitality. The attitude in the U.S. is that "creative destruction" is necessary, and businesses should "fail fast" and move on to the next thing. The romance of starting and running a business and being able to determine one's own work hours has been an ongoing dream of many, even as the landscape itself can be treacherous (with life savings, health, and reputations lost in some endeavors, not to mention opportunity costs) and a tough proving ground. Certainly, with external shocks and the bottom dropping out of the market, the headwinds against business survival increase.

Those who start and run businesses have to be entrepreneurial and risk-taking to put so much on the line. They have to be willing to play to the edge. Others who may not align with such a personality profile may be forced into it by a lack of other available employment, which suggests that a small business is their lifeline to core survival.

Small and Medium(-sized) Enterprises (SMEs).

SMEs are seen as "engines of national economies" (Ruffo, Mnisri, Morin-Esteves, & Gendron, 2020, p. 396). The European Commission asserts that "SMEs represent 99% of all businesses in the European Union…" and created "more than 85% of the new jobs and provided around 2/3 of the total private sector employment in the EU" in the past 5 years (Ruffo, Mnisri, Morin-Esteves, & Gendron, 2020, p. 397). These smaller-scale enterprises play an important role in the U.S. as well. According to the Small Business Profiles for the States and Territories (by the Office of Advocacy, an office in the U.S. Small Business Administration), small businesses in 2019 added "1.8 million net new jobs" in 2018. Further, the U.S. "has 30.7 million small businesses, and they employ 47.3 percent of the private workforce" ("Small businesses…," Apr. 24, 2019). The top three industries of small businesses in the States include the following: "(1) health care and social assistance, (2) accommodation and food services, and (3) retail trade" ("Small businesses…," Apr. 24, 2019). In some locales, unemployment is an important driver for SME formation (Tambunan, 2008a, as cited in Madonono & Barnard, 2020, p. 27) because no other paying jobs are available to parts of the populace. Typically, SMEs are developed and advanced through "exports, innovation, and technology" and require knowledge, creativity, expertise, and investments (Madonono & Barnard, 2020, p. 27). The requirements may be limiting factors for many small firms and organizations.

SMEs experience pressures from larger firms, with greater competitive advantages, and they also experience pressures from the rising expectations of consumers. By dint of their size, SMEs experience "higher chances of failure…due to their liability of smallness and higher institutional pressures coming from their embeddedness in local networks of actors" (Freeman et al., 1983, as cited in Ruffo, Mnisri, Morin-Esteves, & Gendron, 2020, p. 395). SMEs "have fewer resources (i.e. financial, managerial, human and informational), less well-trained managers, and less developed relationships with creditors" (Bruderl & Schussler, 1990, as cited in Ruffo, Mnisri, Morin-Esteves, & Gendron, 2020, p. 398). Such organizations tend to be "preoccupied by immediate issues of the day-to-day survival" and therefore do not have time to strategize "about the future" (Fitjer, 2011, as cited in Ruffo, Mnisri, Morin-Esteves, & Gendron, 2020, p. 398). In relationship to other entities, SMEs experience various power asymmetries and imbalances. Still, they are expected to conduct core functions and simultaneously engage in "corporate social responsibilities" (CSR) and contribute to societal goals, whether voluntarily or through legal requirements (Bikefe, Zubairu, Araga, Maitala, Ediuku, & Anyebe, 2020, p. 17).

The legitimacy of a SME affects its access to resources and ultimately affects its organizational survival. The sense of "acquired legitimacy" of SMEs are based on "instrumental, relational and moral evaluations" but "deferred legitimacy" is based on "mainly instrumental evaluations" (Ruffo, Mnisri, Morin-Esteves, & Gendron, 2020, p. 395). Sources of legitimacy are often taken from "clients and employees" (Ruffo, Mnisri, Morin-Esteves, & Gendron, 2020, p. 395). There are various types of organizational legitimacy: regulatory (based on rules and laws), normative (based on "core technology, key competencies, quality of services, and qualifications of actors"), and cultural-cognitive legitimacy ("cultural beliefs and taken-for-granted assumptions") (Ruffo, Mnisri, Morin-Esteves, & Gendron, 2020, p. 397). SMEs have to satisfy the needs of the so-called dominant stakeholders: "customers, employees, suppliers and investors" (Ruffo, Mnisri, Morin-Esteves, & Gendron, 2020, p. 399) as compared to discretionary ones including "family members, political groups (associations), standard-setting and award-granting organizations and community" (Sen & Cowley, 2013, as cited in Ruffo, Mnisri, Morin-Esteves, & Gendron, 2020, p. 400). Various factors inform how a SME is viewed and its perceived legitimacy.

This pandemic-informed state of affairs has had deleterious effects on small and medium(-sized) enterprises (SMEs), particularly those without much of a financial cushion or so-called rainy day funds. The intuition is that "firms with larger size and more cash, on average, are prone to tolerate the demanding period more effectively by funding themselves" (Song, Yeon, & Lee, 2021, p. 6). Given the common public policy response of enforcing temporary closures of non-essential businesses, SMEs come under increasing risk of failure if these lockdowns occur in a protracted way. One research team in the UK probed the vulnerability of SMEs and found that "only 39% of the...businesses were bolstering their cash balances leading up to COVID-19 which suggests that 61% of businesses may run out of cash, including 8.6% that had no retained earnings whatsoever with micro firms at particular risk" (Cowling, Brown, & Rocha, 2020, p. 593). Only 40% of the studied small firms had been saving for a crisis in the last five years (Cowling, Brown, & Rocha, 2020, p. 600). The scope of the savings were insufficient for a combination of factors such as the present moment. The micro, small, and medium firms were found to be at both immediate- and medium-term risk of failure, with "no retained cash" and "not seen bolstering their cash pile" respectively (Cowling, Brown, & Rocha, 2020, p. 602).

A visual gist of small- and medium-sized firms in the age of COVID-19 may be seen in Figure 1. This shows a word cloud from hundreds of articles published in 2020 about "SMEs and COVID-19". Note the predominance of the disease COVID-19 and the sense of risk, and crisis. For the frequency count, no additional words were added to the stopwords list. NVivo was used for creating this exploratory data visualization.

Figure 1. A Word Frequency Word Cloud of "SME and COVID-19" Articles

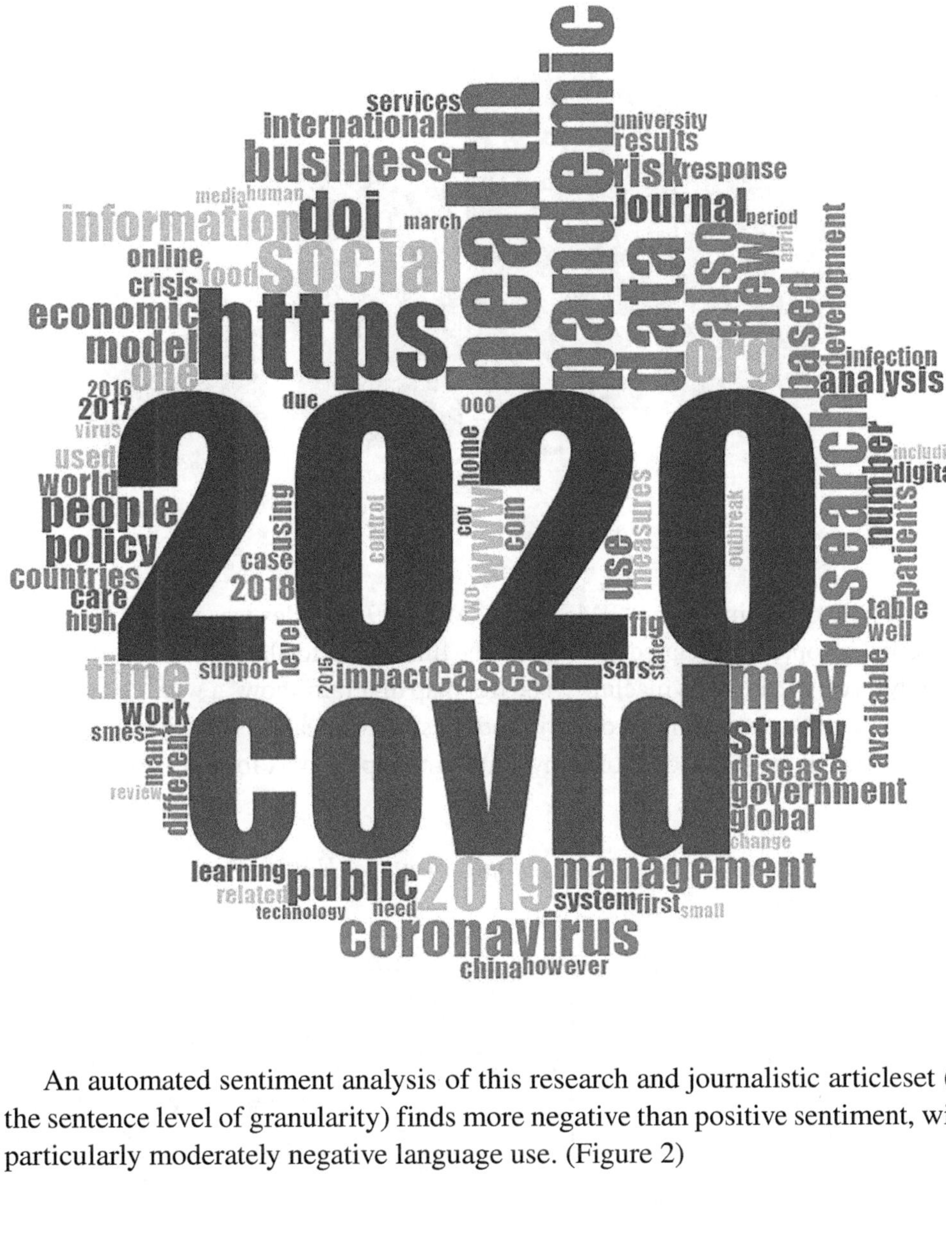

An automated sentiment analysis of this research and journalistic articleset (at the sentence level of granularity) finds more negative than positive sentiment, with particularly moderately negative language use. (Figure 2)

Figure 2. A Sentiment Analysis of "SME and COVID-19" Articles

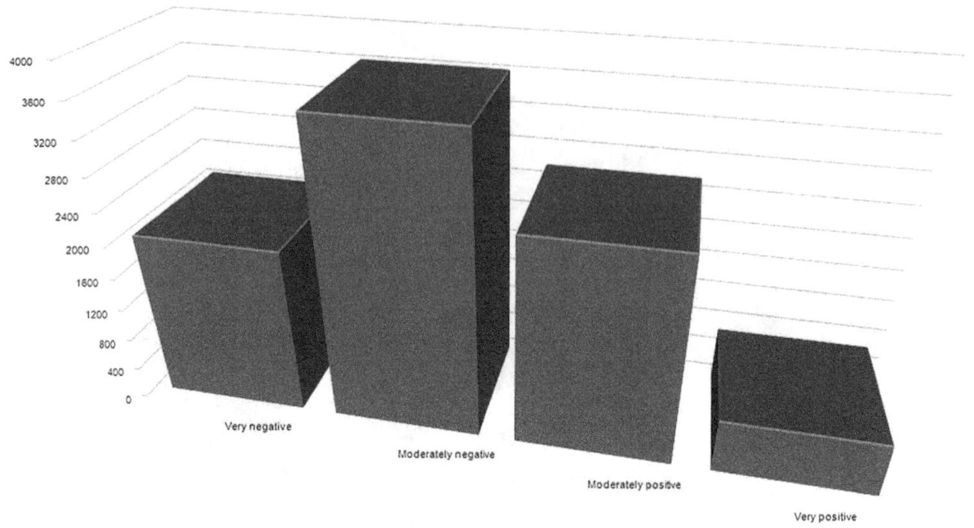

A sample of a third of the "SME and COVID-19" articles was run for the auto-extraction of topics and related subtopics. The full set was too large to run for this type of analysis on the author's machine. The treemap diagram shows a wide complexity of topics, with various dimensionality, and these also speak to logistics. (Figure 3) A complete autocoded codebook is available in Appendix A for more exploration.

Figure 3. Autocoded Topics and Subtopics from a Half-Set of the "SME and COVID-19" Articles

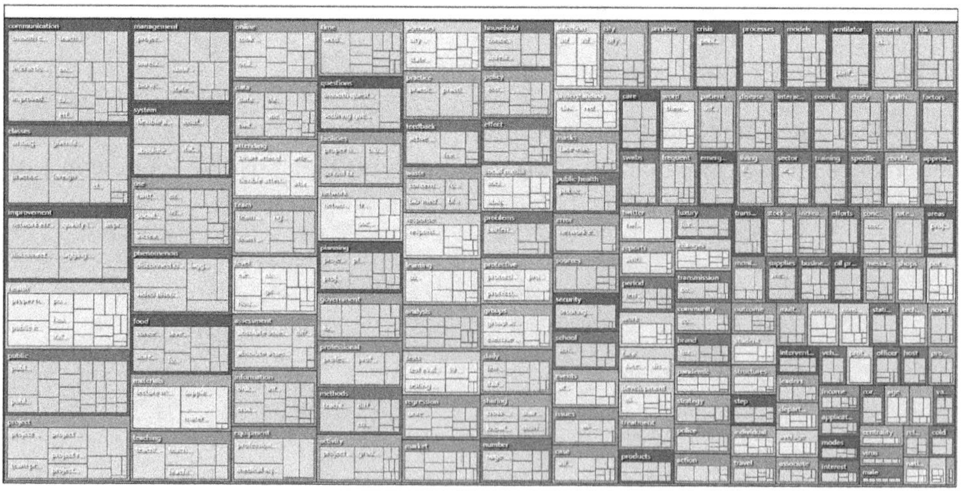

The prior figures provide a visual summary sense of the published academic and journalistic works around SMEs and COVID-19. More in-depth summaries of these works follow.

Perceived Needs of SMEs

An online survey and direct interview study was conducted on 4,807 SMEs in Sichuan Province, a neighboring province to Hubei Province (which contains the city of Wuhan, where COVID-19 apparently broke out in late 2019). With the outbreak, the government "focused on saving lives by conducting stringent control measures, which unavoidably resulted in an economic decline" (Lu, Wu, Peng, & Lu, 2020, p. 338). Transportation was blocked across the country, and "asynchronous work resumption" had effects "on upstream and downstream industrial chains" (Lu, Wu, Peng, & Lu, 2020, p. 335). In many ways, China's experience was of a kind of managed system shutdown, without a clear end in sight. The policy and strict surveillance and enforcement affected various small businesses, among others:

It was found that most SMEs were unable to resume work because of a shortage of epidemic mitigation materials, the inability of employees to return to work, disrupted supply chains, and reduced market demand. Many SMEs were also facing cash flow risks as they had to continue to pay for various fixed expenditures even though they had little or no revenue. (Lu, Wu, Peng, & Lu, 2020, p. 323)

The researchers of this work call for ways to stimulate consumption to bring back market demand; they suggest the importance of financial support for small business owners to ensure cash flow (so they can pay their fixed costs); they propose various forms of relief to get past the dangerous moment (Lu, Wu, Peng, & Lu, 2020), in a state capitalist system (which is shifting from a manufacturing-based export-oriented economy to one focused on internal or domestic population consumption).

Those who are self-employed tend to have earnings that are "relatively low and volatile, a risk that exacerbated during the recent COVID-19 pandemic" and made worse by "psychological distress" (Patel & Rietveld, 2020, p. 1). Compared to wage workers, the self-employed are experiencing more stress because of the sense of financial insecurity defined here as "the chance of running out of money" (Patel & Rietveld, 2020, p. 1). This research recorded a continuum of negative feelings: nervousness and anxiety, depression, loneliness, hopelessness about the future, and even physical reactions like "sweating, trouble breathing, nausea or a pounding heart" (Patel & Rietveld, 2020, p. 7). These researchers found that "the chance of keeping one's job mediates the relationship between self-employment and psychological distress in the sample" (Patel & Rietveld, 2020, p. 8).

There are additional psychosocial pressures from social isolations to limit the spread of the novel coronavirus for the general public (Dubey, et al., 2020, p. 781). The heightened risks for frontline health workers result in documented experiences of "unavoidable stress, fear and anxiety" (Dubey, et al., 2020, p. 781). There are differential impacts on different sub-populations, such as children, elderly people, domestic caregivers, the general public, the homeless, the marginalized (including those experiencing "financial insecurity"), those with pre-existing psychiatric conditions, and others (Dubey, et al., 2020, pp. 782 - 785).

In the Global Epicenter of the COVID-19 Outbreak: The U.S.

In the U.S., Dr. Deborah Birx, White House coronavirus response coordinator, suggested that the Winter 2021 COVID surge will be the "worst event that this country will face" (Higgins, Dec. 6, 2020), with a projected half a million to 750,000 American dead from COVID-19 by Spring 2021. The horrific (and climbing) human toll in the U.S. has been attributed to a lack of "a federal plan or roadmap" and "no federal directive or visible champion for implementing a national strategy" (Hotez, 2020, p. 397). The poor implementation of a public health response has meant that at this present moment, in December 2020, the country is in another effective lockdown while the country itself is the global epicenter of the SARS-CoV-2 outbreak.

The U.S. Congress drafted and passed the Paycheck Protection Program (PPP) through the Small Business Association to protect workers' paychecks, to keep people receiving a paycheck and connected to their workplace. These loans prior to June 5 would mature in two years; those after June 5 would mature in five. The interest rate for these loans was a low 1%, and there were no origination fees. Written into this program was loan forgiveness if certain conditions were met. The government site reads:

Borrowers may be eligible for loan forgiveness if the funds were used for eligible payroll costs, payments on business mortgage interest payments, rent, or utilities during either the 8- or 24-week period after disbursement. A borrower can apply for forgiveness once it has used all loan proceeds for which the borrower is requesting forgiveness. Borrowers can apply for forgiveness any time up to the maturity date of the loan. If borrowers do not apply for forgiveness within 10 months after the last day of the covered period, then PPP loan payments are no longer deferred and borrowers will begin making loan payments to their PPP lender. ("Paycheck Protection Program," n.d.)

The program itself closed August 8, 2020. However, the $669 billion for PPP (as part of the Coronavirus Aid, Relief and Economic Security Act or "CARES

Act") dissipated quickly ("Paycheck Protection Program," Dec. 6, 2020). By late September, 100,000 small businesses that had temporarily shut down had permanently closed (Sraders & Lambert, Sept. 28, 2020). In the intervening months, many more businesses have shuttered permanently. The political palatability of government supports for businesses and individuals in this time has been in question given the ideal of "small government" and "free markets" among Republicans in the U.S.

There are efforts to support European SMEs as well. Researchers suggest that government policies should be sensitive to the respective needs of various small and medium-sized enterprises instead of pursuing a one-size-fits-all approach (Juergensen, Guimón, & Narula, 2020, p. 499). They also suggest the importance of support for SMEs over time. In the short-term, liquidity may be the main issue. In the medium- and long- terms, there may be needs for employee retraining, acquisition and implementation of various technologies, long-term investments, and support for interrelationships with other business entities (Juergensen, Guimón, & Narula, 2020, p. 503). The policy mix could include "reduction of working hours and temporary unemployment; deferral of tax, social security payments, debt payments, and rent and utility payments; loan guarantees; direct lending to SMEs; grants and subsidies" but also in the longer term "support for internationalization; innovation support schemes; training and skills development; teleworking and digitalization; cluster development and networking initiatives; entrepreneurship and start-up support" (Juergensen, Guimón, & Narula, 2020, p. 506).

SURVIVAL STRATEGIES FOR SMEs

In the literature, there are various documented survival strategies for SMEs, which are seen to require constant attention and resources to merely exist.

Crowdfunding as a Survival Strategy

Another survival approach for some small and medium-sized businesses has been to share their stories on crowdfunding sites in order to raise funds from the general public (a majority of which have also been enervated by circumstances). Crowdfunding refers to the practice of eliciting funds from the general public as an "alternate finance option for different purposes of businesses…, individuals…, local communities…, and (the) public sector" (Zhao, Harris, & Lam, 2020, p. 1). A more up-to-date definition of crowdfunding reads as "raising finance for projects from the crowd often through an internet-based platform where project owners pitch their idea to potential backers, who are typically not professional investors" (Kallio & Vuola, 2020, p. 209). One common method used online is for donation-based (charitable) crowdfunding (Zhao, Harris, & Lam, 2020, p. 6), in which donors do not receive a direct return. Crowdfunding is a modern spinoff of "the old concept of crowdsourcing with roots going back to the 1700s" (Zhao, Harris, & Lam, 2020, p. 10). Oftentimes, based on the transparent data shared on crowdfunding sites, the donations are small and piecemeal but can add up given the size of the population willing to engage with their own funds.

Internationalization as a Survival Strategy

Another strategy for SME survival is to be competitive globally by finding export markets abroad. The SMEs with international presences require innovation and risk-taking (Nummela, Vissak, & Francioni, 2020, p. 4).

Digitalization as a Survival Strategy

A study of 518 Chinese SMEs found that going to digitalization and using ICTs enabled them to respond to the public crisis better and to increase efficiencies in their work (Guo, Yang, Huang, & Guo, 2020, p. 1). Digitalization is seen as beneficial both in the short and long terms (Guo, Yang, Huang, & Guo, 2020, p. 10). Another study suggests that the harnessing of digital-enabled connectivity for SMEs to "develop and improve their relational capabilities" benefits organizational resilience (Els, Grobbelaar, & Kennon, 2020, p. 67).

There have been various policy actions taken in the Russian Federation to address the outbreaks there. Credit holidays have been emplaced for those with debt. There has been "a temporary moratorium on bankruptcy at the request of creditors…, insurance contributions…reduced, rent payments delayed (on municipal and state property), and tax, customs and other inspections of small and medium-sized enterprises…suspended" and other endeavors (Malinovsky, Osina, & Trikoz, 2020, p. 284). There are particular state supports for SMEs:

State support measures for SMEs are the following: grant a deferral on loans and all taxes, with the exception of VAT for the next 6 months, and for microenterprises—also provide additional deferrals on insurance contributions to social funds; decrease in half (up to 15%) the amount of insurance contributions by the amount of the salary exceeding the minimum wage; introduce a moratorium on inspections of SMEs, including tax audits, with the exception of issues that pose risks to the life and health of citizens; expand the program for subsidizing the access of SMEs to borrowed funds; restructure loans of the borrower—a subject of SMEs; subsidy…; …temporary postponement (or moratorium) on the payment of rental payments by subjects of SME-tenants of state or municipal property; provide coverage of preferential microloans by SMEs; expand the capabilities of SMEs to obtain soft loans in the absence of collateral; reduce requirements for securing contracts during public procurement from SMEs; not apply penalties, as well as extend terms and price adjustments in 2020… (Malinovsky, Osina, & Trikoz, 2020, pp. 285-286)

Other measures are under consideration to mitigate follow-on impacts as the pandemic continues.

A TALE OF TWO FAMILY-RUN STORES: TARGETED SECTOR SUPPORTS FOR SMES IN THE COVID-19 PANDEMIC ERA

SMEs are "a complex system of cultural, process, and technological components that interact with each other" (DuPreez, Essman, Louw, Schutte, Marais, & Bam, 2009, as cited in Els, Grobbelaar, & Kennon, 2020, p. 69). In the present moment, there are severe external risks to SMEs given the global pandemic and the suppression of consumer purchasing of services and products and highly disruptive changes to people's lifestyles and mobility. A sub-class of SME is the family-owned grocery store and / or restaurant (sometimes linked). Business survival of such entities may be understood as essentially making a profit (taking in more than paying out) through the following:

- Protection of lives and health of the business owners, staff, and customers
- Facilities maintenance
- Security
- Inflow of goods
- Outflow of goods
- Payment of bills
- Recordkeeping, accounting
- Maintenance of customer base (customer loyalty) (customer relationship management)
- Acquisition of new customers (advertising, marketing, special sales)
- Maintenance of relationships with suppliers
- Adherence to legal business practices
- Protection of brand and reputation
- Continuing expression of values
- Maintenance of market share

Essentially, survival means business continuance even if it is markedly not a "business as usual" case. The main *raison d'être* of businesses have to be maintained.

Two Cases *in Vivo*

This work uses real-world primary observations of two family-owned grocery stores (LLCs? Sole proprietorships?) carrying mostly Asian foodstuffs (one of the stores also carries some African foodstuffs) of how they both took different strategies and tactics to survive in the pandemic era. Based on these two cases (n=2), some insights are attained about what may be done locally to mitigate the impacts of SARS-CoV-2 / COVID-19 on a particular type of SME, the family-owned small shop.

These are both in the same town in the American Midwest. One opened in 1984, and the other in 2010, so both have passed the initial tests of survival through some dangerous moments for small businesses.. There are some details masked and hidden, such as the financial performance of each of the privately owned stories, their respective evolutions, and their individual histories. It is not yet clear if either, both, or neither of the stores survives the current stresses and tests. This work is written without the permission of either of the owners because this is not an in-depth analysis of either privately-held business. This work also brings in both academic research and journalistic mass media coverage, given the freshness of the topic and the dearth of other information streams in a time of renewed lockdown.

An additional angle to these cases is the fact that both represent Asian-America in the heartland, in a time when the pandemic is being blamed on the P.R.C. where the virus originated and SARS-CoV-2 is disparagingly referred to as the "China virus" by the U.S. president (apparently to stoke racial animus). That the pandemic has been accompanied by an "infodemic" (information + epidemic) including "outbursts of racism, stigmatization, and xenophobia" (Dubey, et al., 2020, p. 779), which has had implications for psycho-social well-being of many in the populations.

The Resident County and Mobility in Prior Several Months

Both of the stores co-exist in the same county, which is home to a major university and is close to a military base. To offer a geographical context, some mobility data from the "Google COVID-19 Community Mobility Reports" may be informative. The data covers Feb. – Dec. 2020. Figures 4 and 5 show a community still in essential lockdown with much less movement for retail, work-based travel, but some increases in grocery and residential travel (essentials). At the moment of data capture, students were finishing out the Fall Semester 2020, with the campus partially open for de-densified learning and a majority of students taking classes online or in blended fashion (with some on-campus study and some online).

Figure 4. -- County Mobility Data Trends Feb. – Dec. 2020 (scattergraph)
Note: The above data comes from "Google COVID-19 Community Mobility Reports," downloaded Dec. 8, 2020.

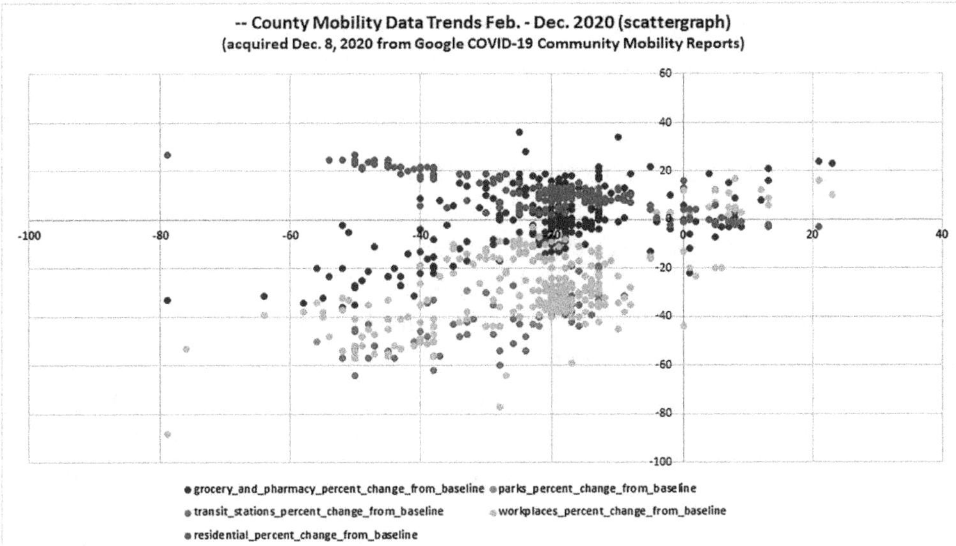

Figure 5. -- County Mobility Data Trends Feb. – Dec. 2020 (linegraph)
Note: The above data comes from "Google COVID-19 Community Mobility Reports," downloaded Dec. 8, 2020.

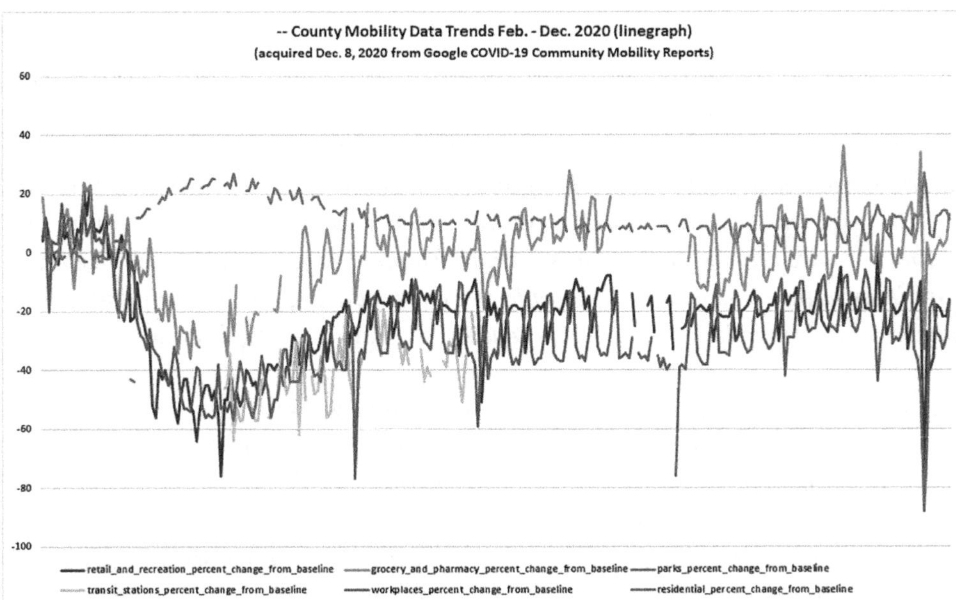

The politics of the town tend towards conservative, with much pushback against masking even against the governor's orders. Her first mask mandate was opted out of by many counties; in the face of surging COVID-19 cases, her second mask mandate was more widely accepted. At the moment, there is a 5% infection rate in the community and a test positivity rate closer to 50% (suggesting a dearth of testing and much hidden spread in the community).

Notes About the Two Competing Stores

Store 1. *For years, I had observed various locals come into the Asian food store run by a husband-and-wife pair. One time, a couple from the community came in looking for either a "fudge" or "brownie" mix. It seemed like that was their first time in the store. Perhaps they walked in from the neighborhood. They missed the signage that indicated that this was a store for Asian food, and there was nothing close to anything chocolate available on the shelves. The cashier-wife-co-owner politely explained that the store did not carry that. And the two—apparent a couple—left on foot.*

Usually, a variety of students from the local university, long-term residents in town, and others would come by for particular ingredients or snack foods or frozen foods. Some would chat with the proprietors in Korean. In the summers, when the college town would empty of students, the proprietors would gently mention that their sales had fallen through the floor because so few came to the shop. One of the downsides of being in a college town is that it can be a little "feast" or "famine" with customers, given that the main draw is the school.

The brand of the store has always been for cleanliness and hygiene. It is known for regular hours. It is known for fair prices. The produce is fresh, and on Tuesdays, when the main truck comes, they may have fresh crabs, fresh-baked goods from Chicago wrapped in plastic, and other goods. Sometimes, there is hand-made gimbap on Styrofoam trays and wrapped in plastic. (Given the fear of the virus riding on various prepared foods, some stores initially stopped serving such foods. Later, as more information was available, people started preparing foods again and selling them.) If one brings in cloth bags, there is even a several-cent discount.

Now, in the middle of the pandemic, whenever the bell rings indicating that someone had come into the store, all heads turn. The eyes go to the face: Is the person wearing a mask and what kind of mask? Is it a singleton or a couple or a group? The shop's aisles had not changed and new spaces created to enable de-densification of people, and anyone walking down the middle aisle would not be 6' away or socially distanced from others in another aisle. The most recent time I went shopping there, I scoped out the gravel parking lot to make sure there were not many cars. There was only that of the owner, so I went in, and I was surprised to see one shopper here (who probably arrived on foot). While shopping, multiple people came in, and then a half-dozen people in their 20s came in. The cashier called out to her husband to stand at the door to stop any others from coming in. The store was suddenly very full and felt dangerous.

The cashier-proprietor who serves as cashier wears crumpled cloth masks that seem to be one-layer and not particularly safe as a barrier, for her or those around her. On the door is only a hand-written sign requesting that people mask. That sign only went up long after the town's commissioners had put in a mask mandate (after rejecting earlier ones earlier in the pandemic). The couple that run the store are pretty laid back, and they do not seem like the type of enforce a mask rule; they do not come across as people who would call the police on potential patrons. Their shop is in a poorer part of town, and their life savings (perhaps multi-general moneys) are apparently invested into it, based on an older interview with a local publication. If they end up antagonizing anyone, the offended know where to find them and know where the shop is. (It is possible, too, that there are remittances abroad from the store's earnings, given family ties back to an originating country.)

And even from a distance, people can complain via social media; they can go to the Better Business Bureau. In a small town, a complaint gets around. If the shop is the location of an outbreak, I think this could easily hit the local grapevine and the local press. If a person came in unmasked, I assume they would just air out the store. But with the advent of colder weather, even that is not a certainty. If it is true that the SARS-CoV-2 virus can hang in the air for up to some 20-days and still be infective, then those going to the shop are taking a pretty big risk. The lack of tracking to know where a person may have gotten infected lessens the potential for accountability.

There may be language barrier issues. The first language of the proprietors is not English. While the proprietors' child is American-born, it is not clear how much information flows to the parents from that channel. It is unclear how much information the proprietors consume about this unprecedented viral spillover with new information virtually daily and complex science involved.

Still, the last two times I was there, once I was done with the shopping basket, it was kept behind the counter to be "sanitized" later (meaning that the handles and other high-touch surfaces are wiped down with soap). There is a small plastic container of hand sanitizer at the counter. There are no three-layer surgical masks (or anything else) that people can use if they did not bring their own face covering. The proprietor herself wears a thin one-layer cloth mask which looks like a minimal effort. Everyone is trying, to varying degrees. The game is to get as much life in as possible without getting infected and taking on all health consequences and medical costs and social stigmas.

If this store is like many with a large percentage of holiday sales making up their annual earnings (anywhere from a third to a half to 80% for various SMEs), then this will be a harsh season for various reasons. The students at the local university have gone home for Thanksgiving and will finish out their term remotely with online courses, to try to slow the spread of SARS-CoV-2 / COVID-19. Many of the regular patrons are older and are leery of going out. (They are often the ones wearing N95s and KN95s, the highest level protection of masks.)

Store 2. *The owners of this Asian food store prides itself on its wide variety of goods from around the world, including products from the Indian subcontinent, Africa, and other locales. This store is part of a small mall with a next-door restaurant, which the family also owns. The store has occasional cellophane-wrapped trays of treats created in the kitchen next door. It has a small room off the main shopping area where fresh meats may be sectioned and packaged for sale. Store 2 has a larger physical footprint than Store 1. Its selection is wider. Its prices are higher. Store 2 does not only for a B2C business; it also has a B2B by providing products to a local restaurant.*

The store proprietors are a mother and two of her daughters. Together, the multigenerational group is bilingual.

The store has a social media presence, which they use to good effect. They share photos of the various goods in the store. They showcase their ties to the broader community: the local military base, the university, and the various professional business groups. One of the co-owners does frequent media appearances on local television and radio.

They take the corporate social responsibility or CSR role seriously, with one of the co-owners coming out strongly for Black Lives Matter (BLM) in the aftermath of George Floyd's suffocation by police. Theirs is a practice of social betterment and social justice. There is also some building of bridges for Asian-Black solidarity.

They have an aggressive social outreach policy. Once after a purchase at the store, one of the co-owners reached out to me via social media (Facebook) and email at the university, wholly unsolicited. Such an approach is highly rare and could be seen as intrusive.

When the county announced required masking, the store had an unfortunate incident when one of their staff became infected with SAR-CoV-2. (The store shared this news on their website albeit without identifying the staff member given HIPAA rules of privacy.) It was unclear if that infection occurred in-store or in some other space. The store immediately shut down for a high-profile sanitation, restricted in-person shopping, and set up an order form on their site for "contactless" purchases and curbside pickup at the store location. Their pivot was near-instantaneous, and their actions were transparently communicated to the broad public through the social networking site, their microblogging account, and various outreaches to mass media and local media (such as a local magazine). They have continued these offered services even as some in-store traffic re-started. (Their delivery service ran for several weeks but was stopped once in-store traffic resumed. In one interview "brag," the store owners described how they once drive half an hour one-way to deliver goods to keep customers supplied.) As more information came out about how to make indoor store spaces safer, they started allowing some limited number of people to shop simultaneously in-store. They hired a "bodyguard" to control the numbers of entrants at the front door. When I drove by several times, though, while I saw the bodyguard and a full parking lot of shoppers, I did not see any line of people waiting. I saw no one waiting in the cars and trucks and vans. It looked like everyone in the parking lot was inside shopping, which seems to have defeated the purpose. There was a sense that the guard was there for security theatre (or social posturing) more than for actual de-densification and optimal bio-safety (or any deep compliance with COVID-19 compliance measures for the service industry). In general, the "game" is to create a sense that the physical store is a bio-safe location or the best approximation of one, against an invisible and lethal airborne and respiratory droplet-borne zoonotic pathogen.

Over the summer, road construction meant that one of two main streets to access the store was blocked for many months. Perhaps that challenge was just one of many in 2020, for that store.

It is unclear whether Store 1 and Store 2 are distressed businesses. Certainly, by sector and likelihood, they are. By direct observations, of lessened traffic, of their messaging, it is likely that both are under pressure.

While observations have been made about how both have adjusted, to varying degrees, neither seems to have changed their amount of inventory as a response, based on visits to both stores. It is important to note that there are upstream businesses that supply both of these stores, from various locales around the world. How these two stores fare will have implications on them, not only on the local community here.

At present, both seem to be "getting by" in this last month of 2020. How they will fare into the future is anyone's guess, at this point.

Other Family-Run Store Survival Strategies in the Pandemic Era

Asian food stores, for some, may carry foundational foods for a diet for some customers; for others, it may carry foods peripheral to a main diet. Based on the consumer preferences, the consumption may be inelastic (not sensitive to the effects of the pandemic in terms of consumer demand) or elastic (sensitive to the effects of the pandemic in terms of consumer demand).

Competitors in the same space should be learning from the competition and applying the lessons to their own spaces. This would suggest that Store 1 could benefit from having an online presence and offering curbside service, for example. (This may not be practical since their slight web presence was updated some years ago.) Some additional potential strategies for survival could include the following:

- Would it be possible to have set-aside hours for shopping by those who are especially vulnerable to bad outcomes if infected with SARS-CoV-2 and progressing to COVID-19 disease?
- Would it be possible to have masks at the door for both locations? And hand sanitizer? [This would be in addition to the wiping down of the carts and baskets.]
- Would it be possible to offer a door-to-door delivery service? A service that uses the mail?
- Would it be possible to have "sidewalk" sales where people may make purchases outdoors (since outdoors is "safer" than indoors in terms of potential airborne viral transmission)?
- Can the stores create senses of events that might drive traffic to their locales?
- Are there air system adjustments that they can install to increase safety in their stores? And then can they advertise more broadly about their accommodations for the present moment?
    - Is crowdfunding (as a form of crowdsourcing) a possibility for funding such adaptations? Are there allies in the community that might help with such endeavors given the importance of both stores to the community?

It is unclear if either business used PPP moneys. It is unclear whether the respective proprietors own their physical locations or are renting.

There are risks to running a family store in the time of a pandemic, with a highly transmissible airborne virus. The store can be a site of a super-spreader event, for example. There can be a range of irretrievable harms. Not running the store—sitting out the season—may be costly in terms of loss of customers, changing customer habits (fragile), income, reputation, and trust. In some cases, it may not be clear how long a pandemic may last, so sitting out a "season" may not be possible; sitting out an indefinite future can mean just closing the store. There are tough choices with attendant tradeoffs, some slightly better than others.

In a time of a pandemic, a SWOT analysis (Strengths, Weaknesses, Opportunities, Threats) for Asian foodstuffs stores in a small town may show serious risks.

Table 1. A Light SWOT Analysis of Asian Grocery Stories in a Small Town During the COVID-19 Pandemic

Strengths	Weaknesses
• Long expertise and experience in the business • Limited competition in terms of provisioning of Asian foodstuffs locally • Known store proprietors in the larger community • Historical presence in the neighborhood • Known brand • Representing for all parts of the community, including some minorities • Connections to mass media • Lower costs of building ownership and / or rent (in a smaller town)	• Limited population of consumers • Less in the way of "rainy day" funding as SMEs • Fewer students in a college town under lockdown and under conditions of online learning (and so fewer customers) • Heightened costs of doing business during a pandemic (masking, deliveries, online ordering, and others) • Heightened costs of goods from various countries in Asia and other locales in the time of a pandemic • Heightened costs of safer air handling (if emplaced) • Personal health risks of staff
Opportunities	**Threats**
• Ability to access PPP funds if eligible • Ability to receive government support for citizens • Ability to take tax write-offs for business expenditures • Ability to earn increased trust from customers and from the larger neighborhood • Increased sympathy and empathy based on media coverage • Chance to rebrand • Chance to think about safer selling and shopping methods	• Racism; discrimination • Sense of risk from anything "Asian" • Community hostility • Reputation (from mass media, from social media, from word-of-mouth) • High unemployment rates affecting a segment of the shoppers • Social disorder in a time of a pandemic

Some suggest that shutdowns lead to pent-up demands that will be expressed when systems are open and available again, but this may not be necessarily so. People may substitute new services and new products for the old ones. They may habituate to ordering groceries online from big box grocery stores and still eschew the local mom-and-pop stores.

Then, too, there have been incidences of racial animus, in this Midwestern town as elsewhere, for those of Asian (and other) backgrounds. These have been reported in the mainstream press and depicted on social media. Chinatowns (Wang, Dec. 14, 2020) and Japantowns (Wang, Dec. 16, 2020) the U.S. have been "decimated" in the pandemic and are in danger of disappearing altogether as businesses close from the pressures of the pandemic. Physical attacks on Asians have resulted in injuries and deaths (Kaur, Feb. 13, 2021). This means that the store proprietors have to walk a fine line in their communications and be very careful in how every customer is treated. This also means a need for maintaining vigilance and investing more in security. (One of the two stores mentioned hiring a bodyguard during some months of the pandemic through the present. Indeed, a young male employee wearing a shirt emblazoned with the term "Security" was seen at the door several days by the author.) On the other hand, there are policies and funding to support minority-owned businesses. In a democratic society, there is a valuing of all citizens, regardless of racial and ethnic differences, in an idealized (and sometimes practical) sense.

If the two focal stores shut down, those who patronize the stores will have to drive between half an hour to an hour to two hours to other stores within the proxemic area for similar goods. Stores in larger metro areas tend to be much larger and carry much more stock and fresh goods; these stores tend to attract people from up to over 100 miles away. Depending on the size of the local clientele, though, some stores only maintain partially filled store shelves. Many may keep dated items there until sold to an unsuspecting customer. Regulatory oversight of such small businesses is slack. (The author visited one such store in the state's capitol and found one store with only about 20% fullness. Most of the shelves were empty. The store was part of a group of buildings in a small retail "mall," and most were closed or out-of-business. Perhaps the store was in the process of closing although there was no signage suggesting that.) If the local stores close, along with so many others, there will not be a place for purchasing canned hot bamboo shoots, tea cake, gel fruit candies, vermicelli noodles, frozen *jiaozi* and *ha gow,* frozen mochi, fresh fruits (*longan*) and vegetables (baby bok choy), and others. Or, if the two stores close, clients may have to go to the "big box" stores with half a store aisle dedicated to "Asian" foods: soy sauce, canned chow mein, dry noodles, and the like. The true diversity of such goods and the ability to special order such goods will no longer be available. Online, such as through Amazon.com, Asian foodstuffs are 3 – 10x more expensive than locally. Perhaps the costs of transferring goods from one location to another just simply adds up. For the larger community, they were receiving a signal that a part of their larger community is no longer visible, and for members of the community, they may feel less at home in their home community. There will not be a physical place where people can gather and chat about shared aspects of culture. The cultural and other losses will stack and accrue.

Many Asians in the pandemic already have been attacked and shunned and blamed, with such severity that the U.S. Legislature had to propose the COVID-19 Hate Crimes Act, and President Joe Biden had to sign it into law on May 20, 2021.

DISCUSSION

The contemporaneous moment presents serious challenges to small business owners: extra expenses to try to ensure biosafety, massive drops in foot traffic (based on leery customers), snarls in supply chains, rising food prices all around, the advance of inflation, and rising fuel costs. The study of two hyperlocal stores for Asian foodstuffs suggests some important ideas for how to support them.
Government:

- Perhaps it would be possible to provide some legislative protections (a liability shield by raising standards for liability, an indemnification fund for businesses sued for infections occurring on their property if businesses followed the best public health guidance they had at the time, and other considerations) against COVID-19 lawsuits, given the challenges of controlling for bio-health especially when the infection levels are high in society. (This is being considered by the U.S. Congress at present.)
- Perhaps insurance companies may be required or incented to provide some coverage for losses from COVID-19 (while being careful not to set precedents that would break the insurance industry).
- Perhaps banks may be further incentivized to make funds available to SMEs for loans beyond the paycheck protections.
- Perhaps the stimulus checks to citizens may include encouragement for particular local expenditures, to benefit SMEs.
- Perhaps point of service tests may be so low-cost and accurate that they may be deployed in such locations.

Community:

- Perhaps the community and local businesses may be encouraged to patronize each other's businesses to keep the money flowing. For example, perhaps a local company may retrofit a shop space for safer airflow and the removal of biohazards from the air.

- Perhaps local customers can be more respectful of social distancing, face masking, hand hygiene, and other considerations for staff and peer-customer safety.
- Perhaps the goodwill built up over years of being a part of a community may mean support even when moneys are scarce and employment elusive.

In some ways, the dearth of other employment opportunities may mean that many family-owned businesses will just endure through severe cost-cutting and grit. They may let go of external employees and just maintain basic business functions with family members or a trusted remaining few. They may do without their own wages or benefits. They may engage in barter, such as trading goods for work from some of their employees. Many have sunk life savings into their business, and they invest their reputations and senses of selves into the work. Their "livelihoods = life" and "livelihoods = life meaning" for many.

An Informative Observation of an Asian Foodstuffs Store Closing in the Town

How some stores disappear may be informed by a prior closing years ago. This town used to have a third Asian food store, which the author also patronized. The proprietors were a husband-and-wife pair, he from the U.S., she from the Philippines. Loquacious and friendly, she was a "mail order bride," according to her, and she shared lurid stories of the early years of their marriage, which was typified by a lot of his hard drinking and their mutual strife. They had settled into a long marriage and shared a child and seemed to have found happiness by the time I met them. She was the one who engaged the customers while he stocked the shelves. They would make long trips in their van down to a supplier in a southern town to acquire their goods and save on delivery costs.

When the couple running it decided to change careers (and they ultimately moved away), they offered their business for sale. They named a price of $110,000 for a few coolers and refrigerators, some dried foodstuffs, an old cash register, and some shelving. They said they would sell the name of the store and the signage. They were renting the space, so the space did not come with the price. And they said they were selling their own customer list, meaning, the ephemeral and fragile habits of the clients who visited their store regularly. A valuing of the store's hard assets would be well less than their asking price.

They could find no takers, and their store closed without much fanfare. Perhaps, as with other store closings, they just offered the various leftover equipment at pennies on the dollar, donated the equipment to a local charity organization, or they may have hired someone to take the equipment to the dump. Older equipment does not retain value. If nothing else, that six-figure asking price was very much pie-in-the-sky and more an expression of aspiration and perhaps greed than anything realistic. And yet, valuating of such businesses can be difficult in a small town without much in the way of diverse foodstuffs. Others may argue that the store was invaluable in the food cultures it enabled and the dietary exploration by others with different palates.

FUTURE RESEARCH DIRECTIONS

There is room for other ideas for how to improve the supports for family-owned businesses, like stores and restaurants. There can be more creative tailoring of supports to help businesses maintain customers, cash flow, physical health, advertising, marketing, and so on. There may be studies of how the pandemic era has had longer-term effects on the respective businesses and their sectors. Other cases from other SME sub-classes may be studied for other insights.

CONCLUSION

A pandemic is an extreme event, and it poses complex and compounding challenges to a country's people, a world's people. It certainly leads to various so-called winners and losers, survivors and non-survivors. Recent research suggests that there has been a 25% drop in the number of baby boomers self-employed or owners of their own businesses in the second quarter of 2020 (Sheng, Nov. 5, 2020). The COVID-19 pandemic has been a mass casualty event in the U.S. with numerous victims, including high-contact SMEs, such as family-owned stores and restaurants. The mass expenditures to shore up the economy have some positive implications currently, but inflation is rising, and there are projected negative externalities for present policies, with so much liquidity in the market.

With so much in play and so many complex responsibilities for governments and communities, such small business may be lost in the shuffle, and their needs may not be sufficiently met for their survival. At this moment, vaccines against SARS-CoV-2 have been approved in multiple countries, and they are being rolled out, even as the pharmaceutical companies are ramping up production. There is hope that humanity can be out of this pandemic a year from the present. It is unclear whether either of the two businesses will be around in a year or if they will join the many hundreds of thousands of SME businesses that have closed around the world, irrecoverably so, and numerous brands ended.

ADDENDUMS

The author recently visited one of the Asian food stores. The proprietor had received her Moderna vaccinations. Earlier, she had slipped on the ice and broken her wrist. In order to have surgery on her wrist, she was tested for whether she had been infected with the SARS-CoV-2 virus. She had not, even though she had run the store daily throughout the pandemic, protected only with paper signs, a cotton face mask, and the "honor system" of those who entered the store. She expressed concern about the lifting of the mask mandates in the county soon even as the city would be maintaining the mask mandates for a short time longer. She said that she could ask people to mask up, but that many already had not listened. She had no enforcement power. At the moment, in mid-May 2021, there is hope that some level of community immunity might be achieved to sufficiently minimize the numbers of infections. There is the sense, though, that small outbreaks can occur anywhere, without warning. Hers is only an n=1. Certainly, the author and others have known many who have become infected, and she has known several who have died of the infection.

Then, in early July, SARS-CoV-2 variants have manifested in various locales, with some more transmissible than others. The Delta variant is said to be able to induce production of itself at levels 1000x higher than other variants, and it is the dominant one across the United States. Both Asian foodstuffs stores remain open. One of the sites, alongside advertising fresh seafood, is inviting applications for jobs. During a visit to the other store, the author was vaccinated and masked. As she was checking out at the counter, a young Asian man approached the door but had no mask. The cashier looked at him and waved him in in a friendly way. It is in no position to turn away business, even as the Fourth Wave of the pandemic has begun stateside.

Meanwhile, in the town, in November, 2021, funerals continue apace. In some months, there are multiple funerals every week. Americans seem to have decided that they can no longer hold the line, and everyone is out and about, often unmasked. Mandates for masking for ended, in many cases. And the unvaccinated are a large part of the population still, even as vaccines against COVID-19 are plentiful and free.

REFERENCES

Abdullah, M., Dias, C., Muley, D., & Shahin, M. (2020). Exploring the impacts of COVID-19 on travel behavior and mode preferences. *Transportation Research Interdisciplinary Perspectives*, *8*(100255), 1–13. doi:10.1016/j.trip.2020.100255 PMID:34173481

Agosto, A., & Giudici, P. (2020). COVID-19 contagion and digital finance. *Digital Finance*, *2*(1-2), 159–167. doi:10.100742521-020-00021-3 PMID:33179008

Altig, D., Baker, S., Barrero, J. M., Bloom, N., Bunn, P., Chen, S., Davis, S. J., Leather, J., Meyer, B., Mihaylov, E., Mizen, P., Parker, N., Renault, T., Smietanka, P., & Thwaites, G. (2020). Economic uncertainty before and during the COVID-19 pandemic. *Journal of Public Economics*, *191*(104274), 1–13. PMID:32921841

Basavaraju, S. V., Patton, M. E., Grimm, K., Rasheed, M. A. U., Lester, S., Mills, L., Stumpf, M., Freeman, B., Tamin, A., Harcourt, J., Schiffer, J., Semenova, V., Li, H., Alston, B., Ategbole, M., Bolcen, S., Boulay, D., Browning, P., Cronin, L., . . . Stramer, S. L. (2020, Nov. 30). Serologic testing of U.S. blood donations to identify SARS-CoV-2-reactive antibodies: December 2019 – January 2020. *Clinical Infectious Diseases.* Retrieved Dec. 8, 2020 from https://academic.oup.com/cid/advance-article/doi/10.1093/cid/ciaa1785/6012472

Beaubien, J. (2020, June 9). *Modelers suggest pandemic lockdowns saved millions from dying of COVID-19.* National Public Radio (NPR).

Beck, M. J., & Hensher, D. A. (2020). Insights into the impact of COVID-19 on household travel and activities in Australia—The early days under restrictions. *Transport Policy*, *96*, 76–93. doi:10.1016/j.tranpol.2020.07.001 PMID:32834680

Bikefe, G., Zubairu, U., Araga, S., Maitala, F., Ediuku, E., & Anyebe, D. (2020). Corporate Social Responsibility (CSR) by small and medium enterprises (SMEs): A systematic review. *Small Business International Review*, *4*(1), 16–33. doi:10.26784bir.v4i1.243

Borgonovi, F., & Andrieu, E. (2020). Bowling together by bowling alone: Social capital and COVID-19. *Social Science & Medicine*, 1–12.

COVID-19 Dashboard. (2020, Dec. 7). *Center for Systems Science and Engineering (CSSE).* Johns Hopkins University & Medicine, Coronavirus Resource Center. Retrieved Dec. 7, 2020, from https://coronavirus.jhu.edu/map.html

Cowling, M., Brown, R., & Rocha, A. (2020). Did you save some cash for a rainy COVID-19 day? The crisis and SMEs. *International Small Business Journal*, *38*(7), 593–604. doi:10.1177/0266242620945102

Dubey, S., Biswas, P., Ghosh, R., Chatterjee, S., Dubey, M. J., Chatterjee, S., Lahiri, D., & Lavie, C. J. (2020). Psychosocial impact of COVID-19. *Diabetes & Metabolic Syndrome*, *14*(5), 779–788. doi:10.1016/j.dsx.2020.05.035 PMID:32526627

Els, C., Grobbelaar, S., & Kennon, D. (2020). Complementary partnerships for SMEs: A relational capability maturity model from an ecosystem perspective. LNCS, 12066, 67 – 78. doi:10.1007/978-3-030-44999-5_6

Google, L. L. C. (2020). *Google COVID-19 Community Mobility Reports*. https://www.google.com/covid19/mobility/

Guo, H., Yang, Z., Huang, R., & Guo, A. (2020). The digitalization and public crisis responses of small and medium enterprises: Implications from a COVID-19 survey. *Frontiers of Business Research in China,* 1 – 25.

Higgins, T. (2020, Dec. 6). *Winter Covid surge is the 'worst event that this country will face,' White House health advisor Birx says.* CNBC.

Hospitality Industry. (2020, Dec. 3). In *Wikipedia*. Retrieved Dec. 10, 2020, from https://en.wikipedia.org/wiki/Hospitality_industry

Hotez, P. (2020). COVID 19 in America: An October plan. *Microbes and Infection, 22*(9), 397–399. doi:10.1016/j.micinf.2020.07.003 PMID:32712199

Huang, A., Makridis, C., Baker, M., Medeiros, M., & Guo, Z. (2020). Understanding the impact of COVID-19 intervention policies on the hospitality labor market. *International Journal of Hospitality Management*, *91*(102660), 1–9. doi:10.1016/j.ijhm.2020.102660 PMID:32904433

Jackson, E. A. (2020). Emerging Innovative Thoughts on Globalization amidst the Contagion of COVID-19. *Springer Nature*, 1 - 12.

Jose, R., Narendran, M., Bindu, A., Beevi, N. L. M., & Benny, P. V. (2020). Public perception and preparedness for the pandemic COVID 19: A Health Belief Model approach. *Clinical Epidemiology and Global Health*, 1–6.

Juergensen, J., Guimón, J., & Narula, R. (2020). European SMEs amidst the COVID-19 crisis: Assessing impact and policy responses. *Economia e Politica Industriale*, *47*, 499–510.

Kallio, A., & Vuola, L. (2020). History of Crowdfunding in the Context of Ever-Changing Modern Financial Markets. In *Advances in Crowdfunding* (pp. 209–239). Palgrave Macmillan.

Kaur, H. (2021, Feb. 13). *As attacks against Asian Americans spike, call for action to protect communities.* CNN.

Keane, M., & Neal, T. (2020). Consumer panic in the COVID-19 pandemic. *Journal of Econometrics*, 1–12.

Lee, A. C. K., Alwan, N. A., & Morling, J. R. (2020). COVID19, race and public health. *Public Health, 185*, A1–A2.

Lorr, B. (2021, Jan. 29). *The American grocery store is all about identity. And it's fueling a broken system.* NBC News.

Lu, Y., Wu, J., Peng, J., & Lu, L. (2020). The perceived impact of the Covid-19 epidemic: Evidence from a sample of 4807 SMEs in Sichuan Province, China. *Environmental Hazards, 19*(4), 323–340.

Madonono, N., & Barnard, B. (2020). The growth perceptions of SMEs. *The IUP Journal of Knowledge Management, 18*(2), 27–69.

Malinovsky, A. A., Osina, D. M., & Trikoz, E. N. (2020). State support for the Russian economy affected by Covid-19 consequences (legal aspects). In *International Scientific and Practical Conference* (pp. 283-287). Springer.

Momaya, K. S. (2020). Return from COVID-19: Thinking differently about export competitiveness and sustainability. *International Journal of Global Business and Competitiveness, 15*, 1–9.

Nummela, N., Vissak, T., & Francioni, B. (2020). The interplay of entrepreneurial and non-entrepreneurial internationalization: An illustrative case of an Italian SME. *The International Entrepreneurship and Management Journal*, 1–31.

Parra, C. M., Gupta, M., & Mikalef, P. (2021). Information and communication technologies (ICT)-enabled severe moral communities and how the (Covid19) pandemic might bring new ones. *International Journal of Information Management*, 1–16.

Patel, P. C., & Rietveld, C. A. (2020). The impact of financial insecurity on the self-employed's short-term psychological distress: Evidence from the COVID-19 pandemic. *Journal of Business Venturing Insights, 14*(e00206), 1–11.

Paycheck Protection Program. (n.d.). *U.S. Small Business Administration*. Retrieved Dec. 7, 2020, from https://www.sba.gov/funding-programs/loans/coronavirus-relief-options/paycheck-protection-program

Paycheck Protection Program. (2020, Dec. 6). In *Wikipedia*. Retrieved Dec. 7, 2020, from https://en.wikipedia.org/wiki/Paycheck_Protection_Program

Prentice, C., Chen, J., & Stantic, B. (2020). Timed intervention in COVID-19 and panic buying. *Journal of Retailing and Consumer Services, 57*(102203), 1–11.

Rowan, N. J., & Laffey, J. G. (2020). Challenges and solutions for addressing critical shortage of supply chain for personal and protective equipment (PPE) arising from coronavirus disease (COVID19) pandemic—Case study from the Republic of Ireland. *The Science of the Total Environment, 725*, 1–9.

Ruffo, O. I., Mnisri, K., Morin-Esteves, C., & Gendron, C. (2020). Judgements of SMEs' legitimacy and its sources. *Journal of Business Ethics, 165*, 395–410.

Sheng, E. (2020, Nov. 5). *The $68 trillion transfer of wealth in America is evaporating amid crisis.* CNBC.

Small and medium-sized enterprises. (2020, Nov. 23). In *Wikipedia*. Retrieved Nov. 27, 2020, from https://en.wikipedia.org/wiki/Small_and_medium-sized_enterprises

Small businesses drive job growth in United States; they account for 1.8 million net new jobs, latest data show. (2019, Apr. 24). Office of Advocacy, U.S. Small Business Administration. Release No. 19-4 ADV.

Smialek, J. (2020, June 8). The U.S. entered a recession in February. *New York Times.*

Song, H. J., Yeon, J., & Lee, S. (2021). Impact of the COVID-19 pandemic: Evidence form the U.S. restaurant industry. *International Journal of Hospitality Management, 92*(102702), 1–7.

Sraders, A., & Lambert, L. (2020, Sept. 28). Nearly 100,000 establishments that temporarily shut down due to the pandemic are now out of business. *Fortune.*

United States. (2020, Dec. 7). Retrieved Dec. 7, 2020, from https://www.worldometers.info/coronavirus/country/us/

Wang, C. (2020, Dec. 14). *A year of loss, heartache, looming eviction—and rescuing itself—for Chinatown.* NBC News.

Wang, C. (2020, Dec. 16). *How the pandemic threatens to destroy America's three remaining Japantowns*. NBC News.

Zhao, Y., Harris, P., & Lam, W. (2020). *Crowdfunding. The Palgrave Encyclopedia of Interest Groups, Lobbying, and Public Affairs*.

ADDITIONAL READING

Hai-Jew, S. (2020, Apr.). Emergent COVID-19 and SARS-CoV-2 in social imagery and social video: Initial three months of viral dispersion. In *Social World Sensing via Social Image Analysis from Social Media.* New Prairie Press. Retrieved Oct. 23, 2020, from https://kstatelibraries.pressbooks.pub/socialworldsensing/chapter/covid19-1/

Hai-Jew, S. (2021). Incisive Real-Time Biosafety Decision-making under Societal Reopening: An Ego-Level Decision-Tree Understructure for A Serious Game (in the COVID-19 Pandemic Era). In Simulation and Game-Based Learning in Emergency and Disaster Management. IGI Global.

Hai-Jew, S. (2021). Observed Mass-Scale Call-Response Dynamics between Public Health Officials and American Public in Surging COVID-19 Pandemic Summer 2020: Content Analysis from Journalistic Articleset and Three-Phased Social Imagesets. In Practical Peer-to-Peer Teaching and Learning on the Social Web. IGI Global.

Hai-Jew, S. (2021). Societal shutdown and reopening and reclosing in the U.S. as expressed in social imagery narratives: COVID-19 pandemic seven/eight months. In Z. Fields (Ed.), *Handbook of Research on Using Global Collective Intelligence and Creativity to Solve Wicked Problems*. IGI Global.

Hai-Jew, S. (2021). Visual gists of home quarantines and self-quarantines from COVID-19 through social imagery: Four months into the SARS-CoV-2 disease outbreak. In Z. Fields (Ed.), *Handbook of Research on Using Global Collective Intelligence and Creativity to Solve Wicked Problems*. IGI Global.

Hai-Jew, S. (2021). Visual stories of COVID-19 social-physical distancing from tagged social imagery. In Z. Fields (Ed.), *Handbook of Research on Using Global Collective Intelligence and Creativity to Solve Wicked Problems*. IGI Global.

KEY TERMS AND DEFINITIONS

Business Continuance: The ability to continue the provision of services in the face of a disaster or crisis; a form of business resilience.

Corporate Social Responsibility: The sense of responsible commitment of a firm or entity to abide by legal and ethical standards to their peers, customers, larger community, and the world across a range of dimensions (social, environmental, economic, political, and others).

Crowdfunding: Going to the mass public through social media accounts to raise funds for particular projects, or endeavors.

Crowdsourcing: Going to the mass public through social media accounts to acquire information or other resources for particular projects or endeavors.

Small and Medium(-Sized) Enterprises: Business with fewer than 100 employees.

Supply Chain: The processes related to the manufacturing and distribution of a particular good or commodity.

APPENDIX A: CODEBOOK FROM THE AUTO-EXTRACTED TOPICS AND SUB-TOPICS FROM A THIRD OF THE "SME AND COVID-19" ACADEMIC AND JOURNALISTIC ARTICLESET

The codebook from the auto-extracted topics from a third of the articles from the "SME and COVID-19" academic and journalistic articleset is kept verbatim, without any of the run-together words or another anomalies "corrected." Using the coding from a software sometimes means having to put up with such anomalies. Reading the terms directly enables sense-making. (Table 2)

Table 2. Codebook from the Auto-Extracted Topics and Subtopics from a Third of the "SME and COVID-19" Academic and Journalistic Articleset

Autocoded Topic	Autocoded Related Sub-Topic
action	
	collective action dilemma
	collective action problems
	coordination dilemmas
	government action
	taking action
activity	
	active transport activity
	activity survey
	childcare activities
	collaborative activities
	group activities
	leisure activities
	normal activity
	physical activities
	project activity
	regular activity
	travel activity
age	
	10 age groups
	age bracket
	age category

Continued on following page

Table 2. Continued

Autocoded Topic	Autocoded Related Sub-Topic
	median age
agencies	
	agency content
	city agencies
	city government agencies
	heterogeneous agents
	individual agencies
	local government agencies
	municipal agencies
	public agencies
	rational agents
	state agencies
	state emergency management agencies
analysis	
	comparative case analysis
	content analysis software leximancer
	discriminant analysis
	dynamic network analysis
	frequent entities analysis
	headline analysis
	innovative analysis
	linear regression analysis
	overarching analysis
	present analysis
	spatial analysis
	spatiotemporal analysis
	statistical analysis
	time series analysis
	topical analysis
	word frequency analysis
applications	
	application program interface
	emerging applications
	key applications

Continued on following page

Table 2. Continued

Autocoded Topic	Autocoded Related Sub-Topic
	recent applications
	regression application
	tracing application
approach	
	classical approach
	comparative case approach
	different approach
	equilibrium approach
	flexible approach
	government approaches
	multi-level approaches
	national approach
	neoclassical approach
	whole-of-government approach
areas	
	area quarantine
	metro area
	project management knowledge areas
	residential areas
	urban areas
	virtual areas
assessment	
	absolute assessment system
	absolute assessment systemswitch
	assessed changes
	assessed disruptions
	different assessment methods
	online assessments
associate	
	associate dean
	associate professor
	meaningful associative relationships
	migrant associations
	suggesting associations

Continued on following page

Table 2. Continued

Autocoded Topic	Autocoded Related Sub-Topic
	words association
attending	
	attending music events
	attending work functions
	flexible attendance system
	smart attendance
average	
	average path length
	average systolic
	historical averages
	moving averages
	sample average
bar	
	bar chart
	error bars
brand	
	brand hate
	branded products
	luxury brand bursts
	luxury brand image
	luxury brand management
	positive brand reputation
	specific brands
business	
	24 business hours
	business closures
	business disruption
	business support initiatives
	everyday business
	local businesses
	reopening business
	supporting businesses
	work-related business
care	

Continued on following page

Table 2. Continued

Autocoded Topic	Autocoded Related Sub-Topic
	cease care
	health care team
	intensive care beds
	intensive care units
	italian health care system
	nursing care
	prenatal care
	qualified health care professional
	seeking care
case	
	aforementioned case series
	case study
	comparative case analysis
	comparative case approach
	cumulative case volume
	fever cases
	infected case
	non-severe cases
	several use cases
category	
	6 food categories
	age category
	income categories
	material category
	middle-age category
centrality	
	central communications office
	in-degree centrality
	network centrality
	out-degree centrality
changes	
	assessed changes
	changing behaviour
	climate change

Continued on following page

Table 2. Continued

Autocoded Topic	Autocoded Related Sub-Topic
	consumer behavior change
	dramatic changes
	extent changes
	planned changes
	service delivery changes
	significant change
	structural change
city	
	5 city blocks
	city agencies
	city content
	city employee
	city government agencies
	city government coordination
	city hall
	city operations
	city services
	multiple city departments
	studying city communication
classes	
	class break phenomenon
	face-to-face classes
	foreign language classes
	givenface-to-face classes
	offline classes
	overall class
	practice classes
	suitable class
	taking classes
	took online classes
	writingcentered classes
cold	
	cold spots
	hot spots

Continued on following page

Table 2. Continued

Autocoded Topic	Autocoded Related Sub-Topic
	significant cold
communication	
	central communications office
	communication criteria
	communication official
	communication procedures
	communication responsibility
	communication sufficiency
	communication tools
	communications problem
	communications technology
	connected communication network
	crisis communication
	effective communication processes
	enhanced interagency communication
	face-to-face communication
	g2012brief communication
	health risk communication
	improved communication
	interactionssmooth communication
	interactive communication
	local government communication
	media communication
	online communication synchrony
	public communication efforts
	smooth communication
	studying city communication
	subsequent communication
	teacher communication
	weekly communication networks
community	
	airport community
	community transmission
	healthy community residents

Continued on following page

Table 2. Continued

Autocoded Topic	Autocoded Related Sub-Topic
	migrant community leaders
	minority communities
	worldwide community efforts
concerns	
	alarming safety concern
	concerns household food waste
	persistent concern
	raising concerns
	theoretical concern
conditions	
	crisis conditions
	current conditions
	equilibrium condition
	living conditions
	maternal condition
	pandemic conditions
	poor health conditions
consumer	
	amplifying consumers
	consumer behavior change
	consumer levels
	discouraging consumer desire
	italian consumers
	negative consumers
	understanding consumer
content	
	agency content
	city content
	content analysis software leximancer
	critical content interpretability
	presenting content
	reuse content
	sharing content
	text content

Continued on following page

Table 2. Continued

Autocoded Topic	Autocoded Related Sub-Topic
coordination	
	city government coordination
	coordination dilemmas
	external coordination challenges
	internal coordination
	multi-agency coordination
	policy coordination
	public sector coordination
	strategic coordination
coronavirus	
	2019 novel coronavirus diseases
	damaging novel coronavirus
	including coronavirus
	infeccion por coronavirus
crisis	
	crisis communication
	crisis conditions
	current crisis
	global crisis
	possible future crisis
	public health crisis child abuse
daily	
	corresponding day
	counting days
	daily data
	daily infections
	daily life
	daily lives
	daily rainfall
	early days
	final days
	previous day
	ten day period
data	

Continued on following page

Table 2. Continued

Autocoded Topic	Autocoded Related Sub-Topic
	aggregate data
	daily data
	data collection
	data cube structure
	data modeling
	data provisionno provision
	digitized data
	final data
	high-quality data
	physiologic data
	primary data
	social network data
	spatiotemporal incident data
	student absenteeism data
	twitter data
	using data
department	
	departments discretion
	different departments
	multiple city departments
	planning department
	police department
development	
	continued development
	developed coding structure
	developed device
	developed fever
	developed mask
	developing pre-requisite
	developing test swabs
	diagnostic equipment development protolabs
	fetal development
	vaccine development
disease	

Continued on following page

Table 2. Continued

Autocoded Topic	Autocoded Related Sub-Topic
	2019 novel coronavirus diseases
	cardiovascular diseases
	coronary artery disease
	disease sequela
	disease vulnerability
	infectious disease pandemic
	inside retirement homes disease
	mild disease
	severe disease
	ular disease
effect	
	direct effect
	effective communication processes
	effective emergency
	effective health safety instruction
	effective online
	effective responses
	expansionary effects
	global effects
	positive effect
	potential effects
	seasonal effects
	significant effect
	viral effects
efforts	
	expediting efforts
	international research efforts
	public communication efforts
	public health efforts
	worldwide community efforts
emergency	
	effective emergency
	emergency management experts
	emergency preparedness

Continued on following page

Table 2. Continued

Autocoded Topic	Autocoded Related Sub-Topic
	public health emergencies
	state emergency management agencies
equipment	
	diagnostic equipment development protolabs
	lawn equipment
	medical equipment volkswagen
	professional equipment
	protective equipment
error	
	error bars
	error terms
	network error improvement
	standard errors
events	
	attending music events
	burst event
	certain event
	key events
	particle collision events
	planned events
	random events
face	
	disposable face
	face masks
	printed face shield
facilities	
	19 testing facility
	biomedical waste management facilities
	bio-medical waste management facilities
	proper health facilities
	school facilities
factors	
	critical success factors
	environmental factor

Continued on following page

Table 2. Continued

Autocoded Topic	Autocoded Related Sub-Topic
	factor loading requirement
	international market risk factors
	several factors
	underlying factors
feedback	
	active feedback
	feedback mechanisms
	immediate feedback
	including feedback
	receiving feedback
	regular feedbacks
food	
	6 food categories
	concerns household food waste
	food losses
	food security
	food shops
	food waste behaviour
	food waste covid
	global food waste
	incorrect food management habits
	italian food
	severe food scarcity
	unrelated regression food management household
frequent	
	analyses word frequency
	frequent complaint
	frequent entities analysis
	frequent mentions
	frequent sanitization
	low frequency bands
	total frequency
	visit frequency
	weighted word frequencies

Continued on following page

Table 2. Continued

Autocoded Topic	Autocoded Related Sub-Topic
	word frequency analysis
government	
	city government agencies
	city government coordination
	government action
	government approaches
	government messages
	government planning
	government reforms
	government services
	government spending
	government transparency
	horizontal government
	local government agencies
	local government communication
	local government officials
groups	
	10 age groups
	allowing groups
	different groups
	diverse groups
	exercise groups
	group activities
	migrant groups
	risk group
	societal groups
health	
	dental health
	effective health safety instruction
	health care team
	health consciousness
	health infrastructure
	health issues
	health risk communication

Continued on following page

Table 2. Continued

Autocoded Topic	Autocoded Related Sub-Topic
	italian health care system
	mental health
	non-symptomatic health persons
	poor health conditions
	preventive health behavior
	proper health facilities
	public health crisis child abuse
	public health efforts
	public health emergencies
	public health initiatives
	public health messages
	qualified health care professional
	regional health system
healthcare	
	access healthcare
	healthcare sector
	healthcare services
	healthcare system
	healthcare workers
	qualified healthcare professional
host	
	determining host tissue specificity
	host cell membrane
	host machinery
	inducing host
	intermediate amplifying host
household	
	concerns household food waste
	household income
	household level
	household travel
	modelling household
	unrelated regression food management household
improvement	

Continued on following page

Table 2. Continued

Autocoded Topic	Autocoded Related Sub-Topic
	disconnection phenomenon improvement
	improved communication
	improving stress regulation skills
	lagging phenomenon improvement
	network error improvement
	quality improvement
income	
	annual income
	before-tax money income
	household income
	income brackets
	income categories
	income increases
	middle income
increasing	
	income increases
	increasing level
	increasing trend
	increasing use
	increasing variability
	profound increases
	sale increase
	sustained increase
individual	
	individual agencies
	individual level
	individual liberties
	individual notices
	individual stops
	individual users
	likely individuals
	optimizing individuals
	risk individuals
infection	

Continued on following page

Table 2. Continued

Autocoded Topic	Autocoded Related Sub-Topic
	confirmed infection
	daily infections
	human infection
	infect others
	infected case
	infected patients
	infecting virus
	infection waves
	receptor-mediated infection
	systemic infection
	viral infection
information	
	akaike information criterion
	bayesian information criterion
	cross-sectoral information sharing
	information evolution
	information overload
	information popularity
	information provision
	information retrieval
	information silos
	online information sources
	posted information
	providing information
	sharing information
	social media information diffusion
	stock market information
interaction	
	complex interaction
	direct interaction
	interactionsno interaction
	public interaction
	smooth interactions
	unilateral interactions

Continued on following page

Table 2. Continued

Autocoded Topic	Autocoded Related Sub-Topic
interest	
	competing interest
	financial interests
	multiples interests
	potential interest
	user interests
interventions	
	interventional policies
	lifestyle interventions
	non-pharmaceutical interventions
	pharmaceutical interventions
	police interventions
	preventive interventions
issues	
	emerging issues
	health issues
	related issues
	respiratory issues
	special issue
	wi-fi issue
leaders	
	lead role
	leading reason
	migrant community leaders
	religious leaders
	team leader
learning	
	learning algorithm
	learning environment
	learning outcomes
	learning process
	learning space
	learning techniques
	online learning

Continued on following page

Table 2. Continued

Autocoded Topic	Autocoded Related Sub-Topic
	remote learning
	supplementary learning materials
level	
	aggregate level
	certain level
	confidence level
	consumer levels
	disaggregate level
	elevating poverty level
	geopolitical risk levels
	hierarchical levels
	household level
	increasing level
	individual level
	mean output level
	single responsibility level
	troponin levels
living	
	daily lives
	elderly living
	live entertainment
	living conditions
	rural living
luxury	
	luxury brand bursts
	luxury brand image
	luxury brand management
	luxury marketing campaign
	luxury products
male	
	male real-time
	male rt-pcr
	specifically male
	year-old male

Continued on following page

Table 2. Continued

Autocoded Topic	Autocoded Related Sub-Topic
	years2 males
	years4 males
management	
	biomedical waste management facilities
	bio-medical waste management facilities
	emergency management experts
	horizontal management
	incorrect food management habits
	internal management capacity
	luxury brand management
	physiologic monitoring treatment management services
	project management knowledge areas
	project management plan
	project resource management
	state emergency management agencies
	unrelated regression food management household
market	
	crude oil markets
	geopolitical risk stock market oil prices
	gold markets
	growing market
	international market risk factors
	live-animal markets
	local markets
	luxury marketing campaign
	marketing message
	social media marketing
	stock market fundamentals
	stock market information
	stock market returns
	stock market volatility
masks	
	developed mask
	face masks
	mask adjusters

Continued on following page

Table 2. Continued

Autocoded Topic	Autocoded Related Sub-Topic
	medical mask
	snorkel mask
	universal masking
	wearing masks
materials	
	acrylonitrile-styrene-acrylate material
	including material composition
	lecture materials
	material category
	supplementary learning materials
	teaching materials
measures	
	air quality measurements
	direct measurement
	governmental measures
	hygienic measures
	policy measure
	risk mitigation measures
messaging	
	constant messaging
	directed messages
	government messages
	marketing message
	ongoing messaging
	proactive messaging vehicle
	public health messages
	regarding message types
methods	
	coherence wavelet method
	deep-learning forecasting methods
	different assessment methods
	direct quantification methods
	existing quantification methods
	in-depth qualitative method

Continued on following page

Table 2. Continued

Autocoded Topic	Autocoded Related Sub-Topic
	surveillance methods
	teaching methods
	using regression method
models	
	asian model
	binomial regression model
	bivariate model
	data modeling
	demand-driven agent-based model
	equation models
	fused deposition modeling
	heuristic model
	linear regression models
	model fit
	modelling household
	multilevel modeling analyses
	nested models
	respective models
	simulation models
	three-level growth curve models
	unrelated regression models
modes	
	active modes
	different modes
	particular mode
	private mode selection
	public mode selection
	public transport modes
monitoring	
	glucose monitoring
	monitoring phases
	monitoring student absenteeism
	monitoring team performance
	physiologic monitoring treatment management services

Continued on following page

Table 2. Continued

Autocoded Topic	Autocoded Related Sub-Topic
multiple	
	multiple attractors
	multiple city departments
	multiple ground-glass-like high-density shadows
	multiple platforms
	multiple representations
	multiples interests
national	
	chinese nationals
	national approach
	national highways
	national stakeholders
	national stereotype
network	
	connected communication network
	dynamic network analysis
	network centrality
	network density
	network diameter
	network error improvement
	network instability
	open network overview
	social network data
	transport networks
	weekly communication networks
novel	
	2019 novel coronavirus diseases
	damaging novel coronavirus
	novel coronaviruses
	novel online
	novel virus
number	
	basic reproduction number
	huge number

Continued on following page

Table 2. Continued

Autocoded Topic	Autocoded Related Sub-Topic
	innumerable numbers
	low number
	maximum number
	mortality numbers
	number users
	overall number
	regionsthe numbers
officer	
	austrian officer
	available officers
	dutch officer
	executive officers
	german officer
	self-quarantined officers
oil prices	
	crude oil markets
	geopolitical risk stock market oil prices
	oil price shocks
	oil price volatility shock
	premium price
online	
	birthday online
	effective online
	novel online
	online assessments
	online communication synchrony
	online evolution
	online exhibits
	online information sources
	online learning
	online shopping
	online survey
	took online classes
outcome	

Continued on following page

Table 2. Continued

Autocoded Topic	Autocoded Related Sub-Topic
	important outcome
	learning outcomes
	main outcome
	positive panic outcome
	pregnancy outcomes
	reproductive outcomes
	specific outcome
pandemic	
	future pandemics
	global pandemic
	infectious disease pandemic
	pandemic conditions
	pandemic outbreak
	pandemic response
	pandemic ventilator project
	pandemic world
	review pandemic influenza plans
panic	
	panic buying
	panic disorder
	panic results
	positive panic outcome
	unexpected panic attacks
patient	
	consecutive patients
	cystic fibrosis patient
	established patient
	hospitalised patients
	infected patients
	patient copays
	positive patients
	pre-recorded patient
period	
	baseline period

Continued on following page

Table 2. Continued

Autocoded Topic	Autocoded Related Sub-Topic
	certain period
	different treatment periods
	expiration period
	month study period
	peri periods
	pre periods
	ten day period
	transition period
	week period
phenomenon	
	class break phenomenon
	disconnection phenomenon improvement
	instabilitylagging phenomenon
	lagging phenomenon improvement
	video disconnection phenomenon prevention
planning	
	covidsafe plan
	government planning
	planned changes
	planned events
	planning department
	planning phase
	planning processes
	planning reliability
	project integration planning
	project management plan
	review pandemic influenza plans
	treatment plan
police	
	police authority
	police cadets
	police department
	police force
	police interventions

Continued on following page

Table 2. Continued

Autocoded Topic	Autocoded Related Sub-Topic
	police response
	realistic police training
	regular police tasks
	regular police training
policy	
	complex policy problems
	economic policy uncertainty
	interventional policies
	policy coordination
	policy goals
	policy measure
	policy responses
	public policy problems
	wicked policy problem
	workplace policy
population	
	civil population
	human populations
	immigrant populations
	urban population
	wild populations
potential	
	potential bat origin
	potential benefits
	potential congestion
	potential effects
	potential exposure risk
	potential interest
	potential psychopathology
	potential trade-off
	potential transmission
practice	
	nursing practice
	practice classes

Continued on following page

Table 2. Continued

Autocoded Topic	Autocoded Related Sub-Topic
	practice subjects
	sanitisation practices
problems	
	buffering problem
	collective action problems
	communications problem
	complex policy problems
	complex problems
	public policy problems
	wicked policy problem
processes	
	cumulative causality process
	effective communication processes
	learning process
	natural language processing
	planning processes
	specific processes
	work-split process
products	
	branded products
	end-user products
	essential products
	innovative products
	luxury products
	overall production
	regular products
	specific product
professional	
	professional equipment
	professional sport
	professional time
	qualified health care professional
	qualified healthcare professional
project	

Continued on following page

Table 2. Continued

Autocoded Topic	Autocoded Related Sub-Topic
	large-complex projects
	oxygen project
	pandemic ventilator project
	project activity
	project execution
	project integration execution
	project integration planning
	project management knowledge areas
	project management plan
	project resource management
	project rules
	team projects
protective	
	property protection
	protecting students
	protective clothing
	protective equipment
	protective gears
	protective gears
	protective gears
protein	
	c-reactive protein
	distinct proteins
	envelope protein
	membrane protein
	spike protein functions
public	
	general public
	public access cable station
	public administration
	public agencies
	public communication efforts
	public compliance
	public co-production

Continued on following page

Table 2. Continued

Autocoded Topic	Autocoded Related Sub-Topic
	public discourse
	public engagement
	public health crisis child abuse
	public health efforts
	public health emergencies
	public health initiatives
	public health messages
	public interaction
	public mode selection
	public outreach
	public policy problems
	public relations
	public response
	public sector coordination
	public service delivery
	public support
	public transport modes
	public understanding
	public health
	public health crisis child abuse
	public health efforts
	public health emergencies
	public health initiatives
	public health messages
questions	
	asking questions
	completed questions
	securing question time
	smooth questioning
regression	
	binomial regression model
	linear regression analysis
	linear regression models
	linear ridge regression

Continued on following page

Table 2. Continued

Autocoded Topic	Autocoded Related Sub-Topic
	regression algorithms
	regression application
	regression decision tree
	regression tree
	unrelated regression food management household
	unrelated regression models
	using regression method
related	
	car use relative
	public relations
	related experts
	related issues
	related terms
reports	
	authentic reports
	different reporting structures
	preferred reporting items
	real-time reporting
	reported observations
	writing reports
response	
	393 student responses
	effective responses
	global response
	immune response
	pandemic response
	police response
	policy responses
	public response
	response rate
	whole-of-government response strategies
risk	
	enhancing risk governance mechanisms
	geopolitical risk levels

Continued on following page

Table 2. Continued

Autocoded Topic	Autocoded Related Sub-Topic
	geopolitical risk stock market oil prices
	health risk communication
	international market risk factors
	potential exposure risk
	risk group
	risk individuals
	risk mitigation measures
school	
	combining school
	offering schools
	school absenteeism
	school closures
	school degree
	school facilities
	school hours
sector	
	biomedical sectors
	healthcare sector
	large sector
	manufacturing sectors
	public sector coordination
	sector items
security	
	casual security guards
	food security
	secure supply chains
	securing question time
	untrained security guards
services	
	city services
	government services
	healthcare services
	nutritional services
	office service

Continued on following page

Table 2. Continued

Autocoded Topic	Autocoded Related Sub-Topic
	physiologic monitoring treatment management services
	public service delivery
	senior services
	service delivery changes
	service delivery tasks
	technologybased service
sharing	
	cross-sectoral information sharing
	knowledge sharing
	sharing content
	sharing information
	sharing thoughts
shops	
	food shops
	general shopping
	online shopping
	small shops
social media	
	media briefing
	media communication
	social media adoption
	social media information diffusion
	social media marketing
	social media platforms
	social media specialists
	social media ties
	social media use
	ubiquitous media
sources	
	emission sources
	key sources
	major source
	online information sources
	reliable source

Continued on following page

Table 2. Continued

Autocoded Topic	Autocoded Related Sub-Topic
	retweeted sources
	source ventilator
	various sources
specific	
	determining host tissue specificity
	specific brands
	specific outcome
	specific place
	specific processes
	specific product
	specific solutions
	specific time
	specifically male
statistically	
	statistical analysis
	statistical elaborations
	statistically significant
	summary statistics
step	
	critical step
	different steps
	important step
	manufacturing steps
	playing step
	prior time step
	third step
stock market	
	500 constituent stocks
	geopolitical risk stock market oil prices
	stock market fundamentals
	stock market information
	stock market returns
	stock market volatility
strategy	

Continued on following page

Table 2. Continued

Autocoded Topic	Autocoded Related Sub-Topic
	alternative strategy
	australian strategy
	important strategy
	search strategy
	training strategies
	whole-of-government response strategies
structures	
	data cube structure
	developed coding structure
	different reporting structures
	embryonic structures
	northern structure
	organizational structure
	thematic structures
student	
	393 student responses
	korean college students
	monitoring student absenteeism
	protecting students
	student absenteeism data
	student–teacher ratio
study	
	case study
	chinese study
	clinical studies
	human challenge studies
	month study period
	present study
	recent studies
	study design
	studying city communication
	thematic analysisthis study
supplies	
	medical supplies

Continued on following page

Table 2. Continued

Autocoded Topic	Autocoded Related Sub-Topic
	secure supply chains
swabs	
	developing test swabs
	nasal swabs
	swab prototype
	swab specimens
	testing swabs carbon3d
system	
	absolute assessment system
	economic system
	federal systems
	flexible attendance system
	healthcare system
	insufficient system utilization
	italian health care system
	macrodynamic systems
	passive system
	regional health system
	remote teaching system
	transit systems
	well-designed sentinel system
teaching	
	different teaching
	remote teaching system
	student–teacher ratio
	teacher communication
	teaching materials
	teaching methods
	traditional classroom teaching
team	
	co-located teams
	cooperative team environments
	health care team
	monitoring team performance

Continued on following page

Table 2. Continued

Autocoded Topic	Autocoded Related Sub-Topic
	research team
	right team member
	team leader
	team projects
	team projectsteamwork
	virtual team
technologies	
	communications technology
	innovative 3dp technologies
	mobile phone technology
	preferred technologies
	technological emergence
	telecommunication technologies
tests	
	19 testing facility
	developing test swabs
	specimen tests
	sphericity tests
	test evaluation
	testing swabs carbon3d
	undergoing testing
	wavelet-based granger causality tests
time	
	certain time
	current time
	diverse time series
	efficient time utilization
	month time slices
	observed time sequence
	prior time step
	professional time
	securing question time
	similar time frame
	space time cube

Continued on following page

Table 2. Continued

Autocoded Topic	Autocoded Related Sub-Topic
	specific time
	time series analysis
	time zone differences
training	
	realistic police training
	regular police tasks
	regular police training
	trained doctors
	training strategies
transmission	
	asymptomatic carrier transmission
	community transmission
	declining malaria transmission
	droplet transmission
	potential transmission
	species transmission
	wild civet-to-human transmission pathway
transport	
	active transport activity
	public transport modes
	sustainable transport future
	transport networks
	transport tool kit
travel	
	2020 vacation travel
	aggregate travel
	holiday travel
	household travel
	longitudinal travel
	reducing travel
	tourist travel
	travel activity
	vehicle travel
treatment	

Continued on following page

Table 2. Continued

Autocoded Topic	Autocoded Related Sub-Topic
	different treatment periods
	malaria treatment failure
	medical treatments
	physiologic monitoring treatment management services
	treatment plan
twitter	
	twitter accounts
	twitter data
	twitter users
understanding	
	classesreduced understanding
	current understanding
	public understanding
	reduced understanding
	scholarly understanding
	understanding consumer
use	
	auto rickshaw users
	car use relative
	external users
	future use
	increasing use
	individual users
	limited use
	next use
	number users
	several use cases
	social media use
	twitter users
	user interests
	using bounded
	using data
	using regression method
	using ridge library

Continued on following page

Table 2. Continued

Autocoded Topic	Autocoded Related Sub-Topic
	using trade credit
	using vts
	vehicle use
values	
	authentic value
	decreasing values
	dollar values
	median value
	symbolic value
vehicle	
	private motor vehicle
	proactive messaging vehicle
	vehicle controls
	vehicle travel
	vehicle use
ventilator	
	manual ventilators
	pandemic ventilator project
	purifying ventilators
	source ventilator
	ventilator bag
	ventilator parts
virus	
	corona virus
	infecting virus
	novel virus
	virus origins
	virus spread
waste	
	biomedical waste management facilities
	bio-medical waste management facilities
	concerns household food waste
	food waste behaviour
	food waste covid

Continued on following page

Table 2. Continued

Autocoded Topic	Autocoded Related Sub-Topic
	global food waste
word	
	analyses word frequency
	important words
	thematic word classification
	weighted word frequencies
	word frequency analysis
	words association
work	
	attending work functions
	flexible work schedule
	healthcare workers
	hospital workers
	ongoing work
	unpaid work
	work experience
	work force
	working hours

Chapter 4
Supply Chain Strategies for Achieving Resilience in the MSMEs:
An Empirical Study

Subhodeep Mukherjee
https://orcid.org/0000-0002-6863-4881
GITAM University (Deemed), India

Manish Mohan Baral
https://orcid.org/0000-0002-9620-1872
GITAM University (Deemed), India

Chittipaka Venkataiah
https://orcid.org/0000-0002-7804-0796
Indira Gandhi National Open University, India

ABSTRACT

Due to COVID-19, the supply chains have been disrupted in many ways. This chapter aims to identify the strategies that can help the MSMEs develop a resilient supply chain strategy that can handle any kind of disruption. Five strategies are determined from the literature review. A questionnaire is being developed for survey-based research in the MSMEs of India. For data analysis, exploratory factor analysis and structural equation modelling are used. In this research, an empirical investigation is carried out to present the research framework. All the proposed hypotheses are accepted, and the developed model satisfied all the parameters.

DOI: 10.4018/978-1-7998-8346-3.ch004

INTRODUCTION

COVID-19 is a virus that infects large numbers of people. Many countries are experiencing significant difficulties as a result of the pandemic. Human lives are lost, and economic activity is slowed. Many industries face problems as their strategies for dealing with the pandemic must be revised (P Barbieri, 2020). The company supply chain (SC) and global SC faced numerous challenges, including seaport closures, airport closures, vehicle movement restrictions, and many others (Antai & Mutshinda, 2021). The COVID-19 outbreak has reduced reliance on the global SC, causing the entire network to collapse. According to Fortune (2020), 94 per cent of the world's top 1000 companies experienced SC disruptions due to the COVID-19 outbreak (D. Das et al., 2021). The SC's uncertainty has grown as a result of the frequent COVID-19 disruptions.

India's Micro Small and Medium Enterprises (MSME) sector is the second-largest job creator after agriculture. The MSME sector will play an essential role within this target, contributing to GDP expected to exceed 50%. The potential of the Indian MSME sector remains untapped, which is one of the reasons why government policies are now more convergent toward creating a resilient ecosystem with greater breadth and depth. It fills in as a good place for business people and pioneers, with critical help in reinforcing the business environment. The assessed number of MSMEs in India is 63 million, with 110 million utilized (S. Das et al., 2020). Various reports, research, and surveys have repeatedly demonstrated that this sector catalyzes the country's socio-economic development. All of this becomes even more important in light of the government's new mission of reaching a $5 trillion economic target by 2025 (Roy et al., 2020).

The declaration of a cross country lockdown tossed MSME proprietors, businesses, and outside partners into a surprising circumstance where nobody had experience managing such a circumstance. The drawn-out lockdown adversely affected completed merchandise supply, unrefined substance acquisition, and representative accessibility to work underway and supply measures. From April to June 2020, the area confronted difficulties identified with obligation reimbursement, compensation/pay rates, legal contribution, etc. (S. Das et al., 2020; Sahoo & Ashwani, 2020). As per review results, disturbances brought about by the Covid-19 pandemic decreased MSMEs profit by 20-50 per cent, with miniature and little endeavours enduring the worst part of the blow, attributable to a liquidity crunch. As far as hindered yet unsurprising incomes, industries in the fundamental item business fared better (Shafi et al., 2020). A few undertakings have advanced by moving their concentration from unnecessary items to essential products, for example, hand sanitizer and toiletries, PPE units, reusable covers, etc., and can get by in testing times (Chaudhary et al., 2020).

MSMEs in remote areas faced numerous challenges due to disrupted SC systems and intrastate lockdown provisions (Barbate et al., 2021). Consumers have less disposable income as a result of the challenges faced by businesses. Numerous organizations laid off specialists because of a failure to pay compensations, abandoned their workplaces to try not to bring about costs, and ended creation because of a drop famous. Equivocalness in future exchange and the arrival of the new typical keeps monetary organizations from expanding any new monetary loaning or covering likely danger (Majumdar et al., 2020). Likewise, the area has replies to basic inquiries like joblessness, neighborhood economic turn of events, financial shortfall, exchange balance, monetary area advancement, SDG arrangement, etc. Private area investment in different bottlenecks of the worth chain and inventory network framework is fundamental for the public authority's various strategies. In India, organizations of all sizes face natural substance obtainment, credit prerequisites, market linkages, quality, normalization, evaluating, business turnaround time, campaigning, and numerous others (Esra Sipahi, 2020).

Supply chain resilience (SCR) is defined as the SC's adaptive capability to prepare for unanticipated events, respond to disruptions, and recover from them by maintaining operations at the desired level of connectedness and control over structure and function (Saikouk et al., 2021; M. Sharma et al., 2021). They defined the connection between strength and viability (Pereira & Soares de Mello, 2021; Scheiwiller & Zizka, 2021). SC weaknesses have expanded in light of the successive interruptions brought about by the pandemic. It affects SC execution just as income age abilities (Nandi et al., 2020). For demand and supply determining before the pandemic, most organizations depended on organization datasets instead of start to finish SC information, a case ordinary of its restricted utilization and mechanized frameworks in SC the board (A Belhadi, 2021; Antai & Mutshinda, 2021).

As a result, businesses could not predict demand and supply constraints when the pandemic struck, resulting in SC disruption. While most organizations have made their SC more astute and quicker after some time, organizations need thoughts to de-hazard their SC against pandemic-like interruptions (Dube et al., 2021; Thaichon, 2021; Xue et al., 2021). This points to a disconnect between the literature's SCR strategies and their implementation in the industry. Organizations are confronting common interest and supply shocks as COVID-19 ranges across the globe. In such a scenario, companies worldwide must urgently improve the resilience of their global SC to deal with future shocks (Pereira & Soares de Mello, 2021; Xue et al., 2021). The current pandemic has demonstrated the need for more SCR research based on real-life events that consider all parameters (Karmaker et al., 2021; P. Kumar & Kumar Singh, 2021). Effective SC risk management can reduce the impact of COVID-19-induced SC disruptions on SCR and robustness (Miani et al., 2021; Scheiwiller & Zizka, 2021).

LITERATURE REVIEW

Resilient Supply Chain (RSC)

The ability of the SC to respond to and recover from disruptions is defined as RSC. Globalization and the use of cutting-edge technologies in SC have been intertwined, resulting in a complex network of entities (Pavlov et al., 2019; Remko, 2020). Such a complex SC is exceptionally vulnerable to disruption. As a result, it has become critical to have the resilience capacity to respond quickly to disruptions (M Christopher, 2004; M. Sharma et al., 2021). The strategic assessment of the SC can help reduce the risk of unforeseen events and assist SC operators and policymakers in developing a collaborative plan for resilience. The customary way of thinking as of late has been that organizations ought to consider needs effectiveness over repetition in their SC (Nandi et al., 2021; R. Sharma et al., 2020). The weakness of this methodology was apparent even before the pandemic, as organizations confronted milder disturbances because of, for instance, higher levies and stricter guidelines. On those occasions, SC execution was hampered by an absence of extra limits and stock cushions and an over-dependence on sole providers (D. Das et al., 2021; J Blackhurst, 2005; A. Sharma et al., 2020). Then, at that point, there was the COVID-19 emergency, which put an uncommon strain on worldwide SC. Because of asset deficiencies, organizations have confronted monstrous interest vulnerability, long deferrals from providers and coordination's accomplices, and activities end (Shahin, 2020; Singh et al., 2020).

Resilience—the capacity to assimilate pressure, recuperate essential usefulness, and flourish in evolving conditions—has arisen as an indispensable part of an organization's general wellbeing (Lopes de Sousa Jabbour et al., 2020). Challenging organizations outflank their companions in three ways: the immediate effect of an extreme shock on their exhibition is lower, the speed of their recovery is quicker, and the degree of their healing is more massive. A tough SC empowers organizations to react to client needs and keep up with high help levels while controlling net working capital and expenses (Hosseini et al., 2019; Ivanov & Das, 2020; Mohammed et al., 2021). Resilient businesses use buffers and strategic inventory to absorb shocks in the day-to-day, end-to-end SC operations more effectively. In case of a considerable disturbance, they decrease the danger of a total organization closure and other severe results by, for instance, changing from essential to auxiliary material stream ways (rebalancing supply throughout the planet) and evolving providers (M. Sharma et al., 2021). Three columns should uphold an organization's endeavours to assimilate shocks: overhauling the worldwide organization, building up new boundaries for SC supports, and overseeing providers proactively (Behzadi et al., 2017).

A formidable stockpile, assembling, and dispersion network accomplish adaptability through the specific utilization of excess, for example, dual sourcing. Different methodologies remember nearshoring to decrease dependence for complex worldwide coordination's and vertical reconciliation to bring essential parts (counting data innovation). While updating an overall organization, a far-reaching hazard appraisal can fill in as the establishment for deciding how to adjust adaptability, proficiency, and adequacy (Ahmed et al., 2021; Amalia et al., 2020; Gouda & Saranga, 2018). An organization should create a viable multi-echelon stock system to advance versatility, prompting new stock focuses in the SC high-instability hubs. Strong organizations assess the criticality of their providers and change provider connections to guarantee asset accessibility (Ali and Gölgeci, 2019; Gölgeci and Kuivalainen, 2020; Karmaker et al., 2021; Sarkis, 2020). They additionally gain perceivability into various levels of providers, permitting them to evaluate upstream dangers thoroughly. Strong organizations utilize spry, storehouse breaking methods of working across multiple capacities and locales to respond rapidly and change following interruptions just as normal unpredictability (Kahiluoto et al., 2020; Sars & Daiichi, 2021; Shashi et al., 2020). They use simulation to develop a forward-looking view of risks and opportunities, and they manage standard deviations through transparency. They also employ robust processes and analytical tools to respond quickly to daily volatility and minor disruptions (Ivanov & Dolgui, 2020; Majumdar et al., 2020; Martínez et al., 2020; Taqi et al., 2020).

Strategy and Hypothesis Development

Companies' current SC strategies and practices are incapable of combating this pandemic. SC professionals and managers must reconsider their strategy (Behzadi et al., 2020; Hosseini et al., 2019). The SC networks must be redesigned, and the RSC strategy must be devised to assist businesses in emerging from the COVID-19 pandemic and sustaining this type of disruption in the long term. The following is the RSC COVID-19 strategy:

Process Automation and Artificial Intelligence (PAAI)

Digital technology is fundamental in SCR on account of its high availability, precision, and straightforwardness. The capacity of an SC to forestall and assimilate changes and return to pre-unsettling influence execution levels is alluded to as SCR (Belhadi et al., 2021). As of late, significant information associations have moved toward measure robotization and manufactured reasoning in their SC activities because of expanded computational force and the fast improvement of cutting-edge examination. Their utilization supports promptly setting off the alert in unavoidable and capricious occasions because of their capacity to—1) cautiously evaluate the circumstance and make opportune moves that assistance to alleviate hazard and increment benefits; 2) manage deviated data and the ability to manage an unsure climate that can't be anticipated completely, with the assistance of learning and reception (Ivanov and Dolgui, 2020; Sarkis, 2020). This essential intercession can help the association by working on prescient abilities and making SC individuals aware of fortifying their SC organizations and settle on convenient choices (Chowdhury, Sarkar, Paul, et al., 2020; Queiroz et al., 2020; Verma & Gustafsson, 2020).

H1: Process automation and artificial intelligence will create an impact on the RSC of the MSMEs.

Outsource of the Business Operation (OBO)

Companies all over the world have adopted outsourcing strategies. Offshoring and outsourcing is a strategic decision to focus on the highest value-added and brand value (Chowdhury, Sarkar, Saha, et al., 2020; McMaster et al., 2020). Firms outsource their business operations to avoid overproduction costs and cycle times (M. S. Kumar et al., 2020; Valdez-Juárez et al., 2021). Outsourcing strategies enable businesses to consider economies of scale, optimize production costs, and increase profit margins (Dannenberg et al., 2020; Rowan & Galanakis, 2020). As a result, businesses can use an outsourcing strategy for crisis management, giving SC agents a competitive advantage during crises and contracting out a specific work process or process to an outside service provider (Rodrigues et al., 2021; Singh et al., 2020). Payroll, accounting, telemarketing, data collection, social media marketing, customer service, and other services may be offered (Ivanov, 2020; Mahmud et al., 2021). It usually provides supplementary — rather than core — business functions in the form of technical or nontechnical services.

H2: Outsourcing of business operations will create an impact on the RSC of the MSMEs.

Geographical Integration of SC Agents (GISCA)

An intertwined supply network in which individual SC must be resilient on a large scale. Suppliers, retailers, manufacturers, wholesalers, customers, and other stakeholders must work together to holistically manage the SC network (M. Sharma & Joshi, 2020; R. Sharma et al., 2020). The mix of SC specialists spread across a topographical area can dispose of data unevenness and exchange boundaries through the free progression of materials, administrations, data, and work on pooled connections. This topographical combination can help specialists decide on proper disturbances and build a strong SC (Remko, 2020). Geographical integration seeks to capitalize on space's comparative advantages, specifically to improve access to markets, labour, parts, and resources. A set of origin/destination relationships between SC actors establishes spatial complementarity (Biswas & Das, 2020; Guan et al., 2020; Končar et al., 2020).

H3: Geographical integration of SC agents will create an impact on the RSC of the MSMEs.

Cost Optimisation (CO)

Customers' satisfaction can be improved by delivering tangible and intangible products at reasonable prices (Cohen, 2020; Ivanov & Dolgui, 2020; Queiroz et al., 2020). Cost optimization, which is required for establishing cost-minimizing distribution networks and logistical routes, is one of the most fundamental aspects of SC management. Thus, cost optimization is essential in building a resilient SC because it improves customer service levels. Cost optimization in the SC includes lowering the purchasing, storing, and transporting of goods (Singh et al., 2020).

H4: Cost optimisation will create an impact on the RSC of the MSMEs.

Inventory Management (IM)

Inventory is a necessary cradle that organizations should continue to manage sudden interest or bullwhips. It is continually at chances with the increasing expense of holding resources. Therefore, powerful stock administration is essential to assist associations with working on their capacity to settle on educated choices about stock stocks and item variation accessibility to fulfil needs during crises (Barbate et al., 2021; Dube et al., 2021; Monmousseau et al., 2020; Zhang et al., 2021). During an emergency, an inventory management strategy allows the company to manage multiple product inventories effectively, reduce inventory pilling risk, optimize holding costs, and achieve SCR (Butu et al., 2020; Fink, 2020; Nandi et al., 2020).

H5: Inventory management will create an impact on the RSC of the MSMEs.

RESEARCH METHODOLOGY

Table 1 (a). Demographics of the respondents

Gender	Number of Respondents	Percentage
Male	214	52.07
Female	197	47.93
Educational Qualification of the respondents		
Polytechnic	93	22.63
Bachelor's degree	142	34.55
Master degree	176	42.82
Work experience of the respondents		
<5 years	58	14.11
6-10 years	115	27.98
11-15 years	92	22.38
>15 years	146	35.52
Year of operation of the firm		
Less than five years	78	18.98
Between 5 years to 10 years	129	31.39
Between 10 years to 20 years	119	28.95
More than 20 years	85	20.68
Number of employees working in the firms		
10-25 employees	32	7.79
26-50 employees	39	9.49
51-100 employees	58	14.11
101-150 employees	95	23.11
151-250 employees	81	19.71
251and above	106	25.79

Data was collected from two sources primary sources and secondary sources. Primary sources data was collected using questionnaires through the survey method. Secondary sources of data were collected from the reports, magazines, websites, and online databases. A questionnaire was being prepared with the help of professionals and academicians in the SC area. The questionnaire contained series of questions that were asked to be filled by the respondents. The target population were the SC professionals working in the various MSMEs of India. The simple random sampling method was used so that there is no biasness in the collection of data. The questionnaire that was sent for collecting the data was 560, out of which 411 questionnaires came back to us, which were used in the data analysis. For data analysis, we had used SPSS 20.0 and AMOS 22.0 software (Henseler et al., 2009). After collecting the data, we had checked whether the data collected is having biasness or not. For that, we had performed a single factor Harman test in the SPSS 20.0. Exploratory factor analysis was committed to checking how much variance the first-factor extract and result came to be 24.134%, below 50% of the recommended value (Podsakoff, 2003). A questionnaire-based survey method was used. Table 1 shows the distribution of respondents based on different industries.

Table 1 (b). Demographics of the respondents

Respondents current position		
Owner	42	10.22
Director	68	16.55
Plant Manager	73	17.76
IT Manager	65	15.82
SC manager	78	18.98
Operational manager	85	20.68
Type of firms		
Micro enterprises	132	32.12
Small enterprises	137	33.33
Medium enterprises	142	34.55
Type of Industry		
Industrial Engineering	32	7.79
Oil, Gas and Coal	23	5.60
Machinery	54	13.14
Packaging material and supplies	31	7.54
Automobile parts and spares	97	23.60
Construction materials	44	10.71
Information technology and services	51	12.41
Agro-based industry	49	11.92
Leather industry	30	7.30

RESULTS

Assessment of reliability helps examine the degree of internal consistency between variable measurement items and its freedom of error at any point in time (Kline, 2015). Cronbach's alpha was utilized to test the reliability of the data (Hair, J. F., Black, W. C., Babin, B. J., Anderson, R. E., & Tatham, 2010; Mukherjee, Chittipaka, et al., 2021). The recommended value should be greater than 0.70 (Nunnally, 1994). Table 2 shows the importance of Cronbach's alpha. Hence, all the values are within the threshold level (Hair, J. F., Black, W. C., Babin, B. J., Anderson, R. E., & Tatham, 2010; Mukherjee, Baral, et al., 2021)

Table 2. Cronbach's alpha

Sl.No.	Variable	Cronbach's Alpha
1	PAAI	0.957
2	OBO	0.904
3	GISCA	0.89
4	CO	0.879
5	IM	0.897
6	RSC_MSMEs	0.866

The first step of the EFA was to evaluate the appropriateness of the sample size. SPSS 20.0 was utilized for EFA. As a result, Kaiser-Meyer-Olkin (KMO) analysis was used to determine whether those items are sufficiently correlated and whether a factor analysis could be performed. The current study's KMO value is 0.828. This statistic's minimum level is 0.60 (Hu & Bentler, 1999; Mukherjee, Mohan Baral, et al., 2021). The extraction method used was principal component analysis. Table 3 shows the values of total variance extracted.

Table 3. Total variance extracted

Component	Initial Eigenvalues			Extraction Sums of Squared Loadings			Rotation Sums of Squared Loadings		
	Total	% of Variance	Cumulative %	Total	% of Variance	Cumulative %	Total	% of Variance	Cumulative %
1	6.300	26.251	26.251	6.300	26.251	26.251	4.916	20.485	20.485
2	3.919	16.328	42.579	3.919	16.328	42.579	4.063	16.930	37.415
3	2.845	11.854	54.433	2.845	11.854	54.433	3.781	15.755	53.169
4	2.495	10.396	64.829	2.495	10.396	64.829	2.545	10.602	63.771
5	2.255	9.396	74.225	2.255	9.396	74.225	2.509	10.453	74.225

The Rotated Component Matrix is required to interpret the results of the analysis. Rotation helps group the items, and each group contains more than two items, simplifying the structure. Table 4 shows the values of the rotated component matrix.

Table 4. Rotated component matrix

Rotated Component Matrix					
	Component				
	1	2	3	4	5
PAAI1	.860				
PAAI2	.919				
PAAI3	.924				
PAAI4	.889				
PAAI5	.863				
PAAI6	.877				
OBO1				.952	
OBO2				.950	
OBO3				.814	
GISCA1		.853			
GISCA2		.825			
GISCA3		.833			
GISCA4		.886			
GISCA5		.458			
GISCA6		.900			
CO1			.778		
CO2			.828		
CO3			.770		
CO4			.776		
CO5			.744		
CO6			.803		
IM1					.898
IM2					.923
IM3					.909

All of the components' composite reliability (CR) was also measured. Because of its ability to produce better results is calculated for internal consistency reliability

(Jenatabadi, 2015). The CR values of the five constructs are more significant than 0.7, indicating that the composite reliability measures are reliable. Table 5 displays the CR values. According to Fornell & Larcker, (1981), AVE > 0.5 indicates convergent validity. The AVE values for the constructs are shown in Table 5. All of the values are greater than 0.5, implying that all constructs have convergent validity (Hair et al., 2014). Fornell & Larcker (1981) proposed that the AVE of the construct must be greater than the square of the correlation between that construct and the other constructs to calculate its validity (Hair et al., 2012). The values for construct correlation and AVE are shown in Table 5. As a result, the extracted variance value is greater than the squared correlation value (Cable & DeRue, 2002).

Table 5. CR, AVE, Divergent validity

	AVE	CR	Variance Extracted Between Factors				
			PAAI	GISCA	CO	OBO	IM
PAAI	0.889	0.958	1				
GISCA	0.793	0.915	0.709	1			
CO	0.783	0.867	0.701	0.621	1		
OBO	0.905	0.933	0.805	0.724	0.716	1	
IM	0.91	0.935	0.809	0.728	0.72	0.824	1

SEM was used to test the hypothesis (Byrne, 2010). Because of its powerful graphic representations and user-friendly interfaces, AMOS 22.0 was used for this research. The model's output is shown here. Figure 1 depicts the final model and the latent variables, their indicators, and the dependent variable. Table 6 shows the model fit values and fits indices. Figure 1 below shows the final structural model generated after analysis in AMOS 22.0.

Table 6. Final Goodness of Fit Indices for the Structural Model

Goodness-of-Fit Indices	Default Model	Benchmark
Absolute goodness-of-fit measure		
CMIN/Df	2.278	Lower Limit: 1.0; Upper Limit 2.0/3.0 or 5.0
GFI	0.890	>0.90
Absolute badness of fit measure		
RMSEA	0.056	⩽0.08
Incremental fit measure		
CFI	0.949	⩾0.90
IFI	0.949	⩾0.90
TLI	0.944	⩾0.90
Parsimony fit measure		
PCFI	0.866	⩾0.50
PNFI	0.833	⩾0.50

The path estimate analysis results are shown in Table 7. The outcome indicates that the five hypotheses are supported by P-value (Hair et al., 2014). Multiple square correlations (R^2) are used to assess how well a regression line predicts actual data points between 0 and 1, stating how well one variable indicates another (Hair et al., 2012). The closer the value, the better the model can predict that technology (Kline, 2012). The proposed model can account for 56 per cent of RSC_MSMEs variance.

Table 7. Structural model results

	Estimate	S.E.	C.R.	P	Hypothesis
RSC_MSMEs <--- GISCA	0.18	0.039	4.62	***	Supported
RSC_MSMEs <--- OBO	0.131	0.032	4.09	***	Supported
RSC_MSMEs <--- PAAI	0.112	0.039	2.87	***	Supported
RSC_MSMEs <--- CO	0.386	0.052	7.42	***	Supported
RSC_MSMEs <--- IM	0.103	0.024	4.29	***	Supported

Figure 1. Model for resilient SC strategies in the MSMEs sector to handle the COVID-19 disruptions

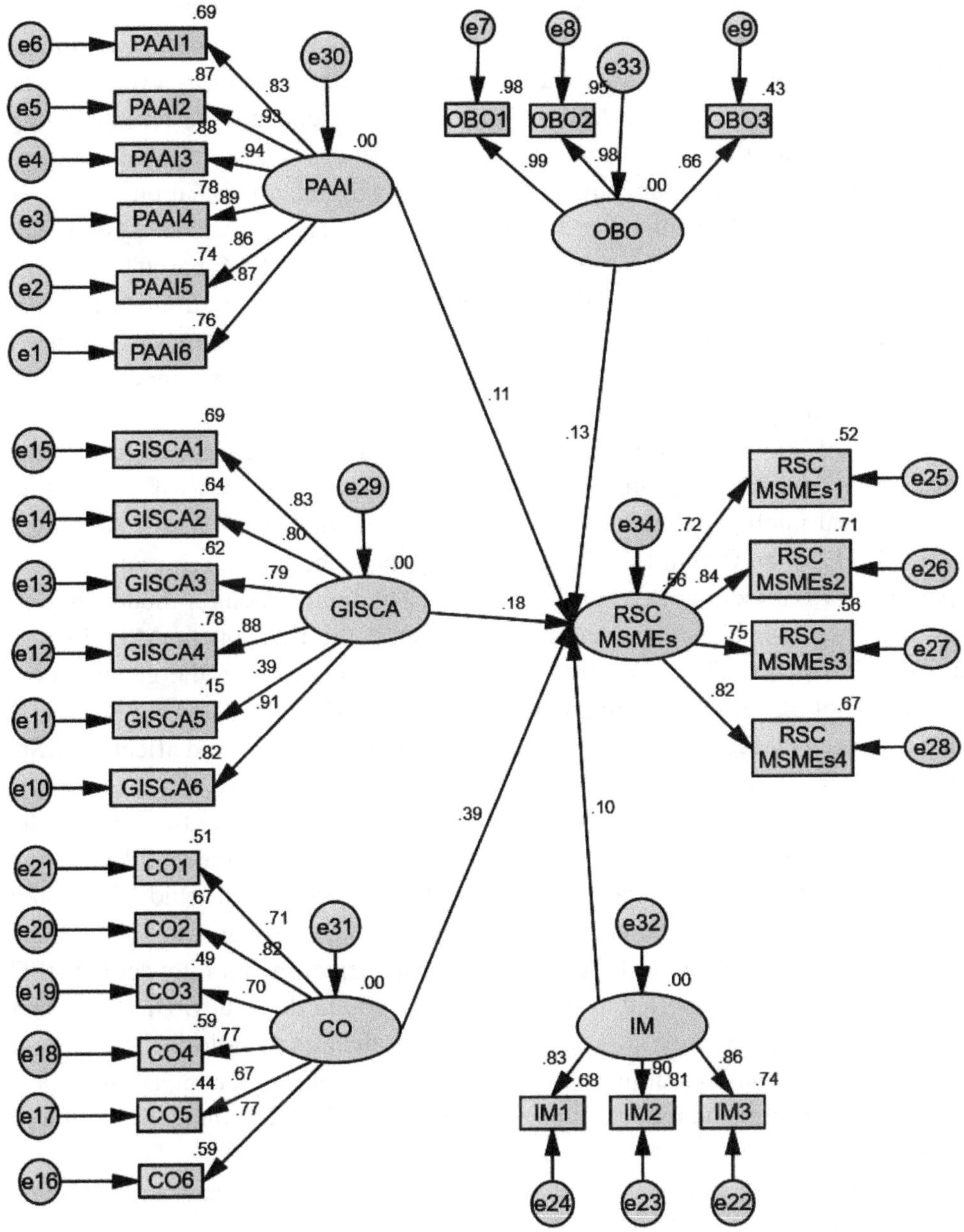

DISCUSSION

Companies must rethink SC policy development to prepare for a potential pandemic. Organisations also need to educate staff about the symptoms and prevention of COVID-19 and adequate health measures that affect the SC (D Das, 2020; D. Das et al., 2021; Karwasra et al., 2021). Companies must concentrate on integrating and working with the federal and core SCs members to reach a unified goal and manage all losses and future gains in reconstructing market foundations (Antai & Mutshinda, 2021; Mohammed et al., 2021). In 2021, The MSME ecosystem will be more robust. Business strength appears to have been aided by phased lockdowns and MSME readiness for external circumstances in the context of digital adoption. Cash flow management will be a defining factor for MSME business success in the future, with lockdowns and restrictions a constant reality in the pandemic world (Roy et al., 2020).

H1 tested how process automation and artificial intelligence will impact the RSC of the MSMEs. The final structural model showed that process automation and artificial intelligence would impact the RSC of the MSMEs was supported as $\beta = 0.112$, $p = .000$ in this study. H2 tested how the outsourcing of business operations will affect the RSC of the MSMEs. The final structural model showed that outsourcing business operations would impact the RSC of the MSMEs was supported as $\beta = 0.131$, $p = .000$ in this study. H3 tested how the geographical integration of SC agents will impact the RSC of the MSMEs. The final structural model showed that the geographical integration of SC agents would affect the RSC of the MSMEs was supported as $\beta = 0.18$, $p = .000$ in this study.

H4 tested how will the cost optimisation create an impact on the RSC of the MSMEs. The final structural model showed that cost optimisation would affect the RSC of the MSMEs was supported as $\beta = 0.386$, $p = .000$ in this study. H5 tested how will inventory management create an impact on the RSC of the MSMEs. The final structural model showed that inventory management would impact the RSC of the MSMEs was supported as $\beta = 0.103$, $p = .000$ in this study. Hardware and tools, electronic appliances, auto parts, building products, and various chemical and industrial specialities are among the industries at high risk. Telecom, automobiles, computer hardware, and industrial conglomerates are the other industries that will be impacted.

Companies that identify and manage SC risks have a better chance of finding a solution or lessening the Corona virus's impact. The best thing to do is to understand the company's SC risks (Ghosh et al., 2020). Fortunately, SC visibility tools have improved, making it easier to analyze risks and address them with appropriate solutions over time (R. Sharma et al., 2020). Companies must also plan for increased costs and the terms of their contract and its enforcement. Customer obligations must be met, and contractual payment terms must be reviewed. For proper backup, allocation requirements and other debts must be met. As the outbreak continues, manufacturers must develop and implement an SC responsive system to reduce risk and address interruptions to their operations (D Das, 2020; P Barbieri, 2020). Companies should communicate with critical suppliers to determine the inventory level carried or that may be in short supply, and they should also deploy resources on alternative suppliers (Dube et al., 2021; Thaichon, 2021).

Factory workers are working around the clock to meet market demand for high-priority goods. To avoid unnecessary scarcity of goods, inventory optimization and reasonable purchase restrictions on items such as toilet paper, wet wipes, protective masks, food grains, and perishable items are required (Agrawal, 2020; Xue et al., 2021). Supply-demand inequity poses a severe problem, and suppliers of essential commodities are struggling to keep up with demand. Suppliers are also concerned about storage and inventory issues. Capacity constraints and unpredictability in the market hamper their decision-making process. Nobody knows for sure how long this crisis will last. Purchasing becomes a difficult task as a result. As the number of infected people grows and the virus spreads, some people are panicking and stockpiling goods and supplies (Iacus et al., 2020; Miani et al., 2021; Scheiwiller & Zizka, 2021).

CONCLUSION

COVID-19 pandemic has created an opportunity for the firms to redesign their SC to sustain any disruptions shortly. This research aims to find out the strategies that could help the industries develop an RSC. Five strategies were identified from the literature which can help the MSMEs for an RSC. The five strategies identified were process automation and artificial intelligence, outsourcing business operations, geographical integration of SC agents, cost optimisation, and inventory management. Five hypotheses were proposed for the five strategies. A questionnaire was being prepared for survey-based research in the MSMEs sector of India. The target population were the employees working in those sectors. After the collection of the data, we performed exploratory factor analysis and a structural equation modelling approach. The model developed satisfied all the parameters, and the five hypotheses were accepted.

REFERENCES

Agrawal, A. (2020). Sustainability of airlines in India with Covid-19: Challenges ahead and possible way-outs. *Journal of Revenue and Pricing Management, 20*(4), 457–472. doi:10.1057/s41272-020-00257-z

Ahmed, S., Taqi, H. M. M., Farabi, Y. I., Sarker, M., Ali, S. M., & Sankaranarayanan, B. (2021). Evaluation of Flexible Strategies to Manage the COVID-19 Pandemic in the Education Sector. *Global Journal of Flexible Systems Management*, 1–25. doi:10.1007/s40171-021-00267-9

Ali, I., & Gölgeci, I. (2019). Where is supply chain resilience research heading? A systematic and co-occurrence analysis. *International Journal of Physical Distribution & Logistics Management*, *49*(8), 793–815. doi:10.1108/IJPDLM-02-2019-0038

Amalia, S., Darma, D. C., & Maria, S. (2020). Supply Chain Management and the Covid-19 Outbreak: Optimizing its Role for Indonesia. *Current Research Journal of Social Sciences and Humanities*, *3*(2), 196–202. doi:10.12944/CRJSSH.3.2.07

Antai, I., & Mutshinda, C. M. (2021). Competitor Identification for Sustainable Survival Strategies: Illustration with Supply Chain Versus Supply Chain Competition. *Sustainability, 13*(14), 7861. doi:10.3390/su13147861

Barbate, V., Gade, R. N., & Raibagkar, S. S. (2021). COVID-19 and Its Impact on the Indian Economy. *Vision: The Journal of Business Perspective*. doi:10.1177/0972262921989126

Barbieri, P., Boffelli, A., Elia, S., Fratocchi, L., Kalchschmidt, M., & Samson, D. (2020). What can we learn about reshoring after Covid-19? *Operations Management Research, 13*(3), 131–136. doi:10.1007/s12063-020-00160-1

Barbieri, P., Boffelli, A., Elia, S., Fratocchi, L., Kalchschmidt, M., & Samson, D. (2020). What can we learn about reshoring after Covid-19? *Oper Manag Res*, *13*(3), 131–136. doi:10.100712063-020-00160-1

Behzadi, G., O'Sullivan, M. J., & Olsen, T. L. (2020). On metrics for supply chain resilience. *European Journal of Operational Research*, *287*(1), 145–158. doi:10.1016/j.ejor.2020.04.040

Behzadi, G., O'Sullivan, M. J., Olsen, T. L., Scrimgeour, F., & Zhang, A. (2017). Robust and resilient strategies for managing supply disruptions in an agribusiness supply chain. *International Journal of Production Economics*, *191*, 207–220. doi:10.1016/j.ijpe.2017.06.018

Belhadi, A., Kamble, S., Jabbour, C. J. C., Gunasekaran, A., Ndubisi, N. O., & Venkatesh, M. (2021). Manufacturing and service supply chain resilience to the COVID-19 outbreak: Lessons learned from the automobile and airline industries. *Technological Forecasting and Social Change*, *163*, 120447. doi:10.1016/j.techfore.2020.120447 PMID:33518818

Belhadi, A., Mani, V., Kamble, S. S., Khan, S. A. R., & Verma, S. (2021). Artificial intelligence-driven innovation for enhancing supply chain resilience and performance under the effect of supply chain dynamism: an empirical investigation. Annals of Operations Research. doi:10.100710479-021-03956-x

Biswas, T. K., & Das, M. C. (2020). Selection of the barriers of supply chain management in Indian manufacturing sectors due to Covid-19 impacts. *Operational Research in Engineering Sciences: Theory and Applications*, *3*(3), 1–12. doi:10.31181/oresta2030301b

Blackhurst, J., Craighead, C. W., Elkins, D., & Handfield, R. B. (2005). An empirically derived agenda of critical research issues for managing supply-chain disruptions. *International Journal of Production Research*, *43*(19), 4067–4081. doi:10.1080/00207540500151549

Butu, A., Brumă, I. S., Tanasă, L., Rodino, S., Vasiliu, C. D., Doboş, S., & Butu, M. (2020). The impact of COVID-19 crisis upon the consumer buying behavior of fresh vegetables directly from local producers. Case study: The quarantined area of Suceava County, Romania. *International Journal of Environmental Research and Public Health*, *17*(15), 1–25. doi:10.3390/ijerph17155485 PMID:32751368

Byrne, B. M. (2010). Structural equation modeling with AMOS: Basic concepts, applications, and programming (multivariate applications series). *Taylor & Francis Group*, *396*, 7384.

Cable, D. M., & DeRue, D. S. (2002). The convergent and discriminant validity of subjective fit perceptions. *The Journal of Applied Psychology*, *87*(5), 875–884. doi:10.1037/0021-9010.87.5.875 PMID:12395812

Chaudhary, M., Sodani, P. R., & Das, S. (2020). Effect of COVID-19 on Economy in India: Some Reflections for Policy and Programme. *Journal of Health Management*, *22*(2), 169–180. doi:10.1177/0972063420935541

Chowdhury, M. T., Sarkar, A., Paul, S. K., & Moktadir, M. A. (2020). *A case study on strategies to deal with the impacts of COVID-19 pandemic in the food and beverage industry*. Operations Management Research. doi:10.100712063-020-00166-9

Chowdhury, M. T., Sarkar, A., Saha, P. K., & Anik, R. H. (2020). Enhancing supply resilience in the COVID-19 pandemic: A case study on beauty and personal care retailers. *Modern Supply Chain Research and Applications*, *2*(3), 143–159. doi:10.1108/MSCRA-07-2020-0018

Christopher, M., & Peck, H. (2004). Building the Resilient Supply Chain. *International Journal of Logistics Management*, *15*(2), 1–14. doi:10.1108/09574090410700275

Cohen, M. J. (2020). *Does the COVID-19 outbreak mark the onset of a sustainable consumption transition?* doi:10.1080/15487733.2020.1740472

Dannenberg, P., Fuchs, M., Riedler, T., & Wiedemann, C. (2020). Digital Transition by COVID-19 Pandemic? The German Food Online Retail. *Tijdschrift voor Economische en Sociale Geografie*, *111*(3), 543–560. doi:10.1111/tesg.12453 PMID:32836487

Das, D., Datta, A., & Kumar, P. (2020). Exit Strategies for COVID 19: An ISM and MICMAC approach. *Asia Pacific Journal of Health Management*, *15*(3), 94–109. doi:10.24083/apjhm.v15i3.423

Das, D., Datta, A., Kumar, P., Kazancoglu, Y., & Ram, M. (2021). Building supply chain resilience in the era of COVID-19: An AHP-DEMATEL approach. *Operations Management Research*, *2021*, 1–19. doi:10.100712063-021-00200-4

Das, S., Basak, S., & Das, G. M. (2020). A Study for Understanding the Problems of MSMEs under Current Pandemic Situation with Special Reference to Kolkata. *The Management Accountant Journal*, *55*(12), 65–67. doi:10.33516/maj.v55i12.65-67p

Dube, K., Nhamo, G., & Chikodzi, D. (2021). COVID-19 pandemic and prospects for recovery of the global aviation industry. *Journal of Air Transport Management*, *92*(December), 102022. doi:10.1016/j.jairtraman.2021.102022

Fink, L. (2020). Conducting Information Systems Research in the Midst of the COVID-19 Pandemic: Opportunities and Challenges. *Information Systems Management*, *37*(4), 256–259. doi:10.1080/10580530.2020.1814460

Fornell, C., & Larcker, D. F. (1981). Evaluating Structural Equation Models with Unobservable Variables and Measurement Error. *JMR, Journal of Marketing Research*, *18*(1), 39–50. doi:10.1177/002224378101800104

Ghosh, A., Nundy, S., & Mallick, T. K. (2020). How India is dealing with COVID-19 pandemic. *Sensors International*, *1*, 100021. doi:10.1016/j.sintl.2020.100021 PMID:34766039

Gölgeci, I., & Kuivalainen, O. (2020). Does social capital matter for supply chain resilience? The role of absorptive capacity and marketing-supply chain management alignment. *Industrial Marketing Management, 84*(September), 63–74. doi:10.1016/j.indmarman.2019.05.006

Gouda, S. K., & Saranga, H. (2018). Sustainable supply chains for supply chain sustainability: Impact of sustainability efforts on supply chain risk. *International Journal of Production Research, 56*(17), 5820–5835. doi:10.1080/00207543.2018.1456695

Guan, Z., Zhang, X., Zhou, M., & Dan, Y. (2020). Demand information sharing in competing supply chains with manufacturer-provided service. *International Journal of Production Economics, 220*, 107450. doi:10.1016/j.ijpe.2019.07.023

Hair, J. F., Black, W. C., Babin, B. J., Anderson, R. E., & Tatham, R. L. (2010). *Multivariate Data Analysis* (7th ed.). Prentice Hall.

Hair, J. F., Sarstedt, M., Hopkins, L., & Kuppelwieser, V. G. (2014). Partial least squares structural equation modeling (PLS-SEM): An emerging tool in business research. European Business Review, 26(2), 106–121. doi:10.1108/EBR-10-2013-0128

Hair, J. F., Sarstedt, M., Ringle, C. M., & Mena, J. A. (2012). An assessment of the use of partial least squares structural equation modeling in marketing research. *Journal of the Academy of Marketing Science, 40*(3), 414–433. doi:10.100711747-011-0261-6

Henseler, J., Ringle, C. M., & Sinkovics, R. R. (2009). The use of partial least squares path modeling in international marketing. Advances in International Marketing, 20, 277–319. doi:10.1108/S1474-7979(2009)0000020014

Hosseini, S., Ivanov, D., & Dolgui, A. (2019). Review of quantitative methods for supply chain resilience analysis. *Transportation Research Part E, Logistics and Transportation Review, 125*, 285–307. doi:10.1016/j.tre.2019.03.001

Hu, L. T., & Bentler, P. M. (1999). Cutoff criteria for fit indexes in covariance structure analysis: Conventional criteria versus new alternatives. *Structural Equation Modeling, 6*(1), 1–55. doi:10.1080/10705519909540118

Iacus, S. M., Natale, F., Santamaria, C., Spyratos, S., & Vespe, M. (2020). Estimating and projecting air passenger traffic during the COVID-19 coronavirus outbreak and its socio-economic impact. *Safety Science, 129*(May), 104791. doi:10.1016/j.ssci.2020.104791 PMID:32377034

Ivanov, D. (2020). Predicting the impacts of epidemic outbreaks on global supply chains: A simulation-based analysis on the coronavirus outbreak (COVID-19/SARS-CoV-2) case. *Transportation Research Part E, Logistics and Transportation Review*, *136*(March), 101922. doi:10.1016/j.tre.2020.101922 PMID:32288597

Ivanov, D., & Das, A. (2020). Coronavirus (COVID-19/SARS-CoV-2) and supply chain resilience: A research note. *International Journal of Integrated Supply Management*, *13*(1), 90–102. doi:10.1504/IJISM.2020.107780

Ivanov, D., & Dolgui, A. (2020). Viability of intertwined supply networks: Extending the supply chain resilience angles towards survivability. A position paper motivated by COVID-19 outbreak. *International Journal of Production Research*, *58*(10), 2904–2915. doi:10.1080/00207543.2020.1750727

Jenatabadi, H. S. (2015). *An Overview of Path Analysis: Mediation Analysis Concept in Structural Equation Modeling*. https://arxiv.org/abs/1504.03441

Kahiluoto, H., Mäkinen, H., & Kaseva, J. (2020). Supplying resilience through assessing diversity of responses to disruption. *International Journal of Operations & Production Management*, *40*(3), 271–292. doi:10.1108/IJOPM-01-2019-0006

Karmaker, C. L., Ahmed, T., Ahmed, S., Ali, S. M., Moktadir, M. A., & Kabir, G. (2021). Improving supply chain sustainability in the context of COVID-19 pandemic in an emerging economy: Exploring drivers using an integrated model. *Sustainable Production and Consumption*, *26*, 411–427. doi:10.1016/j.spc.2020.09.019 PMID:33015267

Karwasra, K., Soni, G., Mangla, S. K., & Kazancoglu, Y. (2021). Assessing dairy supply chain vulnerability during the Covid-19 pandemic. *International Journal of Logistics Research and Applications*, 1–19. doi:10.1080/13675567.2021.1910221

Kline, R. B. (2012). *Assumptions in structural equation modeling*. PsycNET. https://psycnet.apa.org/record/2012-16551-007

Kline, R. B. (2015). *Principles and practice of structural equation modeling*. Guilford publications.

Končar, J., Grubor, A., Marić, R., Vučenović, S., & Vukmirović, G. (2020). Setbacks to IoT implementation in the function of FMCG supply chain sustainability during COVID-19 pandemic. *Sustainability (Switzerland)*, *12*(18), 7391. Advance online publication. doi:10.3390u12187391

Kumar, M. S., Raut, D. R. D., Narwane, D. V. S., & Narkhede, D. B. E. (2020). Applications of industry 4.0 to overcome the COVID-19 operational challenges. *Diabetes & Metabolic Syndrome, 14*(5), 1283–1289. doi:10.1016/j.dsx.2020.07.010 PMID:32755822

Kumar, P., & Kumar Singh, R. (2021). Strategic framework for developing resilience in Agri-Food Supply Chains during COVID 19 pandemic. *International Journal of Logistics Research and Applications*, 1–24. doi:10.1080/13675567.2021.1908524

Lopes de Sousa Jabbour, A. B., Chiappetta Jabbour, C. J., Hingley, M., Vilalta-Perdomo, E. L., Ramsden, G., & Twigg, D. (2020). Sustainability of supply chains in the wake of the coronavirus (COVID-19/SARS-CoV-2) pandemic: Lessons and trends. *Modern Supply Chain Research and Applications, 2*(3), 117–122. doi:10.1108/MSCRA-05-2020-0011

Mahmud, P., Paul, S., Azeem, A., Sustainability, P. C. (2021). *Evaluating Supply Chain Collaboration Barriers in Small-and Medium-Sized Enterprises*. doi:10.3390/su13137449

Majumdar, A., Shaw, M., & Sinha, S. K. (2020). COVID-19 debunks the myth of socially sustainable supply chain: A case of the clothing industry in South Asian countries. *Sustainable Production and Consumption, 24*, 150–155. doi:10.1016/j.spc.2020.07.001

Martínez, C., Paraskevas, J. P., Grimm, C., Corsi, T., & Boyson, S. (2020). The Impact of Environmental Risks in Supply Chain Resilience. *Supply Chain Management and Logistics in Emerging Markets*, 11–39. doi:10.1108/978-1-83909-331-920201002

McMaster, M., Nettleton, C., Tom, C., Xu, B., Cao, C., & Qiao, P. (2020). Risk Management: Rethinking Fashion Supply Chain Management for Multinational Corporations in Light of the COVID-19 Outbreak. *Journal of Risk and Financial Management, 13*(8), 173. doi:10.3390/jrfm13080173

Miani, P., Kille, T., Lee, S. Y., Zhang, Y., & Bates, P. R. (2021). The impact of the COVID-19 pandemic on current tertiary aviation education and future careers: Students' perspective. *Journal of Air Transport Management, 94*(January), 102081. doi:10.1016/j.jairtraman.2021.102081

Mohammed, A., Naghshineh, B., Spiegler, V., & Carvalho, H. (2021). Conceptualising a supply and demand resilience methodology: A hybrid DEMATEL-TOPSIS-possibilistic multi-objective optimization approach. *Computers & Industrial Engineering, 160*, 107589. doi:10.1016/j.cie.2021.107589

Monmousseau, P., Marzuoli, A., Feron, E., & Delahaye, D. (2020). Impact of Covid-19 on passengers and airlines from passenger measurements: Managing customer satisfaction while putting the US Air Transportation System to sleep. *Transportation Research Interdisciplinary Perspectives*, *7*, 100179. doi:10.1016/j.trip.2020.100179 PMID:34173460

Mukherjee, S., Baral, M. M., Chittipaka, V., Srivastava, S. C., & Pal, S. K. (2021). *Discussing the Impact of Industry 4.0 in Agriculture Supply Chain*. Springer. doi:10.1007/978-981-16-3033-0_28

Mukherjee, S., Chittipaka, V., & Baral, M. M. (2021). *Developing a Model to Highlight the Relation of Digital Trust With Privacy and Security for the Blockchain Technology*. doi:10.4018/978-1-7998-8081-3.ch007

Mukherjee, S., Mohan Baral, M., Srivastava, S. C., & Jana, B. (2021). Analyzing the problems faced by fashion retail stores due to COVID-19 outbreak. *Parikalpana-KIIT Journal of Management*, *17*(I), 206. Advance online publication. doi:10.23862/kiit-parikalpana/2021/v17/i1/209031

Nandi, S., Sarkis, J., Hervani, A., & Helms, M. (2020). Do blockchain and circular economy practices improve post COVID-19 supply chains? A resource-based and resource dependence perspective. *Industrial Management &amp. Data Systems*, *121*(2), 333–363. doi:10.1108/IMDS-09-2020-0560

Nandi, S., Sarkis, J., Hervani, A. A., & Helms, M. M. (2021). Redesigning Supply Chains using Blockchain-Enabled Circular Economy and COVID-19 Experiences. *Sustainable Production and Consumption*, *27*, 10–22. doi:10.1016/j.spc.2020.10.019 PMID:33102671

Nunnally, J. C. (1994). *Psychometric theory* (3rd ed.). Tata McGraw-Hill Education.

Pavlov, A., Ivanov, D., Pavlov, D., & Slinko, A. (2019). Optimization of network redundancy and contingency planning in sustainable and resilient supply chain resource management under conditions of structural dynamics. *Annals of Operations Research*, *2019*, 1–30. doi:10.100710479-019-03182-6

Pereira, D. da S., & Soares de Mello, J. C. C. B. (2021). Efficiency evaluation of Brazilian airlines operations considering the Covid-19 outbreak. *Journal of Air Transport Management*, *91*, 101976. doi:10.1016/j.jairtraman.2020.101976 PMID:33235408

Podsakoff, N. P. (2003). Common method biases in behavioral research: a critical review of the literature and recommended remedies. *Journal of Applied Psychology*, *885*(879).

Queiroz, M. M., Ivanov, D., Dolgui, A., & Fosso Wamba, S. (2020). Impacts of epidemic outbreaks on supply chains: mapping a research agenda amid the COVID-19 pandemic through a structured literature review. Annals of Operations Research. doi:10.100710479-020-03685-7

Remko, H. (2020). Research opportunities for a more resilient post-COVID-19 supply chain – closing the gap between research findings and industry practice. *International Journal of Operations and Production Management, 40*(4), 341–355. doi:10.1108/IJOPM-03-2020-0165

Rodrigues, M., Franco, M., Sousa, N., & Silva, R. (2021). COVID 19 and the Business Management Crisis: An Empirical Study in SMEs. *Sustainability, 13*(11), 5912. doi:10.3390/su13115912

Rowan, N. J., & Galanakis, C. M. (2020). Unlocking challenges and opportunities presented by COVID-19 pandemic for cross-cutting disruption in agri-food and green deal innovations: Quo Vadis? In Science of the Total Environment (Vol. 748, p. 141362). Elsevier B.V. doi:10.1016/j.scitotenv.2020.141362

Roy, A., Patnaik, B. C. M., & Satpathy, I. (2020). Impact of Covid-19 crisis on Indian MSME sector: A study on remedial measures. *Eurasian Chemical Communications, 2*(9), 991–1000. doi:10.22034/ecc.2020.114672

Sahoo, P., & Ashwani. (2020). COVID-19 and Indian Economy: Impact on Growth, Manufacturing, Trade and MSME Sector. *Global Business Review, 21*(5), 1159–1183. doi:10.1177/0972150920945687

Saikouk, T., Fattam, N., Angappa, G., & Hamdi, A. (2021). The interplay between inter-personal and inter-organizational relationships in coordinating supply chain activities. *International Journal of Logistics Management, 32*(3), 898–917. doi:10.1108/IJLM-11-2020-0443

Sarkis, J. (2020). Supply chain sustainability: Learning from the COVID-19 pandemic. *International Journal of Operations & Production Management, 41*(1), 63–73. doi:10.1108/IJOPM-08-2020-0568

Sars, T., & Daiichi, F. (2021). Major crises and supply chain disruption: Towards greater sustainability. *Strategic Direction, 37*(4), 36–38. doi:10.1108/SD-01-2021-0008

Scheiwiller, S., & Zizka, L. (2021). Strategic responses by European airlines to the Covid-19 pandemic: A soft landing or a turbulent ride? *Journal of Air Transport Management, 95*, 102103. doi:10.1016/j.jairtraman.2021.102103

Shafi, M., Liu, J., & Ren, W. (2020). Impact of COVID-19 pandemic on micro, small, and medium-sized Enterprises operating in Pakistan. *Research in Globalization, 2*, 100018. doi:10.1016/j.resglo.2020.100018

Shahin, A. (2020). *Supply Chain Risk Management under Covid-19: A Review and Research Agenda.* https://www.researchgate.net/publication/343852256

Sharma, A., Adhikary, A., & Borah, S. B. (2020). Covid-19′s impact on supply chain decisions: Strategic insights from NASDAQ 100 firms using Twitter data. *Journal of Business Research, 117*, 443–449. doi:10.1016/j.jbusres.2020.05.035 PMID:32834209

Sharma, M., & Joshi, S. (2020). Digital supplier selection reinforcing supply chain quality management systems to enhance firm's performance. *The TQM Journal.* Advance online publication. doi:10.1108/TQM-07-2020-0160

Sharma, M., Luthra, S., Joshi, S., & Kumar, A. (2021a). Accelerating retail supply chain performance against pandemic disruption: Adopting resilient strategies to mitigate the long-term effects. *Journal of Enterprise Information Management, 34*(6), 1844–1873. Advance online publication. doi:10.1108/JEIM-07-2020-0286

Sharma, M., Luthra, S., Joshi, S., & Kumar, A. (2021b). Accelerating retail supply chain performance against pandemic disruption: adopting resilient strategies to mitigate the long-term effects. *Journal of Enterprise Information Management.* doi:10.1108/JEIM-07-2020-0286

Sharma, R., Shishodia, A., Kamble, S., Gunasekaran, A., & Belhadi, A. (2020). Agriculture supply chain risks and COVID-19: Mitigation strategies and implications for the practitioners. *International Journal of Logistics Research and Applications, 0*(0), 1–27. doi:10.1080/13675567.2020.1830049

Shashi, C., Centobelli, P., Cerchione, R., & Ertz, M. (2020). Managing supply chain resilience to pursue business and environmental strategies. *Business Strategy and the Environment, 29*(3), 1215–1246. doi:10.1002/bse.2428

Singh, S., Kumar, R., Panchal, R., & Tiwari, M. K. (2020). Impact of COVID-19 on logistics systems and disruptions in food supply chain. *International Journal of Production Research, 0*(0), 1–16. doi:10.1080/00207543.2020.1792000

Sipahi, E. (2020). COVID 19 and MSMEs: A revival framework | Research Journal in Advanced Humanities. *Research Journal in Advanced Humanities, 1*(2). https://royalliteglobal.com/advanced-humanities/article/view/146

Taqi, H. M. M., Ahmed, H. N., Paul, S., Garshasbi, M., Ali, S. M., Kabir, G., & Paul, S. K. (2020). Strategies to manage the impacts of the COVID-19 pandemic in the supply chain: Implications for improving economic and social sustainability. *Sustainability (Switzerland)*, *12*(22), 1–25. doi:10.3390u12229483

Thaichon, P. (2021). COVID in the Aviation Industry: Crisis Management, Its Decisions and Outcomes. *COVID-19. Technology and Marketing*, *2019*, 21–31. doi:10.1007/978-981-16-1442-2_2

Valdez-Juárez, L. E., Gallardo-Vázquez, D., & Ramos-Escobar, E. A. (2021). Online Buyers and Open Innovation: Security, Experience, and Satisfaction. *Journal of Open Innovation*, *7*(1), 37. doi:10.3390/joitmc7010037

Verma, S., & Gustafsson, A. (2020). Investigating the emerging COVID-19 research trends in the field of business and management: A bibliometric analysis approach. *Journal of Business Research*, *118*, 253–261. doi:10.1016/j.jbusres.2020.06.057 PMID:32834211

Xue, D., Liu, Z., Wang, B., & Yang, J. (2021). Impacts of COVID-19 on aircraft usage and fuel consumption: A case study on four Chinese international airports. *Journal of Air Transport Management*, *95*, 102106. doi:10.1016/j.jairtraman.2021.102106 PMID:34548769

Zhang, Z., Srivastava, P. R., Eachempati, P., & Yu, Y. (2021, March 23). An intelligent framework for analyzing supply chain resilience of firms in China: A hybrid multicriteria approach. *International Journal of Logistics Management*. Advance online publication. doi:10.1108/IJLM-11-2020-0452

Chapter 5
Impact of the COVID-19 Pandemic on SMEs in Singapore

Abdul Karim Mohamed Yusoff
Independent Researcher, Singapore

Heather Webb
https://orcid.org/0000-0003-0806-7050
Higher Colleges of Technology, Dubai, UAE

Sean Seery
Higher Colleges of Technology, Dubai, UAE

ABSTRACT

It was reported that almost 3,800 companies closed during the height of the COVID-19 pandemic in Singapore. Sometime between April 2020 to August 2020, the pandemic became the litmus test that shattered the fragile small and medium-sized businesses (SMEs) into dissolution. This chapter discusses the impact of the pandemic on Singaporean SMEs and the challenges ahead post recovery. It also discusses possible strategies for SMEs as well as possible governmental strategies.

IMPACT ON SINGAPORE ECONOMY

At the start of the Covid-19 Pandemic, Singapore imposed a lockdown of the "Circuit Breaker" economy from April 7 to May 4, 2020. Safe distancing measures and tight border control, and travel restrictions have a negatively rippling effect on the Singapore economy. The Ministry of Trade and Industry forecast on growth of

DOI: 10.4018/978-1-7998-8346-3.ch005

Singapore's Gross domestic product was downgraded to - 7% to - 4%. At the end of 2020, the Singapore economy's contraction of 5.4% was registered, and the Singapore economy went into recession. Until the second quarter of 2021, the growth forecast of its Gross domestic product had improved by 14.7%, and Singapore's economy was forecast to rebound to 6 to 7% (Faizal Yahya, 2021).

TOUGH CHALLENGES AHEAD FOR SMEs

The most common and inherent weaknesses of the SMEs are:

1. Lack of access to capital
2. Lack of trained and experienced staff
3. Lack of control over the supply chain
4. Lack of alternative strategies in the business

One factor that becomes the single most contributing cost is the rental of shops for the business. The rental rate is indeed high in Singapore compared to other countries. This huge rental cost led to forming an association called "Singapore Tenants United for Fairness" (SGTUFF). Its main objective is to lead negotiations with landlords for better rental terms. Most of its members come from the food and beverage and retail trades, which were significantly affected by the lockdown, a safe distancing measure implemented by the government.

The lockdown imposed by the Singaporean government, April to June 2020, for safe distancing measures during the Pandemic has created poor sales for businesses. Mr. Terence Yew, Chairman of SGTUFF, mentioned that "10 to 15% of his members had serious financial problems". Almost 1,000 members had already closed their shops. What is direr was his prediction that "5% to 10%" of the shops might continue to shut down for the next 6 to 12 months within the same period. Pessimism among small businesses was rife during the Pandemic (Millet Enriquez, 2021).

THE SMEs IMPACTED THE MOST

The Ministry of Trade and Industry was surveyed in June 2020 to assess the impact of Covid-19 across industries. The results are:

Figure 1. Covid-19 Impact Levels On Singaporean Industries

Severely Affected	Significantly Affected
• Accommodation • Air transport • Arts, entertainment and recreation (AER)	• Food and Beverages • Retail Trade • Land Transport

Moderately Affected(Outward-oriented)	Moderately Affected (domestic-oriented)
• Manufacturing • Wholesale trade • Information and Communication • Professional Services • Finance and Insurance	• Construction • Real estate • Business services • Other services (excluding AER)

In this diagram, the severely affected sector under the accommodation category represents hotels, bread and breakfast joints, hostels for foreign students, etc. This sector also includes "air transport" representing airlines, travel agents, and travel operators. Arts, entertainment, and recreation include cinemas, art exhibitions, event management, conference businesses, stage or theater production, and entertainment and zoos. The tight border control measures and travel restrictions had caused severe financial damage to the SMEs in this sector.

Food and beverage businesses, including restaurants, cafes and bars, and pubs, took a significant beating during the lockdown. Retail trades that depend on physical locations and interactions with customers suffered tremendously. Businesses are making only 10 to 15% gross margins and could hardly pay rent and staff salaries.

Land transport includes taxis, privately operated buses, and a mass rapid transit system. SMEs that operated the taxi system, individually operating taxi services were significantly affected. Meanwhile, there has been an increasing demand for Internet technologies and communication technologies internally. Businesses that have been affected due to lockdown have turned to e-commerce and internet platform to make online sales.

SMEs in the Construction and real estate-related sectors were affected moderately due to workforce shortage. The Border control measures and travel restrictions, inhibiting foreign labor force from coming in, had impeded their ability to fulfill contractual obligations in securing developments to completion. Singapore depends very much on foreign construction labor from India, Malaysia, and Bangladesh. Experiencing economic recession during the Pandemic does not help the real estate industry. With low pessimism among the business owners and cautious buyers of new houses, the real estate market will experience this negative dampening impact (MITI, 2020).

STRATEGIES TO KEEP SMEs AFLOAT

These are the common strategies implemented among SMEs during the Pandemic.

1. Reduce the number of outlets.

Having felt that Covid-19 is here to stay, many business owners have tried to reduce the number of outlets. This will incidentally reduce rentals and the cost of operations. Extra staffing could be diverted to the most promising outlets.

2. Reduce staff headcount.

Excess staff had to be reduced when their operations and margins could not sustain the extra staffing in order to reduce the number of outlets. Thus, many incidences of retrenchments occurred during the Covid-19 pandemic among the SMEs to stay survive.

3. Digitalize operations to improve efficiency and reach the consumers.

The lockdown or "Circuit breaker" from April to June 2020 decreased sales. Many SMEs, especially in the Food and Beverage, land transport, and retail trades, had taken the plunge into digitalizing their operations and invested in e-Commerce platforms to reach their customers. Thus, customers will be able to order their goods through online sales platforms using internet technology.

4. Reorganize existing staff.

Staff retained will undergo specific skills training courses offered by the government to improve overall efficiency. These specific skills courses are offered to the public through financial support from the government. SMEs might be able to claim absentee payrolls for each staff who had undergone these skills training courses.

5. Enhance Collaboration among SMEs to obtain supplies.

SMEs have learned that competition among themselves is not the only way to survive. Through their industry associations, some SMEs have begun collaborating to obtain the common supplies during the Pandemic. The supply chain of critical input factors had been damaged due to travel restrictions and border closure.

6. Seek additional funding.

Lacking access to stable finance affects their monthly cashflows. Some SMEs could not literally pay their rents, staff salaries, and the cost of supplies. SMEs face challenges in obtaining finance from institutional financial organizations. Banks and finance companies may not be accommodative with SMEs during this period. Hence, the Singapore government had started its Bridging Loan Scheme in October 2020 to help out SMEs in dire need during the Pandemic. This extra funding will go towards payments of rents and staff salaries. This initiative will help SMEs retain experienced and trained staff and avoid the already high rate of retrenchments and the impending dampening of the property market.

7. Develop new or alternative businesses for new normal.

Many business owners have started to contemplate developing new ventures or alternative businesses when the ill effect of the Pandemic is felt. Forward-looking business owners began to see new opportunities and plan for expansion after the Covid-19 Pandemic. However, few business owners could plan because of their access to solid financing.

8. Relocate business elsewhere.

Many business owners had also contemplated developing business outside Singapore due to the rising cost of doing business and stiff competition. Despite all the assistance, some SMEs cannot improve their net margins. The rising cost of operating expenses and difficulty in getting trained staff are the two critical factors facing SMEs in Singapore. The new emerging markets of its neighbors, namely Vietnam, Thailand, and Cambodia, become strategic considerations for these business owners.

9. Lay-off extra staff.

The staff of SMEs that do not show improved performance and lack necessary skills were retrenched during the Pandemic. Most SMEs adopted the lean strategy during the Pandemic. The government's scheme to help SMEs in keeping their staff is reflected in the new initiative. Known as the "Job Growth Incentive," SMEs which employ new staff will be eligible to participate, and the government will, in actuality, pay for half of the employees' monthly salary for six months.

10. Encourage group buys.

In order to attract huge traffics and sales orders, SMEs in the Food and beverages and retail trades have encouraged their consumers to do group buys. Coupons with price reduction promises are posted on their websites. Individual customers may join their friends to make an order in large quantities that are discounted. Many SMEs conducting businesses online are now following this trend.

GOVERNMENT SUPPORT AND INCENTIVES FOR SMEs

Amid the intense heat of the Pandemic, the Singapore government decided to alleviate the challenges faced by SMEs by providing direct financial support. The financial support also provides grants for skills upgrading and digitalizing operations and improving operational efficiency, including developing e-commerce capabilities and online presence (MITI, 2020).
These are:

1. Temporary Bridging Loan Program

The temporary bridging loan program is aimed to help local enterprises manage their cash flow needs. This includes payment of rentals, staff salaries, cost of operations, and other running expenses. The project owner, Enterprise Singapore, disburses these loans through participating banks and financial institutions. The enterprises are charged 5% per annum and the loan repayment period is five years. The maximum amount for this loan is SDG 3 million. The government shares the risk element at 70% and 30% for the enterprises. Personal guarantees from the owner of enterprises are still required. The loan program started in April to September 2021 and was extended from October 1, 2021, to March 2022.

2. Enhanced Enterprise Financing schemes - Trade Loans

This loan program aims to finance the local enterprises' inventory other the trade needs such as supplies and raw materials. This loan comes in at the right time when the supply chain disruption takes effect due to the lockdown and restrictions to air travel. Enterprises could therefore look for alternative sources from other supply chain networks. The maximum loan for this program is SDG 10 million. It is also for a period of five years. It is observed that Singapore had spent almost SDG 22 billion to disburse these loans to enterprises, and 25,000 enterprises had received the loans. Almost 99% of these enterprises comprised SMEs.

3. Singapore Dollar facility for Enterprise Singapore Loans

In order to make the above loans practically effective, institutional banks and financial organizations are involved in the execution. The Monetary Authority of Singapore (MAS) devised a loan program named "Dollar Facility for Enterprises Singapore Loans." This facility is aimed to lower costs of funding banks and finance companies in supporting lending to local enterprises. The facility provides Singapore Dollar funding at an interest rate of 0.1% per annum for a period of 2 years to support loans made under the Temporary Bridging Loan Program and Enterprise Funding program. The whole scheme is to lower the cost of funding by banks and financial institutions to keep borrowing costs low for local companies.

4. Working Capital Loan under Enterprise Singapore.

Under the Enterprise Singapore (Government related Organization), a Working capital loan is also available for SMEs. The loan period covers five years, and each borrower is allowed up to SDG 300,000. The risk share is apportioned between 50% SMEs and 50% under Enterprise Singapore.

5. Extended Support Scheme.

This aims to help SMEs defer paying the principal of their loan during the Pandemic. Almost 80% of the principal payment can be deferred for a fully secured loan administered by Enterprise Singapore. Businesses are segmented into certain tiers of administration. Principal payments can be deferred from 1 April to 30 September 2021.

6. Rental Support scheme for SMEs during Covid

This cash payout is aimed to provide relief on rental for SMEs. They are given to owner-occupier or tenant-occupier of commercial properties hit by the Covid-19 lockdown. The cash payouts are not-taxable.

7. Job Support Scheme

The Job Support Scheme aims to provide support for employers to pay salaries of their local employees during the Covid-19 Pandemic. The main focus is to retain employees (Singaporeans and permanent residents) and avoid massive retrenchments during economic uncertainty. Except for government organizations and representative offices, all employers are eligible for this scheme.

Under this scheme, the employer receives a proportion of the first SDG 4,600 gross monthly wages from the government. These subsidies from the government depend on the sector in which the employer operates. Employers can allocate the subsidies for their business operations as necessary to retain their employees and keep the business running. It was originally meant to cover up to March 2021 but has since been extended to September 2021.

In order to be eligible for the Job support scheme payouts, employers are required to make compulsory saving contributions for their local employees, known as the Central Provident fund, within certain stipulated deadlines.

8. A string of advisors to help SMEs with loan applications through affiliate institutions.

With the help of the local Chambers of Commerce and other Non-governmental organizations, Enterprise Singapore provides advice to SME members with their loan applications. The government pays these advisors for such consultations.

9. Courses for SME bosses to improve financial understanding

The Enterprise Singapore, representing the government, had worked jointly with Price Waterhouse, an international accounting firm, to develop training courses to improve SMEs' understanding of financial matters. SME owners must attend these courses as part of the mandatory activities tied to the loan applications.

10. Rebates on foreign workers Levy.

The foreign worker levy is charged on each company's foreign worker in Singapore. It is meant to deter local companies from bringing foreign workers into Singapore. The Singapore government allowed companies to bring in foreign workers during normal times due to the lack of local workers to fill the posts. However, due to the border closing, companies are restrained from bringing foreign workers. Those foreign workers stuck in Singapore during the lockdown may continue to work for these companies. The levy rebate for each worker from SDG 90 per worker per month will increase to SDG 250 per worker per month. Almost 15,000 firms will get these rebates. The sectors that will benefit most are Building and construction, Marine shipyard, and all process-oriented sectors, mainly manufacturing (MITI, 2020).

RESPONSES FROM SMEs

The responses from SMEs were mixed concerning governmental support and their ability to cope with the Pandemic.

1. Digitalization initiatives and government support.

Even though the digitalization of operations was the way forward during the Covid-19 Pandemic, not all SMEs were ready for it. A study conducted by the Association of Small and Medium-sized Enterprises (ASME) and Microsoft (Singapore) showed that 83% have plans to digitalize their operations. Only 2 out of 5 SMEs were deemed to have a successful implementation. And 54% of those surveyed mentioned that Covid-19 lockdown had delayed their plans, while 56% of those surveyed said digitalization efforts are very costly.

The other barriers that stymied digitalization efforts were uncertain business environment, lack of digitally skilled employees, lack of government support, and wrong choice of technology used. In the study, respondents among SMEs mentioned that the lack of clarity of business needs before selecting digitalized solutions has led to poor-outcome and sub-optimal use of such technologies.

While SMEs could smoothly take off their digitalization effort, others with successful experience registered 400% productivity improvements. Their efforts paid off with fully optimized operational processes and enhanced employee-customer engagement (Hariz Baharuddin, 2020).

2. Responses from each sector across industries on government support schemes

Figure 2. Types of Support Schemes, Sectors and % Favouring the Scheme

	Types of Support Scheme	Sectors	Responses favouring the scheme in %	Remarks
1	Job Support Scheme	Retail	44	Retail sector responded the hiahest
		Food & Beverage	25	
		Building & Constructions	26	
2	Working Capital Loan	Retail	36	Food &Beverage and Buildina & Construction
		Food & Beverage	43	
		Building & Construction	43	
3	Foreign Worker Levy rebates and waiver of levy	Retail	1.0	Food &Beverage and Building &consctuctions favor the scheme well
		Food & Beverage	3.0	
		Building & Construction	22	
4	Rental relief scheme	Retail	7.0	Retail seems to favor well this scheme.
		Food & Beverage	Nil	
		Building & Construction	1.0	

The Development Bank of Singapore had conducted a "Pulse Check Survey" in early October 2020 on 250 SMEs about their responses on government support schemes to ride over the Pandemic. The results were as follows:

The survey found that 7 out of 10 were confident of meeting repayment obligations for the Temporary bridging loan program, Enhanced financing scheme, and working capital loan scheme when it becomes due. They sacrificed their expansion plans and scaled-down business operations to meet these obligations. Only 3% surveyed felt they could not make the repayment obligations in 2021 and felt that they would wind down their businesses. The retail sector well favored the job support scheme. This is due to the labor-intensive aspect of the sector that requires trained manpower and managerial segments that command higher salaries. As for the working capital loan, the three sectors have a somewhat favorable demand. The highest among them is the Building and Construction as they need higher levels of working capital to buy raw materials and operational costs. The Building and Construction sector responded well that the foreign worker levy and its rebates seem to be favorable on this sector. Most of their workers are foreign laborers coming from countries with relations with Singapore. The retail sector favors the rental relief scheme. The majority of the SMEs conducting retail business are renting premises from property owners for their outlets (Development Bank of Singapore, 2021).

CONCLUSION

There are various perspectives to analyze this situation. We might conclude that:

1. SMEs lack business contingency planning and mindsets

SMEs do not have a business continuity mindset in planning their businesses. Thus, sudden environmental changes might outspend their resources, and their business comes around. Business planning must be an avowed skill of any SME entrepreneur, and this includes riding over contingencies like widespread pandemics or social disturbances.

2. SMEs need to improve the predictability of the supply chain and critical human resources

The Covid-19 Pandemic, with its highly viral and transitive effect, disrupts the community's social and business life. SMEs cannot afford the supply chain disruption and dissipation of their critical human resources due to the safe management measures. Singapore depends very much on the availability of trained and highly skilled foreign employees for the Food & Beverage, manufacturing, and building & construction sectors. Some SMEs in the construction sector could not fulfill their obligations to complete their projects on time and face penalties. In the manufacturing sector, existing local employees and foreign employees who could not go home due to timely border closure had to double their efforts to meet deadlines.

3. SMEs should improve decisions on the choice of technology

SMEs should not rush to take on the digitalization route. There should be careful planning on the types of technology which is appropriate and suitable to their needs and operational conditions. Rushing to digitalize their operations without proper planning might end up in wasteful efforts and frustrations among employees.

REFERENCES

Baharuddin, H. (2020). Over half of SMEs beam digitalization delay on Coronavirus. *The Straits Times*. https://www.straitstimes.com/singapore/over-half-of-smes-blame-digitalisation-delay-On-virus

Development Bank of Singapore. (2021). DBS survey reveals government assisted financing schemes paying off proportion of SMEs flagging cash flow as top concern more than halves since February 2020. *DBS Newsletter*. https://www.dbs.com/newsroom/

Enriquez, M. (2021). *Survival strategies for SMEs as Singapore moves from pandemic to endemic*. Channel News Asia. https://www.channelnewsasia.com/business/survival-strategies-smes-singapore-moves-pandemic-endemic-2158541

Kit. (2020). *About 3,800 companies closed down in April; expect uptick in coming months: Chee Hong Tat.* Channel New Asia. https://www.channelnewsasia.com/business/3800-business-closures-april-uptick-ahead-covid19-coronavirus-648176

Ministry of Trade and Industry. (2020). Impact of covid 19 pandemic on Singapore economy. *MITI Newsletter.* https://www.mti.gov.sg/Resources/feature-articles/2020/Impact-of-the-COVID-19-Pandemic-on-the-Singapore-Economy

Yahya, F. (2021). *Commentary: Singapore should focus on economic growth rather than redistributing a smaller pie as it reopens*. Channel News Asia. https://www.channelnewsasia.com/commentary/singapore-growth-help-low-wage-workers-income-households-2125671

Chapter 6
The Impact of the COVID-19 Pandemic:
Service Quality in Reviving the United Arab Emirates Hospitality Sector

Anca Bocanet
Higher Colleges of Technology, Dubai, UAE

Heather Webb
https://orcid.org/0000-0003-0806-7050
Higher Colleges of Technology, Dubai, UAE

Humaid Almulla
Higher Colleges of Technology, Dubai, UAE

ABSTRACT

The purpose of the study is to explore the role of service quality in reviving the United Arab Emirates hospitality sector post COVID-19 pandemic. Various factors contribute to the success of the hospitality industry in UAE; some of them are strategic location, leisure facilities, and business-friendly policies. Nevertheless, the COVID-19 pandemic has impacted the hospitality industry all over the world. Therefore, it is necessary to find ways to revive the hospitality sector during and post pandemic. Thus, the findings of this research give insight into customer preference and expectations as well as the need to invest and implement technology to deliver exceptional service. Therefore, it emphasizes that organizations operating in the hospitality sector should understand the customer needs, develop appropriate strategies, and invest in technology. Specifically, this research stresses that service quality dimensions improve customer satisfaction, enhances customer loyalty, and regain trust with consumers.

DOI: 10.4018/978-1-7998-8346-3.ch006

INTRODUCTION

In the last two decades, the United Arab Emirates (UAE) has focused on strengthening the hospitality sector for sustainable growth. Undeniably, the hospitality sector contributes to a significant segment towards Gross Domestic Product (GDP) and generates employment. The UAE Government has taken initiatives to enhance infrastructure and other aspects that boost this sector. Market analysis during 2007 – 2017 reveals that the tourism and hospitality sector's direct contribution to GDP saw significant growth by 138%. Furthermore, it generated employment by 119% during the same period (Mordor Intelligence, 2020). Although the hospitality sector was performing above the global average, the COVID-19 Pandemic crisis hit the industry hard. Currently, gradual growth predicts a recovery. The improvement in global market sentiment, brand safety measures, and assurance is crucial to creating demand and stimulating people to travel. The travel restrictions, resumption of airline activities influence the recovery speed (Abbas, 2020).

The COVID-19 Pandemic has led to changes in customer needs. Therefore, all the stakeholders in the hospitality industry have to focus on changes in customer experience, customer perceptions, consumption patterns, and quality asset management. Specifically, 'Service Excellence' is fundamental to add value to the products and improve market competitiveness (Bhattacharya, 2020), making a difference in how quickly the UAE recovers to pre-pandemic levels.

Al Ababneh (2017) points out that service quality is vital to gain sustainable competitive advantage and customer confidence and trust. Thus, service quality is a significant and critical success factor for the hospitality industry. Service quality dimensions include reliability, assurance, empathy, tangibility, and responsiveness. Additionally, organizations can enhance their service quality that results in service excellence by aligning service quality dimensions with customer experience, patterns, and other factors. Thus, the present study aims to fill the gap by identifying the critical service quality dimensions that help gain customer confidence and trust to revive the hospitality sector in the UAE post-COVID-19 Pandemic. This research answers the following questions:

1. Why is service quality essential in the hospitality sector?
2. How service quality enables us to gain customer confidence and trust?
3. In what ways do the recent UAE Government measures influence service quality in the hospitality sector?
4. Which service quality dimension is more focused in the current COVID-19 Pandemic context?

UAE HOSPITALITY SECTOR

The insights of the session on the "UAE Hospitality 2020 and beyond" in 2017 examined opportunities and challenges by industry leaders, emphasized Dubai is a buoyant hospitality market and performs better than the global average, and predicted to increase by 5 percent annually. Expo 2020 is not a challenge for Dubai, but it has to create opportunities and new trends. Post Expo 2020 survival depends on innovation, so hotels need to be more experiential and satisfy diverse groups (TTN, 2017). According to the World Tourism Organization (UNWTO), the global tourism and hospitality industry faces enormous losses posed by COVID-19. The domestic and international restrictions cause revenue loss between the US $1.2 – the US $ 3.3 trillion, and to come to form, it depends on recovery time from the Pandemic (Hotelier India, 2020). Although the hospitality industry was performing ahead of the global average and contributed more towards GDP, the COVID-19 Pandemic made to postpone Dubai Expo 2020 to 2021, and globally, the industry saw a dip.

In order to fully recover by 2024 to pre-pandemic levels, the hospitability sector has to focus on customer experience as expectations will differ. Therefore, for the hospitality sector, the new norms will have to be benchmarked. Such changes include perception shifts in the safety of food choices and new patterns such as online platforms to improve and maintain interaction with guests (Maadad, 2020).

With the reduction in infection cases and higher recovery rate, the UAE "reopened" the country to tourists from July 2020 (Bhattacharya, 2020). Almost all the hotels offered discounts on room rates and food and beverages to attract families. In May 2021, the domestic tourism market in the UAE increased with the likes of staycations. Especially in Dubai, beach properties occupancy rate increased to over 80% during the weekend. Bhattacharya (2020) says it is necessary to follow stringent protocols that focus on maintaining high health and safety standards in order to meet the new norm.

Furthermore, certified health and safety measures increased confidence for both domestic and international travelers. For example, Jumeirah and other Dubai-based luxury hotels received the prestigious Bureau Veritas Safeguard label. The Bureau Veritas Safeguard label is when Dubai Tourism, a government entity, approves and issues a 'DUBAI ASSURED' stamp to reinforce its positioning as one of the world's safest destinations. Due to COVID-19 Pandemic, the sector was hit hard with lockdowns and lack of traveling from tourists. Still, in the recovery phase, organizations need to focus on differentiation to gain customer confidence. The hospitality sector in the UAE, especially in Dubai, is highly competitive. Thus, this sector requires competitive differentiation for organizations to succeed.

SERVICE QUALITY AND INNOVATION

Service quality is one of the fundamental elements for securing sustainable competitive advantage and customers' confidence. Service quality refers to physical facilities, employees, and materials. Moreover, it includes the five dimensions: assurance, reliability, responsiveness, tangibility, and empathy (Al Ababneh, 2017). The tangibles dimension relates to the appearance of physical facilities, personal, equipment, and communication materials. Reliability considers the ability to perform the promised service dependably and accurately. Responsiveness displays willingness to help customers and provide prompt service. Assurance is about the knowledge and courtesy of employees and their ability to convey trust and confidence. At the same time, empathy refers to the care, individualized attention given to customers (Arien, 2020). By understanding the concept of service quality, the hospitality sector can measure the quality aspects of tangibles and intangibles.

It is necessary to understand the influence of service quality on various levels such as customer trust, customer satisfaction, customer loyalty, customer confidence. Lemy et al. (2019) examined the relationship between the personnel, physical environment, service quality, relationship quality, service innovation, and customer loyalty in five-star hotels in Indonesia. They found that there is a correlation between personnel and service quality and customer loyalty. Thus, when an organization focuses on service excellence, they receive higher levels of customer satisfaction, trust, and commitment to be returning customers.

Technological advancement and dynamic changes in the business environment encourage organizations to focus on innovative ways to manage the business efficiently. Even after introducing technological advancement in the industry, service quality still holds a place in influencing customer satisfaction, customer loyalty, and trust. Moreover, organizations are finding alternatives to deliver exceptional services to their customers during the pandemic period by using technology to reduce human contact and ensure health and safety. In this scenario, service quality innovation benefits the organizations operating in this sector.

Service Quality Dimensions Ranking

Service quality dimensions ranking differs from country to country. It depends on customers' perceptions because there is a change in customer perceptions and consuming patterns due to the COVID-19 Pandemic (Bhattacharya, 2020). Therefore, considering the service quality dimension ranking during the Pandemic adds value.

The hotel star rating moderates the relationship between service quality and customer satisfaction. Nunkoo et al. (2019) found that accommodation infrastructure and employee expertise determine customer satisfaction in low-end hotels. Thus, understanding the service quality factors that determine customer satisfaction in the UAE context adds value to making business organizations more attentive to these factors that help revive the industry.

Moreover, the UAE Tourism Authorities encourage implementing innovative strategies to boost the tourism and hospitality sector during and after the COVID-19 Pandemic. Consequently, it makes organizations consider the technological advancements to improve their service delivery by assuring health and safety to the domestic and international visitors. In this context, Jiang and Wen's (2020) study highlights the need to focus on deploying artificial intelligence (AI) and robotics, hygiene and cleanliness, and health and healthcare. AI and robotics have a role in managing health crises and hotel management during the Pandemic. Furthermore, customer perception of cleanliness and hygiene differs before and after the Pandemic. Indeed, hygiene is now probably much more highly considered for the average consumer than pre-pandemic times. Besides, AI also allows serving better and delighting guests through innovation. Thus, AI becomes a new service concept (Jiang and Wen, 2020).

Djeebet (2020) points out the need to consider empathy, responsiveness, and assurance factors along with tangibles. The Pandemic brought changes in the business operations, customer needs, and expectations. Andrews (2020) highlights the differences in procedures that ensure health and safety as a priority. It focuses on hygiene and sanitation and provides physical evidence that health and safety are a chief concern. Besides, hotels should provide essential facilities and employees to meet customer needs. Additionally, it stresses the emergence of new practices in the hospitality sector (Andrews, 2020). To deliver contactless service, organizations have to depend on advanced technologies that ensure health and safety as well as provide exceptional service to the customers. Hotels, travel agents, airlines, retail outlets, and other tourist destinations started operating with limited employees. They utilized AI functions and started using online platforms such as websites and social media for booking, payments, and other parts. They increased their online awareness, which is a positive outcome of the Pandemic.

Therefore, all these studies reveal that all these service quality dimensions are essential. Still, changes in consumer perception and consumption patterns influence the dimensions ranking. It indicates that dimension ranking differs based on various elements such as hotel ranking, customer perception, and consuming patterns. Consequently, gaining insight into the service quality dimension that gain more value during and after the Pandemic benefits the business organizations in the hospitality industry.

Gaining Customer Confidence and Trust Pre/Post COVID-19

It is vital to remember that during and after the COVID-19, organizations in the hospitality sector have to gain customer confidence and customer satisfaction. The hospitality sector is a service sector; hence they have to provide a high standard of service at all times. Consequently, it enables to enhance customer satisfaction and gain customer loyalty. Moreover, customer satisfaction and loyalty result in profitability. Priyo et al. (2019) support that hotels can improve customer satisfaction by providing high-standard services and ensure customer loyalty. However, the study highlights that customer satisfaction is not enough to maintain customer loyalty. Therefore, to maintain customer loyalty, it is necessary to provide excellent service in terms of reliability, tangible responsiveness, and other services. As a result, customers will recommend the service organization to others and revisit as well as be ready to pay premium pricing for the services (Priyo et al., 2019).

To overcome the impact of the COVID-19 crisis, Hao et al. (2020) emphasize the anti-pandemic strategies for hospitality industries as service strategies aim to restore customer confidence. These strategies include the following: leadership and communication, human resource, service, corporate social responsibility, finance, and finally, disaster management standard operating procedures.

While considering the relationship between the brand and consumer, the initial step is to regain customer confidence to overcome the crisis. Companies operating in the hospitality sector have to focus on strict sanitary and hygiene measures and follow new practices to monitor and control the business environment. Besides, communication plays a vital role in reassuring customers about safety concerns. Also, it is essential to consider the emotional factors to understand customer needs and expectations (Djeebet, 2020). By considering these aspects, the service organizations can be back to normalcy as customers gain confidence in the services. Word of mouth will increase amongst returning customers. Thus, it is possible to charge premium pricing for the services from loyal customers.

UAE Government Initiatives Impacting Service Quality

The UAE Government developed various strategies to revive the hospitality sector. As a part of it, it encourages private and government entities to develop innovative strategies. Dubai Tourism authorities created a framework for reaching beyond the expectations of all its stakeholders and partners with innovative initiatives. The Corporation for Tourism and Commerce Marketing (DCTCM) ensured that to follow a zero-tolerance approach in managing health and safety measures at hotels, tourist attractions, and retail outlets. With regular monitoring of compliance, tourists gain confidence.

Dubai Tourism's 'DUBAI ASSURED' stamp reinforces the emirate's positioning as the world's safest destination. To obtain the 'DUBAI ASSURED' stamp, organizations must adhere to high safety and health precautions standards. World Travel and Tourism Council (WTTC) acknowledged the measures of Dubai's to combat COVID-19 by giving the city a 'Safe Travel' stamp. Emirates Airlines is the first airline that provides free medical coverage for COVID-19 related medical expenses if a passenger is diagnosed with COVID-19. The free medical coverage strategy boosts tourists' confidence and encourages them to travel worldwide with Emirates Airlines. Additionally, engaging marketing campaigns by Dubai Tourism promotes businesses by coordinating with over 3,000 partners across the globe to attract bookings. #Till We Meet Again and #We Will See You Soon were successful digital campaigns before reopening international tourists with the #Ready When You Are campaign (Hotelier India, 2020).

The UAE has been using Artificial Intelligence (AI) to help with safety protocols. Similar to the Internet of Things (IoT), Microsoft (2020) highlights a case in China where IoT helped to deliver new experiences for hotel guests. Duotel utilizes an electronic box with an integrated touch screen interface that allows controlling standard hotel devices such as TV, lights, thermostat, and other features. 'Air Safety Guard' helps to monitor sleep and air quality as well as to kill bacteria and viruses with UV rays. Additionally, the device allows guests to interact with hotel employees to avail room service, payments, language translation. Consequently, it eliminates face-to-face contact to deliver contactless service. As a result, it enhances the safety of hotels and regains customers' confidence. Microsoft's IoT Azure Hub supports the functions of Duotel. Mehmood Hotel, New Century Hotels and Resorts, and Youxi Movie Hotel successfully using Duotel to deliver exceptional service during the Pandemic (Microsoft Asia News Center, 2020). As mentioned earlier, organizations in the hospitality sector can benefit from service innovation during the Pandemic and revive the industry by enhancing customer loyalty (Lemy et al., 2019). As the UAE government involves all the stakeholders to revive the tourism and hospitality sector, it is the right time to bring technological innovation and new practices appropriate to the industry.

METHODOLOGY

The research explores the service quality impact on reviving the hospitality industry. Therefore, the study follows an exploratory approach (Dudovskiy, 2018) that uses qualitative and quantitative methods to understand the topic from customers' perspectives. The study incorporates both primary data and secondary data. Primary data was collected through an online survey to reach more participants. The primary data gathered from customers allows us to obtain answers to research questions. The survey questions cover five dimensions of service quality: reliability, assurance, empathy, tangibility, and responsiveness.

Along with demographic information, the survey question includes closed-ended questions related to service quality dimensions. The closed-ended statement of the survey is in the form of a Five-point Likert Scale (Strongly disagree, disagree, neither/nor, agree, and strongly agree). The secondary data comprises journal articles, previous research studies, articles, and reports from credible online sources appropriate to address research objectives. The study follows a qualitative method, thus, permits to select a non-probability sampling method. The target population is customers of the hospitality sector, so they come from diverse organizations related to aviation, hotels and resorts, travel agents, tour operations, entertainment centers, etc.

Data Collection

The research questionnaire includes demographic information – age, gender, marital status, and closed-ended questions related to the SERVQUAL dimensions and hospitality industry. Despite the limitations of the survey method, the questionnaire was appropriate. It was designed to ensure that it covers all the significant factors based on the literature review to overcome the limitations of the survey. The SERVQUAL dimensions were used for the study because it relates to the customer satisfaction in the hospitality industry and widely used by various researchers (Al Ababneh, 2017; Arien, 2020; Lemy et al., 2019; Priyo et al., 2019). Besides, secondary research includes questions referring to the service innovation, technological adaptation, changes in the processing after the COVID-19 Pandemic, and certifications.

FINDINGS

Demographic Variables

The survey sample represents all the age groups from 18 years to above 50 years. The majority of the participants were in the age group of 31-40 years, with 30%. Moreover, it includes both male and female participation at 56% and 44%, respectively. The marital status shows 38% were married whereas 34% were single and 28% divorced. Thus, the findings show married and divorced populations took part in the survey and the age group 31- 40 years correlates with the marital status. The survey revealed that married individuals give priority to safety and other factors during and post-pandemic. However, mostly, they travel or utilize hospitality services with their family. Specifically, the expatriate population visits their home country with family or with family visit other countries for vacation. Therefore, their perspective helps to understand what service quality aspects influence their decision. Moreover, statement related to other factors, such as pricing, satisfaction, recommendation, DUBAI ASSURED, and Safe Travel stamps gives us insight about customer perception and expectation on the hospitality industry.

Tangibility

Participants emphasized the preference for a neat and clean environment (96%), contactless services such as touch-free handles, automated check-in using Apps, voice-controlled lifts, and other modes (94%). Besides, they also expect that hotels and airlines should provide gloves, sanitizers, and other such products while checking in hotels or airlines (92%). It is also interesting to note that it is expected to utilize technology to ensure air quality and kill bacteria and viruses using UV rays (96%). Moreover, anticipate that all the places should have clear signboards displaying the guidelines, clean certifications, cleaning, or sanitizing cues (94%). It is interesting to know that there is no disagreement with these statements as well as the neutral score is less compared to an agreement. Moreover, it regularly monitors that business establishments adhere to rules and regulators and get certified. Therefore, tangible scores show that it gains importance in gaining customer confidence and satisfaction.

Reliability

The primary data shows that 94% of the respondents expect that organizations should provide the promised service. Also, the organization should act responsibly by insisting customers follow guidelines or procedures during travel or stay (96%).

Responsiveness

Customers prioritize hygienic conductions (98%) and expect employees to show a willingness to support or help customers (96%).

Assurance

The way employees behave with customers should instill confidence (92%) that the place is safe, and the organization ensures that customer safety is on priority in all possible ways. Besides, the hospitality sector requires employees to be consistently courteous (96%). Moreover, customers expect that if the employees are knowledgeable, they answer the questions or provide appropriate answers to eliminate their doubts (96%).

Empathy

Especially during and post-pandemic situation, customers expect individual attention (92%) to ensure their safety as well as make them enjoy their trip. Moreover, they expect that organizations act by keeping the customer's best interest at heart (98%); only 2% disagree with the statement. Additionally, the pandemic situation would have brought changes in customer needs, so employees must have the ability to understand the specific needs of customers (98%). The response for the five service quality dimensions shows that except for 2% disagreement, all the statements have a higher score for a strongly agree and agree. Thus, it shows that customers prioritize all the dimensions of service quality in the post-pandemic situation. Moreover, it supports that service quality impacts customer satisfaction, customer loyalty, customer trust, customer confidence (Al Ababneh, 2017; Arien, 2020; Lemy et al., 2019).

Service Innovation

Then there is a strong belief that the UAE hospitality industry implements service innovation (100%) (Lemy et al., 2019). Besides, respondents expect that organizations in the hospitality sector would have brought changes in their processing and other activities to ensure customer safety (Battacharya, 2020; Hao et al., 2020). Moreover, it also correlates with tangibles, as customers expect service innovation as a part of it and expect organizations to utilize the technology to its maximum to deliver contactless services to their customers.

Service Standard

All the respondents stress that the high-standard service makes them satisfied. Moreover, customers are ready to pay premium prices to ensure safety (Priyo et al., 2019). When customers are satisfied with the service and gain confidence, they recommend it to their friends and family (Djeebet, 2020). In a way, DUBAI ASSURED and Safe Travels stamps/certifications enhance confidence to travel or stay in the UAE (98%) (Djeebet, 2020; Battacharya, 2020; Hao et al., 2020; Priyo et al., 2019). These also show that service quality dimensions support the organization in delivering exceptional service to their customers, understanding the customer needs, and giving them confidence with appropriate measures consistently. As a result, customer satisfaction and confidence level increase, leading them to refer their family and friends. However, the DUBAI ASSURED and Safe Travel stamps/certifications help regain customer confidence because customers know that after ensuring and assessing the hotels and other organizations in the hospitality sector, it is possible to get these certifications.

DISCUSSION

The UAE authorities are taking initiatives to support the hospitality industry by creating relevant and supportive government policies. Moreover, DUBAI ASSURED is a Government initiative; and domestic tourism saw a rise in recent months. It shows the customer confidence because they are aware that organizations adhere to the regulations or guidelines of health authorities and other authorities in combating the COVID-19 Pandemic in all the emirates. The main weakness is that it is exceedingly difficult to develop strategies and differentiate from the competitors quickly in the market; moreover, it requires investment. The opportunities show utilizing technological advancement and marketing strategies and targeting leisure tourism and medical tourism supports to boost the industry. There are threats from regional competitors such as Qatar and Oman and changes in customer behavior, plus the continual impact of the Pandemic.

Secondary data points out that there is a change in customer behavior and needs due to the Pandemic. Thus, implementing technologies, bringing service innovation, and developing strategies are vital.

The primary data also supports that customers give attention to all the service quality dimensions and expect changes in the processing and all the activities after the Pandemic. Therefore, the hospitality sector requires investment to update the technologies and deliver exceptional service and exceptional customer experience to regain confidence and customer loyalty. Moreover, the primary data supports the secondary data discussed in the literature review by showing that service quality dimensions boost customer confidence, customer satisfaction, customer loyalty. However, utilizing the technology and implementing service innovation helps the organization differentiate them from their competitors and gain customer confidence. Besides, it also supports ensuring safety, and if the service is exceptional, customers do not hesitate to pay premium prices. Therefore, it is necessary to ensure that all service quality dimensions require attention. In addition, after implementing appropriate technologies and strategies, charging premium prices does not impact the industry.

The discussion of the strengths and limitations of the study is vital. Therefore, the findings of the study contribute knowledge from the customer perspective. Although there is limited or scarce research related to the hospitality industry revival or after the impact of a pandemic; still, it gives insight for future research that is more specific to airlines and hotels as well as tourist destinations such as theme parks. While the previous research journals related to the tourism industry relevant to the UAE context are limited, government initiatives and other measures are still informative. The study covers various aspects such as service quality dimensions (tangibles, responsiveness, reliability, empathy, and assurance), service innovation, certifications, premium pricing, customer satisfaction, and recommendation to their friends and family.

There are some limitations, especially sample size. The sample size was 50. It might be due to the short duration for data collection, and the pandemic situation might be a valid reason for the less sample size. Another notable limitation is the lack of expertise.

CONCLUSION

In conclusion, service quality plays a vital role in reviving the UAE Hospitality Sector. The study shows that customers give attention to all the dimensions of service quality – tangibility, responsiveness, assurance, reliability, and empathy. Hence, it is necessary to focus on these elements to regain customer confidence, boost customer satisfaction and customer loyalty. As a result, they recommend the organization to their friends and family. Moreover, these service quality dimensions comprise tangibles and intangibles. The findings reveal expectations and preferences to witness the changes in the service delivery and deployment of technology. Besides, it also shows that service innovation and innovative strategies are vital to delivering exceptional service to the customers, gaining their confidence, and satisfying them. Therefore, organizations operating in the hospitality sector need to invest in technology and update the strategies to satisfy the changing customer needs and behavior. Furthermore, they can also charge premium pricing if they invest in these technologies to deliver services that ensure customer safety. Finally, organizations have to develop excellent marketing strategies and utilize the technologies to target the various customer segments from leisure to medical tourism.

Moreover, organizations operating in the hospitality sector can differentiate using service quality to gain customer confidence. Besides, exceptional service quality permits to charge premium pricing for the services from loyal customers and gain more referrals through them. Thus, organizations planning to deploy technology to provide contactless service and innovative service by focusing on the safety measures, understating the customer needs, and consuming patterns can charge premium pricing by gaining customer confidence and satisfaction.

As customer expectation increases, government authorities also enhance their strategies, and its UAE Vision reveals the country is ahead in various ways. The UAE wants to be a template for other GCC countries and across the world. Now is the right time to bring changes in business practices in the hospitality sector. Therefore, it is crucial to encourage AI, Big Data, IoT to deliver services to the customers that ensure high safety standards and gain the confidence of tourists and visitors. Also, service innovation improves customer loyalty. Thus, understanding the service quality impact on customer confidence and customer satisfaction during the pandemic era gives insight into reviving the industry. Moreover, service innovation and service quality dimensions add value to develop appropriate strategies to meet customers with new practices to gain their confidence.

RECOMMENDATION

The primary data showcases that all the dimensions of service quality are crucial. These ensure that the organizations in the hospitality sector take precautionary measures and make sure their guests or customers strictly follow them. The study gives insight into the changes in customer needs and expectations or preferences. Therefore, organizations operating in the hospitality sector must focus on tangibles, reliability, responsiveness, assurance, and empathy. It not only results in customer satisfaction but also contributes to enhancing customer loyalty. Therefore, it makes customers recommend the organization in their friends and family circle as well as show interest to avail premium services (Priyo et al., 2019)

In the current scenario, investing in technology to deliver contactless services is essential. Moreover, utilizing Duotel like facilities enhances contactless services and lets the customers gain new and excellent experiences. Because investing in Duotel, such as integrates touch screen interface, controls standard hotel devices like TV, lights, and thermostat. Besides, it also provides facilities such as interact with employees to get room service, payments, and language translation. Moreover, it has an Air Safety Guard to monitor sleep and UV rays to kill the virus and bacteria. Consequently, it enhances the safety of hotels and supports to regain customers' confidence (Microsoft Asia News Center, 2020).

REFERENCES

Abbas, W. (2020, May 7). *We look forward to welcoming you soon: UAE Hospitality Sector sees recovery in Q4*. Retrieved September 10, 2020, from Khaleej Times: https://www.khaleejtimes.com/business/local/see-you-soon-uae-hospitality-sector-sees-recovery-in-q4-

Al Ababneh, M. M. (2017). Service Quality in the Hospitality Industry. *Journal of Tourism & Hospitality (Los Angeles, Calif.)*, *6*(1). Advance online publication. doi:10.4172/2167-0269.1000e133

Al-Saadi, H. (2014). Demystifying Ontology and Epistemology in research methods. *Research Gate*, *1*(1), 1–10.

Andrews, S. (2020, April 28). *Impact of COVID-19 on the hotel industry and suggestions for post-pandemic recovery*. Retrieved September 22, 2020, from Hospitality Economic Times: https://hospitality.economictimes.indiatimes.com/blog/impact-of-covid-19-on-the-hotel-industry-and-suggestions-for-post-pandemic-recovery/4214

Arien, C. (2020). *The 5 Service Dimensions All Customers Care About*. Retrieved September 22, 2020, from Service Performance: https://www.serviceperformance.com/the-5-service-dimensions-all-customers-care-about/

Bhattacharya, A. (2020, February). *Hospitality Industry After COVID-19: How to Survive?* Retrieved September 10, 2020, from EHL Insights: https://hospitalityinsights.ehl.edu/hospitality-covid19-crisis

Djeebet, H. (2020, April 9). *What is the impact of COVID-19 on Global Hospitality Industry*. Retrieved September 22, 2020, from Hospitalitynet: https://www.hospitalitynet.org/opinion/4098062.html

Dudovskiy, J. (2018). *The Ultimate Guide to Writing a Dissertation in Business Studies: A step by step assistance*. Academic Press.

Frost, J. (2018). *How To Interpret R-squared in Regression Analysis*. Retrieved October 25, 2020, from Statistics by Jim: https://statisticsbyjim.com/regression/interpret-r-squared-regression/

Hao, F., Xiao, Q., & Chon, K. (2020, August 5). COVID-19 and China's Hotel Industry: Impacts, a Disaster Management Framework, and Post-Pandemic Agenda. *International Journal of Hospitality Management, 90*, 102636. Advance online publication. doi:10.1016/j.ijhm.2020.102636 PMID:32834356

Hotelier India. (2020, August 10). *Dubai's tourism and hospitality sectors see green shoots of revival*. Retrieved September 10, 2020, from Hotelier India: https://www.hotelierindia.com/business/11752-dubais-tourism-and-hospitality-sectors-see-green-shoots-of-revival

Hotelier India. (2020, August 10). *Dubai's tourism and hospitality sectors see green shoots of revival*. Retrieved September 22, 2020, from Hotelier India: https://www.hotelierindia.com/business/11752-dubais-tourism-and-hospitality-sectors-see-green-shoots-of-revival

Jiang, Y., & Wen, J. (2020). Effects of COVID-19 on hotel marketing and management: A perspective article. *International Journal of Contemporary Hospitality Management, 32*(8), 2563–2573. doi:10.1108/IJCHM-03-2020-0237

Lemy, D., Goh, E., & Ferry, J. (2019, January 3). Moving out of the silo: How service quality innovations can develop customer loyalty in Indonesia's hotel. *Journal of Vacation Marketing*, *25*(4), 462–479. Advance online publication. doi:10.1177/1356766718819658

Maadad, N. (2020, July 12). *It's a long and hard road for UAE hospitality Industry*. Retrieved September 10, 2020, from Gulf News: https://gulfnews.com/business/analysis/its-a-long-and-hard-road-for-uae-hospitality-industry-1.72549820

Microsoft Asia News Center. (2020, June 17). *Healthy hotels in the age of COVID-19*. Retrieved September 2020, 2020, from Microsoft: https://news.microsoft.com/apac/2020/06/17/healthy-hotels-in-the-age-of-covid-19/

Mordor Intelligence. (2020). *Hospitality Industry in the United Arab Emirates - Growth, Trends, and Forecasts (2020 - 2025)*. Mordor Intelligence. Retrieved September 10, 2020, from https://www.mordorintelligence.com/industry-reports/hospitality-industry-in-the-united-arab-emirates

Nunkoo, R., Teeroovengadum, V., Ringle, C., & Sunnassee, V. (2019). Service quality and customer satisfaction: The moderating effects of hotel star rating. *International Journal of Hospitality Management*. Advance online publication. doi:10.1016/j.ijhm.2019.102414

Priyo, J., Mohamad, B., & Adetunji, R. (2019, February). An Examination of the Effects of Service Quality and Customer Satisfaction on Customer Loyalty in the Hotel Industry. *International Journal of Supply Chain Management*, *8*(1), 653–663.

TTN. (2017, October). *UAE hospitality 2020 and beyond*. Retrieved September 10, 2020, from Travel & Tourism News Middle East: http://www.ttnworldwide.com/Article/268130/-UAE-hospitality-2020-and-beyond

Chapter 7
The Impact of COVID-19 on Bank Consumers in the UAE:
A Dubai-Based Literature Review

Hussain Ali Al Numairy
https://orcid.org/0000-0002-5948-0972
Higher Colleges of Technology, Dubai, UAE

Shaikha Rashid Al Essa
Higher Colleges of Technology, Dubai, UAE

Aliya Saleh Alshamsi
Higher Colleges of Technology, Dubai, UAE

Hamda Ibrahim Ahli
Higher Colleges of Technology, Dubai, UAE

Shamma Ahmed Al Zarooni
Higher Colleges of Technology, Dubai, UAE

Heather Webb
https://orcid.org/0000-0003-0806-7050
Higher Colleges of Technology, Dubai, UAE

ABSTRACT

Pandemics generally affect businesses due to their nature. Business owners have little to no knowledge of when crises such as pandemics will occur or how severe they will be. Each pandemic is different in nature as its spreadability is different; therefore, the outcome of no two pandemics can be the same. This chapter discusses the historical impact previous pandemics had on businesses. Then it presents information about the COVID-19 pandemic and how the United Arab Emirates (UAE) government and businesses dealt with this particular pandemic. More specifically, the authors focus on Dubai's banking sector response.

DOI: 10.4018/978-1-7998-8346-3.ch007

INTRODUCTION

Pandemics throughout history have had a significant impact on society as a whole and, most significantly, the economy. The fear of catching the infectious disease may result in loss of business as business owners and customers fear for their safety and well-being. This will then result in business shutdowns and city lockdowns resulting in major financial crunches for business owners. While many would then prefer to stay safe and not reopen, others forced to shut down would lose their main sources of income, which would drive them into bankruptcy.

This chapter discusses the historical impact of previous pandemics had on businesses. Then it presents information about Covid-19 Pandemic and how the United Arab Emirates (UAE) government and businesses dealt with this particular pandemic. More specifically, we focus on Dubai's banking sector response.

Pandemics in General

Pandemics generally affect businesses due to their nature, which are unforeseeable events. Business owners have little to no knowledge of when crises such as pandemics will occur or how severe they will be. Each pandemic is different in nature as its spreadability is different; therefore, the outcome of no two pandemics can be the same (Tisdell, 2021).

The plague of 1348-1350 was given the name of 'The Black Death' (Langer, 1964) and was one of the most altering pandemics to the European economy as it claimed the lives of up to 60% of its population (Herlihy and Cohn, 1997). The Black Death Pandemic resulted in a shortage of labor throughout Europe, which caused an influx of new labor from Asia and Africa. However, this did not cover the need for skilled labor as many of them could only perform unskilled tasks that did not require intricate work.

Moreover, the demand for goods and services was dislocated. The price of agricultural food products like grain was low, making the income of 'peasants' at that time lower. Nevertheless, the plague positively impacted their standard of living as it improved. The demand for luxury goods spiked in counties like Italy, where manufacturers manufactured and sold goods at a high rate (Routt, 2008).

The 1918 influenza crisis, commonly known as 'the Spanish Flu,' is one of the first pandemics of the 20th century and is still one of the most catastrophic pandemics to date. The flu lasted from 1918-1919, and nearly 100 million people were killed due to getting infected (Aassve et al., 2021). The flu itself was highly infectious and spread due to hundreds and thousands of soldiers in the First World War, as they were in confined spaces, such as tents, making it easy for the virus to be transmitted (Oxford et al., 2005).

Small and medium-sized companies (SMEs) mainly felt the effects of this virus due to them not getting recognition. They were deemed not essential and non-deserving of government subsidies, as the priority was given to big multi-national companies. This resulted in MNC's coming out of the pandemic possibly even more substantial, and SME's suffering grave losses to go bankrupt (Bodenhorn, 2020).

Covid-19 Pandemic

Covid-19 is a severe acute respiratory syndrome coronavirus 2 (SARS-CoV-2. It Is the seventh human coronavirus and was discovered in Wuhan, Hubei province, China Ciotti, (Marco, et al., 2020). It is a global health crisis that has affected more than 222 countries and territories, with cases increasing at a drastic and unprecedented rate due to travel. Cases have neared 300 million and continue to rise.

Tourism, one of the most affected sectors due to government-imposed lockdowns, has seen a drastic fall in demand for air travel resulting in layovers of employees; the sector makes up 10% of the global GDP as well as 10% of global employment. This resulted in a decrease in the demand for oil due to large companies' demand falling due to travel bans, and individual demand fell due to curfews and the work from home schemes. This resulted in a price war between major oil exporters, Russia and Saudi Arabia, and a drop in oil prices as there was an over-supply, and demand did not meet that supply (Açikgöz & Günay, 2020).

Furthermore, arguably the most affected was employment. Due to business closers and government lockdowns, many companies made a percentage of their employees redundant. This resulted in a decrease in demand for labor as demand for goods and services decreased. Moreover, as many sectors transformed their operations into e-commerce, they required fewer employees. Due to tight cost controls, many other businesses did not add new additions to their workforce.

As consumption for goods and services reduced, a pattern of demand and supply shocks was identified. Supply shocks were due to many businesses being limited; therefore, their capacity to produce goods and services was affected. This can be observed in cases like the restaurant or service sector, where staff could not operate due to government lockdowns and restrictions. Moreover, demand shocks were observed as people avoided restaurants and public spaces to avoid the risk of infection. Additionally, as employees lost their jobs, demand for goods and services was reduced, or what can be termed a sectoral demand shock (Brinca et al., 2020).

The United Arab Emirates and Covid-19

The UAE consists of seven emirates that cooperate in planning the development of the society to maintain and reinforce national unity, promote ongoing economic progress, and improve personal health and well-being. The Department of Health in Abu Dhabi, the Dubai Health Authority, and the Ministry of Health and Prevention, which oversees the remaining five Emirates, are the three central authorities in charge of the UAE health system (Al-Hosani et al., 2021).

Covid-19 is a global pandemic that could be categorized as an uncertain catastrophe that impacted the UAE as a whole. However, the UAE was slightly impacted due to the quick response in mitigating and controlling such issues (Sundarakani & Onyia, 2021). As the UAE's economy depends on trade in general and tourism, it is quite challenging to adapt to those sudden changes rapidly since it threatens its economy. For instance, many people avoided traveling due to the fear and possibility of getting the virus, so the percentage of tourism has decreased dramatically. Based on that, each country needs to develop new strategies and studies that go along with the current situation to avert the extent of collapsing or the trough stage in the businesses. As shown below, the business cycle troughs are evaluated in the bottom frame (Chauvet & Piger, 2005).

Figure 1. Business Cycle Troughs

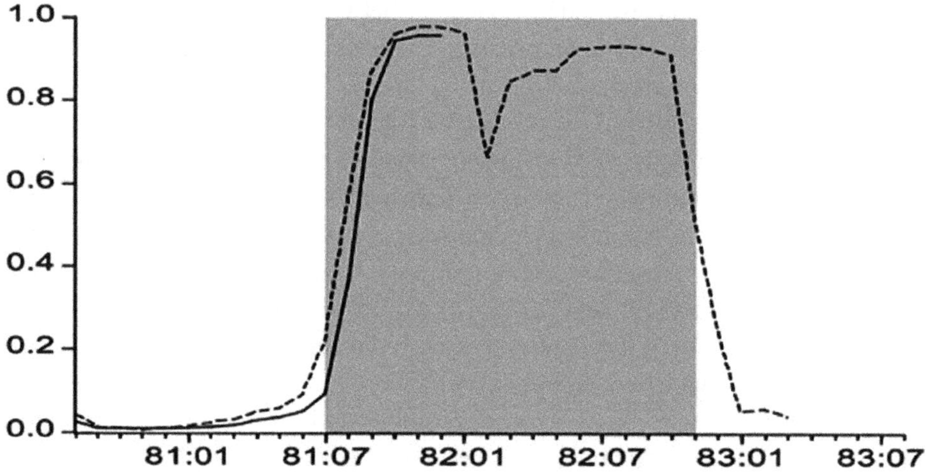

The UAE launched a free application named ALHOSN, specifically the healthcare regulatory authorities, to facilitate the process of tracking Covid-19 positive cases and allow users to view their covid-19 test results and know how many days they have completed a PCR test.

On January 29, 2020, the first case of Covid-19 was detected in the UAE (Al-Hosani et al., 2021). The UAE government was very cautious about it and had to provide the control and prevention measures to overcome the pandemic, such as; enforcing full lockdown, social distancing, closing schools, and restricting the activity of internal and external flights. Sundarakani and Onyia (2021) stated that the UAE Government deserves international commendation for pumping additional bailout funding into the systems. This has enabled financial institutions to assist the supply chain and logistics operators. Although the imported and exported activities from goods and products traded with the other countries were restricted, the UAE's effort towards reacting to such situations early created a significant difference. For example, the UAE avoided running out of stock in the stores that provided life's necessities and everything available before the pandemic. This reflected positively on the country's reputation. Afterward, on 11 March 2020, the World Health Organization officially announced the Covid-19 as a pandemic (Al-Hosani et al., 2021). As shown below, new announcements were made between now and then since Covid-19 cases kept on increasing (Thomas et al., 2020).

Figure 2. Covid-19 cases

Date announced	Effective date	Emirate	No. of cases	No. of deaths	Control and prevention measures
Mar 3	Mar 8	UAE	6		All nurseries, schools and universities closed
Mar 12	Mar 14	Abu Dhabi	85		Remote working enacted for non-key workers
Mar 16	Mar 17	UAE	98		Places of worship closed
Mar 21	Mar 21	UAE	140	2	Closing of public recreational spaces (i.e., beach, parks)
Mar 22	Mar 22	Dubai			Social distancing in stores (1.5 m)
Mar 23	Mar 24	UAE	198		Closure of all shops and malls
	Mar 25	UAE			Grounding of flights
	Mar 26	UAE	333		3- days disinfection Program and Night curfew
	Mar 28	Abu Dhabi	468	4	First testing center opens
	Apr 5	Dubai	1,799	8	Movement permit requirements implemented
	Apr 7	Dubai	2,359	10	First drive through testing center open
	Apr 9	UAE	2,990	14	13 drive through testing centers open
	Apr 9	UAE			Mosques, churches, places of worship to stay closed as Ramadan approaches
	Apr 12	UAE		28	Home testing program for people of determination
Apr 15	Apr 16	Dubai	5,375		Field hospital with capacity to treat 3,000 COVID-19 patients opened
	Apr 28	Abu Dhabi	11,380		Mandatory COVD-19 test for mall employees before reopening Abu Dhabi malls

Due to the precautions taken against the pandemic, the UAE took on financial losses to diminish the spread of Covid-19 and ensure the residents' safety. For instance, EXPO 2020 was postponed to 2021, which was one of the UAE's sacrifices. The country's economy was about to revive and prosper due to the predicted millions of visitors and the enormous income that EXPO would have generated.

SEHA, the Emirate of Abu Dhabi's main governmental health care provider, was instrumental in establishing the mass testing program across the seven Emirates. On March 29, 2020, it opened its first drive-through screening location (Al-Hosani et al., 2021). The Covid-19 test prioritized a specific category of people made for free due to their age or experiencing covid symptoms. According to others and individuals who desire to check for reassurance, the test cost was around 360 Dhs, but then it reduced to 150 Dhs. SEHA had treated more than 9000 patients whether they were in their hospitals or the specialized hotels for quarantine. Moreover, the Cleveland Clinic also treated Covid-19 patients from March to May 2020 (Al-Hosani et al., 2021). As Covid-19 cases were increasing and more patients were required to be treated in the hospitals, Abu Dhabi established a field hospital to provide treatment and medications to the patients and in order to reduce the pressure on the regular hospitals. The Abu Dhabi Healthcare Company currently runs 23 drive-through centers around the UAE.

A Specific Approach in Dubai

During the pandemic, telemedicine through a telephonic encounter with patients using a standardized strategy for case triage proved to be beneficial in managing the enormous number of positive cases (Elhennawy, Alsalem, Bahri, & Alarfaj, 2021). In Dubai, telemedicine was very effective and successful as it enabled identifying the patients' medical needs according to their clinical condition. Based on that, a decision is made whether home or hospital isolation is required. The availability of the 24/7 channels was provided for the covid-19 patients for any medical inquiries such as; Dubai Health Authority (DHA) call center, DHA website, covid-19 DXB smartphone application, etc.

In addition, the rapid spread of Covid-19 has led Dubai schools to look for alternative teaching techniques as soon as possible. As shown below, the Knowledge and Human Development Authority (KHDA) announced the closure of Dubai schools to ensure the students' and faculty's safety (Moghazy, 2020).

Figure 3. KHDA

Moghazy (2020) mentions the government partnership with Hamdan bin Mohammed Smart University launched the "Learning from A Far" initiative, and more than 42,000 UAE teachers were trained on virtual teaching and learning (Mansoor, 2020). This means that shifting to a new and unusual teaching technique requires several training sessions in order to adapt in a short period to proceed with the academic year successfully, efficiently, and effectively. Moreover, the KHDA established the #InThisTogetherDubai campaign (Moghazy, 2020). In September 2020, the Dubai government decided to start implementing different teaching modes, which are the mix of online learning and hybrid learning (Moghazy, 2020).

As for the work, shifting to 'work from home' has been challenging as it requires sound technical knowledge and a home atmosphere capable of being productive. Many private-sector businesses have implemented more flexible working arrangements such as; remote working for their employees to help employees maintain their health and guarantee business continuity and operating during the crisis (Khan, 2020). However, this working mode requires mutual exchange from both, such as company trust in their employees and the employees' loyalty in return to the organization in performing their work. Few could face difficulties due to the internet connection, lack of laptop or computer at home, etc.

Banking Industry

As a consequence of the worldwide reaction to the spread of Covid-19, businesses have been severely disrupted, asset prices and currency exchange rates have become more unpredictable, and interest rates have dropped significantly (KPMG, 2020). Supply and demand shocks are likely to continue, leading to more disruptions. Additionally, liquidity issues may affect businesses and people, such as a lack of credit. This might, in turn, lead to a rise in corporate loan defaults, particularly in the speculative-grade (*Banking and Capital Markets: Implications of COVID-19 | Deloitte Insights*, 2020).

The banks' management strategies will influence the economy's recovery after the CoVid-19 crisis. Banks are a crucial driving force behind the economy because they promote domestic and foreign commerce. Any society would be adversely affected if its banking system were severely disrupted (Marcu, 2021).

The Approach of Global Banks to Covid-19

According to Notteboom et al. (2021), like the financial crisis of 2008/2009, Covid-19 has also caused financial barriers across the globe. Central banks throughout the globe have already taken action to stabilize the global market and signal their willingness to use all appropriate steps. The Federal Reserve of the United States just lowered the federal funds rate by 50 basis points (Liesman, 2020), their first emergency step since the crisis of 2008. Additional liquidity is being added to the repo market via active intervention by the Federal Reserve (Liesman, 2020). Meanwhile, the Bank of Japan (BoJ) released an emergency statement indicating that it will increase asset purchases to infuse liquidity into the market (*IMF*, 2021). More than US$240 bn of liquidity has also been injected into the banking system by the People's Bank of China (PBoC) (Capital Markets in the Current Climate I Vistra, 2020). Additional initiatives have been revealed by the Bank of England and the European Central Bank to oppose COVID-19 in the near future.

Nonetheless, as things progress, additional action from governments, legislators, and central banks may be necessary, necessitating rapid collaboration at a global level. A global mobilisation is underway to limit COVID-19's impact on day-to-day operations in banks and financial markets throughout the globe. These plans include alternative workplace arrangements such as split work locations, remote workers, and rotating shifts for all sorts of workers — including traders — to ensure company continuity in the event of an emergency. Many have also imposed blanket travel restrictions, even outside the most affected nations, and canceled major events.

Organizations have also increased their efforts to protect the health and safety of their workers. Banks have asked regulators to relax their reserve requirements. Firms covered by COVID-19 have been given dispensation from regulatory financial reporting by authorities such as the US Securities and Exchange Commission (SEC). There are a number of international banking institutions doing their part as good citizens by providing loans to those in need, renegotiating credit conditions, and even handing out face masks to customers.

The Approach of the UAE Banks to Covid-19

According to Demirgüç-Kunt et al. (2021), Covid-19 has influenced the banking industry, though primarily indirectly. It has been observed that since the banks were able to provide services remotely without making any physical contact with the clients, services have extended the Covid-19 crisis' harmful impact on banks and other financial organizations (Sundarakani & Onyia, 2021). Instead of being affected, the banking sector has been observed to be an active part of the solution. Arrangements for personnel to work from home were quickly made during the lockdown, and branches were reconfigured to meet the increased hygiene criteria. While the epidemic has a detrimental impact on the financial industry, it is also necessary for economic recovery. On the other hand, the crisis worsens competitive pressures on banks by speeding up trends toward digitalization such as "working from home." Consumer expectations in the banking industry are changing quickly in the UAE, according to new research released today by AlQutob et al. (2020). This is especially true given how rapidly Covid-19 still continues to spread.Simultaneously, the banking industry has a role to play in aiding businesses and individuals through this era of lower revenues and incomes, which has driven financial regulators and governments to adopt necessary regulatory steps. Due to Covid-19, the banking sector has experienced poor financial conditions due to the high range of debtor's payments, where people in Dubai face difficulties in managing their financing payments (Reuters, 2021). This uncertainty is now quite manageable after the consideration from Sharia banks to raise funds as buying & selling and profit share. That strategy works in managing the financial conditions of the banks, following the Sharia/Islamic principles, which are also helping people to manage their financing payments.

Companies that have halted operations have been reported to lose revenue, and as a result, may be unable to repay obligations. Similarly, families with members who have lost their employment may find themselves unable to repay their loans due to a lack of income. Not only has this resulted in lost income, but it has also resulted in losses, both of which will have a damaging impact on earnings and bank capital (Gerth, Ramiah, Toufaily, & Muschert, 2021). As a speedy recovery becomes impossible, banks may expect considerable losses forcing the need for increased provisions, gradually destroying their profitability and capital position. At the same time, as a result of the uncertainty created by Covid-19, Dubai banks are experiencing a spike in loan demand, as companies, in particular, seek more cash flow to meet their bills even while sales are flat or dropping. As a result of the increasing demand, some borrowers have reduced their credit limits. In return, clients' behaviour has been affected negatively. As per the survey conducted by BCG (2020) with 2000 Dubai Bank customers, 76% have stated that they are willing to switch banks, while 70% have agreed to search for new bank offers.

In Dubai banks, all the clients differed in behavior in a pre-Covid situation or around 2018. All of them were structured and processed through the conventional systematic banking system approach (Ibrahim, 2014). Thus, all the clients of Dubai banks were integrated with the conventional systems of banks. Through those systems, the consumers or clients could operate all the information and functions of their accounts. Digital transactions or digital banking systems were not so popular or effective in terms of usability at that moment. All of them were using credit cards, ATMs, cheque-book systems, and other system components as well (Marie et al., 2013). In addition to that, in a pre-Covid situation, all of the bank transactions well basically slow. Even net banking was not so popular or trusted for the clients of Dubai banks. Before Covid-19, the customers in Dubai were looking for high usage rates on savings, current, and investment accounts where the satisfaction rate relies on these factors. On the other hand, after Covid-19, similar customers faced difficulties in managing their financing payments where the support from Sharia banks helped them manage their relationships with banks (OECD, 2021).

In terms of profitability, Dubai banks clients were different in terms of behaviour in the pre-Covid situation where all of those bank clients have trust in the banking system and interest rates. A considerable percentage of Dubai bank clients were not in the stock market or crypto investments. These digitalized investment methods or systems have come into focus after the Covid post-period. In that case, people were willing to put all of their money and investment values into the banks. For this significant reason, the whole banking sector of Dubai got high profitability from their clients regularly (Al-Tamimi et al., 2016). The most recent development in the Dubai banking sector is raised due to the high demand for digital products from customers, which led to the requirement of end-to-end digital banking solutions, which referred to the strong appetite of digital banks of the clients (CNBC, 2021). With concern to this factor, Sharia banks are highly focused on integrating Omnichannel experience and increasing their investment over digital tools to meet client needs. That reflects the shift in consumer demand due to Covid-19.

UAE Central Bank

Since the crisis began, the UAE Central Bank has reduced its main policy rate twice and announced an AED 256 billion (USD 27.2 billion) stimulus plan to assist banks' lending to the economy (*COVID-19 Crisis Response in MENA Countries*, 2020). This involves deferring loan repayments, decreasing bank reserve requirements, and providing banks with zero-interest collateralized loans to help SMEs. The UAE government has announced a total of AED 26.5 billion (*COVID-19 Crisis Response in MENA Countries*, 2020) in fiscal measures to mitigate the crisis's consequences and ensure economic continuity. The steps seek to reduce the costs for businesses by decreasing labour charges and other Ministry of Economy expenses, postponing the collection of administrative penalties, extending the deadline for tax payments, and reducing work permits and other service fees for firms. Locally, numerous emirates' administrations have implemented financial aid policies, which have often taken the form of lowered or eliminated customs taxes, township fees, and energy costs (*COVID-19 Crisis Response in MENA Countries*, 2020).

The CBUAE has made many efforts to help the industry in the UAE. It enabled the UAE banks to increase loans by releasing statutory cash reserves. They will have accessibility to zero-interest borrowings secured by collateral from the CBUAE. They will be permitted to utilize up to 60% of their capital conservation buffer, while those classified as systemically significant will be permitted to use 100% of their supplementary capital buffer. Additionally, the CBUAE is decreasing the number of capital banks must retain for loans to SMEs from 15% to 25%, facilitating this sector's access to funding (*COVID-19: Impact on the Banking Sector - KPMG Global*, 2020).

Additionally, the current cap on banks' exposure to the real estate industry is being reviewed. Banks will be permitted to expand it to 30% but will be obliged to maintain additional capital. The UAE's major banks have been proactive in giving clients financial assistance, following the CBUAE's AED 256 billion economic stimulus plan.

Additionally, post-Covid or living with Covid, those conventional systems and high profitability rates made the whole banking structure stable and regular in nature. The banks did not often propose new policies or new investment plans to the clients (VEERANKI, 2021). All the Dubai banks clients saved and invested their money in the same policies and structures. Hence, it is understood that the banking structure was regular with conventional investment policies and rates and interest rates. There were digital processes for money transactions through the bank, but people were not used to those yet. These conventional factors also help determine the differences between the pre-Covid and post-Covid situations in banks or Dubai.

However, it is evident that Fintech, the financial technology business, has looked to be resistant to the pandemic's threats and has largely projected to grow as consumers shift to digital-only services (IBSI, 2021). This technological aspect has motivated the client behaviour of Dubai Banks to show their willingness to open an account with a branchless digital bank only. This aligns with the worldwide benchmark of BCG (2020), which found that more than 53% of UAE banking clients increased their mobile app usage for banking during the pandemic, with more than 50% enrolling in digital banking for the first time as a result of the crisis.

CONCLUSION

Throughout history, pandemics have played a role in reshaping the economy around the world. Demand for goods and services increased and decreased without past precedent. The sectors affected in each pandemic vary, and the short- and long-term effects of each pandemic cannot be said to be the same as their nature differs, and so does the century they initiated in.

Globally, central banks have been strong and far-reaching in their activities. Along with the steps taken by local banks, some international banks have taken the following measures: donated 0.5 percent of all debit card spending in March to the fight against Covid-19; reduced monthly installments by 75 percent with significantly lower interest; a repayment holiday without interest or fees for personal loans, mortgages, and car loans; and school fees paid with a credit card meet the criteria for a flexible repayment plan of up to 6 months ***(COVID-19: Impact on***

***the Banking Sector - KPMG Global*, 2020)**. Under such circumstances, banks and the financial markets must maintain a constant state of vigilance. As long as the COVID-19 situation remains unresolved, they must actively examine the ramifications of the financial, risk, and regulatory compliance.

In terms of banking, service interaction changed because of the ever-changing client preferences due to the pandemic. Thus, banks must look for new ways to improve their services across channels, which involves investing in digital and building an experience to fulfill customer expectations. As a result, it can be claimed that Dubai banks have a significant chance to disrupt the industry, and taking rapid action to fulfill growing client expectations will be critical in retaining business and navigating the road ahead.

In conclusion, the effect of the pandemic was significant globally; however, the UAE was able to recover from it faster than the more prominent countries due to their quick response in providing risk management plans and strategies. Furthermore, the UAE had the opportunity to help other countries with a shortage of medical supplies and medications. As per the efforts and implementations made at the beginning of the pandemic to reduce its spread, the UAE is currently one of the countries open to tourists.

REFERENCES

Aassve, A., Alfani, G., Gandolfi, F., & Le Moglie, M. (2021). *Epidemics and trust: The case of the Spanish Flu.* Available at: https://onlinelibrary.wiley.com/doi/full/10.1002/hec.4218

Açikgöz, Ö., & Günay, A. (2020). The early impact of the Covid-19 pandemic on the global and Turkish economy. *Turkish Journal of Medical Sciences*, *50*(SI-1), 520–526. doi:10.3906ag-2004-6 PMID:32283904

Al-Hosani, F., Al-Mazrouei, S., Al-Memari, S., Al-Yafei, Z., Paulo, M. S., & Koornneef, E. (2021). *Policy and practice reviews. A Review of COVID-19 Mass Testing in the United Arab Emirates*. Academic Press.

Al-Tamimi, H. A. H., Lafi, A. S., & Uddin, M. H. (2016). Bank image in the UAE: Comparing Islamic and conventional banks. In *Islamic Finance* (pp. 46–65). Palgrave Macmillan.

AlQutob, R., Moonesar, I., Tarawneh, M., Al Nsour, M., & Khader, Y. (2020). Public health strategies for the gradual lifting of the public sector lockdown in Jordan and United Arab Emirates during the COVID-19 crisis. *JMIR Public Health and Surveillance*, 20478.

Banking and capital markets: Implications of COVID-19. (2020, March 16). *Deloitte Insights*. https://www2.deloitte.com/us/en/insights/economy/covid-19/banking-and-capital-markets-impact-covid-19.html

BCG. (2020). *COVID-19 is rapidly changing customer's banking demands, as 76 percent of UAE respondents expressed the interest to switch to banks that meet their needs*. Retrieved Dec 3, 2021, from https://www.bcg.com/en-mideast/press/5october2020-covid-19-is-rapidly-changing-customers-banking-demands

Bodenhorn, H. 2020. Business in a time of Spanish influenza (No. w27495). National Bureau of Economic Research.

BrincaP.DuarteJ. B.Faria-e-CastroM. (2020). Is the COVID-19 pandemic a supply or a demand shock? doi:10.20955/es.2020.31

Capital Markets in the current climate. (2020, April 22). *Vistra; Vistra Insights*. https://www.vistra.com/insights/capital-markets-current-climate

Chauvet, M., & Piger, J. (2005). *A Comparison of the Real-Time Performance of Business Cycle Dating Methods*. Academic Press.

Ciotti, M., Ciccozzi, M., Terrinoni, A., Jiang, W. C., Wang, C. B., & Bernardini, S. (2020). The COVID-19 pandemic. *Critical Reviews in Clinical Laboratory Sciences*, *57*(6), 365–388. doi:10.1080/10408363.2020.1783198 PMID:32645276

CNBC. (2021, December 4). *Fierce competition as UAE digital bank Zand prepares for launch*. Retrieved from CNBC: https://www.cnbc.com/2021/06/24/fierce-competition-as-uae-digital-bank-zand-prepares-for-launch.html

COVID-19. Impact on the banking sector. (2020, June 24). *KPMG*. https://home.kpmg/xx/en/home/insights/2020/07/covid-19-impact-on-banking-m-and-a-2020.html

COVID-19 crisis response in MENA countries. (2020, November 6). *OECD*. https://www.oecd.org/coronavirus/policy-responses/covid-19-crisis-response-in-mena-countries-4b366396/

Demirgüç-Kunt, A., Pedraza, A., & Ruiz-Ortega, C. (2021). Banking sector performance during the covid-19 crisis. *Journal of Banking & Finance*, 106305.

Elhennawy, A., Alsalem, F. A., Bahri, S., & Alarfaj, N. (2021). *Telemedicine versus Physical Examination in Patients' Assessment during COVID-19 Pandemic: The Dubai Experience*. Academic Press.

Gerth, F., Ramiah, V., Toufaily, E., & Muschert, G. (2021). Assessing the effectiveness of Covid-19 financial product innovations in supporting financially distressed firms and households in the UAE. *Journal of Financial Services Marketing*, 1–11.

Herlihy, D., & Cohn, S. H. (1997). *The Black Death and the transformation of the West*. Harvard University Press.

Ibrahim, M. (2014). A comparative performance of two Banks in United Arab Emirates. *Research Journal of Finance and Accounting*, *5*(21), 24–29.

IBSI. (2021). *5 FinTech companies making waves in the UAE market*. Retrieved Dec 3, 2021, from https://ibsintelligence.com/ibsi-news/5-fintech-companies-making-waves-in-the-uae-market/

IMF. (2021). https://www.imf.org/en/Topics/imf-and-covid19/Policy-Responses-to-COVID-19#J

Khan, M. (2020). *UAE's successful policies against COVID-19*. Academic Press.

KPMG. (2020). *A catalyst for change for bank branches*. https://home.kpmg/xx/en/blogs/home/posts/2020/04/a-catalyst-for-changefor-bank-branches.html

Langer, W. L. (1964). The black death. *Scientific American*, *210*(2), 114–121. doi :10.1038cientificamerican0264-114 PMID:14121747

Liesman, S. (2020, March 15). *Federal Reserve cuts rates to zero and launches massive $700 billion quantitative easing program*. CNBC. https://www.cnbc.com/2020/03/15/federal-reserve-cuts-rates-to-zero-and-launches-massive-700-billion-quantitative-easing-program.html

Marcu, M. R. (2021). The impact of the COVID-19 pandemic on the banking sector. *Management Dynamics in the Knowledge Economy*, *9*(2), 205–223.

Marie, A., Al-Nasser, A., & Ibrahim, M. (2013). Operational-Profitability-Quality Performance of Dubai's Banks. *Journal of Management Research*, *13*(1), 25–34.

Moghazy, M. A. (2020). *Teaching and learning Arabic as a second language online: a case study of Dubai during COVID-19 pandemic*. Academic Press.

Notteboom, T., Pallis, T., & Rodrigue, J. (2021). Disruptions and resilience in global container shipping and ports: The COVID-19 pandemic versus the 2008–2009 financial crisis. *Maritime Economics & Logistics*, *23*(2), 179–210.

OECD. (2021, December 4). *COVID-19 crisis response in MENA countries*. OECD. Retrieved from OECD: https://www.oecd.org/coronavirus/policy-responses/covid-19-crisis-response-in-mena-countries-4b366396/

Oxford, J. S., Lambkin, R., Sefton, A., Daniels, R., Elliot, A., Brown, R., & Gill, D. (2005). A hypothesis: The conjunction of soldiers, gas, pigs, ducks, geese and horses in Northern France during the Great War provided the conditions for the emergence of the "Spanish" influenza pandemic of 1918–1919. *Vaccine*, *23*(7), 940–945. doi:10.1016/j.vaccine.2004.06.035 PMID:15603896

Reuters. (2021, December 4). *Deserted debts stir disquiet in the mysterious world of Dubai Inc*. Retrieved from Reuters: https://www.reuters.com/article/dubai-debt-insight-int-idUSKBN2A9118

Routt, D. (2008). The economic impact of the Black Death. *EH.net Encyclopedia.*

Sundarakani, B., & Onyia, O. (2021). Fast, furious and focused approach to Covid-19 response: An examination of the financial and business resilience of the UAE logistics industry. *Journal of Financial Services Marketing*, 1–22.

Sundarakani, B., & Onyia, O. P. (2021). *Fast, furious and focused approach to Covid-19 response. An examination of the financial and business resilience of the UAE logistics industry*. Academic Press.

Thomas, J., Barbato, M., Verlinden, M., Gaspar, C., Moussa, M., Ghorayeb, J., . . . Bentall, R. P. (2020). *Psychosocial Correlates of Depression and Anxiety in the United Arab Emirates During the COVID-19 Pandemic*. Academic Press.

Tisdell, C. A. (2021). Determinants of the Economic Vulnerability of Businesses to Pandemics and Similar Events. *Journal of Risk and Financial Management, 14*(11), 532. doi:10.3390/jrfm14110532

Veeranki, Y. (2021). *Relative analysis of private and public sector banks–Pre and post COVID* (Doctoral dissertation). SRM University.

Chapter 8
Strategies for Growth Adopted by Indian Businesses Amid the COVID-19 Crisis

Vivek Joshi
https://orcid.org/0000-0002-1869-7569
Creative Head Consultants, India

Supreet Ahluwalia
Creative Head Consultants, India

ABSTRACT

This chapter makes an effort to highlight the challenges faced and strategies adopted by businesses in India. An effort has been made to describe the economic condition of the economy before the onset of the COVID pandemic and the resulting outcome of the havoc so created by the pandemic and resulting lockdowns. An analysis has been done to clarify how large corporations and small businesses faced the combined blunt of poor economy and COVID. Case story-based approach has been adopted to highlight responses of few large corporations and how they turned the pandemic into an economic opportunity to churn out super normal profits. The chapter also highlights how the number of billionaires in India has increased during this time. Struggles of small businesses are also highlighted, and how they struggled for survival and sustenance and changes they have made in the way they function or carry out day-to-day business operations have also been discussed. A very small proportion of businesses did stand up for the welfare of the public and made an effort to facilitate their workforce.

DOI: 10.4018/978-1-7998-8346-3.ch008

INTRODUCTION

Every economy works as well and as effectively as the participants or a constituent within the economic system. Indian economy is no exception to the rule. The country struggled as the country's governments failed to plan the lockdown and later failed to provide any economic impetus or stimulus for the businesses. Hence, the crisis gave rise to an extraordinary breed of business class, especially those originating from the middle class. These businesses resisted accepting the drawbacks of lockdown and decided to adopt innovative practices and change the business outlook to survive, sustain and grow. These brave-hearts' never-say-die attitudes put commoners' belief in the economic system and gave them hope for economic recovery and survival. All Businesses whether big or small followed certain stratagems to survive, sustain and grow in this troubled socio-economic turbulence. The stratagems or strategies so opted for depended upon size, availability and strengths of each economic participant or the business. The range of strategies so played varied from intensive cost cutting to changing the complete line of business.

Several authors have contributed to the field of strategy, and several definitions have been given over the time to highlight the role that a strategy plays in success of a business in challenging times. To initiate a strategy is the executive action taken to facilitate the attainment of organizational goals.

A strategy could also be explained as a specific track or path opted by a company and its associated components to accomplish chosen state or competitive position in the future. Most strategies revolve around growth, profitability, and creating a competitive advantage that helps a business organization gain an edge over rival firms. The competitive advantage attained via strategy helps generate a unique market position resulting in higher profits.

In the commercial domain, profit is not a 'DIRTY' word. The most sought-after objective is complete market domination and profitability in the form of supernormal profits. Supernormal profits are all the excess profit a firm makes above the minimum return necessary to keep a firm in business. Thus, corporations select several alternative routes to attain the desired objective. These routes are nothing more than the strategy adopted and deployed by any business entity to achieve desired objectives and outperform the competitors.

Theories and other research on strategy suggest several strategies to attain desired objectives. Though few strategies might induce the businesses to do something completely new or try new ways of doing old tricks prompting the enterprise to take up the innovation or introduce invention into the market.

Most of the strategies discussed are challenging to implement and take a lot of effort, time, and resource commitment. Any strategy selected to be executed may deliver benefits in the long run as it usually takes consistent efforts of five to eight years to build up any strategic advantage to result in consistent cash flows. Furthermore, for how long the selected strategy would be sustainable again a question mark.

Strategic Choice and Strategy Implementation is a long-term process, whereas a pandemic is not a long-term phenomenon (instead of a short to medium-term portent). The pandemic is either an opportunity or a threat that could alter the game and change the fortunes of organizations if they do not play smart or try to outlive the pandemic and its aftereffects. Organizations should fine-tune their actions and draw plans to face this extraordinary challenge and effectively meet their economic, social, and business obligations.

New Strategies are needed during a pandemic to grow and outsmart the competition. Moreover, strategies are required to convert the challenges posed by the pandemic into an opportunity to make short-term profits and gain more market access. If developed and executed smartly, strategies would help create a competitive advantage that any close competitor could not replicate in the short run. Such innovative strategies would keep a business in a better position than its rivals.

Considering pandemic as a short-term opportunity, most corporate houses (few serious exceptions were there) geared up to use cost-cutting and other easy-to-implement strategies to maximize the bottom line. Businesses focused on making easy money moreover to showcase a healthy bottom-line in the short run. All cost-cutting efforts so adopted resulted in job losses, reduced pay, hiked working hours, and exploitation of constrained demand conditions for raw material.

The strategies adopted during the pandemic to maximize profitability impacted the community in a big way. For instance, reducing or cutting jobs altogether, reducing wages and salaries, buying raw materials at unfairly low prices, charging higher prices for finished products, cutting supplies, demanding higher profits, closing down offices, not paying rents and old dues, demanding for loan waivers all in the name of pandemic became the ways or few of the preferred strategies of Indian businesses to generate higher profits.

Some of the executive actions, strategies, and paths opted by Indian businesses to attain objectives might not seem acceptable on minimum social and ethical grounds. However, these deviations are neither uncommon nor unacceptable in the world of business. Breaching socially acceptable norms and ethical principles for attaining profits and creating a monopoly is very common.

The pandemic was nerve-racking, and there was nervous energy all around as the people worldwide were scared, and the uncertainty loomed largely. Loss of livelihoods, loss of life, losing loved ones, and losing health were prime concerns that people faced and expected some support from those who controlled maximum resources of society and controlled maximum wealth.

Expectation from a business was not to share wealth but to stand in solidarity with society. Businesses were expected to extend support and give the common people confidence that life to normalcy would soon return. To tell the masses that the affluent stand with them, provide support in these difficult times. Unfortunately, in India, most of the population, especially the middle class, were left alone at the mercy of fate to face the pandemic and fight the war of their own.

In order to lay out the complete scene that existed in India as the pandemic hit the country, this chapter first discusses the social scenario and economic environment that existed when the pandemic set off in the country. After discussions of the Socio-economic scenario, it deliberates on the various strategies, whether good or bad, adopted by businesses and big corporations in India. This approach was essential to orient the reader about the setting of overall environmental factors that existed before the onset of the pandemic moreover to provide an insight into how the country was not ready or prepared at the least to face the global chaos 'COVID -19 Pandemic'.

To a great extent, the chapter follows a case study-based style and tries to integrate one after another series of examples or cases that highlights the strategies and tactics adopted by Indian businesses and corporations.

In order to understand the panoramic view of the Indian corporate sector and strategies adopted by various companies in India, we would look at few Big Players (the Big Caps or the Mughals of Indian Economy). This discussion would facilitate to understand the kind of response that India Incorporation had towards the Pandemic and how they have utilised all opportunities to make extra-ordinary profit. There were some smaller businesses that responded innovatively and vigorously to survive in the face of the challenge. Very small group of Big Caps or corporates did gave upon profit objective and made efforts to serve the public and protect their workforce by extending all measures and support possible under the circumstances.

The Start of the Pandemic and Its Economic Impact

COVID-19 pandemic has wreaked havoc on all economies throughout the world. Businesses have struggled to survive and are forced to learn new tricks to sustain through this turbulence. Though the already slowing economy was jolted by the pandemic and resulted in the negative growth rate of 23.9% in the first quarter of 2020-2021, the World Bank report for the Indian economy was not surprising (World Bank, 2020).

In gross value terms, the economy contracted by 22.8%. The pandemic forced Indian corporates to restrict commercial activities and resulted in great job loss; an estimated 122 million lost their livelihood. The unemployment rate rose to 27.1% in India primarily due to the severe lockdown imposed in the last week of March 2020 (PTI, 2021).

Job loss was worse in Micro, Small, and Medium-Sized Enterprises (MSME) and the unorganized sector though they provide the maximum proportion of jobs to unskilled and semi-skilled labour (Singh, 2020). The job losses were in almost all sectors, and now the more substantial second wave seems to add more numbers to unemployment. The rise in the numbers of the unemployed population was not the only issue being faced by the economy. Hundreds of millions suffered pay cuts and are still reeling under the financial stress of managing their obligations to support the family.

Amid this scenario, most major corporations, primarily the large companies and big corporate houses, especially those who fall under the category of Large Caps (Market Capitalization of USD 10 billion or more), used this pandemic as an opportunity. They made good by adding substantial profitability in the financial year 2020-2021. The Sultans of India Incorporation saw a golden opportunity being presented by the pandemic. These big corporations were cash and resource-rich and had powerful lobbying abilities and high-profile political connections facilitating access to several large projects and new policy changes taking place much before their smaller or cash-strapped contemporaries.

The Draconian Lockdown

The first COVID-19 case was reported in India in late January 2020. After a single day of curfew on March 22, 2020, the country announced a nationwide 21-day lockdown on March 25, 2020, that time confirmed that COVID positive cases in India were just a mark above 500. This lockdown was further extended in a phased manner and continued till May 17, 2020, and later in a gradually phased manner, the unlocking of the economy started. This sudden call for lockdown and lack of financial support and assistance from any government, either federal or state, resulted in heavy financial losses and set off a financial Tsunami for the vast middle class of the country and small business owners (Singh, 2020).

The lockdown initiated a panic and frenzy amongst people and a lot of small business owners. Millions lost their jobs without being paid for the work they did before the lockdown. Additionally, employees were forced to accept lesser pays or unreasonable pay cuts, and these wages and pay cuts ranged from 10% to 60% (McKinsey and Co., 2020).

More than 12 million lost their jobs. The economy had no chance to rebound as the weak economy was poorly performing even before the onset of the pandemic (CMIE, 2021).

The situation was quite evident from the Public Debt to Gross Domestic Product (GDP) ratio, which highlights the level of a country's government borrowings as a %age of the nation's Gross Domestic Product. This ratio was gradually moving towards 83% at the time of the introduction of lockdown. Although, it was close to

74% in 2019, and by the end of 2020, it was almost 90% (89.4%). However, it finally climbed to 90.23% at the start of the year 2021 (World Bank, 2020).

Those who could work from home were allowed to work from home, and it made corporations realize that they are overstaffed and could quickly reduce their present workforce by another 20%-30% to gain better bottom-line numbers for the quarter and maybe for the financial year.

Though several restrictions were being relaxed and the lockdown was eased after the first week of May 2020, the official unlocks phase started from June 1, 2020, and continued till the end of November in the same year.

Surging Profits Amidst Lockdown

During the gruesome lockdown period in India, almost four thousand (4000) plus listed companies stated collective profits of INR 1.52 Trillion in the second quarter of the year, almost after the lockdown was made liberal (July-September 2020). The figure so quoted is the peak profit geared by all listed companies within India in any quarter (Online, 2020).

These listed companies have accomplished to produce supernormal profits amidst the lockdown. Additionally, the declared profit figure (INR 1.52 Trillion) was almost 31% greater than the previously held record of INR 1180 billion in Quarter 4 (January-March) of FY2014, geared toward the effort of 4,854 listed companies. The combined profits of 4,076 companies increased 171% from INR 0.57 billion in the same quarter last year (Online, 2020).

Manufacturing Companies Leading From the Front

Although banks, NBFCs, construction companies all added to the phenomenal growth in profits of the listed companies in the second quarter, almost 50% of the profits were generated by manufacturing companies (Online, 2020).

The period was marked by a decline in sales, lesser other income or non-operating incomes, and famished net extraordinary income, if any, hardly generated. The manufacturing firms generated record-high collective profits, although their overhead was higher and more significant taxes.

It has listed 1,675 manufacturing companies geared up INR 726 Billion in net profits. The value generated is the highest profit ever engendered by these companies, severely ailing India during the pandemic. The profit so created was 16.82% more when compared to the previously recorded value of around INR 622 Billion in 2019 (Online, 2020).

The Reverse - Sales Fall and Profits Soars

Higher sales lead to more revenue and increased profitability. The pandemic showed us the reverse. Shrinkage in demand was noted and visible throughout the first phase of the pandemic in the year 2020 still, and the manufacturing companies garnered bumper profit despite a major somewhat historic shriveling of INR 961 Billion in net sales backed by acute contraction in long-term demand (Online, 2020).

Another interesting phenomenon observed during the period was the fall in operating expenses that fuelled further the growth in profits. Operating expenses over the spectrum got reduced by INR 1030 Billion in the period. The contraction in operating costs was due to much-reduced spending on raw materials, labour, and finished goods (Mohan, 2021).

Though for profits earned in Quarter 2 (Q2) or the September quarter of the Financial Year 2020-2021, India Incorporation has done significantly well in the face of the disturbances caused by the pandemic. The collective net profit of listed companies touched a new high of INR 1.52 trillion — up two and a half times on a year-on-year (YoY) basis (Kant, 2020).

The oil and gas sector also performed surprisingly well, especially the oil marketer like Indian Oil, Bharat Petroleum, and Hindustan Petroleum, all registered extreme profits on inventory gains. However, a registered 21% plus drop in their net sales (Kant, 2020).

The gains attained during this period, at one point, seemed temporary. They were assumed to vanish soon, but support from the government of India and continuous price rise by the oil marketing companies has changed the story of supernormal gains as the phenomenon resulted in historically high petrol and diesel prices in India (Kant, 2020).

Reasons for the Profits – The Changing Scenario

There were several reasons for the hike in profits. The Indian Incorporation left no stone unturned to ensure that they converted this pandemic into an opportunity to add more money to their coffers. In the manufacturing sector, profits and earnings improved due to a severe weakening in costs or the input prices that facilitate gross and operating margins in most sectors.

To top it all, several other manufactured goods such as tyres, iron, cement, glass, and metals, saw a harsh prices increase thanks to an amalgamation of interruption in domestic manufacturing and severely imposed import restrictions. Further support to the corporate initiative for profit maximization was provided by corporate tax rate cuts as introduced by the Government of India in several policy initiatives. The reduction in corporate tax rates helped India Incorporation to witness further robust plus sturdy growth in PAT (Profit after Tax) in Quarter2 (Q2) of Financial Year 2021 (Thomas, 2021).

The key reasons that could be easily highlighted for the generation of the steep profits in India Incorporation during COVID -19 lockdown are as follows:

1. Low Prices of Raw Material
2. Low cost of Labour
3. Low spends on Finished Goods
4. Reduced Competition in the market

Falling Raw Material Prices – Broken-back Micro Industry and Perishing Smaller Businesses

The pandemic witnessed historically low raw material prices as most of the raw material providers in India are in grey or unorganized markets (sectors of economic activity) and are very small to impact the demand and supply equation. These small or micro-businesses were neither supported nor protected by the government. As the lockdown was announced, these raw material suppliers got exposed to the harsh realities of the pandemic and frail economic system. Lack of government support, missing financial safety net, and non-availability of social security system in the country made the situation worse (Mohan, 2021).

These raw material providers started to sell their raw material at any price (whatever they could realize from the market) that they could fetch to generate sufficient liquidity and keep their households running.

A crucial factor that hit them hard was the need for hard cash as there was constantly growing demand for funds due to severe lockdown, and most of these vendors had large debts that were needed to be serviced. Funds (especially cash) were hard to come, and the need to effectively meet our debt obligations was on priority as financial institutions' pressure was mounting (Biswas, 2020). Most of these small businesses usually operate on credit and are provided with minimal credit periods. The situation warranted to pay creditors at the earliest as most creditors to are small businesses. Overall the scene was tense and grim, mandating thwarting decisions and actions to salvage whatever could be saved quickly.

Raw Material providers also had a shortage of demand due to several small businesses closing their shops due to unavailability of cash and inability to face the dire financial consequences of COVID lockdown. COVID-19, and resulting lockdowns, forced the small raw material suppliers to sell their assets and shops to utilize available cash. This hindered the restoration of businesses when the lockdown was taken back, resulting in several small manufacturers ultimately losing their businesses or closing their shops.

The effects of lockdown began to emerge in manufacturing and all economic activities such as hospitality, food processing, consumer durables, construction, real estate, oil mills, and even agriculture and grocery shops. The gruesome effects of lockdown were left untouched, and a steep fall in overall consumer demand was observed (Biswas, 2020).

The closing of shops and businesses and a fall in overall demand forced the raw material suppliers to sell their products to listed companies or cash-rich companies, especially in the manufacturing sector. The situation thus resulted in a further fall in negotiating abilities of these small businesses. These raw material suppliers started selling at any price (lowest possible prices dictated by buyers) they could get to salvage their finances and protect themselves against any odds of losing or closing their businesses permanently.

Low Cost of Labour

Low demand and excessive supply of labour helped bring down the cost of labour up to a great extent (Mohan, 2021).

Most of the small and unviable industries and manufacturing units did close down. A ban on exports plus the restricted movement of goods and services out of the country forced several others to close their shops as there was an excess supply of goods and no market to sell. Few other businesses were short of cash and could not meet our fixed costs, including wages and salaries, and locked their facilities.

The environment was conducive and ripe for job shortages due to lockdown, the uncertainty that loomed large on the employers, and the eagerness of Micro, Small and Medium enterprises to close shop and save as much cash as possible. The movement of Migrant labour and their plight further added to the woes pushing the cost of labour further down as there were no jobs or alternative employment opportunities available. The reverse migration trend started from metros cities to native places in small cities, towns, and villages.

Low Spends on Finished Goods

Business spending on finished goods also went low due to easy transport availability; goods' transportation time to move from factories to outlets was also reduced due to empty roads, thanks to the lockdown. Cost of transportation went downwards as transporters had very few opportunities available due to lockdown and movement hesitancy due to the pandemic. Transporters accepted whatever assignments they could get at an optimal price. Several thousands of transporters who updated their fleet in the last six months to a year were under heavy debt burden and were pushed by banks to meet their payment deadline and service their debt obligations effectively.

The mounting pressure from banks also forced transporters to accept sub-optimal assignments. Another peculiar observation that needs to be mentioned is that transporters also tried to make supernormal profits as they used to deliver goods. While returning from the delivery, they started carrying migrant labour without permission and permits, charging 20 to 30 times the cost of travel by the public transportation system. This trend started due to the absence of public transports and other means of commuting (Jha, 2020).

Some transporters started planning and running round trips to illegally transport migrant labour charging INR 500,000 for a single trip for 17 and 19 feet trucks to carry the load of 5-8 tons, giving them INR 1 million or more per return trip (Singh, 2020).

Warehousing also had difficult times due to reduced production and shrinkage in imports and production for exports. Empty warehouses and lack of mobility of goods further added to the woes of warehouse owners pushing warehousing costs down and giving manufacturers a low-cost advantage on storage of finished goods.

Reduced Competition in Indian Market

Due to the pandemic and lockdown, supply chains and movement of goods externally were restricted. Smaller players were closing the shop, and these changes reduced the competition within the Indian Market. The condensed competition gave more opportunities to earn to domestic players, especially to those more prominent players who had a large resource base or were cash-rich. The customers were also forced to consume what was available within the country as they were short of choices, and international brands' availability was consistently short.

The Corporate's Search for Profits

Businesses and corporates exist for earning profits, and the search for profit is universal and all-pervasive. India is no exception, corporates of the country were searching for profit, and the pandemic failed to make any dent in this pursuit. The willingness to make a profit and that too at any cost does hurt humanity's sentiment, and notion and question the ethical framework these corporate houses claim to honor and follow.

The stressful time of the pandemic witnessed the wealth of Indian billionaires skyrocketing and hiking by more than 35%. The total wealth of Indian billionaires grew multifold through the initial phase of a pandemic to reach INR 3 trillion (Chandra, 2021).

Mukesh Ambani, Chairman of Reliance Industries, emerged as the richest man in India and Asia, with his net worth touching $83 billion. He also became the 8th

richest man in the world. Mukesh Ambani earned INR 1.9 billion per hour through the pandemic when more than 24% of the population of India were just having monthly earnings of less than INR 3,000 in the middle of severe lockdown (Nahar, 2021).

In spirit and word, the Covid-19 Pandemic has indeed created a more significant divide between the rich and the poor. Rich, they become super-rich, and the poor, they are progressively getting poorer. Some economists also tab the Corona Virus as the inequality virus as it has helped the rich add more wealth and made the poor more pitiable. One of the reports suggests that the amount Mukesh Ambani, the richest man in India, makes in an hour, an unskilled worker would take almost ten thousand years to make the same amount (Bhargava, 2021).

The list of Indian billionaires grew, plus the wealth of these billionaires also increased several folds, Mukesh Ambani being the richest in Asia. Mukesh was followed by Adani Group's Gautam Adani as the second richest person in the country, with Adani's wealth almost doubled to $32 billion during the pandemic (Sasi, 2020).

Other Indian Billionaires who made great wealth during the pandemic were HCL's Shiv Nadar, with $27 billion. Shiv Nadar became the third richest man in India, followed by ArcelorMittal's Lakshmi Mittal, whose net worth touched $19 billion. India's largest vaccine manufacturer Serum Institute's Chairman Cyrus Poonawalla's net worth crossed $18.5 billion and is expected to increase further due to the government giving him clearance to manufacture other foreign vaccines within India. The net worth of Hinduja Group's Hinduja Brothers reached $18 billion. They preceded Uday Kotak of Kotak Mahindra Bank, whose wealth reached $15 billion (Chandra, 2021).

One interesting fact emerges from this list, most of these business leaders, who have earned and whose wealth has skyrocketed in these testing times, are considered very close to the political circles in India. Most have supported the current ruling party in the past and endorsed each policy. This is especially so even in recent turmoil when the commoner of the country is finding it difficult to make their ends meet (Varma, 2019).

Ways to Wealth

Best suited cases to highlight how rich Indian corporate honchos become super rich, two corporate leaders both close to Indian political power center could be named. Two Indian super rich Mukesh Ambani of Reliance and Gautam Adani of Adani Group made lot of money and amassed tremendous wealth during this testing period. Looking separately at both Mukesh Ambani and Gautam, Adani seems to have adopted different strategies. The domains of operations moreover business focuses for both also look diverged and very much sector aligned. The only standard variables seem to be the closeness to political power center and following constant search for higher profits. A closer look would surely help find out way more similarities between the two corporate giants than that could be caught without in-depth analysis.

Both Billionaires Mukesh Ambani and Gautam Adani amassed great wealth during a pandemic. The strategies used were simple and had a dash of luck to support them. Both groups had high profitability besides being financially stable even before the onset of the pandemic through the entire Indian economy at the time was in doldrums besides economic growth rate was in tethers.

These billionaires followed very simple business policies to follow. The strategic initiatives were focused on controlling expenses by cutting down costs, especially fixed costs and unnecessary overheads. To buy new businesses, assets and make capital investments cheap when nobody else was in a position to buy or invest.

The clear policy focus was to make sure not even a single penny was wasted or left without generating enough returns. However, these high returns on Investment (ROI) may have to come at the cost of curtailing charity works or donations at the time of thoroughgoing needs.

Reliance and Adani Group aligned their businesses quite closely with the policies of the Government of India. Both corporate houses made considerable investments in the sectors. Their success showcases the successful lobbying and negotiation skills of the two gentlemen (Varma, 2019).

Both Corporate houses are known for limitless diversification. Given an opportunity by pandemic, they further diversified themselves by adding new businesses and initiating continuous heavy investments in new verticals ranging from green energy, retail, to agricultural produces, IT infrastructure, and platform development at one end of the spectrum to producing medical grade oxygen and manufacturing PPE kits, Masks, Sanitizers along with the development of protective therapies against CORONA at the other (Sharma & qz.com, 2021).

Monopoly Practices and Demand for Curtailing Economic Power of International Players Like Amazon etc.

Several Indian businesses raised their voice against big international brands operating in India especially against giants like Amazon and Flipkart. These voices though seem to be the concerns of small players but in reality any action against these global super houses would benefit Indian corporate giants like Reliance.

Before the pandemic, India's online market was anticipated to be valued at nearly about $85.3 billion by 2024. Facebook, Walmart, and several others have joined Amazon, investing heavily in India. With changing policy frameworks and difficult economic situations, these companies find that game is becoming increasingly difficult to play (Singh, 2020).

Shrinkage in economic activity and effects of the pandemic resulted in severe stagnation in market demand. Fall in demand and shortage of resources and liquidity needed for sustenance forced business enterprises to take drastic steps and give out loud shouts to the government to save them. Failure of the government to respond appropriately added to the woes. The grim economic atmosphere created led the Indian businesses, mostly small businesses, to turn against foreign players. An alternative anti-foreign business strategy and attacking foreign online players seemed to be gaining momentum in India.

There has been continuous demand during the pandemic by Indian businesses, whether big or small, besides some political quarters to cut short the power and position of foreign players operating within the Indian economy.

Continuous voice-outs or out roars against online platforms and players like Walmart Wholesale, Amazon, and Flipkart. Smaller shopkeepers and businesses to Mukesh Ambani found an inherent threat in Walmart, Amazon, and Flipkart. Each business or player devised a strategy to tackle the threat as per their capabilities and available resources. All businesses, big or small, put pressure on the government to curtail the economic power and freedom to play enjoyed by the prominent foreign players in the Indian market.

Questions were raised about the business ethics of large foreign players, along with questioning their ability to buy cheap and sell cheap (a competitive advantage that Indian businesses might not be able to generate and sustain). Concerns were raised about foreign players' ability to generate supernormal profits from India during the pandemic. In addition to the concerns showcased, some domestic businesses went on to the extent of seeking protection against these large foreign businesses.

Looking at the challenging environment and difficulty to sustain business in India, some small businesses have even asked the country's government for full closure or complete withdrawal of foreign companies in order to protect the interest of small Indian businesses could be safeguarded.

Amazon lost a fiercely fought battle against Indian giant reliance industries to acquire Future retail (Future Group). However, Amazon was the first mover and the first bidder for Future Group's retail business.

Amazon started the proceedings two years before Reliance plus even decided to invest in Future Group. However, Amazon is a foreign company that was pressured by Indian Authorities on several grounds. Looking at the situation worsening every day, Amazon decided to settle the deal via Arbitration in Singapore (newssapp. Com, 2021).

The deal became difficult as Reliance overpowered and bought Future Group, and the game became nasty and reached to Supreme Court of India. In the Supreme Court of India, Amazon lost the final battle as the Supreme Court of India ruled in favour of Mukesh Ambani's Reliance Industries (newssapp.Com, 2021).

In order to get a better view of the economic situation, the legal environment needs to be discussed. The laws in India are somewhat loft-sided and mostly favor big local players pitted against more efficient foreign players. The legal framework supports these inefficient business corporations with protectionist measures that too in the name of guarding the interests of mom and pop stores.

To understand the Indian market and its dynamics better, understanding the composition of India population distribution becomes critical. More than 65% of the Indian population is of average 30 years of age.

The large and young populations provide great incentive and prospects to any International company venturing into India. India was also considered a close competitor to China, and the world expected India to stop the Chinese progression and dominance around the globe. All these factors clubbed with the big middle class, and sizeable consuming population made India an attractive marketplace and a potential launch-pad to several other sunrise sectors.

To make the matters grimmer, the Reserve Bank of India (BRI), and the Enforcement Directorate (ED), India's federal crime-fighting agency, have initiated investigations against the world's biggest online retail platform Amazon for suspected breach of India's Foreign Investment Laws (Sethi, 2021).

Flipkart, another e-tailer belonging to Walmart along with Amazon, is contesting another legal suit. Both Flipkart and Amazon face an investigation being pursued by India's antitrust regulator Competition Commission of India, which has raised concerns and doubts about their sales practices. A formal investigation has been launched after permission was given by the Government of India based upon the complaints made by several local retailers and small businesses. These businesses have been raising voices for quite some time now against the two retail platform giants besides demanding that the government should bar these two foreign e-tailers from operating in India (Sethi, 2021).

There has been a populist sentiment being flagellated against foreign forces for quite some time now, especially in IT, ITeS, and online retail segments. This anti-foreign player propaganda is part of a mandate to develop domestic industries besides providing more opportunities to small companies in retailing, manufacturing, the internet, and ITeS, to name a few.

The environment within the country now seems quite conducive for the formation of a few big conglomerates that would later monopolize the market. The phenomenal growth of Reliance and Adani groups and the expansion trajectory of their activities indicate that these two groups will soon dominate the Indian markets.

In addition to controlling the Indian market, both corporates are set to control maximum economic activities within the nation. The Adani - Ambani duo are cash-rich and well supported by the government of the country. Along with having a wide range of present and potential investors, the current pandemic has presented these two big corporations with an ideal opportunity to expand further and beyond their current line of activities. Political lobbying and pandemic have given them a chance to diversify into new segments where they had no presence before the onset of the pandemic. Competitive Business has been made more opportunistic and favorable for Indian players by cutting down the economic power of big global players to provide an edge to the selected Indian corporations.

The Other Face of Corporations

Public Service and serving the community to the attainment of larger good is also a strategy followed by several business entities. The strategy to serve the public and society at large does serve well most of the time. Whenever the businesses kept the society in the front of their economic activity or the business operations, the community has always respected and appreciated such businesses plus rewarded them with huge profits.

Though the picture presented so far looked pale and infested with greed, the discussion would not be over without mentioning the few who worked relentlessly to serve the public. It was not that every corporate house was running after the money. Several reputed business families and billionaires took several efforts to help and pay back the society at this most critical juncture of human crisis.

Godrej Consumer Products Limited (GCPL), TataSons, Hindustan Uniliver, Wipro, and Amway Enterprises India have taken several steps to serve society and keep their workforce intact, safe, and well protected through insurance protection (Roy, 2020).

These corporations also conducted heavy testing and carried out mandatory vaccination drives that too free of cost for the employees and their family members. The coverage of insurance and vaccine was also extended to the vendors and channels partners (Mukherji, 2021).

These business houses contributed to societal wellbeing by making large donations to charity organizations, distributing PPE kits, Sanitizers, Face Masks, Food packets, Oxygen concentrators, Ventilators, and medicines.

Moreover, these businesses also dropped the prices of their home essential or personal care products. The price drop was to help those who have lost their substantial income due to COVID. The focus was on the large chunk of the population, so people do not have to make living quality compromises besides providing easy access to essentialities for consumers to live a dignified life.

Innovation and Change in Strategy as Survival and Sustainability Mantra – MSME's Route to Grow and Thrive

The arrival of COVID-19 rang alarm bells for the Micro Small and Medium Enterprises (MSME) in India, as several of them were already struggling before the arrival of the pandemic due to poor economic conditions. Significant challenges faced by these small businesses ranged from the challenge of continuity of business to maintaining current customers besides managing supply-side challenges posed by lockdown and post lockdown as the money supply slumped.

More than 60% of the businesses came under threat of closure. Out of these, almost 42% finally closed the shop. This resulted in a fall in GDP and rise in unemployment as this sector used to employ a bit higher than 122 million people and contributed quite significantly to the GDP of India (CMIE, 2021).

New challenges and deteriorating financial conditions raised cash management, supply chain management, and revenue management concerns. The prolonged continuation of the pandemic brought a new challenge, something these small businesses were not expecting so soon. The critical challenge being faced was a change in consumption patterns and preferences (Drolia, 2021).

Significant challenges faced by small businesses or the MSME sectors were as follows:

1. Changes in Cash Management Practices – Only 24% of businesses had the cash holding capacity or cash in hand that would have helped them to remain operational if COVID persisted beyond six months. However, at the start of the pandemic, this number was as high as 73% (Drolia, 2021).
2. Managing the Revenue – 34% of small businesses reported a complete loss of revenue by the end of 2020. Nearly 40% of the companies quoted that they have suffered losses between 15% to 30%, only 11% reported revenue increase (mint, 2020).
3. Supply Chain Difficulties – Difficulty in domestic transportation, non-availability of imports, and critical fall in Chinese imports (affected first) presented significant tests. Almost 48% of small businesses reported disruptions in the supply chain (Now, n.d.).

Changed situations and questions on survival forced these businesses to completely transform how they used to do the business and how they used to carry out their daily operations.

There were several strategies adopted and significant changes that were introduced in their business practices. Some of these changes were as follows: (Singh, 2021)

- The majority of small businesses decided to become lean as they fired additional staff or employees and curtailed those activities which were not adding real value to the business.
- Retaining Efficient Employees
- Low-cost hiring practices were adopted as expensive employees were made to exit from their jobs.
- Small innovations in products, business processes were adopted to reduce the cost of operations.
- Local sourcing was preferred, and alternative arrangements were made to bring corrections in the Supply-side.
- Low-cost alternatives were adopted to adjust to consumers' pockets forcing consumption habits to change.
- Warehousing and other ancillary costs were reduced. Stock management and ordering operations were made more prompt and cost-effective by only ordering when the need arose and ordering small quantities pooled with others from the same business to push for sufficient volume to get lower prices.
- Management of cash flows by cutting costs and reducing operating expenses
- Non-essential or non-operative assets were sold off to make up for revenue losses
- Online existence was now considered a significant move and was adopted by several, but there was a surprising move, and several small businesses started raising concerns and demands for closing foreign online platforms or e-tailers such as Flipkart and Amazon
- Diversification in businesses and the creation of more revenue verticals was considered by those who could afford, or some completely changed their line of business
- Adoption of technology was another strategy that MSME adopted, but it was too little too late
- Several Small traders adopted the role of aggregators, or they became channel partners to big corporations like Reliance industries

CONCLUSION

This story of the extraordinary struggle for survival of small businesses and struggle to grow and thrive is just one dimension of the story. It does give us immense pride and faith in fairness, values, and business ethics. The other side of the story is of Big Cash-rich corporate houses that went for no hold-bar battle for business growth, expansions, supernormal profits, and using the pandemic as an opportunity to make abnormal profits at any cost.

The Indian economic environment also witnessed a frenzy of strategic alliances, especially mergers and takeovers. Some big corporations saw an opportunity to amass wealth by buying smaller businesses and chains at paltry prices or by lobbying to put the political pressure on competitive businesses to sell their strategic operations to powerful big business corporations for far lower prices. Some of the businesses were brought at much lower prices than the higher bid made by foreign businesses. All this was done in the name of national interest and protecting the Indian Economy.

Taking unfair advantage of the economic situation and exploiting the same for benefits, some large corporations could even pay back their large debts that were supposed to be settled in 3 years to 5 years tenure, just in the time frame of 8-10 months. All thanks to measures adopted such as cost-cutting practices, buying cheap raw material as the vendors have no option but to sell it to large cash wealthy corporations at dirt-low prices. These small vendors, especially in the unorganized and primary sectors, were forced due to pressure for survival and keeping themselves in business. Liquidity crunch was another constraint faced by smaller businesses that were also exploited for advantage by big corporations.

COVID-19 Crisis has changed the world, and a lot more is still in the balance, but the current crisis failed to change the old business practices. Several Strategies were adopted in the recent past to sustain the business. Several short-term business tactics were used to earn supernormal profits and attain phenomenal growth in corporate wealth. Some small and micro enterprises did struggle and changed the way they do their business.

The smaller businesses adopted innovative practices or took too significant risks to sustain under the given environment. Cash Rich, large corporate houses with many resources expanded their business operations using their economic power, political proximity at the peak time of crisis, circumventing the laws and provisions of the land. Several powerful corporations got support from the governments or aligned their businesses with the wishes of the country's government. The constant search for growth and supernormal profits continued even during this pandemic. Major corporations saw the COVID-19 pandemic as an opportunity to earn enormous profits during this great human crisis.

REFERENCES

Al Jazeera. (2021, January 18). *Two of India's richest men face farmers' ire over new laws*. Retrieved August 5, 2021, from Al Jazeera website: https://www.aljazeera.com/economy/2021/1/18/bbtwo-of-indias-richest-men-face-ire-over-its-new-farm-laws

Amazon battles Mukesh ambani for India's E-commerce future - newssapp.com. (2021, June 7). Retrieved July 12, 2021, from Newssapp.com website: https://newssapp.com/2021/06/07/business/amazon-battles-mukesh-ambani-for-indias-e-commerce-future/

Bhargava, Y. (2021, March 2). *In 2020, the world added three billionaires every two days, India added one every week.* Retrieved May 2, 2021, from The Hindu. https://www.thehindu.com/news/national/india-adds-40-billionaires-in-pandemic-year-adani-ambani-see-rise-in-wealth-report/article33970268.ece

Biswas, S. (2020, March 30). *Coronavirus: India's pandemic lockdown turns into a human tragedy.* Retrieved July 13, 2021from BBC. https://www.bbc.com/news/world-asia-india-52086274

Bloomberg. (2021, June 3). *Mukesh Ambani plans to tackle Covid with cheaper tests, tapeworm drugs.* Retrieved June 15, 2021, from Economic Times website: https://economictimes.indiatimes.com/news/company/corporate-trends/mukesh-ambani-plans-to-tackle-covid-with-cheaper-tests-tapeworm-drug/articleshow/83200963.cms

Business Insider India. (2021, January 25). *From Mukesh Ambani to Gautam Adani — India's top billionaires increased their wealth by 35% during COVID-19 pandemic.* Retrieved April 11, 2021, from Business Insider India website: https://www.businessinsider.in/finance/news/from-mukesh-ambani-to-gautam-adani-indias-top-billionaires-increased-their-wealth-by-35-during-covid-19-pandemic/articleshow/80445646.cms

Chandra, J. (2021, January 25). *Indian billionaires increased their wealth by 35% during the lockdown, says Oxfam report.* Retrieved May 8, 2021, from The Hindu. https://www.thehindu.com/news/national/oxfam-study-shows-rich-got-richer-during-pandemic/article33655044.ece

Chatterjee, P. (2020, April 12). *The pandemic exposes India's apathy toward migrant workers.* Retrieved May 12, 2021, from Atlantic Monthly (Boston, Mass.: 1993). https://www.theatlantic.com/ideas/archive/2020/04/the-pandemic-exposes-indias-two-worlds/609838/

Chatterjee, S. (n.d.). *Farm laws versus field realities: Understanding India's agricultural markets.* Retrieved July 26, 2021, from Psu.edu website: https://www.personal.psu.edu/sc20/papers/SC_MK_farmlaws.pdf

Corporate social responsibility practices in the times of COVID-19: A study of India's BFSI sector. (n.d.). Retrieved August 9, 2021, from Org.in website: https://www.downtoearth.org.in/blog/governance/corporate-social-responsibility-practices-in-the-times-of-covid-19-a-study-of-india-s-bfsi-sector-74583

COVID-19. Implications for business. (2020, March 1). *McKinsey & Company*. Retrieved May 18, 2021 from McKinsey and Company website: https://www.mckinsey.com/business-functions/risk-and-resilience/our-insights/covid-19-implications-for-business

Drolia, T. (2021, May 10). *Navigating through SME lending challenges during the pandemic*. Retrieved July 1, 2021, from Yourstory.com website: https://yourstory.com/smbstory/sme-lending-fintech-msmes-covid-19/amp

Gopalan, A. (2021, June 19). *India's vaccine makers are pandemic profiteers, not humanitarians*. Retrieved August 8, 2021, from The Intercept website: https://theintercept.com/2021/06/19/india-covid-vaccine-profiteering/

How businesses have successfully pivoted during the pandemic. (2020, July 7). *Harvard Business Review*. Retrieved May 21, 2021, from https://hbr.org/2020/07/how-businesses-have-successfully-pivoted-during-the-pandemic

India's unemployment in 2020 at worst level in 29 years, shows study. (n.d.). *Business Today*. Retrieved September 2, 2021, from https://www.businesstoday.in/jobs/story/india-unemployment-in-2020-at-worst-level-in-29-years-shows-study-297195-2021-05-28

Jha, A. N. (2020, August 23). *Middlemen make money as workers from Bihar return to other states*. Retrieved May 23, 2021, from The Hindustan Times. https://www.hindustantimes.com/india-news/middlemen-make-money-as-workers-from-bihar-return-to-other-states/story-ec7mIfteBIfB9vE5mjoxWJ.html

John, C. (2020, August 27). *How musk, Bezos, Zuckerberg, Ambani got richer amid the pandemic*. Retrieved July 5, 2021, from Thequint.com website: https://www.thequint.com/tech-and-auto/tech-news/how-jeff-bezos-elon-musk-mark-zuckerberg-and-mukesh-ambani-made-more-billions-during-the-covid-19-pandemic

Kant, K. (2020, November 17). *India Inc gains despite Covid-19 disruptions; combined profit at Rs 1.5 trn*. Retrieved April 28, 2021, Business-Standard.Com. https://www.business-standard.com/article/companies/india-inc-gains-despite-covid-19-disruptions-combined-profit-at-rs-1-5-trn-120111700077_1.html

Kapoor, M. (n.d.). *Serum Institute founder Cyrus Poonawalla's wealth rises 85% in 5 months to $13.8 bn*. Retrieved August 18, 2021, from Business Today website: https://www.businesstoday.in/latest/corporate/story/serum-institute-founder-cyrus-poonawalla-adar-wealth-85pc-to-138-bn-271174-2020-08-26

Kaur, M. (2020, September 9). *Adani Wilmar's continuing double-digit growth.* Retrieved June 25, 2021, from Indifoodbev.com website: https://indifoodbev.com/uncategorized/adani-wilmar/

Lockett, H., & Findlay, S. (2020, November 13). 'Modi's Rockefeller': Gautam Adani and the concentration of power in India. *Financial Times*. Retrieved May 3, 2021 from https://www.ft.com/content/474706d6-1243-4f1e-b365-891d4c5d528b

Madhok, D., & Business, C. N. N. (2021, April 29). Asia's richest man wants to build the next tech giant. *CNN*. Retrieved May 13, 2021, from https://edition.cnn.com/videos/business/2020/05/29/mukesh-ambani-jio-platforms-orig.cnn-business

Managing the impact of COVID-19 on India's supply chains. (n.d.). Retrieved June 22, 2021, from https://assets.ey.com/content/dam/ey-sites/ey-com/en_in/topics/government-and-public-sector/2020/09/managing-the-impact-of-covid-19-on-india-supply-chains.pdf

Mint. (2020, October 25). *Opinion*. Retrieved August 8, 2021, from mint website: https://www.livemint.com/opinion/online-views/opinion-covid-and-its-impact-on-economy-and-msmes-11603604611652.html

Mohan, D. (2021, March 26). *How daily wage workers in India suffered in the lockdown – and continue to struggle months later*. Retrieved on June 6, 2021, Scroll. In. https://scroll.in/article/989258/how-daily-wage-workers-in-india-suffered-in-the-lockdown-and-continue-to-struggle-months-later

Mukesh Ambani wants to build the next tech giant with Jio Platforms. (2021, April 29). *CNN*. Retrieved from https://www.cnn.com/videos/business/2020/05/29/mukesh-ambani-jio-platforms-orig.cnn-business

Mukherjee, A., & Opinion, B. (2021, June 26). *Mukesh Ambani and Gautam Adani. Two billionaires, one green ambition*. Retrieved June 28, 2021, from Business-standard.com website: https://www.business-standard.com/article/companies/ambani-and-adani-two-billionaires-one-clean-energy-ambition-121062600112_1.html

Mukherji, B. (2021, May 26). *Lifetime salaries and college tuition: Indian companies are compensating the families of COVID victims*. Retrieved July 18, 2021, from Fortune website: https://fortune.com/2021/05/26/corporate-india-covid-compensation-tata-oyo-borsi/

Nahar, P. (2021, June 30). *Mukesh Ambani, Gautam Adani, 4 other Indians earned $45 billion in 6 months.* Retrieved July 8, 2021, from Economic Times website: https://economictimes.indiatimes.com/markets/stocks/news/mukesh-ambani-gautam-adani-4-other-indians-earned-45-billion-in-6-months/articleshow/83980938.cms

Online, F. E. (2020a, April 11). Cooking oil production down 40% amid Coronavirus pandemic: Adani Wilmar. *The Financial Express.* Retrieved May 21, 2021 from https://www.financialexpress.com/industry/cooking-oil-production-down-40-per-cent-amid-coronavirus-pandemic-adani-wilmar/1925558/

Online, F. E. (2020b, August 25). Covid vaccine boost: Serum Institute founder adds $3.6 billion to his wealth in just under 4 months. *The Financial Express.* Retrieved July 26, 2021 from https://www.financialexpress.com/industry/covid-vaccine-boost-serum-institute-founder-adds-3-6-billion-to-his-wealth-in-just-under-4-months/2064217/

Online, F. E. (2020c, November 26). *Listed companies post bumper profits despite lockdown; manufacturing firms steal the show.* Retrieved June 27, 2021 from The Financial Express. https://www.financialexpress.com/industry/listed-companies-post-bumper-profits-despite-lockdown-manufacturing-firms-steal-the-show/2136984/

Press Trust of India. (2021, June 8). *Why are fuel prices rising in India? Here's what oil minister says.* Retrieved July 5, 2021, from Indiatoday.in website: https://www.indiatoday.in/business/story/why-are-fuel-prices-rising-in-india-here-s-what-oil-minister-says-1811952-2021-06-08

PTI. (2021, June 8). *World Bank projects India to grow at 8.3% in 2021.* Retrieved on July 6, 2021, from Economic Times. https://economictimes.indiatimes.com/news/economy/indicators/world-bank-projects-india-to-grow-at-8-3-per-cent-in-2021/articleshow/83340761.cms

Reliance to buy Future Group's retail arm for $3.38 billion. (2020, August 29). *Reuters.* Retrieved May 14, 2021, from https://www.reuters.com/article/us-future-enterprises-m-a-reliance-indus-idUSKBN25P0N6

Roy, A. (2021, April 28). We are witnessing a crime against humanity: Arundhati Roy on India's Covid catastrophe. *The Guardian.* Retrieved July 16, 2021 from https://www.theguardian.com/news/2021/apr/28/crime-against-humanity-arundhati-roy-india-covid-catastrophe

Roy, S. (2020, March 30). *How Indian companies are contributing to the war against coronavirus*. Retrieved July 9, 2021, from Business-standard.com website: https://www.business-standard.com/podcast/current-affairs/how-indian-companies-are-contributing-to-the-war-against-coronavirus-120033001663_1.html

Sachdev, T. (2021, March 15). *Gautam Adani's wealth stoops up by 50% during the pandemic, congress leaders question the integrity of the surge. While all other income groups suffering from the crisis, how come billionaires kept on increasing their wealth so enormously?* Inventiva. Retrieved June 25, 2021, from Inventiva.co.in website: https://www.inventiva.co.in/stories/tanish/gautam-adanis-wealth-stoops-up-by-50-during-the-pandemic-congress-leaders-question-the-integrity-of-the-surge-while-all-other-income-groups-suffering-from-the-crisis-how-come-billionaires-kept-on/

Sasi, A. (2020, July 1). Explained: Why, despite the pandemic, some billionaires are becoming richer. *The Indian Express*. Retrieved May 27, 2021, from https://indianexpress.com/article/explained/coronavirus-pandemic-billionaires-wealth-unemployment-6480380/

Sazonov, A., Shrivastava, B., & Sanjai, P. R. (2020, December 14). *The story of Gautam Adani's rise — from kidnapping & 26/11 survivor to Mukesh Ambani rival*. Retrieved July 3, 2021, from The print.in website: https://theprint.in/india/the-story-of-gautam-adanis-rise-from-kidnapping-26-11-survivor-to-mukesh-ambani-rival/566169/

Sethi, A. (2021, June 7). Why Amazon is confronting the richest man in India. *The New York Times*. Retrieved July 9, 2021, from https://www.nytimes.com/2021/06/07/business/amazon-reliance-ambani-future.html

Sharma, N. (2020, December 8). *Why Indian farmers believe new laws are rigged to favour India's richest man*. Retrieved April 25, 2021, from Quartz website: https://qz.com/india/1942448/indias-protesting-farmers-think-new-laws-benefit-ambani-adani/

Sharma, N. (2020, June 22). *How Reliance Industries cleared its $21-billion debt amid the coronavirus pandemic*. Retrieved April 25, 2021, from Scroll.in website: https://scroll.in/article/965263/how-reliance-industries-cleared-its-21-billion-debt-amid-the-coronavirus-pandemic

Sharma, N. (2021, May 4). *Have India's ultra-rich done enough to help in the country's fight against Covid-19?* Retrieved June 17, 2021, from Scroll.in website: https://scroll.in/article/993957/have-indias-ultra-rich-done-enough-to-help-in-the-countrys-fight-against-covid-19

Singh, A. (2021, April 28). *Making MSMEs competitive in the post COVID-19 era.* Retrieved August 28, 2021, from Sap.com website: https://news.sap.com/india/2021/04/making-msmes-competitive-post-covid-19/

Singh, D. (2020, May 12). *Lockdown: Truck drivers make big bucks transporting stranded migrants.* Retrieved August 8, 2021 from Indiatoday.In; India Today. https://www.indiatoday.in/india/story/lockdown-truck-drivers-make-big-bucks-transporting-stranded-migrants-1677298-2020-05-12

Singh, K. (2020, September 21). *COVID-19 has pushed the Indian economy into a tailspin. But there's a way out.* Retrieved May 4, 2021, from https://thewire.in/economy/covid-19-india-economic-recovery

Spotlight, E. T. (2021, February 24). *MSME sector is the key to unlock India's economic growth.* Retrieved May 15, 2021, from Economic Times website: https://economictimes.indiatimes.com/small-biz/sme-sector/msme-sector-is-the-key-to-unlock-indias-economic-growth/articleshow/81188321.cms

Supernormal profits: Latest News & Videos, Photos about Supernormal profits. (n.d.). Retrieved May 3, 2021, from https://economictimes.indiatimes.com/topic/Super-normal-profits

Ten million lost jobs in Covid 2nd wave, 97% households' income declined: CMIE. (n.d.). *Business Today.* Retrieved September 2, 2021, from https://www.businesstoday.in/latest/economy-politics/story/income-of-97-households-declined-since-covid-19-pandemic-began-cmie-298381-2021-06-01

The global economic outlook during the COVID-19 pandemic: A changed world. (n.d.). Retrieved April 2, 2021, from https://www.worldbank.org/en/news/feature/2020/06/08/the-global-economic-outlook-during-the-covid-19-pandemic-a-changed-world

Thomas, T. (2021, March 17). *Steel companies will use supernormal profits to pay back ₹35,000 crore debt.* Retrieved July 5, 2021 from Mint. https://www.livemint.com/news/india/steel-companies-will-use-supernormal-profits-to-pay-back-rs-35-000-crore-debt-11615985829160.html

Vanshika. (2020, April 11). *Edible oil production dropped by 40% due to Coronavirus.* Retrieved July 5, 2021, from Inventiva.co.in website: https://www.inventiva.co.in/trends/vanshika/edible-oil-production-dropped-by-40-due-to-coronavirus/

Varma, S. (2019, October 13). *Under Modi rule, Ambani, Adani have doubled their wealth.* Retrieved June 17, 2021, from Newsclick.in website: https://www.newsclick.in/Under-Modi-Rule-Ambani-Adani-Have-Doubled-Their-Wealth

Verma, P. A. (2021, January 15). *Why technology is the only path to sustained growth for MSMEs.* Retrieved July 10, 2021, from Economic Times website: https://economictimes.indiatimes.com/small-biz/sme-sector/why-technology-is-the-only-path-to-sustained-growth-for-msmes/articleshow/80281133.cms

Vidya, S. (n.d.). HR challenge! Justifying expenditure on reskilling employees. *Business Today*. Retrieved April 12, 2021, from https://www.businesstoday.in/jobs/story/hr-challenge-justifying-expenditure-on-reskilling-employees-293262-2021-04-12

World Bank. (2020). *India Development Update*. Retrieved May 13, 2021, from worldbank.org: https://openknowledge.worldbank.org/bitstream/handle/10986/34367/India-Development-Update.pdf?sequence=1&isAllowed=y

Chapter 9
Plight of Employees, Migrant Workers, and the Middle Class in India During COVID-19

Vivek Joshi
https://orcid.org/0000-0002-1869-7569
Creative Head Consultants, India

Supreet Ahluwalia
Creative Head Consultants, India

ABSTRACT

The chapter discusses condition of employees, migrant workers, and middle classes in India during COVID-19. How each of them faced the pandemic and how their conditions deteriorated drastically are explored. The chapter highlights how labour laws changed, how training and development programs were shelved, and how millions of employees ended up losing jobs during the pandemic. Impact of job loss and its trickledown effects changed the way the Indian middle class was living and forced them to take up a war of their own. It changed the socio-economic scenario and forced several micro, small, and medium enterprises to close shop. SMEs rose to the challenge and either changed the line of business or adopted innovative business practices so as to survive and sustain. Changed scoio-economic environment further became more complex and volatile as few large corporations, pharmaceutical companies, healthcare providers, and hospitals in India started considering the pandemic an opportunity to make super normal profits. The Indian middle class rose to the challenge and proved their never say die attitude!

DOI: 10.4018/978-1-7998-8346-3.ch009

INTRODUCTION

The COVID-19 Pandemic had a significant impact on employees in India, more specifically, the ones belonging to middle class. The impact was felt within every industry, but incredibly more rigid on a vulnerable group such as the migrant workers. The lockdown increased inequality as incomes were wiped out. Individuals found ways, though, on how to adapt and cope.

The other side of this story emerged from those smaller innovative and creative players who accepted the challenges and made swift and faster decisions. Some closed their old shops, took significant risks, and started completely new ventures writing astounding success stories.

The success stories that emerged were either fairytales or the ones that would question the presence of business ethics. The chapter discusses an important element of the Indian socio-economic system, the Migrant Workers. Indian Middle Class and Migrant workers are closely related and constitute majority of the population considered for the study. Any change that affects the middle class and migrant workers in India involves the entire economic system and profoundly impacts the nation's socio-economic fabric.

The plight of migrant workers and the condition of middle-class Indian Families are two critical considerations that are needed to be discussed at length as almost 82% population is covered by these two population segments (Chatterjee, 2020).

As discussed, the middle class and migrant workers comprise the country's maximum population. Understanding these two would help visualize what the country was going through and the sentiments of large part of the population. The challenges were too many, but both the Indian Middle Class and Migrant Workers, presented extraordinary resistance and emerged victors due to their attitude of never saying die.

The Indian Middle Class – Perfect Example of Never Say Die Attitude

India is vastly defined by its massive middle class, people who are neither too rich nor too poor but are keeping the nation's economic engine running. The middle class comprises diverse sections of people from different walks of life and professions: public sector employees, carpenters, cab drivers, healthcare staff, engineers, lawyers, traders, small shopkeepers, and people in business.

The immense middle class in India makes it pretty challenging to put this class and its constituents in a water-tight compartment or to define them with a clear-cut classification. As per the definition given by the McKinsey Global Institute, the middle-income segment is households with real annual disposable incomes between INR. 200,000 and INR. 1,000,000 (Narayanswamy & Zainulbhai, 2015).

The current Finance Minister of India, Ms. Nirmala Sitaraman, demarcated the Indian middle class with an annual income below Rs. 1.8 million and above the poverty line. Though, the representative income based upon the ground reality considered approximately INR. 600,000 per year. Economists from Mumbai University categorized the Indian middle class as consumers who could spend anywhere between US $2 to the US $10 per capita per day.

To define the middle class in numbers and make its strength visible, we need to find the number that shows its presence within the economy to look at the magnitude; approximately 600 million of India's population forms the great Indian middle class. Furthermore, the actual numbers keep on increasing. It was expected that almost 80% of the households would be in the middle segment in the coming years, but the reverse happened. Instead, almost 17% of the middle class dropped down to below the poverty line (Wadhwa, 2021) thanks to the pandemic!

The current second wave of COVID hit India badly. The economy and the social classification were severely hit, and the dream of tens of millions to join the Indian middle class did get shattered. In the year 2020-2021, the COVID hit the finances of about 32 million-plus people in India. Hundreds of thousands were compelled to dive and live in poverty (COVID-19 first wave pushed 23 crore Indians into poverty: Azim Premji University, n.d.).

The Plight of Migrant Workers

Most of India's 470 million workers are labeled as informal labor due to low or no skills. Amongst these low-skilled or no-skilled workers, around 120 million comprises migrants or migrant workers (Chatterjee, 2020).

These Migrants mostly emerge from rural areas or semi-urban areas of India. These workers come to the big or metro cities to escape grave poverty and the traditional feudal social order deeply rooted in Indian rural areas. Such a vast number of migrants show the social calamity that has been caused by the failure of the country's economic planning since independence. This poor migrant labour is "the proletarians of the proletariat" as they are distinctive from the ceremonial recognized working class.

Migrant Labour – Sad Story of Losing Job and Hopes

The struggle of migrant labour started a few days after the announcement of lockdown number one. As the lockdown - 1 was announced, nothing was planned. In addition, no measures were taken to protect and safeguard migrant labour. They constituted the large base of India's workforce employed in the grey market or unorganized sector. Almost 35% of these migrants were employed in the SME sector (Small and Medium Enterprises) (First Post, 2021).

The informal workers were the worst hit; of 123 million who had lost their jobs, 75% were from the informal sector (ILO Decent work team for South Asia and Country Office for India, 2018).

A total of 92.38 million jobs vanished in the informal sector in India's first wave of the pandemic. More than 300 informal workers died during the reverse migration thanks to poor facilities, unlivable conditions, hunger, suicides, exhaustion, accidents during commutes, police brutality, and refutation of medical care on time (Business Today, 2021).

These Migrants with low-skilled or semi-skilled jobs were asked to leave. They were fired without being compensated, or several hundred thousand were not even paid their dues (last Month's salaries and wages) as the business owners themselves were scared and running short of funds and liquidity. No money was moving, and these migrants were not having alternative incomes and great savings to sustain themselves in big cities. They started working on compromised rates and started accepting menial jobs and giving their services for their earlier income. The phenomenon of compromising on labor reduced the labor cost. The vast availability of labor further added to the woes of these migrants as the labor market war intensified as everyone wanted to put some food on the family table.

Migrant Workforces soon realized, in addition to being exposed to the harsh reality that manufacturing units would not help them, most of the manufacturing units were using the situation to their advantage. As the pain of failure to make sufficient money and failure to survive and sustain in big cities was realized by migrants, they started going back to their home towns and villages, beginning the trend of reverse migration.

Labour Laws Have Gone for a Toss by Government Legislation to Facilitate Factory Owners and to Attract International Investments in the Country

As if what has happened was not enough for the labour, the labour laws were also shelved by the several state governments. The decision to do away with labour laws further added to the injuries of migrant labours as their basic rights were also compromised.

Several State governments of India (Uttar Pradesh, Madhya Pradesh, Gujarat, Assam, and Orissa, to name a few), especially the ones ruled by the party in power within the country and the party running the central government or the federal government of India decided to do away with the labour laws of the country.

The laws were suspended from attracting more investments from abroad. The move was to provide employers a free hand to run their organizations without being concerned about labor and costs associated with labour well-being besides maintaining safety work standards that would ensure labor safety during working hours or when on the job. Another argument given was to generate more employment and sustainable development for labour (Singh, 2020).

The move was initiated by bringing just one amendment, 35 out of 38 labor laws have been suspended for almost four years (1200 days) starting from 2020 (Daigavane & Belmannu, 2020).

With this single move (Amendment made), the guaranteed wages or minimum pay, insurance coverage, and good working conditions were eradicated. This amendment also resulted in the withdrawal of rights to form unions and labours' right to negotiate with employers.

This ensured that private and public employers could retrench or fire employees at their whims and fancies without paying them any compensation. Even the payment of minimum wages is not mandatory. Payment of dues is also at the mercy and wishes of the employers (Mohan, 2021).

Hence, the suspension of labour laws created this environment that would make the Indian labour market more lucrative and pretty cheap. Moreover, it is easy to exploit for international investment as they do not have to do anything to safeguard the interest of the Indian labour nor pay a fixed amount of wages and salaries to the labour hired.

No labour laws, pandemic, and rise in a reverse migration of labor and large joblessness in the country provided an idle environment for foreign companies to hire and fire people at will. The situation so emerged allowed employers to use the workforce at dirt cheap rates as many unemployed workers were seeking employment and were ready to work for as little as two meals a day for the family (Biswas, 2020).

The reasons given for the labour law amendment were that they had been implemented in the wake of the ongoing global pandemic and the nationwide lockdown. The dilution or complete scrapping of specific labour laws would help curtail the bearing of the pandemic on the public and commercial institutions; this would guarantee the minutest possible interruption in the supply chain and so on.

The reasoning given to support such draconian actions is that the amendment brought is an important measure to encourage investment and employment under current extraordinary situations.

The idea floated and propagated behindhand of the deferment plus attenuation of labour laws is that in the current scenario, there is an urgent requisite bringing in flexibility in operations for business and industry so they could provide better to the needs of employment the workers. The focus has to be on those who have reverse migrated to the states and safeguard the remaining employment of workers (Daigavane & Belmannu, 2020).

This step is exactly the opposite of what other countries have done. India ignored how other nations have responded by making continuous efforts to cut down the lay-offs by offering wage subsidies and closely following the United Nation's call to minimalize the effect of the pandemic on the marginal workers.

The scrapping of labor laws left the labor force at the whims and fancy of the employers, who could use their free will on the majority of decisions concerning labour affairs. Several employers would surely benefit from the disadvantage of the labour in the given situation. In addition, these employers would fire the employees without needing to comply with the legal formalities (Chatterjee, 2020).

Additionally, to make matters worse, the suspension of laws means that even trade unions are made useless and helpless as they are made ineffective. All the chaos so created adds to the injury of hapless workers as they are left without a grievance redressal mechanism (Singh, 2020).

The decision taken on justifying economic development, generating more employment, and attracting higher international investment has led to the violation of poor workers' right to live dignified life. Moreover, the right to earn livelihood has also been put into severe danger as labour would not guarantee fixed minimum wages or salaries along with the compromised or almost no protection against retrenchment or layoffs (Daigavane & Belmannu, 2020).

Ironically India, the country known for upholding human rights, has taken these measures too in troubled and socio-economically difficult times for labour and employees. In contradiction, the actions taken by other nations, especially from countries like the UK, Canada, and Australia, have proved to be very effective and positive to support the employees and employers in this time of the pandemic.

Training and Developmental Programs Were Shelved so Were Bonuses and Increments

It was not only the blue collared or the wage earners that were hit by the legislation, the executives also came in the line of fire as any opportunities for them to be trained and grow was compromised by the corporations. The changed economic situation and human resource dynamics hit the working population badly. The working population (salaried employee class) mostly constitutes the middle class so the decisions to do away with labour laws and cutting the training and development expenses bot hit the middle class either directly or indirectly.

Most industries BFSI to Telecom and IT to Consumer Durables all stopped hiring processes, and expenditure on Training and Developmental Program reduced by over 40%. More than 43% of organizations either shifted their training commitments for later dates or altogether canceled them (Vidya, n.d.).

The trend further gained momentum as the infection rates increased and the spending patterns of the organizations changed. The focus was to bring down the cost of operations and retrench the workforce, especially those with a certain level of high bracket cutoff salaries. Recruits relatively younger recruits with better education and willingness to work for much lower salaries were hired.

The low-cost hiring trend was made more profitable with the help of workflow changes. Therefore, one person could work longer hours and fulfill the duties of 3 employees, thereby getting the work of 3 employees done by one and increasing the work productivity per person three times, thereby workforce was reduced to 1. The employee was made to work equal to work accomplished by 3, resulting in higher profits (Daigavane & Belmannu, 2020).

Most Indian Technology companies, even the top 5, adopted the conservative approach and shelved several of their training programs, and cut off their training and developmental budget by 60%. In contrast, their global counterparts maintained the spending, and some even increased it by roughly 18% to effectively meet the workflow challenges thrown by conditions of the pandemic (Nevins, 2020).

The money so saved has also added to the profits. In India, the money spent on training and development is considered an expenditure, and the pandemic allowed corporations to cut down on training and development costs.

Profit at Any Cost – Story of Pharmaceuticals, Vaccine Manufacturers and Health Care Providers

Adding to the woes of middle class was the increasing cost of living and sky rocketing expenses of health care that too at the time of crises when health care became a bare necessity for the masses. Hospitals, Vaccine Manufacturers, Pharmaceutical Companies, and Healthcare providers all considered COVID a lifetime opportunity to make money. Moreover, it was for them a chance to endear supernormal profits. India witnessed the severe second wave of infection that jolted the nation and the normalcy of life to make matters worse. There were shortages all around, especially in life-saving drugs, oxygen, beds in hospitals, and above all, the crucial COVID vaccines (Economic Times, 2021).

The shortage so faced in the availability of vaccines helped vaccine manufacturers demand a higher price and push their agendas to the government that had no intention or interest to end the illegitimate demands of these vaccine providers. Several policy changes were observed, and the entire vaccination drive went hey-ware several times due to the inflexible attitude of the vaccine manufacturers and the lack of the will of the Government of India to bear the cost of vaccination of public in India.

An example of how one pharmaceutical faired from this pandemic is Serum Institute's Cyrus Poonawalla's mercurial rise in ranks within the list of billionaires. He climbed 57 places to become the 86th richest person in the world (Kapoor, n.d.).

Cyrus Poonawalla's wealth increased at a phenomenal rate (more than a 25% increase) amid Indian billionaires, also the fifth-fastest increase in the world in the course of the pandemic. This feat was achieved just because of the nature of his business besides strong impending business possibilities for his company. All this was attained due to the single deal his company has made with AstraZeneca to produce 1 billion doses of COVID-19 vaccine developed by Oxford University (Online, 2020).

Later looking at the compromised efficacy of the vaccine developed by Oxford University, European Union bans. The Indian Government's control on the prices and supply of AstraZeneca/Oxford University Vaccine within India made Poonawalla seek the Government of India's permission to produce two other vaccines and sell domestically as well as be imported without restrictions (GQ Staff, 2021).

Several Pharmaceutical companies sided with vaccine manufacturers' demand to fix prices of vaccine doses independently. Demand was to charge a premium on the justification that these companies have invested billions of dollars and several years in Research and Development and building production capacities that could be used in extraordinary situations like these. Most believed moreover tried to prove that the pandemic is an ideal earning opportunity for them to make supernormal profits and recover their past investments in failed R&D initiatives (Gopalan, 2021).

During the critical phase of the second wave, pharmaceutical companies started controlling supplies of essential drugs and medicines. The pharmacies and suppliers (middlemen) started hoarding the stock to create the artificial shortage and practice differential pricing. Several lifesaving drugs, injections, and medicines whose actual prices were nearly $30-$35 per dose were sold for as high as $800 per dose. Faulty ventilators and faulty oxygen concentrators were sold to the poor public for ten times their actual market price, almost 1200% profit.

Hospitals and healthcare providers were also not at the backend of this gambit as they realized the public's dependence on them. Due to the scarcity of beds and limited availability of health care services during the second wave, hospitals and healthcare providers started charging skyrocketed fees and prices.

Most healthcare institutions and hospitals even denied recognizing government-sponsored health insurance schemes stating that they are being paid too low for their services. Some even stated that they would not like to work for low payments as there is high traffic of patients and demand for healthcare is high compared to the supply. Private or corporate hospitals were caught quoting that working for low payments would be a miss on the opportunity to earn higher returns and would not be justified in front of the stockholders and Board of Directors. facility was available.

One needs to pay priority charges which might be 300% above the basic test prices fixed by the government and health regulatory bodies in India.

Fear and panic were made more volatile by the added pressure from vaccine manufacturers, doctors, pharmaceutical companies, pharmacies, and hospitals. All were following the single-pronged strategy of exploiting the opportunity of Demand being higher than Supply. Moreover, few of the players in the healthcare sector even went a step ahead and created artificial shortages in drugs, oxygen, and life-support systems so the situation of shortage could be sustained for a longer time resulting in higher profits.

Though few governments of the states fixed the rates of hospitalization services, corporate hospitals and several private players denied accepting those rates as these rates applicable did not justify their Return on Investment (ROI) and the opportunity costs. Average billing for one COVID patient's treatment in a corporate or private hospital for two weeks cost around US$3000 that too for not so severe infection for severe cases the billing was almost four-folds.

Pathological labs hiked the pricing of their services and started charging arbitrary prices even for RT-PCR testing for COVID. Other diseases testing was only done for premium pricing that too when the facility was available or you need to pay priority charges which might be 300 percent above the basic test prices fixed by the government and health regulatory bodies in India.

The environment of fear and panic was made more volatile by the added pressure from vaccine manufacturers, doctors, pharmaceutical companies, pharmacies and hospitals. All were following single pronged strategy of exploiting the opportunity of Demand being higher than Supply. Moreover few of the players in healthcare sector even went a step ahead and created artificial shortages in drugs, oxygen and life-supports systems so the situation of shortage could be sustained for longer time resulting into higher profits.

The Great Indian Oil Story – Story of Soaring Petrol and Diesel Prices and It Continues

Cost of transportation got hiked and resulted in further increase in cost of living adding to the inflation, hitting the Indian Middle class below the belt, all this, thanks to ever rising petrol and diesel prices in the country.

In India, everything moves on petrol and diesel though being an importer, India still is one of the largest consumers of petrol and diesel. Limited availability and further limited capability to extract petroleum and other liquids make matters worse. One very interesting phenomenon was observed in the country as the global prices of crude were falling besides everywhere on the globe, the prices of fuel were moving southward. In India, petrol and diesel prices performed well and moved up slow and steadily, seemingly to follow an old proverb that 'slow and steady wins the race.'

Numerous factors govern undoubtedly Petrol, and diesel prices and global production could not be controlled or governed by a single country. Still, none of the world's governments or any petroleum or diesel marketing companies could state simply that they cannot control or reduce the final price offered to the country's consumers. None of the petroleum marketers could state no say or control on the Final Retail Price (FRP) of fuel within the domestic market.

The final retail price of petrol in the domestic market is the sum of various factors such as international crude prices, transportation charges, and taxation by various governments. To make things more understandable following formula could be used as a guide:

Domestic Retail Price/Final Retail Price (FRP) = International price of crude oil (per barrel) + charges of the refinery + transport charges + Commission charged by in-country distributors and dealers + Central Government of the Country Imposed Excise Duty + Surcharges Collected by Central Government of the country + Value Added Tax (VAT) & duty collected by the state government.

Looking at the above formulae and the various factors constituted therein, several factors play a decisive role in determining the fuel prices in a country. The two most important factors were responsible for determining domestic price being the International Prices of Crude and the tax collected by the governments thereon. The two mentioned factors contribute maximum towards the price rise, but it does not mean that charges by refinery and commission charged by distributors and dealers do not have a role to play. Readiness to compromise a little bit of revenue on the part of government and petroleum marketing companies would have relieved Indian consumers, but none was ready to make a compromise.

Looking at the behaviour of each component of fuel prices during the period would provide a better understanding of the situation that marred the budgets of Indian middle-class households.

The first factor to check is the International crude prices. The prices of crude internationally were falling for a long time but in India start of the New Year 2021 witnessed the continuation of petrol and diesel price hike just like the year before. After unlocking the economy in June-July 2020, petrol and diesel both started to witness a consistent price hike. The same practice continued till the Third Quarter of 2021 (Jayaswal, 2021).

Second in order are charges of the refinery. They did get revised, but this increase was not substantial. Next is Transportation Charges definitely would increase as the majority of transportation again depends upon petrol and diesel. Higher fuel prices would result in hiked transportation costs, resulting again in escalated costs and prices. In India, Dealers' and Distributors' commissions are fixed and stringently regulated.

Now what is left is Central Government's excise duty, surcharges, VAT, and charges by State Governments. These taxes in India have increased consistently and progressively, and now the taxes constitute almost 70% plus of the Final Retail Price of fuel in India (Press Trust of India, 2021).

In present times (as of April-June 2021), the scenario has not changed as central and state taxes now amounts to more than two-thirds of the price of the fuel in the retail market, plus one-third of the price consists of crude oil price, freight charges, commissions, and other recurrent charges. India has one of the highly taxed fuels in the world. The Government of India justifies the continuous increase in fuel tax due to high government expenditure and revenue losses due to COVID (Press Trust of India, 2021).

The Indian Government has explained the reason behind tax increase as more revenue is needed to spend on the country's welfare schemes and economic stability. The government of India also blames Saudi Arabia and other countries for cutting down on oil supplies due to low international demands on COVID (Press Trust of India, 2021).

Therefore, by looking at the equilibrium situation as marked by the interplay of demand and supplies. Low supplies and sudden spurts in fuel demands as the countries move out of the lockdown also imbalances the international demand-supply equilibrium, causing crude prices to move upwards. The upward trend so emerged has to be short-lived, and soon prices should be stabilized. In India, the prices of petroleum and diesel did not reduce nor stabilize. Even after, the crude prices went down to as low as almost $19 per barrel in the international markets (Jayaswal, 2021).

At the lowest of the international prices, the benefit was not passed on to the Indian public because of low revenues for oil marketing companies due to low demand and low tax collection for the government of India. The decision was that most of the industries were closed because of the sudden lockdown executed in the country. The government lost much revenue and bled money in managing the pandemic. However absurd it may sound, the reasoning was that the money so collected is needed to stabilize the economy. The government had to make some harsh decisions (Press Trust of India, 2021).

For the last three years, leading economists in India and the world over have suggested that the Government of India (GoI) move petrol and diesel in the domain of GST (Goods & Services Tax). If fuel prices do come under GST, collection of taxes on taxes will be vastly reduced or altogether circumvented; hence the retail prices of fuel would be reduced in India. The Government of India is postponing the decision stating that the GST council has to decide what should be included under GST and what should not. Petrol Dealers and Marketing companies also do not raise their voice and concerns over skyrocketing prices, nor do they call out for the implementation of GST on fuel.

Role Played by Banks and Financial Sector – Demand for Credit Vanishes but Profit Soars

Ease of access to finance and government lending programs in any nation are supposed to be the much needed breather for the country's Middle Class, especially in testing times like a Pandemic. In India the middle class of the country once again paid the price and were brought under the knife so as to bear the brunt of the pandemic and ended up being the source of profiteering for the financing institutions both in public and private sectors.

Keeping up with the performance of listed manufacturing and oil companies, the banking and financial sector also did well. On the Financial front, the earnings from banks (consolidation of Balance-sheet) also ended the Q2 on a high note as the banks did not have to report bad loans or hike in NPAs (Non-Performing Assets). Banks also took advantage of the lockdown and less demand for credit and felt they need not make any provisions for bad credit or NPAs (RBI, 2021).

Another breather or opportunity for financial institutions and banking to maximize profitability came in a moratorium on loans, ordered by the Supreme Court of India. The maximum clients availed a three-month moratorium period so announced by Supreme Court of the banks thinking it is a three-month interest-free period. Later, to realize that this moratorium was just an extension by the supreme court to pay interest/EMI after three months, meaning the four months installments is to be paid in one go. Any non-conformity or failure to pay the entire amount in the fourth month would charge interest even on the total outstanding amount, including that accrued due to the moratorium period (interest would now be charged on the Amount = Outstanding Principal + Accrued Interest).

The overall result of the moratorium was a severe escalation in profits regardless of muffled growth in disbursal and approval of new loans. Further to the events discussed above, the decline in interest rates paid by financial institutions or banks on Fixed Deposits and Savings accounts to customers also helped the banks by bringing down their payment obligations or interest charges on liability. The decision to reduce the interest rate payable on savings and investment instruments hurt the Indian middle class, especially the elderly or those living on to their savings after losing employment (RBI, 2021a).

Further to the above, on the announcement of the economic relief package, it was estimated that there would be hiked demand for credit next quarter. The so-called economic relief package declared by The Government of India was nothing more than introducing different credit schemes to prompt public plus SMEs to take loans rather than provide money directly into people's savings accounts. There were no efforts by the government to reduce the direct taxation burden on the public or scrap GST to make things inexpensive in the country and boost demand (Singh, 2020).

Failure of the Indian National Government to understand market dynamics and lack of will to spend money for social welfare made the situation worse. The government's search for more revenues to run election campaigns or finance their pet projects hurt the economy further. There was no spectacular hike in demand for credit as the government expected, and the money in banks stayed with them. Banks continued to save money on cost reduction by firing temporary staff and other ancillary support staff. Accrued interest on the moratorium period and failure of the people to service their debt obligations further opened flood gates of the hefty profits for Indian banks. Consequentially Reserve Bank of India (Indian Central Bank) in May 2021 decided to hand over a whopping surplus of INR. 991.22 Billion to the Government of India (RBI, 2021).

As discussed above, the manufacturing, oil and gas, banking, and finance industry were not the only sectors making profit during the pandemic. The EAT or Earnings after Tax of several companies such as telecommunications also went up by 7.83% yearly. In contrast, adjusted net profits for these companies increased by 3.61% on a Year-on-Year basis in Quarter 2 of the year 2020-2021 (ANI, 2021).

Overall sales of the telecommunication companies' though showed a negative trend and declined by more than 3.0% on Year on Year compared to 31.5% Year on Year shrinkage in Quarter 1(Q1) of Financial Year 2021 (Economic Times, 2020).

CONCLUSION

The COVID-19 pandemic caused poor living conditions to increase in large cities, and existing policies failed to protect migrants or other labourers in remote areas. India has the drive to survive, but only if there is a comprehensive recovery policy been developed and executed with pure political motivation. This will then enable the Indian economy and the employees to emerge quickly and strongly from this crisis. Thus, long-term policies need to be designed to focus on the middle class, especially the migrant workers and blue collar employees.

The efforts hence require an integrated support system. Organizations also need to critically analyse the crucial roles that they are needed to play in success of Indian economy post-Covid-19 Pandemic.

An internal analysis by the companies with regards to their policies and strategic framework is much needed as their cost cutting efforts clubbed with government led initiatives to pass on the expenditure to the middle class is badly hurting the purchasing power. The Actions so taken by the corporates and the India government would in short run cause serious issues for the Indian economy. Situation of lack of purchasing power clubbed with high price rise might put Indian middle class in serious trouble hurting the long term well-being of the nation and its strongest pillar the Indian Middle class.

Hopefully the Indian Middle Class as usual would showcase its strength and would fight against all odds to come out victorious and it's never say die attitude would prevail. Success of Indian Middle Class would be the victory of India as the country over the challenges thrown by the pandemic.

REFERENCES

80% of India's informal workers lost jobs during COVID lockdown, 63% survived on two meals a day, shows data. (2021, February 2). Retrieved July 11, 2021, from Firstpost.Com. https://www.firstpost.com/india/80-of-indias-informal-workers-lost-jobs-during-covid-lockdown-63-survived-on-two-meals-a-day-shows-data-9264141.html

ANI. (2021, September 10). *Indian banks' improved performance in contrast to stress from Covid: Fitch.* Retrieved December 14, 2021, from Business-standard.com website: https://www.business-standard.com/article/finance/indian-banks-improved-performance-in-contrast-to-stress-from-covid-fitch-121091000513_1.html

Biswas, S. (2020, March 30). *Coronavirus: India's pandemic lockdown turns into a human tragedy*. Retrieved July 13, 2021from BBC. https://www.bbc.com/news/world-asia-india-52086274

Chatterjee, P. (2020, April 12). *The pandemic exposes India's apathy toward migrant workers*. Retrieved May 12, 2021, from Atlantic Monthly (Boston, Mass.: 1993). https://www.theatlantic.com/ideas/archive/2020/04/the-pandemic-exposes-indias-two-worlds/609838/

Chatterjee, S. (n.d.). *Farm laws versus field realities: Understanding India's agricultural markets*. Retrieved July 26, 2021, from Psu.edu website: https://www.personal.psu.edu/sc20/papers/SC_MK_farmlaws.pdf

COVID-19. Implications for business. (2020, March 1). *McKinsey & Company*. Retrieved May 18, 2021 from McKinsey and Company website: https://www.mckinsey.com/business-functions/risk-and-resilience/our-insights/covid-19-implications-for-business

COVID-19 first wave pushed 23 crore Indians into poverty: Azim Premji University. (n.d.). *Business Today*. Retrieved August 2, 2021, from Business Today: https://www.businesstoday.in/jobs/story/covid-19-first-wave-pushed-23-crore-indians-into-poverty-azim-premji-university-295173-2021-05-06

Daigavane, W., & Belmannu, P. (n.d.). *Impact of the global pandemic on Indian labor laws*. Retrieved April 18, 2021, from Jurist.org website: https://www.jurist.org/commentary/2020/05/daigavane-belmannu-labor-law-suspensions-india/

Gopalan, A. (2021, June 19). *India's vaccine makers are pandemic profiteers, not humanitarians*. Retrieved August 8, 2021, from The Intercept website: https://theintercept.com/2021/06/19/india-covid-vaccine-profiteering/

ILO Decent work team for South Asia and Country Office for India. (2018). *India Wage Report - Wage policies for decent work and inclusive growth.* Retrieved April 9, 2021 from ILO website: https://www.ilo.org/wcmsp5/groups/public/---asia/---ro-bangkok/---sro-new_delhi/documents/publication/wcms_638305.pdf

India's unemployment in 2020 at worst level in 29 years, shows study. (n.d.). *Business Today*. Retrieved September 2, 2021, from https://www.businesstoday.in/jobs/story/india-unemployment-in-2020-at-worst-level-in-29-years-shows-study-297195-2021-05-28

Jayaswal, R. (2021, July 10). Fuel price surge continues, petrol at ₹100.91 per litre in Delhi. *The Hindustan Times*. Retrieved July 12, 2021 from https://www.hindustantimes.com/india-news/fuel-price-surge-continues-petrol-at-100-91-per-litre-in-delhi-101625941654714.html

Jha, A. N. (2020, August 23). *Middlemen make money as workers from Bihar return to other states*. Retrieved May 23, 2021, from The Hindustan Times. https://www.hindustantimes.com/india-news/middlemen-make-money-as-workers-from-bihar-return-to-other-states/story-ec7mIfteBIfB9vE5mjoxWJ.html

Kapoor, M. (n.d.). *Serum Institute founder Cyrus Poonawalla's wealth rises 85% in 5 months to $13.8 bn*. Retrieved August 18, 2021, from Business Today website: https://www.businesstoday.in/latest/corporate/story/serum-institute-founder-cyrus-poonawalla-adar-wealth-85pc-to-138-bn-271174-2020-08-26

Mohan, D. (2021, March 26). *How daily wage workers in India suffered in the lockdown – and continue to struggle months later*. Retrieved on June 6, 2021, Scroll. In. https://scroll.in/article/989258/how-daily-wage-workers-in-india-suffered-in-the-lockdown-and-continue-to-struggle-months-later

Narayanswamy, S., & Zainulbhai, A. (2015, October 30). *India's consumer evolution*. Retrieved April 22, 2021, from Mckinsey.Com; McKinsey & Company. https://www.mckinsey.com/mgi/overview/in-the-news/consumer-evolution-in-india

Nevins, M. (2020, July 18). Re-thinking training and development in a post-covid world: A case study. *Forbes Magazine*. Retrieved August 08, 2021 from forbes.com. https://www.forbes.com/sites/hillennevins/2020/07/18/re-thinking-training-and-development-in-a-post-covid-world-a-case-study/

Online, F. E. (2020a, August 25). Covid vaccine boost: Serum Institute founder adds $3.6 billion to his wealth in just under 4 months. *The Financial Express*. Retrieved July 26, 2021 from https://www.financialexpress.com/industry/covid-vaccine-boost-serum-institute-founder-adds-3-6-billion-to-his-wealth-in-just-under-4-months/2064217/

Online, F. E. (2020b, November 26). *Listed companies post bumper profits despite lockdown; manufacturing firms steal the show*. Retrieved June 27, 2021 from The Financial Express. https://www.financialexpress.com/industry/listed-companies-post-bumper-profits-despite-lockdown-manufacturing-firms-steal-the-show/2136984/

Press Trust of India. (2021, June 8). *Why are fuel prices rising in India? Here's what oil minister says.* Retrieved July 5, 2021, from Indiatoday.in website: https://www.indiatoday.in/business/story/why-are-fuel-prices-rising-in-india-here-s-what-oil-minister-says-1811952-2021-06-08

PTI. (2021, June 8). *World Bank projects India to grow at 8.3% in 2021*. Retrieved on July 6, 2021, from Economic Times. https://economictimes.indiatimes.com/news/economy/indicators/world-bank-projects-india-to-grow-at-8-3-per-cent-in-2021/articleshow/83340761.cms

RBI. (2021a). *Economic Review*. Retrieved July 2, 2021, from RBI website. https://rbidocs.rbi.org.in/rdocs/AnnualReport/PDFs/IIECONOMICREVIEW650084A9F3494152939D99449E63D040.PDF

RBI. (2021b). *Financial Stability Report*. Retrieved August 8, 2021, from RBI website. https://rbidocs.rbi.org.in/rdocs/PublicationReport/Pdfs/5CHAPTER13F7BC1B353D241828187E91649DF1584.PDF

Singh, N. (2020, July 3). *Suspension of Labour Rights during the Covid-19 Pandemic: Possible Implications under the revised draft*. Retrieved April 14, 2021 from Cambridge.Org. https://www.cambridge.org/core/blog/2020/07/03/suspension-of-labour-rights-during-the-covid-19-pandemic-possible-implications-under-the-revised-draft/

Singh, K. (2020, September 21). *COVID-19 has pushed the Indian economy into a tailspin. But there's a way out*. Retrieved May 4, 2021, from https://thewire.in/economy/covid-19-india-economic-recovery

Staff, G. Q. (2021, January 15). *This is the net worth of Adar Poonawalla's father & Serum Institute's founder, Dr. Cyrus Poonawalla*. Retrieved July 8, 2021, from GQ India website: https://www.gqindia.com/get-smart/content/this-is-the-net-worth-of-adar-poonawallas-father-and-serum-institutes-founder-dr-cyrus-poonawalla

Supernormal profits: Latest News & Videos, Photos about Supernormal profits. (n.d.). Retrieved May 3, 2021, from https://economictimes.indiatimes.com/topic/Super-normal-profits

Ten million lost jobs in Covid 2nd wave, 97% households' income declined: CMIE. (n.d.). *Business Today*. Retrieved September 2, 2021, from https://www.businesstoday.in/latest/economy-politics/story/income-of-97-households-declined-since-covid-19-pandemic-began-cmie-298381-2021-06-01

Vidya, S. (n.d.). HR challenge! Justifying expenditure on reskilling employees. *Business Today*. Retrieved April 12, 2021, from https://www.businesstoday.in/jobs/story/hr-challenge-justifying-expenditure-on-reskilling-employees-293262-2021-04-12

Wadhwa, P. (2021, March 16). *633,000 "New Middle Class" households In India: Hurun India report*. Retrieved August 13, 2021, from Business-standard.com website: https://www.business-standard.com/article/economy-policy/633-000-new-middle-class-households-in-india-hurun-india-report-121031600357_1.html

Compilation of References

80% of India's informal workers lost jobs during COVID lockdown, 63% survived on two meals a day, shows data. (2021, February 2). Retrieved July 11, 2021, from Firstpost.Com. https://www.firstpost.com/india/80-of-indias-informal-workers-lost-jobs-during-covid-lockdown-63-survived-on-two-meals-a-day-shows-data-9264141.html

Aassve, A., Alfani, G., Gandolfi, F., & Le Moglie, M. (2021). *Epidemics and trust: The case of the Spanish Flu.* Available at: https://onlinelibrary.wiley.com/doi/full/10.1002/hec.4218

Abbas, W. (2020, May 7). *We look forward to welcoming you soon: UAE Hospitality Sector sees recovery in Q4*. Retrieved September 10, 2020, from Khaleej Times: https://www.khaleejtimes.com/business/local/see-you-soon-uae-hospitality-sector-sees-recovery-in-q4-

Açikgöz, Ö., & Günay, A. (2020). The early impact of the Covid-19 pandemic on the global and Turkish economy. *Turkish Journal of Medical Sciences*, *50*(SI-1), 520–526. doi:10.3906ag-2004-6 PMID:32283904

Agrawal, A. (2020). Sustainability of airlines in India with Covid-19: Challenges ahead and possible way-outs. *Journal of Revenue and Pricing Management, 20*(4), 457–472. doi:10.1057/s41272-020-00257-z

Ahmed, S., Taqi, H. M. M., Farabi, Y. I., Sarker, M., Ali, S. M., & Sankaranarayanan, B. (2021). Evaluation of Flexible Strategies to Manage the COVID-19 Pandemic in the Education Sector. *Global Journal of Flexible Systems Management*, 1–25. doi:10.1007/s40171-021-00267-9

Al Ababneh, M. M. (2017). Service Quality in the Hospitality Industry. *Journal of Tourism & Hospitality (Los Angeles, Calif.)*, *6*(1). Advance online publication. doi:10.4172/2167-0269.1000e133

Al Jazeera. (2021, January 18). *Two of India's richest men face farmers' ire over new laws.* Retrieved August 5, 2021, from Al Jazeera website: https://www.aljazeera.com/economy/2021/1/18/bbtwo-of-indias-richest-men-face-ire-over-its-new-farm-laws

Al-Hosani, F., Al-Mazrouei, S., Al-Memari, S., Al-Yafei, Z., Paulo, M. S., & Koornneef, E. (2021). *Policy and practice reviews. A Review of COVID-19 Mass Testing in the United Arab Emirates*. Academic Press.

Ali, I., & Gölgeci, I. (2019). Where is supply chain resilience research heading? A systematic and co-occurrence analysis. *International Journal of Physical Distribution & Logistics Management, 49*(8), 793–815. doi:10.1108/IJPDLM-02-2019-0038

Alonso, A. D., Kok, S. K., Bressan, A., O'Shea, M., Sakellarios, N., Koresis, A., Solis, M.A.B., & Santoni, L. J. (2020). COVID-19, aftermath, impacts, and hospitality firms: An international perspective. *International Journal of Hospitality Management, 91*, 1 – 11.

AlQutob, R., Moonesar, I., Tarawneh, M., Al Nsour, M., & Khader, Y. (2020). Public health strategies for the gradual lifting of the public sector lockdown in Jordan and United Arab Emirates during the COVID-19 crisis. *JMIR Public Health and Surveillance*, 20478.

Al-Saadi, H. (2014). Demystifying Ontology and Epistemology in research methods. *Research Gate, 1*(1), 1–10.

Alsharif, M. (2020, Nov. 27). *A Toronto restaurant owner was arrested after allegedly continuing to violate public health orders.* CNN.

Al-Tamimi, H. A. H., Lafi, A. S., & Uddin, M. H. (2016). Bank image in the UAE: Comparing Islamic and conventional banks. In *Islamic Finance* (pp. 46–65). Palgrave Macmillan.

Amalia, S., Darma, D. C., & Maria, S. (2020). Supply Chain Management and the Covid-19 Outbreak: Optimizing its Role for Indonesia. *Current Research Journal of Social Sciences and Humanities, 3*(2), 196–202. doi:10.12944/CRJSSH.3.2.07

Amazon battles Mukesh ambani for India's E-commerce future - newssapp.com. (2021, June 7). Retrieved July 12, 2021, from Newssapp.com website: https://newssapp.com/2021/06/07/business/amazon-battles-mukesh-ambani-for-indias-e-commerce-future/

Anderson, C. (2020, Aug. 10). *Many landmark restaurants, bars won't reopen after virus.* ABC News.

Andrews, S. (2020, April 28). *Impact of COVID-19 on the hotel industry and suggestions for post-pandemic recovery.* Retrieved September 22, 2020, from Hospitality Economic Times: https://hospitality.economictimes.indiatimes.com/blog/impact-of-covid-19-on-the-hotel-industry-and-suggestions-for-post-pandemic-recovery/4214

ANI. (2021, September 10). *Indian banks' improved performance in contrast to stress from Covid: Fitch.* Retrieved December 14, 2021, from Business-standard.com website: https://www.business-standard.com/article/finance/indian-banks-improved-performance-in-contrast-to-stress-from-covid-fitch-121091000513_1.html

Antai, I., & Mutshinda, C. M. (2021). Competitor Identification for Sustainable Survival Strategies: Illustration with Supply Chain Versus Supply Chain Competition. *Sustainability, 13*(14), 7861. doi:10.3390/su13147861

Arien, C. (2020). *The 5 Service Dimensions All Customers Care About.* Retrieved September 22, 2020, from Service Performance: https://www.serviceperformance.com/the-5-service-dimensions-all-customers-care-about/

Arthi, V., & Parman, J. (2020). Disease, downturns, and wellbeing: Economic history and the long-run impacts of COVID-19. *Explorations in Economic History, 101381*, 1–20. PMID:33162564

Attwood, S., & Hajat, C. (2020, August 12). How will the COVID-19 pandemic shape the future of meat consumption? *Public Health Nutrition, 23*(17), 3116–3120. doi:10.1017/S136898002000316X PMID:32782062

Auerbach, S., & Kilmann, P. (1977). Crisis intervention: A review of outcome research. *Psychological Bulletin, 84*(6), 1189–1217. doi:10.1037/0033-2909.84.6.1189 PMID:928575

Azuma, K., Yanagi, U., Kagi, N., Kim, H., Ogata, M., & Hayashi, M. (2020). Environmental factors involved in SARS-CoV-2 transmission: Effect and role of indoor environmental quality in the strategy for COVID-19 infection control. *Environmental Health and Preventive Medicine, 25*(1), 1–16. doi:10.118612199-020-00904-2 PMID:33143660

Baek, S., Mohanty, S. K., & Glambosky, M. (2020). COVID-19 and stock market volatility: An industry level analysis. *Finance Research Letters, 37*(101748), 1–10. doi:10.1016/j.frl.2020.101748 PMID:32895607

Baharuddin, H. (2020). Over half of SMEs beam digitalization delay on Coronavirus. *The Straits Times.* https://www.straitstimes.com/singapore/over-half-of-smes-blame-digitalisation-delay-On-virus

Banking and capital markets: Implications of COVID-19. (2020, March 16). *Deloitte Insights.* https://www2.deloitte.com/us/en/insights/economy/covid-19/banking-and-capital-markets-impact-covid-19.html

Barbate, V., Gade, R. N., & Raibagkar, S. S. (2021). COVID-19 and Its Impact on the Indian Economy. *Vision: The Journal of Business Perspective.* doi:10.1177/0972262921989126

Barbieri, P., Boffelli, A., Elia, S., Fratocchi, L., Kalchschmidt, M., & Samson, D. (2020). What can we learn about reshoring after Covid-19? *Operations Management Research, 13*(3), 131–136. doi:10.1007/s12063-020-00160-1

Bartik, A. W., Bertrand, M., Cullen, Z. B., Glaeser, E. L., Luca, M., & Stanton, C. T. (2020, Apr.) *How are small businesses adjusting to COVID-19? Early evidence from a survey.* Working Paper 26989. National Bureau of Economic Research. NBER Working Paper Series.

Bartik, A. W., Bertrand, M., Cullen, Z., Glaeser, E. L., Luca, M., & Stanton, C. (2020, July 28). The impact of COVID-19 on small business outcomes and expectations. *Proceedings of the National Academy of Sciences of the United States of America, 117*(3), 17656–17666. doi:10.1073/pnas.2006991117 PMID:32651281

Batat, W. (2020). How Michelin-starred chefs are being transformed into social bricoleurs? An online qualitative study of luxury foodservice during the pandemic crisis. *Journal of Service Management, 32*(1), 1–13. doi:10.1108/JOSM-05-2020-0142

BCG. (2020). *COVID-19 is rapidly changing customer's banking demands, as 76 percent of UAE respondents expressed the interest to switch to banks that meet their needs*. Retrieved Dec 3, 2021, from https://www.bcg.com/en-mideast/press/5october2020-covid-19-is-rapidly-changing-customers-banking-demands

Behzadi, G., O'Sullivan, M. J., & Olsen, T. L. (2020). On metrics for supply chain resilience. *European Journal of Operational Research, 287*(1), 145–158. doi:10.1016/j.ejor.2020.04.040

Behzadi, G., O'Sullivan, M. J., Olsen, T. L., Scrimgeour, F., & Zhang, A. (2017). Robust and resilient strategies for managing supply disruptions in an agribusiness supply chain. *International Journal of Production Economics, 191*, 207–220. doi:10.1016/j.ijpe.2017.06.018

Belhadi, A., Mani, V., Kamble, S. S., Khan, S. A. R., & Verma, S. (2021). Artificial intelligence-driven innovation for enhancing supply chain resilience and performance under the effect of supply chain dynamism: an empirical investigation. Annals of Operations Research. doi:10.100710479-021-03956-x

Belhadi, A., Kamble, S., Jabbour, C. J. C., Gunasekaran, A., Ndubisi, N. O., & Venkatesh, M. (2021). Manufacturing and service supply chain resilience to the COVID-19 outbreak: Lessons learned from the automobile and airline industries. *Technological Forecasting and Social Change, 163*, 120447. doi:10.1016/j.techfore.2020.120447 PMID:33518818

Bhagat, R. K., Wykes, M. D., Dalziel, S. B., & Linden, P. F. (2020). Effects of ventilation on the indoor spread of COVID-19. *Journal of Fluid Mechanics, 903*.

Bhargava, Y. (2021, March 2). *In 2020, the world added three billionaires every two days, India added one every week*. Retrieved May 2, 2021, from The Hindu. https://www.thehindu.com/news/national/india-adds-40-billionaires-in-pandemic-year-adani-ambani-see-rise-in-wealth-report/article33970268.ece

Bhattacharya, A. (2020, February). *Hospitality Industry After COVID-19: How to Survive?* Retrieved September 10, 2020, from EHL Insights: https://hospitalityinsights.ehl.edu/hospitality-covid19-crisis

Biswas, S. (2020, March 30). *Coronavirus: India's pandemic lockdown turns into a human tragedy*. Retrieved July 13, 2021 from BBC. https://www.bbc.com/news/world-asia-india-52086274

Biswas, T. K., & Das, M. C. (2020). Selection of the barriers of supply chain management in Indian manufacturing sectors due to Covid-19 impacts. *Operational Research in Engineering Sciences: Theory and Applications, 3*(3), 1–12. doi:10.31181/oresta2030301b

Blackhurst, J., Craighead, C. W., Elkins, D., & Handfield, R. B. (2005). An empirically derived agenda of critical research issues for managing supply-chain disruptions. *International Journal of Production Research, 43*(19), 4067–4081. doi:10.1080/00207540500151549

Bloomberg. (2021, June 3). *Mukesh Ambani plans to tackle Covid with cheaper tests, tapeworm drugs*. Retrieved June 15, 2021, from Economic Times website: https://economictimes.indiatimes.com/news/company/corporate-trends/mukesh-ambani-plans-to-tackle-covid-with-cheaper-tests-tapeworm-drug/articleshow/83200963.cms

Bodenhorn, H. 2020. Business in a time of Spanish influenza (No. w27495). National Bureau of Economic Research.

Breier, M., Kallmuenzer, A., Clauss, T., Gast, J., Kraus, S., & Tiberius, V. (n.d.). The role of business model innovation in the hospitality industry during the COVID-19 crisis. *International Journal of Hospitality Management, 92*, 1 - 12.

Brennen, J. S., Simon, F. M., & Nielsen, R. K. (2020). Beyond (Mis) Representation: Visuals in COVID-19 Misinformation. *The International Journal of Press/Politics*, 1–26.

BrincaP.DuarteJ. B.Faria-e-CastroM. (2020). Is the COVID-19 pandemic a supply or a demand shock? doi:10.20955/es.2020.31

Brizek, M. G., Frash, R. E., McLeod, B., & Patience, M. M. (2020). Independent restaurant operator perspectives in the wake of the COVID-19 pandemic (R3). *International Journal of Hospitality Management*, 102766. PMID:33230361

Brunner, M. (2020, July 17). *Riley Co. extends restrictions on bars, restaurants.* WIBW.

Bucak, T., & Yiğit, S. (2021). The future of the chef occupation and the food and beverage sector after the COVID-19 outbreak: Opinions of Turkish chefs. *International Journal of Hospitality Management*, *92*(102682), 1–8. doi:10.1016/j.ijhm.2020.102682 PMID:33071426

Bufquin, D., Park, J. Y., Back, R. M., de Souza Meira, J. V., & Hight, S. K. (2021, February). Employee work status, mental health, substance use, and career turnover intentions: An examination of restaurant employees during COVID-19. *International Journal of Hospitality Management*, *93*(102764), 1–9. doi:10.1016/j.ijhm.2020.102764

Burki, T. (2020, Sept.). The origin of SARS-CoV-2. *The Lancet.* Retrieved Dec. 17, 2020, from https://www.thelancet.com/journals/laninf/article/PIIS1473-3099(20)30641-1/fulltext

Business Insider India. (2021, January 25). *From Mukesh Ambani to Gautam Adani — India's top billionaires increased their wealth by 35% during COVID-19 pandemic*. Retrieved April 11, 2021, from Business Insider India website: https://www.businessinsider.in/finance/news/from-mukesh-ambani-to-gautam-adani-indias-top-billionaires-increased-their-wealth-by-35-during-covid-19-pandemic/articleshow/80445646.cms

Butu, A., Brumă, I. S., Tanasă, L., Rodino, S., Vasiliu, C. D., Doboş, S., & Butu, M. (2020). The impact of COVID-19 crisis upon the consumer buying behavior of fresh vegetables directly from local producers. Case study: The quarantined area of Suceava County, Romania. *International Journal of Environmental Research and Public Health*, *17*(15), 1–25. doi:10.3390/ijerph17155485 PMID:32751368

Byrne, B. M. (2010). Structural equation modeling with AMOS: Basic concepts, applications, and programming (multivariate applications series). *Taylor & Francis Group, 396*, 7384.

Cable, D. M., & DeRue, D. S. (2002). The convergent and discriminant validity of subjective fit perceptions. *The Journal of Applied Psychology, 87*(5), 875–884. doi:10.1037/0021-9010.87.5.875 PMID:12395812

Capital Markets in the current climate. (2020, April 22). *Vistra; Vistra Insights*. https://www.vistra.com/insights/capital-markets-current-climate

Carrasco C. (2021). *Digital Marketplaces, and how to survive COVID-19*. Smefinanceforum.org

Casert, R. (2020, Oct. 25). *Virus is pummeling Europe's eateries—and winter is coming*. ABC News.

CCAF, World Bank, & World Economic Forum. (2020). *The Global COVID-19 FinTech Market Rapid Assessment Report*. University of Cambridge, World Bank Group, and the World Economic Forum.

Chadee, D., Ren, S., & Tang, G. (2021). Is digital technology the magic bullet for performing work at home? Lessons learned for post COVID-19 recovery in hospitality management. *International Journal of Hospitality Management, 92*(102718), 1–8. doi:10.1016/j.ijhm.2020.102718 PMID:33071425

Chandra, J. (2021, January 25). *Indian billionaires increased their wealth by 35% during the lockdown, says Oxfam report.* Retrieved May 8, 2021, from The Hindu. https://www.thehindu.com/news/national/oxfam-study-shows-rich-got-richer-during-pandemic/article33655044.ece

Chang, H.-H., & Meyerhoefer, C.D. (2020). COVID-19 and the demand for online food shopping services: Empirical evidence from Taiwan. *American Journal of Agricultural Economics,* 1 – 18.

Chang, S., Pierson, E., Koh, P. W., Gerardin, J., Redbird, B., Grusky, D., & Leskovec, J. (2020, November 10). Mobility network models of COVID-19 explain inequities and inform reopening. *Nature*. PMID:33171481

Chappell, B. (2020, Dec. 9). *The coronavirus crisis: 'Cruise to Nowhere' returns to Singapore early after positive coronavirus test.* NPR.

Chart: Each State's COVID-19 Reopening and Reclosing Plans and Mask Requirements. (2020, Dec. 14). *National Academic for State Health Policy*. Retrieved Dec. 15, 2020, from https://www.nashp.org/governors-prioritize-health-for-all/

Chatterjee, P. (2020, April 12). *The pandemic exposes India's apathy toward migrant workers*. Retrieved May 12, 2021, from Atlantic Monthly (Boston, Mass.: 1993). https://www.theatlantic.com/ideas/archive/2020/04/the-pandemic-exposes-indias-two-worlds/609838/

Chatterjee, S. (n.d.). *Farm laws versus field realities: Understanding India's agricultural markets*. Retrieved July 26, 2021, from Psu.edu website: https://www.personal.psu.edu/sc20/papers/SC_MK_farmlaws.pdf

Chaudhary, M., Sodani, P. R., & Das, S. (2020). Effect of COVID-19 on Economy in India: Some Reflections for Policy and Programme. *Journal of Health Management, 22*(2), 169–180. doi:10.1177/0972063420935541

Chauvet, M., & Piger, J. (2005). *A Comparison of the Real-Time Performance of Business Cycle Dating Methods*. Academic Press.

Chenarides, L., Manfredo, M., & Richards, T.J. (2020). COVID-19 and food supply chains. *Applied Economic Perspectives and Policy*, 1 – 10.

Chetty, R., Friedman, J. N., Hendren, N., & Stepner, M. (2020). Real-time economics: A new platform to track the impacts of COVID-19 on people, businesses, and communities using private sector data. *NBER Working Paper, 27431*, 1 – 26.

Chetty, R., Friedman, J. N., Hendren, N., Stepner, M., & the The Opportunity Insights Team. (2020, June). *How did COVID-19 and stabilization policies affect spending and employment? A new real-time economic tracker based on private sector data*. National Bureau of Economic Research. NBER Working Paper Series. Working Paper 27431.

Chowdhury, M. T., Sarkar, A., Paul, S. K., & Moktadir, M. A. (2020). *A case study on strategies to deal with the impacts of COVID-19 pandemic in the food and beverage industry*. Operations Management Research. doi:10.100712063-020-00166-9

Chowdhury, M. T., Sarkar, A., Saha, P. K., & Anik, R. H. (2020). Enhancing supply resilience in the COVID-19 pandemic: A case study on beauty and personal care retailers. *Modern Supply Chain Research and Applications, 2*(3), 143–159. doi:10.1108/MSCRA-07-2020-0018

Christopher, M., & Peck, H. (2004). Building the Resilient Supply Chain. *International Journal of Logistics Management, 15*(2), 1–14. doi:10.1108/09574090410700275

Ciotti, M., Ciccozzi, M., Terrinoni, A., Jiang, W. C., Wang, C. B., & Bernardini, S. (2020). The COVID-19 pandemic. *Critical Reviews in Clinical Laboratory Sciences, 57*(6), 365–388. doi:10.1080/10408363.2020.1783198 PMID:32645276

CNBC. (2021, December 4). *Fierce competition as UAE digital bank Zand prepares for launch*. Retrieved from CNBC: https://www.cnbc.com/2021/06/24/fierce-competition-as-uae-digital-bank-zand-prepares-for-launch.html

Cohen, M. J. (2020). *Does the COVID-19 outbreak mark the onset of a sustainable consumption transition?* doi:10.1080/15487733.2020.1740472

Coibion, O., Gorodnichenko, Y., & Weber, M. (2020, May). *The cost of the Covid-19 crisis: Lockdowns, macroeconomic expectations, and consumer spending*. National Bureau of Economic Research. NBER Working Paper 27141.

Community, work, and school: Information for where you live, work, learn, and play. (2020, Nov. 13). *U.S. Centers for Disease Control and Prevention*. Retrieved Dec. 14, 2020, from https://www.cdc.gov/coronavirus/2019-ncov/community/index.html

Coronavirus: Robot dog enforces social distancing in Singapore park. (2020, May 11). BBC News.

Corporate social responsibility practices in the times of COVID-19: A study of India's BFSI sector. (n.d.). Retrieved August 9, 2021, from Org.in website: https://www.downtoearth.org.in/blog/governance/corporate-social-responsibility-practices-in-the-times-of-covid-19-a-study-of-india-s-bfsi-sector-74583

COVID-19 crisis response in MENA countries. (2020, November 6). *OECD.* https://www.oecd.org/coronavirus/policy-responses/covid-19-crisis-response-in-mena-countries-4b366396/

COVID-19 first wave pushed 23 crore Indians into poverty: Azim Premji University. (n.d.). *Business Today*. Retrieved August 2, 2021, from Business Today: https://www.businesstoday.in/jobs/story/covid-19-first-wave-pushed-23-crore-indians-into-poverty-azim-premji-university-295173-2021-05-06

COVID-19 science update released: Nov. 24, 2020 Edition 66. (2020, Nov. 24). *U.S. Centers for Disease Control and Prevention (CDC).* Retrieved Dec. 20, 2020, from https://www.cdc.gov/library/covid19/112420_covidupdate.html

COVID-19. Impact on the banking sector. (2020, June 24). *KPMG.* https://home.kpmg/xx/en/home/insights/2020/07/covid-19-impact-on-banking-m-and-a-2020.html

COVID-19. Implications for business. (2020, March 1). *McKinsey & Company*. Retrieved May 18, 2021 from McKinsey and Company website: https://www.mckinsey.com/business-functions/risk-and-resilience/our-insights/covid-19-implications-for-business

Crowley, C. (2020, Oct. 2). What is the RESTAURANTS Act—and can it really save the hospitality industry? *Grub Street.*

Da, B. L., Im, G. Y., & Schiano, T. D. (2020). COVID-19 hangover: A rising tide of alcohol use disorder and alcohol-associated liver disease. *Hepatology (Baltimore, Md.)*, *72*(3), 1102–1108.

Daigavane, W., & Belmannu, P. (n.d.). *Impact of the global pandemic on Indian labor laws*. Retrieved April 18, 2021, from Jurist.org website: https://www.jurist.org/commentary/2020/05/daigavane-belmannu-labor-law-suspensions-india/

Dannenberg, P., Fuchs, M., Riedler, T., & Wiedemann, C. (2020). Digital Transition by COVID-19 Pandemic? The German Food Online Retail. *Tijdschrift voor Economische en Sociale Geografie*, *111*(3), 543–560. doi:10.1111/tesg.12453 PMID:32836487

Das, D., Datta, A., & Kumar, P. (2020). Exit Strategies for COVID 19: An ISM and MICMAC approach. *Asia Pacific Journal of Health Management*, *15*(3), 94–109. doi:10.24083/apjhm.v15i3.423

Das, D., Datta, A., Kumar, P., Kazancoglu, Y., & Ram, M. (2021). Building supply chain resilience in the era of COVID-19: An AHP-DEMATEL approach. *Operations Management Research*, *2021*, 1–19. doi:10.100712063-021-00200-4

Das, S., Basak, S., & Das, G. M. (2020). A Study for Understanding the Problems of MSMEs under Current Pandemic Situation with Special Reference to Kolkata. *The Management Accountant Journal*, *55*(12), 65–67. doi:10.33516/maj.v55i12.65-67p

Dave, D., McNichols, D., & Sabia, J. J. (2020). The contagion externality of a superspreading event: The Sturgis Motorcycle Rally and COVID-19. *Southern Economic Journal*, 1–39.

del Rio-Chanona, R. M., Mealy, P., Pichler, A., Lafond, F., & Farmer, D. (2020). *Supply and demand shocks in the COVID-19 pandemic: An industry and occupation perspective*. arXiv preprint arXiv:2004.06759.

Deloitte. (2020). *Addressing the impact of COVID-19: Crisis management and resilience planning*. Author.

Deloitte. (2020). *Beyond COVID-19: New opportunities for fintech companies*. Deloitte Center for Financial Services.

Demirgüç-Kunt, A., Pedraza, A., & Ruiz-Ortega, C. (2021). Banking sector performance during the covid-19 crisis. *Journal of Banking & Finance*, 106305.

Development Bank of Singapore. (2021). DBS survey reveals government assisted financing schemes paying off proportion of SMEs flagging cash flow as top concern more than halves since February 2020. *DBS Newsletter*. https://www.dbs.com/newsroom/

Dijk, M. N. (2020). *How entrepreneur resilience impacts the utilization of innovation in dealing with adversities like the COVID-19 pandemic in the restaurant industry in the Netherlands* (Bachelor's thesis). University of Twente.

Djeebet, H. (2020, April 9). *What is the impact of COVID-19 on Global Hospitality Industry*. Retrieved September 22, 2020, from Hospitalitynet: https://www.hospitalitynet.org/opinion/4098062.html

Dobrowolski, Z. (2020). After COVID-19: Reorientation of crisis management in crisis. *Entrepreneurship and Sustainability Issues*, *8*(2), 1–12.

Drolia, T. (2021, May 10). *Navigating through SME lending challenges during the pandemic*. Retrieved July 1, 2021, from Yourstory.com website: https://yourstory.com/smbstory/sme-lending-fintech-msmes-covid-19/amp

Dube, K., Nhamo, G., & Chikodzi, D. (2021). COVID-19 pandemic and prospects for recovery of the global aviation industry. *Journal of Air Transport Management, 92*(December), 102022. doi:10.1016/j.jairtraman.2021.102022

Duda-Chodak, A., Lukasiewicz, M., Zięć, G., Florkiewicz, A., & Filipiak-Florkiewicz, A. (2020). Covid-19 pandemic and food: Present knowledge, risks, consumers fears and safety. *Trends in Food Science & Technology*, *105*, 145–160.

Dudovskiy, J. (2018). *The Ultimate Guide to Writing a Dissertation in Business Studies: A step by step assistance*. Academic Press.

Eco, U. (1991). *Travels in Hyperreality*. Harcourt Brace & Company.

Elassar, A. (2020, Dec. 20). *A customer at an Ohio restaurant left a $5,600 tip to split among the entire staff for Christmas*. CNN.

Elhennawy, A., Alsalem, F. A., Bahri, S., & Alarfaj, N. (2021). *Telemedicine versus Physical Examination in Patients' Assessment during COVID-19 Pandemic: The Dubai Experience*. Academic Press.

Enriquez, M. (2021). *Survival strategies for SMEs as Singapore moves from pandemic to endemic*. Channel News Asia. https://www.channelnewsasia.com/business/survival-strategies-smes-singapore-moves-pandemic-endemic-2158541

Fantozzi, J. (2020, Nov. 13). *Indoor dining major cause of COVID-19 'superspreader' events, Stanford-led study suggests*. Nation's Restaurant News (NRN).

Fasth, J., Elliot, V., & Styhre, A. (2021). Crisis management as practice in small-and medium-sized enterprises during the first period of COVID-19. *Journal of Contingencies and Crisis Management*, 1–10.

Fetzer, T. (2020). Subsidizing the spread of COVID19: Evidence from the UK's Eat-Out-to-Help-Out scheme (No. 1310). University of Warwick, Department of Economics.

Feuer, W. (2020, Mar. 28). *CDC says coronavirus RNA found in Princess Cruise ship cabins up to 17 days after passengers left*. CNBC.

Fink, L. (2020). Conducting Information Systems Research in the Midst of the COVID-19 Pandemic: Opportunities and Challenges. *Information Systems Management*, *37*(4), 256–259. doi:10.1080/10580530.2020.1814460

Fornell, C., & Larcker, D. F. (1981). Evaluating Structural Equation Models with Unobservable Variables and Measurement Error. *JMR, Journal of Marketing Research*, *18*(1), 39–50. doi:10.1177/002224378101800104

Foroudi, P., Tabaghdehi, A. H., & Marvi, R. (2021). The gloom of the COVID-19 shock in the hospitality industry: A study of consumer risk perception and adaptive belief in the dark cloud of a pandemic. *International Journal of Hospitality Management*, *92*(102717), 1–10.

Frost, J. (2018). *How To Interpret R-squared in Regression Analysis*. Retrieved October 25, 2020, from Statistics by Jim: https://statisticsbyjim.com/regression/interpret-r-squared-regression/

Fu & Mishra. (2020). *The Global Impact of COVID-19 on Fintech Adoption*. Swiss Finance Institute Research Paper Series 20-38, Swiss Finance Institute.

Gerth, F., Ramiah, V., Toufaily, E., & Muschert, G. (2021). Assessing the effectiveness of Covid-19 financial product innovations in supporting financially distressed firms and households in the UAE. *Journal of Financial Services Marketing*, 1–11.

Ghosh, A., Nundy, S., & Mallick, T. K. (2020). How India is dealing with COVID-19 pandemic. *Sensors International, 1*, 100021. doi:10.1016/j.sintl.2020.100021 PMID:34766039

Gibson, K. (2020, June 17). *After reopening, restaurants again shutting their doors as coronavirus flares.* MoneyWatch. CBS News.

Gillison, S. (2020, May 22). *Thought Experiment: Samantha Gillison: Is the coronavirus the end for fancy restaurants—and the start of a new dining era.* NBC News.

Giordani & Rullani. (2020). *The Digital Revolution and COVID-19.* Working Papers 6, Department of Management, Università Ca' Foscari Venezia.

Glaeser, E. (2020, May 1). Looking beyond the urban jobs Armageddon. In How life in our cities will look after the coronavirus pandemic. Foreign Policy.

Glaeser, E. L., Jin, G. Z., Leyden, B. T., & Luca, M. (2020, Aug.). *Learning from deregulation: The asymmetric impact of lockdown and reopening on risky behavior during COVID-19.* National Bureau of Economic Research. NBER Working Paper 27650.

Global Dashboard on COVID-19 Government Policies. (n.d.). *U.S. Chamber of Commerce.* Retrieved Dec. 17, 2020, from https://www.uschamber.com/international-affairs-division/covid-dashboard

Gölgeci, I., & Kuivalainen, O. (2020). Does social capital matter for supply chain resilience? The role of absorptive capacity and marketing-supply chain management alignment. *Industrial Marketing Management, 84*(September), 63–74. doi:10.1016/j.indmarman.2019.05.006

Goolsbee, A., & Syverson, C. (2021). Fear, lockdown, and diversion: Comparing drivers of pandemic economic decline 2020. *Journal of Public Economics, 193*(104311), 1–8.

Gopalan, A. (2021, June 19). *India's vaccine makers are pandemic profiteers, not humanitarians.* Retrieved August 8, 2021, from The Intercept website: https://theintercept.com/2021/06/19/india-covid-vaccine-profiteering/

Gössling, S., Scott, D., & Hall, C. M. (2021). Pandemics, tourism and global change: A rapid assessment of COVID-19. *Journal of Sustainable Tourism, 29*(1), 1–20.

Gottlieb, S. (2020, Dec. 7). *Dr. Scott Gottlieb on future of COVID-19, vaccine, and Pfizer.* USA Today. Retrieved Dec. 20, 2020, from https://youtu.be/PxJO8MrlGcg

Gouda, S. K., & Saranga, H. (2018). Sustainable supply chains for supply chain sustainability: Impact of sustainability efforts on supply chain risk. *International Journal of Production Research, 56*(17), 5820–5835. doi:10.1080/00207543.2018.1456695

Guan, Z., Zhang, X., Zhou, M., & Dan, Y. (2020). Demand information sharing in competing supply chains with manufacturer-provided service. *International Journal of Production Economics, 220*, 107450. doi:10.1016/j.ijpe.2019.07.023

Gursoy, D., & Chi, C. G. (2020). Effects of COVID-19 pandemic on hospitality industry: Review of the current situations and a research agenda. *Journal of Hospitality Marketing & Management, 29*(5), 527–529.

Hai-Jew, S. (2020, Apr.). Emergent COVID-19 and SARS-CoV-2 in social imagery and social video: Initial three months of viral dispersion. In *Social World Sensing via Social Image Analysis from Social Media.* New Prairie Press. Retrieved Oct. 23, 2020, from https://kstatelibraries.pressbooks.pub/socialworldsensing/chapter/covid19-1/

Hai-Jew, S. (2021). Societal shutdown and reopening and reclosing in the U.S. as expressed in social imagery narratives: COVID-19 pandemic seven/eight months. In Z. Fields' (Ed.), *Handbook of Research on Using Global Collective Intelligence and Creativity to Solve Wicked Problems*. IGI Global.

Hailu, G. (2020, Apr. 18). Economic thoughts on COVID-19 for Canadian food processors. *Canadian Journal of Agricultural Economics/Revue canadienne d'agroeconomie*, 163 – 169.

Hair, J. F., Sarstedt, M., Hopkins, L., & Kuppelwieser, V. G. (2014). Partial least squares structural equation modeling (PLS-SEM): An emerging tool in business research. European Business Review, 26(2), 106–121. doi:10.1108/EBR-10-2013-0128

Hair, J. F., Black, W. C., Babin, B. J., Anderson, R. E., & Tatham, R. L. (2010). *Multivariate Data Analysis* (7th ed.). Prentice Hall.

Hair, J. F., Sarstedt, M., Ringle, C. M., & Mena, J. A. (2012). An assessment of the use of partial least squares structural equation modeling in marketing research. *Journal of the Academy of Marketing Science, 40*(3), 414–433. doi:10.100711747-011-0261-6

Hamner, L., Dubbel, P., Capron, I., Ross, A., Jordan, A., Lee, J., Lynn, J., Ball, A., Narwal, S., Russell, S., Patric, D., & Leibrand, H. (2020, May 15). *High SARS-CoV-2 attack rate following exposure at a choir practice – Skagit County, Washington, March 2020.* Morbidity and Mortality Weekly Report (MMWR). U.S. Centers for Disease Control and Prevention. Retrieved Dec. 17, 2020, from https://www.cdc.gov/mmwr/volumes/69/wr/mm6919e6.htm

Hao, F., Xiao, Q., & Chon, K. (2020, August 5). COVID-19 and China's Hotel Industry: Impacts, a Disaster Management Framework, and Post-Pandemic Agenda. *International Journal of Hospitality Management, 90*, 102636. Advance online publication. doi:10.1016/j.ijhm.2020.102636 PMID:32834356

Harrell, A. J. (2008). Factors that influence the recovery of small family-owned residential-care facilities for senior citizens in New Orleans, Louisiana after Hurricane Katrina. *Academy of Strategic Management Journal, 7*, 49–53.

Harris, J. E. (2020). Data from the COVID-19 epidemic in Florida suggest that younger cohorts have been transmitting their infections to less socially mobile older adults. *Review of Economics of the Household*, 1019–1037.

Hassan, A. (2020, May 19). *Masks required, fewer games, buffet closed: Idaho casino offers glimpse of gambling's future*. NBC News.

Hassen, T.B., El Bilali, H., & S Allahyari, M. (2020). Impact of COVID-19 on Food Behavior and Consumption in Qatar. *Sustainability, 12*(17), 1 - 18.

Havice, E., Marschke, M., & Vandergeest, P. (2020, June 8). Industrial seafood systems in the immobilizing COVID-19 moment. *Agriculture and Human Values*, 1–2.

Henseler, J., Ringle, C. M., & Sinkovics, R. R. (2009). The use of partial least squares path modeling in international marketing. Advances in International Marketing, 20, 277–319. doi:10.1108/S1474-7979(2009)0000020014

Herlihy, D., & Cohn, S. H. (1997). *The Black Death and the transformation of the West*. Harvard University Press.

Hermann, C. F. (1972). *International Crises: Insights from Behaviour Research*. The Free Press.

Higgins-Dunn, N. (2020, July 13). *California to close indoor restaurants, movie theaters and bars statewide as coronavirus cases rise*. CNBC.

Hobbs, J. E. (2020, April 21). Food supply chains during the COVID-19 pandemic. *Canadian Journal of Agricultural Economics*, 1–18.

Holmes, K., & Valencia, N. (2020, May 13). *CDC guidelines shelved by Trump administration spell out far stricter road map to reopening*. CNN.

Hosseini, S., Ivanov, D., & Dolgui, A. (2019). Review of quantitative methods for supply chain resilience analysis. *Transportation Research Part E, Logistics and Transportation Review, 125*, 285–307. doi:10.1016/j.tre.2019.03.001

Hotelier India. (2020, August 10). *Dubai's tourism and hospitality sectors see green shoots of revival*. Retrieved September 10, 2020, from Hotelier India: https://www.hotelierindia.com/business/11752-dubais-tourism-and-hospitality-sectors-see-green-shoots-of-revival

Hotelier India. (2020, August 10). *Dubai's tourism and hospitality sectors see green shoots of revival*. Retrieved September 22, 2020, from Hotelier India: https://www.hotelierindia.com/business/11752-dubais-tourism-and-hospitality-sectors-see-green-shoots-of-revival

How businesses have successfully pivoted during the pandemic. (2020, July 7). *Harvard Business Review*. Retrieved May 21, 2021, from https://hbr.org/2020/07/how-businesses-have-successfully-pivoted-during-the-pandemic

Huang, A., Makridis, C., Baker, M., Medeiros, M., & Guo, Z. (2020). Understanding the impact of COVID-19 intervention policies on the hospitality labor market. *International Journal of Hospitality Management, 91*, 1 – 9.

Hu, L. T., & Bentler, P. M. (1999). Cutoff criteria for fit indexes in covariance structure analysis: Conventional criteria versus new alternatives. *Structural Equation Modeling*, *6*(1), 1–55. doi:10.1080/10705519909540118

Hu, X., Yan, H., Casey, T., & Wu, C. H. (2020). Creating a safe haven during the crisis: How organizations can achieve deep compliance with COVID-19 safety measures in the hospitality industry. *International Journal of Hospitality Management*, *92*, 102662.

Iacus, S. M., Natale, F., Santamaria, C., Spyratos, S., & Vespe, M. (2020). Estimating and projecting air passenger traffic during the COVID-19 coronavirus outbreak and its socio-economic impact. *Safety Science*, *129*(May), 104791. doi:10.1016/j.ssci.2020.104791 PMID:32377034

Ibrahim, M. (2014). A comparative performance of two Banks in United Arab Emirates. *Research Journal of Finance and Accounting*, *5*(21), 24–29.

IBSI. (2021). *5 FinTech companies making waves in the UAE market*. Retrieved Dec 3, 2021, from https://ibsintelligence.com/ibsi-news/5-fintech-companies-making-waves-in-the-uae-market/

IFC. (2020). *The early impact of Covid-19 on financial institutions. In Insights from a survey of IFC financial institution clients*. IFC.

IFC. (2021). *The Effects of COVID-19 and the Need for Bank Restructuring*. IFC.

IHME COVID-19 Forecasting Team. (2020, October 23). Modeling COVID-19 scenarios for the United States. *Nature*.

Iles, A., & de Wit, M. M. (2020). Who gets to define 'the COVID-19 problem'? Expert politics in a pandemic. *Agriculture and Human Values*, 1–2.

ILO Decent work team for South Asia and Country Office for India. (2018). *India Wage Report - Wage policies for decent work and inclusive growth.* Retrieved April 9, 2021 from ILO website: https://www.ilo.org/wcmsp5/groups/public/---asia/---ro-bangkok/---sro-new_delhi/documents/publication/wcms_638305.pdf

IMF. (2021). https://www.imf.org/en/Topics/imf-and-covid19/Policy-Responses-to-COVID-19#J

Im, J., Kim, H., & Miao, L. (2021). CEO letters: Hospitality corporate narratives during the COVID-19 pandemic. *International Journal of Hospitality Management*, *92*, 1–9.

India's unemployment in 2020 at worst level in 29 years, shows study. (n.d.). *Business Today*. Retrieved September 2, 2021, from https://www.businesstoday.in/jobs/story/india-unemployment-in-2020-at-worst-level-in-29-years-shows-study-297195-2021-05-28

Ivanov, D. (2020). Predicting the impacts of epidemic outbreaks on global supply chains: A simulation-based analysis on the coronavirus outbreak (COVID-19/SARS-CoV-2) case. *Transportation Research Part E, Logistics and Transportation Review*, *136*(March), 101922. doi:10.1016/j.tre.2020.101922 PMID:32288597

Ivanov, D., & Das, A. (2020). Coronavirus (COVID-19/SARS-CoV-2) and supply chain resilience: A research note. *International Journal of Integrated Supply Management*, *13*(1), 90–102. doi:10.1504/IJISM.2020.107780

Ivanov, D., & Dolgui, A. (2020). Viability of intertwined supply networks: Extending the supply chain resilience angles towards survivability. A position paper motivated by COVID-19 outbreak. *International Journal of Production Research*, *58*(10), 2904–2915. doi:10.1080/00207543.2020.1750727

Jaques, T. (2010). Reshaping crisis management: The challenge for organizational design. *Organization Development Journal*, *28*(1), 9–17.

Jayaswal, R. (2021, July 10). Fuel price surge continues, petrol at ₹100.91 per litre in Delhi. *The Hindustan Times*. Retrieved July 12, 2021 from https://www.hindustantimes.com/india-news/fuel-price-surge-continues-petrol-at-100-91-per-litre-in-delhi-101625941654714.html

Jenatabadi, H. S. (2015). *An Overview of Path Analysis: Mediation Analysis Concept in Structural Equation Modeling*. https://arxiv.org/abs/1504.03441

Jha, A. N. (2020, August 23). *Middlemen make money as workers from Bihar return to other states*. Retrieved May 23, 2021, from The Hindustan Times. https://www.hindustantimes.com/india-news/middlemen-make-money-as-workers-from-bihar-return-to-other-states/story-ec7mIfteBIfB9vE5mjoxWJ.html

Jiang, Y., & Wen, J. (2020). Effects of COVID-19 on hotel marketing and management: A perspective article. *International Journal of Contemporary Hospitality Management*, *32*(8), 2563–2573. doi:10.1108/IJCHM-03-2020-0237

John, C. (2020, August 27). *How musk, Bezos, Zuckerberg, Ambani got richer amid the pandemic*. Retrieved July 5, 2021, from Thequint.com website: https://www.thequint.com/tech-and-auto/tech-news/how-jeff-bezos-elon-musk-mark-zuckerberg-and-mukesh-ambani-made-more-billions-during-the-covid-19-pandemic

Jung, H. S., Jung, Y. S., & Yoon, H. H. (2021). COVID-19: The effects of job insecurity on the job engagement and turnover intent of deluxe hotel employees and the moderating role of generational characteristics. *International Journal of Hospitality Management*, *92*(102703), 1–9.

Kahiluoto, H., Mäkinen, H., & Kaseva, J. (2020). Supplying resilience through assessing diversity of responses to disruption. *International Journal of Operations & Production Management*, *40*(3), 271–292. doi:10.1108/IJOPM-01-2019-0006

Kant, K. (2020, November 17). *India Inc gains despite Covid-19 disruptions; combined profit at Rs 1.5 trn*. Retrieved April 28, 2021, Business-Standard.Com. https://www.business-standard.com/article/companies/india-inc-gains-despite-covid-19-disruptions-combined-profit-at-rs-1-5-trn-120111700077_1.html

Kapoor, M. (n.d.). *Serum Institute founder Cyrus Poonawalla's wealth rises 85% in 5 months to $13.8 bn.* Retrieved August 18, 2021, from Business Today website: https://www.businesstoday.in/latest/corporate/story/serum-institute-founder-cyrus-poonawalla-adar-wealth-85pc-to-138-bn-271174-2020-08-26

Karimi, F. (2020, May 15). *The focus is shifting from trying to eliminate coronavirus to reducing the risks, a doctor says.* CNN.

Karmaker, C. L., Ahmed, T., Ahmed, S., Ali, S. M., Moktadir, M. A., & Kabir, G. (2021). Improving supply chain sustainability in the context of COVID-19 pandemic in an emerging economy: Exploring drivers using an integrated model. *Sustainable Production and Consumption*, *26*, 411–427. doi:10.1016/j.spc.2020.09.019 PMID:33015267

Karwasra, K., Soni, G., Mangla, S. K., & Kazancoglu, Y. (2021). Assessing dairy supply chain vulnerability during the Covid-19 pandemic. *International Journal of Logistics Research and Applications*, 1–19. doi:10.1080/13675567.2021.1910221

Kaur, M. (2020, September 9). *Adani Wilmar's continuing double-digit growth.* Retrieved June 25, 2021, from Indifoodbev.com website: https://indifoodbev.com/uncategorized/adani-wilmar/

Kaushal, V., & Srivastava, S. (2021). Hospitality and tourism industry amid COVID-19 pandemic: Perspectives on challenges and learnings from India. *International Journal of Hospitality Management*, *92*(102707), 1–9.

Kesslen, B. (2020, Oct. 30). *'I'm going to church more': Restaurant owners wonder whether they'll survive winter.* NBC News.

Khan, M. (2020). *UAE's successful policies against COVID-19.* Academic Press.

Khan, K. S., Mamun, M. A., Griffiths, M. D., & Ullah, I. (2020). The mental health impact of the COVID-19 pandemic across different cohorts. *International Journal of Mental Health and Addiction*, 1–7.

Kim, A. (2020, May 21). *More than 1,200 pastors say they'll defy California's state order and resume in-person services.* CNN.

Kim, J., Kim, J., & Wang, Y. (2021). Uncertainty risks and strategic reaction of restaurant firms amid COVID-19: Evidence from China. *International Journal of Hospitality Management*, *92*(102752), 1–10.

Kim, J., & Lee, J. C. (2020). Effects of COVID-19 on preferences for private dining facilities in restaurants. *Journal of Hospitality and Tourism Management*, *45*, 67–70.

Kit. (2020). *About 3,800 companies closed down in April; expect uptick in coming months: Chee Hong Tat.* Channel New Asia. https://www.channelnewsasia.com/business/3800-business-closures-april-uptick-ahead-covid19-coronavirus-648176

Kline, R. B. (2012). *Assumptions in structural equation modeling.* PsycNET. https://psycnet.apa.org/record/2012-16551-007

Kline, R. B. (2015). *Principles and practice of structural equation modeling*. Guilford publications.

Knowles, J., Ettenson, R., Lynch, P., & Dollens, J. (2020). Growth opportunities for brands during the COVID-19 crisis. *MIT Sloan Management Review*, 1–6.

Kok, G., Jonkers, R., Gelissen, R., Meertens, R., Schaalma, H., & de Zwart, O. (2010). Behavioural intentions in response to an influenza pandemic. *BMC Public Health*, *10*(174), 1–19.

Končar, J., Grubor, A., Marić, R., Vučenović, S., & Vukmirović, G. (2020). Setbacks to IoT implementation in the function of FMCG supply chain sustainability during COVID-19 pandemic. *Sustainability (Switzerland)*, *12*(18), 7391. Advance online publication. doi:10.3390u12187391

Kong, E., & Prinz, D. (2020). Disentangling policy effects using proxy data: Which shutdown policies affected unemployment during the COVID-19 pandemic? *Journal of Public Economics*, *189*(104257), 1–39.

Kornfield, M. (2020, May 23). Rats are getting aggressive hunting for food amid restaurant closures, CDC warns. *The Washington Post.*

KPMG. (2020). *A catalyst for change for bank branches*. https://home.kpmg/xx/en/blogs/home/posts/2020/04/a-catalyst-for-changefor-bank-branches.html

Kumar, P., & Kumar Singh, R. (2021). Strategic framework for developing resilience in Agri-Food Supply Chains during COVID 19 pandemic. *International Journal of Logistics Research and Applications*, 1–24. doi:10.1080/13675567.2021.1908524

Kumar, M. S., Raut, D. R. D., Narwane, D. V. S., & Narkhede, D. B. E. (2020). Applications of industry 4.0 to overcome the COVID-19 operational challenges. *Diabetes & Metabolic Syndrome*, *14*(5), 1283–1289. doi:10.1016/j.dsx.2020.07.010 PMID:32755822

Langer, W. L. (1964). The black death. *Scientific American*, *210*(2), 114–121. doi:10.1038cien tificamerican0264-114 PMID:14121747

Lara. (2020). *Need financing because of the pandemic? SMEs turn to fintech companies*. IFC.

Leatherby, L., & McCann, A. (2020, May 15). Sweden stayed open. A deadly month shows the risks. *The New York Times.*

Lemy, D., Goh, E., & Ferry, J. (2019, January 3). Moving out of the silo: How service quality innovations can develop customer loyalty in Indonesia's hotel. *Journal of Vacation Marketing*, *25*(4), 462–479. Advance online publication. doi:10.1177/1356766718819658

Li, Q., Bessell, L., Xiao, X., Fan, C., Gao, X., & Mostafavi, A. (2020, June 25). *Disparate patterns of movements and visits to points of interests located in urban hotspots across U.S. metropolitan cities during COVID-19*. arXiv.

Liesman, S. (2020, March 15). *Federal Reserve cuts rates to zero and launches massive $700 billion quantitative easing program.* CNBC. https://www.cnbc.com/2020/03/15/federal-reserve-cuts-rates-to-zero-and-launches-massive-700-billion-quantitative-easing-program.html

Lock, S. (2020, Dec. 11). *Restaurant industry in the U.S. – statistics & facts.* Statista.

Lockett, H., & Findlay, S. (2020, November 13). 'Modi's Rockefeller': Gautam Adani and the concentration of power in India. *Financial Times*. Retrieved May 3, 2021 from https://www.ft.com/content/474706d6-1243-4f1e-b365-891d4c5d528b

Loi, K. I., Lei, W. S., & Lourenço, F. (2020). Understanding the reactions of government and gaming concessionaires on COVID-19 through the neo-institutional theory–The case of Macao. *International Journal of Hospitality Management, 102755,* 1 - 11.

Lopes de Sousa Jabbour, A. B., Chiappetta Jabbour, C. J., Hingley, M., Vilalta-Perdomo, E. L., Ramsden, G., & Twigg, D. (2020). Sustainability of supply chains in the wake of the coronavirus (COVID-19/SARS-CoV-2) pandemic: Lessons and trends. *Modern Supply Chain Research and Applications*, *2*(3), 117–122. doi:10.1108/MSCRA-05-2020-0011

Love, D., Allison, E., Asche, F., Belton, B., Cottrell, R., Froelich, H., Gephart, J.A., Hicks, C.C., Little, D.C., Nussbaumer, E.M., Pinto da Silva, P., Poulain, F., Rubio, A., Stoll, J.S., Tlusty, M.F., Thorne-Lyman, A.L., Troell, M., & Zhang, W. (2020). *Emerging COVID-19 impacts, responses, and lessons for building resilience in the seafood system.* Academic Press.

Lu, J., Gu, J., Li, K., Xu, C., Su, W., Lai, Z., Zhou, D., Yu, C., Xu, B., & Yang, Z. (2020, July). COVID-19 outbreak associated with air conditioning in restaurant, Guangzhou, China, 2020. Research Letter. *Emerging Infectious Diseases*, *26*(7).

Luna, N. (2020, Sept. 16). Compensation: Pandemic forces restaurant industry to rethink wages, tip credit. *Nation's Restaurant News*, 1 – 8.

Lyons, A., Kass-Hanna, J., & Polato e Fava, A. (2021). Fintech Development and Savings, Borrowing and Remittances: A Comparative Study of Emerging Economies. *Borrowing and Remittances: A Comparative Study of Emerging Economies.*

Maadad, N. (2020, July 12). *It's a long and hard road for UAE hospitality Industry.* Retrieved September 10, 2020, from Gulf News: https://gulfnews.com/business/analysis/its-a-long-and-hard-road-for-uae-hospitality-industry-1.72549820

Madhok, D., & Business, C. N. N. (2021, April 29). Asia's richest man wants to build the next tech giant. *CNN*. Retrieved May 13, 2021, from https://edition.cnn.com/videos/business/2020/05/29/mukesh-ambani-jio-platforms-orig.cnn-business

Mahmud, P., Paul, S., Azeem, A., Sustainability, P. C. (2021). *Evaluating Supply Chain Collaboration Barriers in Small-and Medium-Sized Enterprises.* doi:10.3390/su13137449

Majumdar, A., Shaw, M., & Sinha, S. K. (2020). COVID-19 debunks the myth of socially sustainable supply chain: A case of the clothing industry in South Asian countries. *Sustainable Production and Consumption*, *24*, 150–155. doi:10.1016/j.spc.2020.07.001

Makridis, C.A., & Hartley, J.S. (2020, Apr. 6). *The cost of COVID-19: A rough estimate of the 2020 US GDP impact.* Policy Brief, Mercatus Center, George Mason University.

Managing the impact of COVID-19 on India's supply chains. (n.d.). Retrieved June 22, 2021, from https://assets.ey.com/content/dam/ey-sites/ey-com/en_in/topics/government-and-public-sector/2020/09/managing-the-impact-of-covid-19-on-india-supply-chains.pdf

Mandal, A. (2020, May 26). Simulated sunlight kills SARS CoV-2 on surfaces in 7 to 14 minutes. *News Medical-Life Sciences.*

Maples, J.G., Thompson, J.M., Anderson, J.D., & Anderson, D.P. (2020). Estimating COVID019 impacts on the broiler industry. *Applied Economic Perspectives and Policy,* 1 – 14.

Marcu, M. R. (2021). The impact of the COVID-19 pandemic on the banking sector. *Management Dynamics in the Knowledge Economy*, *9*(2), 205–223.

Marie, A., Al-Nasser, A., & Ibrahim, M. (2013). Operational-Profitability-Quality Performance of Dubai's Banks. *Journal of Management Research*, *13*(1), 25–34.

Martin, A., Markhvida, M., Hallegatte, S., & Walsh, B. (2020). Socio-economic impacts of COVID-19 on household consumption and poverty. *Economics of Disasters and Climate Change*, *4*, 453–479.

Martínez, C., Paraskevas, J. P., Grimm, C., Corsi, T., & Boyson, S. (2020). The Impact of Environmental Risks in Supply Chain Resilience. *Supply Chain Management and Logistics in Emerging Markets*, 11–39. doi:10.1108/978-1-83909-331-920201002

Martinez, C.C., Maples, J.G., & Benavidez, J. (2020). Beef cattle markets and COVID-19. *Applied Economic Perspectives and Policy*, 1 – 11.

Ma, S., Kim, D. D., Cohen, J. T., & Neumann, P. J. (2020). Measuring "fearonomic effects" in valuing therapies: An application to COVID-19 in China. *Value in Health*, *23*(11), 1405–1408.

Mathai, V., Das, A., Bailey, J. A., & Breuer, K. (2020, December 4). Airflows inside passenger cars and implications for airborne disease transmission. *Science Advances.*

McCarthy, K. (2020, July 24). *Nearly 16,000 restaurants have closed permanently due to the pandemic, Yelp data shows.* ABC News.

McMaster, M., Nettleton, C., Tom, C., Xu, B., Cao, C., & Qiao, P. (2020). Risk Management: Rethinking Fashion Supply Chain Management for Multinational Corporations in Light of the COVID-19 Outbreak. *Journal of Risk and Financial Management*, *13*(8), 173. doi:10.3390/jrfm13080173

Meyer, Z. (2020, Oct. 23). The ugly truth about tipping waitstaff during COVID-19. *Fast Company.*

Miani, P., Kille, T., Lee, S. Y., Zhang, Y., & Bates, P. R. (2021). The impact of the COVID-19 pandemic on current tertiary aviation education and future careers: Students' perspective. *Journal of Air Transport Management*, *94*(January), 102081. doi:10.1016/j.jairtraman.2021.102081

Microsoft Asia News Center. (2020, June 17). *Healthy hotels in the age of COVID-19*. Retrieved September 2020, 2020, from Microsoft: https://news.microsoft.com/apac/2020/06/17/healthy-hotels-in-the-age-of-covid-19/

Ministry of Trade and Industry. (2020). Impact of covid 19 pandemic on Singapore economy. *MITI Newsletter.* https://www.mti.gov.sg/Resources/feature-articles/2020/Impact-of-the-COVID-19-Pandemic-on-the-Singapore-Economy

Mint. (2020, October 25). *Opinion.* Retrieved August 8, 2021, from mint website: https://www.livemint.com/opinion/online-views/opinion-covid-and-its-impact-on-economy-and-msmes-11603604611652.html

Moghazy, M. A. (2020). *Teaching and learning Arabic as a second language online: a case study of Dubai during COVID-19 pandemic*. Academic Press.

Mohammed, A., Naghshineh, B., Spiegler, V., & Carvalho, H. (2021). Conceptualising a supply and demand resilience methodology: A hybrid DEMATEL-TOPSIS-possibilistic multi-objective optimization approach. *Computers & Industrial Engineering*, *160*, 107589. doi:10.1016/j.cie.2021.107589

Mohan, D. (2021, March 26). *How daily wage workers in India suffered in the lockdown – and continue to struggle months later*. Retrieved on June 6, 2021, Scroll.In. https://scroll.in/article/989258/how-daily-wage-workers-in-india-suffered-in-the-lockdown-and-continue-to-struggle-months-later

Monmousseau, P., Marzuoli, A., Feron, E., & Delahaye, D. (2020). Impact of Covid-19 on passengers and airlines from passenger measurements: Managing customer satisfaction while putting the US Air Transportation System to sleep. *Transportation Research Interdisciplinary Perspectives*, *7*, 100179. doi:10.1016/j.trip.2020.100179 PMID:34173460

Mordor Intelligence. (2020). *Hospitality Industry in the United Arab Emirates - Growth, Trends, and Forecasts (2020 - 2025)*. Mordor Intelligence. Retrieved September 10, 2020, from https://www.mordorintelligence.com/industry-reports/hospitality-industry-in-the-united-arab-emirates

Mukesh Ambani wants to build the next tech giant with Jio Platforms. (2021, April 29). *CNN*. Retrieved from https://www.cnn.com/videos/business/2020/05/29/mukesh-ambani-jio-platforms-orig.cnn-business

Mukherjee, A., & Opinion, B. (2021, June 26). *Mukesh Ambani and Gautam Adani. Two billionaires, one green ambition*. Retrieved June 28, 2021, from Business-standard.com website: https://www.business-standard.com/article/companies/ambani-and-adani-two-billionaires-one-clean-energy-ambition-121062600112_1.html

Mukherjee, S., Baral, M. M., Chittipaka, V., Srivastava, S. C., & Pal, S. K. (2021). *Discussing the Impact of Industry 4.0 in Agriculture Supply Chain*. Springer. doi:10.1007/978-981-16-3033-0_28

Mukherjee, S., Chittipaka, V., & Baral, M. M. (2021). *Developing a Model to Highlight the Relation of Digital Trust With Privacy and Security for the Blockchain Technology*. doi:10.4018/978-1-7998-8081-3.ch007

Mukherjee, S., Mohan Baral, M., Srivastava, S. C., & Jana, B. (2021). Analyzing the problems faced by fashion retail stores due to COVID-19 outbreak. *Parikalpana-KIIT Journal of Management*, *17*(I), 206. Advance online publication. doi:10.23862/kiit-parikalpana/2021/v17/i1/209031

Mukherji, B. (2021, May 26). *Lifetime salaries and college tuition: Indian companies are compensating the families of COVID victims*. Retrieved July 18, 2021, from Fortune website: https://fortune.com/2021/05/26/corporate-india-covid-compensation-tata-oyo-borsi/

Nahar, P. (2021, June 30). *Mukesh Ambani, Gautam Adani, 4 other Indians earned $45 billion in 6 months*. Retrieved July 8, 2021, from Economic Times website: https://economictimes.indiatimes.com/markets/stocks/news/mukesh-ambani-gautam-adani-4-other-indians-earned-45-billion-in-6-months/articleshow/83980938.cms

Najaf, Subramaniam, & Atayah. (2021). Understanding the implications of FinTech Peer-to-Peer (P2P) lending during the COVID-19 pandemic. *Journal of Sustainable Finance & Investment*, 1-16.

Nandi, S., Sarkis, J., Hervani, A. A., & Helms, M. M. (2021). Redesigning Supply Chains using Blockchain-Enabled Circular Economy and COVID-19 Experiences. *Sustainable Production and Consumption*, *27*, 10–22. doi:10.1016/j.spc.2020.10.019 PMID:33102671

Nandi, S., Sarkis, J., Hervani, A., & Helms, M. (2020). Do blockchain and circular economy practices improve post COVID-19 supply chains? A resource-based and resource dependence perspective. *Industrial Management &amp. Data Systems*, *121*(2), 333–363. doi:10.1108/IMDS-09-2020-0560

Narayanswamy, S., & Zainulbhai, A. (2015, October 30). *India's consumer evolution*. Retrieved April 22, 2021, from Mckinsey.Com; McKinsey & Company. https://www.mckinsey.com/mgi/overview/in-the-news/consumer-evolution-in-india

Nevins, M. (2020, July 18). Re-thinking training and development in a post-covid world: A case study. *Forbes Magazine*. Retrieved August 08, 2021 from forbes.com. https://www.forbes.com/sites/hillennevins/2020/07/18/re-thinking-training-and-development-in-a-post-covid-world-a-case-study/

Notteboom, T., Pallis, T., & Rodrigue, J. (2021). Disruptions and resilience in global container shipping and ports: The COVID-19 pandemic versus the 2008–2009 financial crisis. *Maritime Economics & Logistics*, *23*(2), 179–210.

Nunkoo, R., Teeroovengadum, V., Ringle, C., & Sunnassee, V. (2019). Service quality and customer satisfaction: The moderating effects of hotel star rating. *International Journal of Hospitality Management*. Advance online publication. doi:10.1016/j.ijhm.2019.102414

Nunnally, J. C. (1994). *Psychometric theory* (3rd ed.). Tata McGraw-Hill Education.

OECD. (2021, December 4). *COVID-19 crisis response in MENA countries*. OECD. Retrieved from OECD: https://www.oecd.org/coronavirus/policy-responses/covid-19-crisis-response-in-mena-countries-4b366396/

Online, F. E. (2020a, April 11). Cooking oil production down 40% amid Coronavirus pandemic: Adani Wilmar. *The Financial Express*. Retrieved May 21, 2021 from https://www.financialexpress.com/industry/cooking-oil-production-down-40-per-cent-amid-coronavirus-pandemic-adani-wilmar/1925558/

Online, F. E. (2020a, August 25). Covid vaccine boost: Serum Institute founder adds $3.6 billion to his wealth in just under 4 months. *The Financial Express*. Retrieved July 26, 2021 from https://www.financialexpress.com/industry/covid-vaccine-boost-serum-institute-founder-adds-3-6-billion-to-his-wealth-in-just-under-4-months/2064217/

Online, F. E. (2020b, August 25). Covid vaccine boost: Serum Institute founder adds $3.6 billion to his wealth in just under 4 months. *The Financial Express*. Retrieved July 26, 2021 from https://www.financialexpress.com/industry/covid-vaccine-boost-serum-institute-founder-adds-3-6-billion-to-his-wealth-in-just-under-4-months/2064217/

Online, F. E. (2020b, November 26). *Listed companies post bumper profits despite lockdown; manufacturing firms steal the show*. Retrieved June 27, 2021 from The Financial Express. https://www.financialexpress.com/industry/listed-companies-post-bumper-profits-despite-lockdown-manufacturing-firms-steal-the-show/2136984/

Online, F. E. (2020c, November 26). *Listed companies post bumper profits despite lockdown; manufacturing firms steal the show*. Retrieved June 27, 2021 from The Financial Express. https://www.financialexpress.com/industry/listed-companies-post-bumper-profits-despite-lockdown-manufacturing-firms-steal-the-show/2136984/

Ou, J., Wong, I. A., & Huang, G. I. (2021). The coevolutionary process of restaurant CSR in the time of mega disruption. *International Journal of Hospitality Management*, *92*(102684), 1–10.

Oxford, J. S., Lambkin, R., Sefton, A., Daniels, R., Elliot, A., Brown, R., & Gill, D. (2005). A hypothesis: The conjunction of soldiers, gas, pigs, ducks, geese and horses in Northern France during the Great War provided the conditions for the emergence of the "Spanish" influenza pandemic of 1918–1919. *Vaccine*, *23*(7), 940–945. doi:10.1016/j.vaccine.2004.06.035 PMID:15603896

Ozili, P. K. (2020). *Financial inclusion and Fintech during COVID-19 crisis: Policy solutions*. Academic Press.

Pasquini, M. (2020, May 28). TGI Fridays CEO says 20% of U.S. restaurants could close for good due to coronavirus crisis. *People Magazine*.

Pavlov, A., Ivanov, D., Pavlov, D., & Slinko, A. (2019). Optimization of network redundancy and contingency planning in sustainable and resilient supply chain resource management under conditions of structural dynamics. *Annals of Operations Research*, *2019*, 1–30. doi:10.100710479-019-03182-6

Pearson, C., & Clair, J. (1998). Reframing Crisis Management. *Academy of Management Review*, *23*(1), 59–76. doi:10.2307/259099

Pedroso, R., Reverdosa, M., & Darlington, S. (2020, July 2). *"Sending the population to the slaughterhouse": Restaurants and bars open in Rio, as experts warn worst is yet to come.* CNN.

Pereira, D. da S., & Soares de Mello, J. C. C. B. (2021). Efficiency evaluation of Brazilian airlines operations considering the Covid-19 outbreak. *Journal of Air Transport Management*, *91*, 101976. doi:10.1016/j.jairtraman.2020.101976 PMID:33235408

Peters, A. (2020, Sept. 3). If you're in the hospital with COVID-19, this robot dog might come take your vital signs. *Fast Company.*

Pinsker, J. (2020, May 7). A guide to staying safe as states reopen. *Atlantic (Boston, Mass.).*

Podsakoff, N. P. (2003). Common method biases in behavioral research: a critical review of the literature and recommended remedies. *Journal of Applied Psychology, 885*(879).

Press Trust of India. (2021, June 8). *Why are fuel prices rising in India? Here's what oil minister says.* Retrieved July 5, 2021, from Indiatoday.in website: https://www.indiatoday.in/business/story/why-are-fuel-prices-rising-in-india-here-s-what-oil-minister-says-1811952-2021-06-08

Priyo, J., Mohamad, B., & Adetunji, R. (2019, February). An Examination of the Effects of Service Quality and Customer Satisfaction on Customer Loyalty in the Hotel Industry. *International Journal of Supply Chain Management*, *8*(1), 653–663.

PTI. (2021, June 8). *World Bank projects India to grow at 8.3% in 2021.* Retrieved on July 6, 2021, from Economic Times. https://economictimes.indiatimes.com/news/economy/indicators/world-bank-projects-india-to-grow-at-8-3-per-cent-in-2021/articleshow/83340761.cms

Qin, X., Huang, G., Shen, H., & Fu, M. (2020). COVID-19 pandemic and firm-level cash holding—Moderating effect of goodwill and goodwill impairment. *Emerging Markets Finance & Trade*, *56*(10), 2243–2258.

Queiroz, M. M., Ivanov, D., Dolgui, A., & Fosso Wamba, S. (2020). Impacts of epidemic outbreaks on supply chains: mapping a research agenda amid the COVID-19 pandemic through a structured literature review. Annals of Operations Research. doi:10.100710479-020-03685-7

Raj, M., Sundararajan, A., & You, C. (2020). *COVID-19 and digital resilience: Evidence from Uber Eats.* arXiv preprint arXiv:2006.07204.

Ranka, S. (2020, June). How corona virus could affect the culture of eating, special reference to street food: The New Normal. *IOSR Journal of Business and Management*, *22*(6), 1–7.

Ratnesar-Shumate, S., Williams, G., Green, B., Krause, M., Holland, B., Wood, S., Bohannon, J., Boydston, J., Freeburger, D., Hooper, I., Beck, K., Yeager, J., Altamura, L. A., Biryukov, J., Yolitz, J., Schuit, M., Wahl, V., Hevey, M., & Dabisch, P. (2020, May 20). Simulated Sunlight Rapidly Inactivates SARS-CoV-2 on Surfaces. *The Journal of Infectious Diseases*. doi:10.1093/infdis/jiaa274

RBI. (2021a). *Economic Review*. Retrieved July 2, 2021, from RBI website. https://rbidocs.rbi.org.in/rdocs/AnnualReport/PDFs/IIECONOMICREVIEW650084A9F3494152939D99449E63D040.PDF

RBI. (2021b). *Financial Stability Report*. Retrieved August 8, 2021, from RBI website. https://rbidocs.rbi.org.in/rdocs/PublicationReport/Pdfs/5CHAPTER13F7BC1B353D241828187E91649DF1584.PDF

Reliance to buy Future Group's retail arm for $3.38 billion. (2020, August 29). *Reuters*. Retrieved May 14, 2021, from https://www.reuters.com/article/us-future-enterprises-m-a-reliance-indus-idUSKBN25P0N6

Remko, H. (2020). Research opportunities for a more resilient post-COVID-19 supply chain – closing the gap between research findings and industry practice. *International Journal of Operations and Production Management, 40*(4), 341–355. doi:10.1108/IJOPM-03-2020-0165

Remolina, N. (2020). Towards a data-driven financial system: the impact of COVID-19. *SMU Centre for AI & Data Governance Research Paper*, *8*, 1-24.

Reuters. (2021, December 4). *Deserted debts stir disquiet in the mysterious world of Dubai Inc.* Retrieved from Reuters: https://www.reuters.com/article/dubai-debt-insight-int-idUSKBN2A9118

Richards, T.J., & Rickard, B. (2020, Apr. 13). COVID-19 impact on fruit and vegetable markets. *Canadian Journal of Agricultural Economics/Revue canadienne d'agroeconomie*, 189 - 194.

Richter, A., & Wilson, T. C. (2020). Covid-19: Implications for insurer risk management and the insurability of pandemic risk. *The Geneva Risk and Insurance Review*, *45*, 171–199.

Rizou, M., Galanakis, I. M., Aldawoud, T. M., & Galanakis, C. M. (2020). Safety of foods, food supply chain and environment within the COVID-19 pandemic. *Trends in Food Science & Technology*, *102*, 293–299.

Rodrigues, M., Franco, M., Sousa, N., & Silva, R. (2021). COVID 19 and the Business Management Crisis: An Empirical Study in SMEs. *Sustainability, 13*(11), 5912. doi:10.3390/su13115912

Routt, D. (2008). The economic impact of the Black Death. *EH.net Encyclopedia*.

Rowan, N. J., & Galanakis, C. M. (2020). Unlocking challenges and opportunities presented by COVID-19 pandemic for cross-cutting disruption in agri-food and green deal innovations: Quo Vadis? In Science of the Total Environment (Vol. 748, p. 141362). Elsevier B.V. doi:10.1016/j.scitotenv.2020.141362

Roy, A. (2021, April 28). We are witnessing a crime against humanity: Arundhati Roy on India's Covid catastrophe. *The Guardian*. Retrieved July 16, 2021 from https://www.theguardian.com/news/2021/apr/28/crime-against-humanity-arundhati-roy-india-covid-catastrophe

Roy, S. (2020, March 30). *How Indian companies are contributing to the war against coronavirus*. Retrieved July 9, 2021, from Business-standard.com website: https://www.business-standard.com/podcast/current-affairs/how-indian-companies-are-contributing-to-the-war-against-coronavirus-120033001663_1.html

Roy, A., Patnaik, B. C. M., & Satpathy, I. (2020). Impact of Covid-19 crisis on Indian MSME sector: A study on remedial measures. *Eurasian Chemical Communications*, *2*(9), 991–1000. doi:10.22034/ecc.2020.114672

Runyan, R. (2006). Small Business in the Face of Crisis: Identifying Barriers to Recovery from a Natural Disaster1. *Journal of Contingencies and Crisis Management*, *14*(1), 12–26. doi:10.1111/j.1468-5973.2006.00477.x

Sachdev, T. (2021, March 15). *Gautam Adani's wealth stoops up by 50% during the pandemic, congress leaders question the integrity of the surge. While all other income groups suffering from the crisis, how come billionaires kept on increasing their wealth so enormously?* Inventiva. Retrieved June 25, 2021, from Inventiva.co.in website: https://www.inventiva.co.in/stories/tanish/gautam-adanis-wealth-stoops-up-by-50-during-the-pandemic-congress-leaders-question-the-integrity-of-the-surge-while-all-other-income-groups-suffering-from-the-crisis-how-come-billionaires-kept-on/

Sahay, R., Eriksson von Allmen, U., Lahreche, A., Khera, P., Ogawa, S., Bazarbash, M., & Beaton, K. (2020). *The Promise of Fintech, Financial Inclusion in the Post COVID-19 Era. Departmental Paper No. 20/09*. IMF.

Sahoo, P., & Ashwani. (2020). COVID-19 and Indian Economy: Impact on Growth, Manufacturing, Trade and MSME Sector. *Global Business Review*, *21*(5), 1159–1183. doi:10.1177/0972150920945687

Saikouk, T., Fattam, N., Angappa, G., & Hamdi, A. (2021). The interplay between inter-personal and inter-organizational relationships in coordinating supply chain activities. *International Journal of Logistics Management*, *32*(3), 898–917. doi:10.1108/IJLM-11-2020-0443

Sarkis, J. (2020). Supply chain sustainability: Learning from the COVID-19 pandemic. *International Journal of Operations & Production Management*, *41*(1), 63–73. doi:10.1108/IJOPM-08-2020-0568

Sars, T., & Daiichi, F. (2021). Major crises and supply chain disruption: Towards greater sustainability. *Strategic Direction*, *37*(4), 36–38. doi:10.1108/SD-01-2021-0008

Sasi, A. (2020, July 1). Explained: Why, despite the pandemic, some billionaires are becoming richer. *The Indian Express*. Retrieved May 27, 2021, from https://indianexpress.com/article/explained/coronavirus-pandemic-billionaires-wealth-unemployment-6480380/

Saxena, J. (2020, Dec. 1). Survey finds that pandemic has exacerbated sexual harassment of tipped workers. *Eater.*

Saxenian, A. (1996). Regional Advantage: Culture and Competition in Silicon Valley and Route 128. Harvard University Press.

Sazonov, A., Shrivastava, B., & Sanjai, P. R. (2020, December 14). *The story of Gautam Adani's rise —from kidnapping & 26/11 survivor to Mukesh Ambani rival.* Retrieved July 3, 2021, from The print.in website: https://theprint.in/india/the-story-of-gautam-adanis-rise-from-kidnapping-26-11-survivor-to-mukesh-ambani-rival/566169/

Scerri, M., & Grech, V. (2020, Nov. 12). *To wear or not to wear? Adherence to face mask use during the COVID-19 and Spanish influenza pandemics.* US National Library of Medicine National Institutes of Health.

Scheiwiller, S., & Zizka, L. (2021). Strategic responses by European airlines to the Covid-19 pandemic: A soft landing or a turbulent ride? *Journal of Air Transport Management*, *95*, 102103. doi:10.1016/j.jairtraman.2021.102103

Seetharaman, P. (2020). Business models shifts: Impact of Covid-19. *International Journal of Information Management*, *54*(102173), 1–4.

Sethi, A. (2021, June 7). Why Amazon is confronting the richest man in India. *The New York Times*. Retrieved July 9, 2021, from https://www.nytimes.com/2021/06/07/business/amazon-reliance-ambani-future.html

Seymour, M., & Moore, S. (2000). *Effective crisis management: Worldwide principles and practice*. Cassell.

Shafi, M., Liu, J., & Ren, W. (2020). Impact of COVID-19 pandemic on micro, small, and medium-sized Enterprises operating in Pakistan. *Research in Globalization*, *2*, 100018. doi:10.1016/j.resglo.2020.100018

Shahin, A. (2020). *Supply Chain Risk Management under Covid-19: A Review and Research Agenda.* https://www.researchgate.net/publication/343852256

Sharma, N. (2020, December 8). *Why Indian farmers believe new laws are rigged to favour India's richest man*. Retrieved April 25, 2021, from Quartz website: https://qz.com/india/1942448/indias-protesting-farmers-think-new-laws-benefit-ambani-adani/

Sharma, N. (2020, June 22). *How Reliance Industries cleared its $21-billion debt amid the coronavirus pandemic*. Retrieved April 25, 2021, from Scroll.in website: https://scroll.in/article/965263/how-reliance-industries-cleared-its-21-billion-debt-amid-the-coronavirus-pandemic

Sharma, N. (2021, May 4). *Have India's ultra-rich done enough to help in the country's fight against Covid-19?* Retrieved June 17, 2021, from Scroll.in website: https://scroll.in/article/993957/have-indias-ultra-rich-done-enough-to-help-in-the-countrys-fight-against-covid-19

Sharma, A., Adhikary, A., & Borah, S. B. (2020). Covid-19's impact on supply chain decisions: Strategic insights from NASDAQ 100 firms using Twitter data. *Journal of Business Research*, *117*, 443–449. doi:10.1016/j.jbusres.2020.05.035 PMID:32834209

Sharma, M., & Joshi, S. (2020). Digital supplier selection reinforcing supply chain quality management systems to enhance firm's performance. *The TQM Journal*. Advance online publication. doi:10.1108/TQM-07-2020-0160

Sharma, M., Luthra, S., Joshi, S., & Kumar, A. (2021a). Accelerating retail supply chain performance against pandemic disruption: Adopting resilient strategies to mitigate the long-term effects. *Journal of Enterprise Information Management*, *34*(6), 1844–1873. Advance online publication. doi:10.1108/JEIM-07-2020-0286

Sharma, R., Shishodia, A., Kamble, S., Gunasekaran, A., & Belhadi, A. (2020). Agriculture supply chain risks and COVID-19: Mitigation strategies and implications for the practitioners. *International Journal of Logistics Research and Applications*, *0*(0), 1–27. doi:10.1080/13675567.2020.1830049

Shashi, C., Centobelli, P., Cerchione, R., & Ertz, M. (2020). Managing supply chain resilience to pursue business and environmental strategies. *Business Strategy and the Environment*, *29*(3), 1215–1246. doi:10.1002/bse.2428

Sheng, E. (2020, Nov. 5). *The $68 trillion transfer of wealth in America is evaporating amid crisis.* CNBC.

Shutt, J., & Lerman, D. (2020, Dec. 20). Deal reached on $900B coronavirus relief package; votes likely Monday. *Roll Call.*

Simmons, D. (2020, Oct. 13). *City of Manhattan installing outdoor dining platforms in front of seven downtown restaurants.* KMAN 1350 AM.

Singh, A. (2021, April 28). *Making MSMEs competitive in the post COVID-19 era.* Retrieved August 28, 2021, from Sap.com website: https://news.sap.com/india/2021/04/making-msmes-competitive-post-covid-19/

Singh, D. (2020, May 12). *Lockdown: Truck drivers make big bucks transporting stranded migrants.* Retrieved August 8, 2021 from Indiatoday.In; India Today. https://www.indiatoday.in/india/story/lockdown-truck-drivers-make-big-bucks-transporting-stranded-migrants-1677298-2020-05-12

Singh, K. (2020, September 21). *COVID-19 has pushed the Indian economy into a tailspin. But there's a way out.* Retrieved May 4, 2021, from https://thewire.in/economy/covid-19-india-economic-recovery

Singh, N. (2020, July 3). *Suspension of Labour Rights during the Covid-19 Pandemic: Possible Implications under the revised draft.* Retrieved April 14, 2021 from Cambridge.Org. https://www.cambridge.org/core/blog/2020/07/03/suspension-of-labour-rights-during-the-covid-19-pandemic-possible-implications-under-the-revised-draft/

Singh, J. (1994). Organizational Niches and the Dynamics of Organizational Mortality. *American Journal of Sociology*, *100*(2), 346–380. doi:10.1086/230540

Singh, S., Kumar, R., Panchal, R., & Tiwari, M. K. (2020). Impact of COVID-19 on logistics systems and disruptions in food supply chain. *International Journal of Production Research*, *0*(0), 1–16. doi:10.1080/00207543.2020.1792000

Singu, S., Acharya, A., Challagundla, K., & Byrareddy, S. N. (2020). Impact of social determinants of health on the emerging COVID-19 pandemic in the United States. *Frontiers in Public Health*, *8*, 1–18.

Sipahi, E. (2020). COVID 19 and MSMEs: A revival framework | Research Journal in Advanced Humanities. *Research Journal in Advanced Humanities, 1*(2). https://royalliteglobal.com/advanced-humanities/article/view/146

Smith, T.C. (2020, May 16). *Tara C. Smith Coronavirus vaccine and quarantine protesters in America form an unholy COVID-19 alliance. Thought experiment.* NBC News.

Song, H. J., Yeon, J., & Lee, S. (2021). Impact of the COVID-19 pandemic: Evidence from the U.S. restaurant industry. *International Journal of Hospitality Management*, *92*(102702), 1–7.

Sönmez, S., Apostolopoulos, Y., & Lemke, M.K. (2020). Understanding the effects of COVID-19 on the health and safety of immigrant hospitality workers in the United States. *Tourism Management Perspectives*, *35*(100717), 1–7.

Spotlight, E. T. (2021, February 24). *MSME sector is the key to unlock India's economic growth.* Retrieved May 15, 2021, from Economic Times website: https://economictimes.indiatimes.com/small-biz/sme-sector/msme-sector-is-the-key-to-unlock-indias-economic-growth/articleshow/81188321.cms

Sridhar & Gamser. (2020). *Member Survey Results on the Impact of COVID-19.* UKRI.

Staff, G. Q. (2021, January 15). *This is the net worth of Adar Poonawalla's father & Serum Institute's founder, Dr. Cyrus Poonawalla.* Retrieved July 8, 2021, from GQ India website: https://www.gqindia.com/get-smart/content/this-is-the-net-worth-of-adar-poonawallas-father-and-serum-institutes-founder-dr-cyrus-poonawalla

Sun, C., & Zhai, Z. (2020). The efficacy of social distance and ventilation effectiveness in preventing COVID-19 transmission. *Sustainable Cities and Society, 62*, 1 - 10.

Sundarakani, B., & Onyia, O. P. (2021). *Fast, furious and focused approach to Covid-19 response. An examination of the financial and business resilience of the UAE logistics industry*. Academic Press.

Sundarakani, B., & Onyia, O. (2021). Fast, furious and focused approach to Covid-19 response: An examination of the financial and business resilience of the UAE logistics industry. *Journal of Financial Services Marketing*, 1–22.

Supernormal profits: Latest News & Videos, Photos about Supernormal profits. (n.d.). Retrieved May 3, 2021, from https://economictimes.indiatimes.com/topic/Super-normal-profits

Taqi, H. M. M., Ahmed, H. N., Paul, S., Garshasbi, M., Ali, S. M., Kabir, G., & Paul, S. K. (2020). Strategies to manage the impacts of the COVID-19 pandemic in the supply chain: Implications for improving economic and social sustainability. *Sustainability (Switzerland), 12*(22), 1–25. doi:10.3390u12229483

Taylor, S. (2020). The socially distant servicescape: An investigation of consumer preference's during the re-opening phase. *International Journal of Hospitality Management, 91*(102692), 1–9.

Ten million lost jobs in Covid 2nd wave, 97% households' income declined: CMIE. (n.d.). *Business Today*. Retrieved September 2, 2021, from https://www.businesstoday.in/latest/economy-politics/story/income-of-97-households-declined-since-covid-19-pandemic-began-cmie-298381-2021-06-01

Thaichon, P. (2021). COVID in the Aviation Industry: Crisis Management, Its Decisions and Outcomes. *COVID-19. Technology and Marketing, 2019*, 21–31. doi:10.1007/978-981-16-1442-2_2

The global economic outlook during the COVID-19 pandemic: A changed world. (n.d.). Retrieved April 2, 2021, from https://www.worldbank.org/en/news/feature/2020/06/08/the-global-economic-outlook-during-the-covid-19-pandemic-a-changed-world

Thomas, J., Barbato, M., Verlinden, M., Gaspar, C., Moussa, M., Ghorayeb, J., . . . Bentall, R. P. (2020). *Psychosocial Correlates of Depression and Anxiety in the United Arab Emirates During the COVID-19 Pandemic*. Academic Press.

Thomas, T. (2021, March 17). *Steel companies will use supernormal profits to pay back ₹35,000 crore debt.* Retrieved July 5, 2021 from Mint. https://www.livemint.com/news/india/steel-companies-will-use-supernormal-profits-to-pay-back-rs-35-000-crore-debt-11615985829160.html

Tisdell, C. A. (2021). Determinants of the Economic Vulnerability of Businesses to Pandemics and Similar Events. *Journal of Risk and Financial Management, 14*(11), 532. doi:10.3390/jrfm14110532

TTN. (2017, October). *UAE hospitality 2020 and beyond.* Retrieved September 10, 2020, from Travel & Tourism News Middle East: http://www.ttnworldwide.com/Article/268130/-UAE-hospitality-2020-and-beyond

Tufekc, Z. (2020, May 12). How Hong Kong Did It: With the government flailing, the city's citizens decided to organize their own coronavirus response. *Atlantic (Boston, Mass.)*.

Valdez-Juárez, L. E., Gallardo-Vázquez, D., & Ramos-Escobar, E. A. (2021). Online Buyers and Open Innovation: Security, Experience, and Satisfaction. *Journal of Open Innovation, 7*(1), 37. doi:10.3390/joitmc7010037

Valencia, N., & Kelly, C. (2020, May 19). *CDC releases detailed guidance on reopening that had previously been shelved by White House.* CNN.

Valinsky, J. (2020, Dec. 12). *The 30 retailers and restaurant chains that filed for bankruptcy in 2020*. CNN.

Vanshika. (2020, April 11). *Edible oil production dropped by 40% due to Coronavirus*. Retrieved July 5, 2021, from Inventiva.co.in website: https://www.inventiva.co.in/trends/vanshika/edible-oil-production-dropped-by-40-due-to-coronavirus/

Varma, J., & Saxena, S. (2021). *Impact of COVID-19 on FinTechs*. Academic Press.

Varma, S. (2019, October 13). *Under Modi rule, Ambani, Adani have doubled their wealth*. Retrieved June 17, 2021, from Newsclick.in website: https://www.newsclick.in/Under-Modi-Rule-Ambani-Adani-Have-Doubled-Their-Wealth

Veeranki, Y. (2021). *Relative analysis of private and public sector banks–Pre and post COVID* (Doctoral dissertation). SRM University.

Verma, P. A. (2021, January 15). *Why technology is the only path to sustained growth for MSMEs*. Retrieved July 10, 2021, from Economic Times website: https://economictimes.indiatimes.com/small-biz/sme-sector/why-technology-is-the-only-path-to-sustained-growth-for-msmes/articleshow/80281133.cms

Verma, S., & Gustafsson, A. (2020). Investigating the emerging COVID-19 research trends in the field of business and management: A bibliometric analysis approach. *Journal of Business Research*, *118*, 253–261. doi:10.1016/j.jbusres.2020.06.057 PMID:32834211

Vidya, S. (n.d.). HR challenge! Justifying expenditure on reskilling employees. *Business Today*. Retrieved April 12, 2021, from https://www.businesstoday.in/jobs/story/hr-challenge-justifying-expenditure-on-reskilling-employees-293262-2021-04-12

Wadhwa, P. (2021, March 16). *633,000 "New Middle Class" households In India: Hurun India report*. Retrieved August 13, 2021, from Business-standard.com website: https://www.business-standard.com/article/economy-policy/633-000-new-middle-class-households-in-india-hurun-india-report-121031600357_1.html

Wafai, Y. (2020, May 22). Reopening phases in Washington state: When you can get a haircut, go to the gym, or eat at restaurants as coronavirus lockdowns are lifted. *The Seattle Times*.

Webel, M., & Freeman, M. C. (2020, June 5). *Compare the flu pandemic of 1918 and COVID-19 with caution*. University of Pittsburgh Medical School. https://inside.upmc.com/compare-the-flu-pandemic-of-1918-and-covid-19-with-caution/

Wen, J., Kozak, M., Yang, S., & Liu, F. (2020). COVID-19 potential effects on Chinese citizens' lifestyle and travel. *Tourism Review*, 1–19.

Willens, K., Shaffrey, T., & Hajela, D. (2020, Dec. 11). *New York City bars, restaurants pursue adaptation to survive*. ABC News.

Williams, C., & Kayaoglu, A. (2020). COVID-19 and undeclared work: Impacts and policy responses in Europe. *Service Industries Journal*, 1–32.

World Bank. (2020). *India Development Update.* Retrieved May 13, 2021, from worldbank.org: https://openknowledge.worldbank.org/bitstream/handle/10986/34367/India-Development-Update.pdf?sequence=1&isAllowed=y

Xue, D., Liu, Z., Wang, B., & Yang, J. (2021). Impacts of COVID-19 on aircraft usage and fuel consumption: A case study on four Chinese international airports. *Journal of Air Transport Management, 95*, 102106. doi:10.1016/j.jairtraman.2021.102106 PMID:34548769

Yahya, F. (2021). *Commentary: Singapore should focus on economic growth rather than redistributing a smaller pie as it reopens.* Channel News Asia. https://www.channelnewsasia.com/commentary/singapore-growth-help-low-wage-workers-income-households-2125671

Yan, H., & Maxouris, C. (2020, May 18.) *Reopening the US: States relax rules, but some could return to stay-at-home orders if coronavirus cases surge.* CNN.

Youn, H., Hua, N., & Lee, S. (2015). Does size matter? Corporate social responsibility and firm performance in the restaurant industry. *International Journal of Hospitality Management, 51*, 127–134.

Zachariadis, M., Ozcan, P., & Dinçkol, D. (2020). The Covid-19 impact on fintech: now is the time to boost investment. *LSE Business Review*, 1-3.

Zdziarski, E., Dunkel, N., & Rollo, J. (2007). *Campus crisis management.* Jossey-Bass.

Zeng, Z., Chen, P.-J., & Lew, A. A. (2020). From high-touch to high-tech: COVID-19 drives robotics adoption. *Tourism Geographies*, 1–11.

Zhang, Z., Srivastava, P. R., Eachempati, P., & Yu, Y. (2021, March 23). An intelligent framework for analyzing supply chain resilience of firms in China: A hybrid multicriteria approach. *International Journal of Logistics Management*. Advance online publication. doi:10.1108/IJLM-11-2020-0452

About the Contributors

Supreet Ahluwalia is Senior Consultant and Partner at Creative Head Consultants. She is seasoned professional with more than 13 years of experience working with several big corporate clients in India and abroad.

Shamma Alzarooni is a final year student at the Higher Colleges of Technology Dubai majoring in finance with a minor in investments.

Manish Mohan Baral is working as an Assistant Professor in the Department of Operations, GITAM Institute of Management, GITAM (Deemed to be University), Visakhapatnam. He is an engineering graduate from KIIT University, Bhubaneswar, Odisha, MBA in International Business from GITAM University, Visakhapatnam, and pursued his Ph.D. in Management from Birla Institute of Technology Mesra, Ranchi. He has publications in reputed journals and high indexed book chapters. He has published in reputed journals like the International Journal of Logistics Management, FIIB Business Review, etc. He has presented more than 12 papers in various conferences and has also received three best papers and best paper presented awards. His research areas include Information Technology, Cloud Computing, Supply Chain Management, Artificial Intelligence, Operations Research, and Quality Management. He has expertise in statistical techniques like SEM and MCDM techniques like TOPSIS, Fuzzy TOPSIS, etc.

Anca Bocanet is currently an Assistant Professor and Program Team Leader at the Higher Colleges of Technology in the UAE. She earned her Ph.D. in Science and Technology Management from the University of Naples Federico II. Her current research interests include innovation and entrepreneurship, organizational dynamics, complexity theory and systems, sustainable development. Her latest research contributes to the debate on corporate innovation–productivity trade-off in the context of new venture creation. Her paper presents a novel application of the entrepreneurial learning approach in the context of new venture creation.

Shalin Hai-Jew works as an instructional designer at Kansas State University (K-State). She has taught at the university and college levels for many years (including four years in the People's Republic of China) and was tenured at Shoreline Community College but left tenure to pursue instructional design work. She has Bachelor's degrees in English and psychology, a Master's degree in Creative Writing from the University of Washington (Hugh Paradise Scholar), and an Ed.D in Educational Leadership with a focus on public administration from Seattle University (where she was a Morford Scholar). She tested into the University of Washington at 14. She reviews for several publishers and publications. She has worked on a number of instructional design projects, including public health, biosecurity, one health, mental health, PTSD, grain science, turfgrass management, social justice, English language learning, and others. She has authored and edited a number of books. Hai-Jew was born in Huntsville, Alabama, in the U.S.

Vivek Joshi has 20 years of experience in Academics, Corporate Training and Consulting. Currently he is working as Director Creative Head Consultants and Founder of EdgeVantage, a consulting firm operating in USA, Singapore and India. Vivek has worked with several recognised corporations and executed consulting and training projects in UK, UAE, Malaysia, China, India, Singapore, and Africa.

Vasilios Stouraitis is a lecturer in International Business and Management at Glasgow Caledonian University in the UK and visiting lecturer in several institutions abroad including Italy and Panama. Specializing in small and medium-sized enterprises and with a background in International Business and Economics, he holds a PhD from Henley Business School/University of Reading, an Msc in Development studies from University College London and an MBA and Bsc from the University of Kent. He has worked on development issues (agribusiness and governance) for the United Nations (Food and Agriculture Organization and the International Fund for Agricultural Development) and European Commission (DG Enterprise and Industry) and is also a published author in international business strategy and entrepreneurship. Regarding academic work, he has taught in several institutions (Edinburgh Business School at Athens, The American University of Rome, Link Campus Rome, Swiss School of Management Rome) and supervised several BA/BSc and MA/MSc theses on International Business topics and Food Economics.

Heather Webb is an Assistant Professor of Business at Higher Colleges of Technology, Dubai Men's College where she teaches strategy, entrepreneurship, strategic marketing, project management and other international business courses. She received both her PhD in Management and her MSc in International Business and Emerging Markets (IBEM) from the University of Edinburgh, and her BA in History from the University of Washington. Her research focuses on aspects of strategy, culture, innovation, sustainability, and artificial intelligence. She has successfully published research on mobile payment systems, sectoral system of innovation, Internet of Things, green marketing, and sustainable innovation.

Index

M

P

Q

R

S

T

U

www.ingramcontent.com/pod-product-compliance
Lightning Source LLC
LaVergne TN
LVHW081333300926
849161LV00008B/1962
* 9 7 8 1 7 9 9 8 8 3 4 6 3 *